NIEUPORT 28

The NIEUPORT 28

AMERICA's FIRST FIGHTER

Theodore Hamady

Schiffer Military History
Atglen, PA

Special Notes

The correct designation for the Nieuport 28 fighter is Nieuport 28C.1 – C for Chasse or pursuit (as a fighter was then called), and 1 for single place. The aircraft is referred to in this book as the Nieuport 28, or the Nieuport 28A, if it is the modified version of the aircraft that was manufactured towards the end of and after the war.

Victory claims for American pilots mentioned in this book, derive from *USAF Historical Study No. 133*, entitled *U.S. Air Service Victory Credits: World War I*. This listing, published in June 1969, records the victory credits officially awarded to members of the U.S. Army who served with the Air Service, American Expeditionary Force.

All images contained in this book are from the author's collection except those marked as copyrighted by others or attributed to other individuals or organizations.

This book is dedicated to the memory of my father,
Robert Michael Hamady.

Book design by Robert Biondi.

Library of Congress Catalog Number: 2008923978.

Printed in China.
ISBN: 978-0-7643-2933-3

Published by Schiffer Publishing Ltd.
4880 Lower Valley Road
Atglen, PA 19310
Phone: (610) 593-1777
FAX: (610) 593-2002
E-mail: Info@schifferbooks.com.
Visit our web site at: www.schifferbooks.com
Please write for a free catalog.
This book may be purchased from the publisher.
Please include $5.00 postage.
Try your bookstore first.

In Europe, Schiffer books are distributed by:
Bushwood Books
6 Marksbury Ave.
Kew Gardens, Surrey TW9 4JF
England
Phone: 44 (0)20 8392-8585
FAX: 44 (0)20 8392-9876
E-mail: info@bushwoodbooks.co.uk
www.bushwoodbooks.co.uk
Free postage in the UK. Europe: air mail at cost.
Try your bookstore first.

FOREWORD

One of the small joys of my life was the opportunity to see and hear an original Nieuport 28 in a simulated aerial combat above the Old Rhinebeck Aerodrome some forty years ago, mixing it up with a nearly original Fokker D.VII, and making wonderfully tight turns to elude the otherwise superior German fighter aircraft. To complete the experience, as the last flying example of the nimble little rotary-engined biplane passed low over the crowd, it left a slight mist of expended castor oil lubricant with the unforgettable aroma I had only read about. That and subsequent visits to Rhinebeck, to see Cole Palen's plane in action, have given me Nieuport 28 memories that remain so vibrant that I can easily understand Ted Hamady's devotion to that aircraft, which resulted in this book.

Author-historian Peter Kilduff, at left, with German Ace Paul Strähle. Peter Kilduff

After becoming acquainted with the restored Rhinebeck Nieuport – decked out as the famous "10" of the 94th Aero Squadron – I met the original's greatest admirer, World War I American Ace Douglas Campbell, and he solidified the image and feel of the Nieuport 28 in my mind. He earned a place in history as the first American-trained pilot to score an aerial victory, and in a Nieuport 28, all of which Ted covers wonderfully well in this book. Doug Campbell told his story many times and, having heard it several times, I can attest that each telling remained fresh and clear, as the Ace truly enjoyed talking about those early days in military aviation and, especially, about the Nieuport 28.

The next step in my learning about World War I aviation history from firsthand sources came in April 1967 during visits with two former German adversaries of Nieuport fighters. Hanns-Gerd Rabe, an observer in two-seat reconnaissance aircraft, had a healthy respect for Nieuports. He said they were "like gnats in the morning sun, hard to see and a damned nuisance – but a dangerous nuisance." Fortunately for Rabe, most of his encounters were while he was in a Rumpler C.VII, the highest-flying German aircraft of World War I, which could easily out-climb the Nieuports. On the other hand, 15-victory fighter Ace Paul Strähle encountered Nieuports in their lower-level combat environment. He managed to shoot down two Nieuports, but only after lengthy, hard-fought combats. "They all twisted and turned like the devil himself," Strähle said, "and they could be on your neck in a second."

So it is with this background that I became familiar with Ted Hamady's research and appreciated his devotion to the Nieuport 28. In my view, Ted has portrayed all of the necessary details and truly captured the spirit of these remarkable aircraft. There is much to be learned from and enjoyed in this book.

Peter Kilduff
New Britain, Connecticut
September 2007

CONTENTS

Foreword 5

Acknowledgments 8

Chapter 1 **First Combat: 14 April 1918 .....10**

Chapter 2 **The Great War in the Air: 1914–1917 .....21**

The French Take the Lead 21

World War I 25

Chapter 3 **Fighting Machines for the Air Service, AEF 38**

America Mobilizes 39

Meanwhile … the War on the Ground 49

Chapter 4 **Four Months of Combat 50**

Gearing Up 50

To the Toul Sector … and Combat 54

The Competition in the Toul Sector 60

Problems Develop 62

The Death of Lufbery 68

The Nieuport 28 Is Cashiered … Temporarily 70

The Genesis of the Nieuport 28A 72

The German Spring Offensives 72

The Real War Looms for the First Pursuit Group 73

From Toul to Touquin 75

The Tide Turns 78

Rickenbacker Brings Home a SPAD XIII 80

From Touquin to Saints for the Final German Offensive 81

Outnumbered and Vulnerable 82

The "Black Day of the 27th" 88

Epilogue 96

Chapter 5 **An Assessment of the Nieuport 28's Combat Role 99**
Performance 99
Mission Capability 102
The Toul Sector 103
The Château-Thierry Sector 104
The St. Mihiel and the Meuse-Argonne Offensives 104
Operational Readiness 106
Command Effectiveness 108
Conclusion 110

Chapter 6 **The Nieuport 28 in Postwar Service 112**
The U.S. Air Service, AEF: Winding Down 112
The U.S. Air Service Stateside 115
Scouting for the Fleet 117
In Swiss Colors 124
Fuerza Aérea Argentina 131

Chapter 7 **In Civilian Hands 135**
Barnstorming and Airshows 135
The Hollywood Years 139

Chapter 8 **The Survivors 157**
NASM Restores a Nieuport 28 157
Photo Essay of NASM's Nieuport 28 Restoration 159
The Survivors 167
Ex-Movie Stars 169
Others in Museums and Works in Progress 177
Flying Reproductions: Past, Present … and Future 183

Appendices
Appendix A: Flying the Nieuport 28 188
Appendix B: The Design Evolution of the Nieuport 28 193
Appendix C: The Nieuport 28 - General Characteristics and Specifications 204
Appendix D: Destined to Fail - The Nieuport 28 Wing 230
Appendix E: Production Orders, Deliveries, and Known Serial Numbers 241
Appendix F: Colors and Markings 249

Notes 264
Bibliography 273
Index 275

ACKNOWLEDGMENTS

I am very grateful to many friends who have made significant contributions to this book on the Nieuport 28. They have very kindly shared their expertise, information and imagery, offered encouragement and useful criticism, and helped guide my research and writing throughout a very long process. I am fortunate because many of the contributors share my interest in World War I military aviation, as well as an affection for this elegant fighter.

I owe special thanks to my son Michael, who spent countless hours patiently scanning and enhancing every image that appears in this book. I marvel at his talent and deeply appreciate his willingness to undertake this laborious task.

I am very grateful to my friend, Alan Toelle, who very generously shared his expert knowledge, artwork, and many valuable images from his treasure-trove of photographs; his work is much in evidence throughout this book.

Peter Kilduff offered to write the foreword to this book, and he has been exceptionally helpful in many ways ... thank you, Peter.

Jim and Zona Appleby offered their wonderful hospitality and a wealth of practitioners' knowledge about the intricacies of building and flying Nieuport 28 replicas – no one knows more about the Nieuport 28 than Jim Appleby. I thank Jim and Zona for their patience in answering my deluge of questions. I am also indebted to Roger Freeman of Vintage Aviation, and to Andrew King and Fred Murrin. All are experienced airplane builders, restorers, and flyers who freely shared their knowledge of the Nieuport 28's airframe and systems, including the Gnôme 9N rotary engine.

I thank Bob Biondi, editor at Schiffer Publishing Ltd., for his encouragement from the very start of this project ... and his patience until the book was finally completed.

Megen Princehouse scrutinized every sentence in the book and pointed out more grammatical and other errors than I'm willing to admit to. Her diligence in catching and correcting every fault, however, kept me at ease. Her growing interest in the story of the Nieuport 28 and contemporary aircraft became evident after she started checking out early volumes of *Jane's All The World's Aircraft* from the University of Colorado Libraries ... thank you, Megen, for your much needed assistance.

I appreciate the interest and efforts of Major General James Randolph, USAF (ret.), Lieutenant Colonel Roy Houchin, USAF, Bill Moran, Ray Voss, Charles Walthall, and my son Peter; they critiqued various chapters and made many helpful suggestions.

I am deeply grateful to Juanita Franzi of Aero Illustrations, whose graphic art appears throughout the book. Juanita's consummate artistic skills and knowledge of aircraft systems are impressive, and she was a joy to work with. I also thank my friends Colin Owers and Michael O'Neal, who contributed their art and drafting skills to the book.

I was delighted to meet and host Gérard and Bertrand Pommier, grandsons of Edouard Nieuport, pioneer aviator-engineer and founder of what became S.A. des Établissements Nieuport. The brothers Pommier provided stunning photographs of the early days of the Nieuport Company.

My long association as a volunteer research historian with the Aeronautics Department of the National Air and Space Museum (NASM), has been immensely rewarding for me. Everyone sharing my passion for aviation history should be as fortunate, for I was always able to consult with the experts about myriad subject matters and find answers to the most difficult questions. I owe much to my friend Peter L. Jakab, Curator of Early Flight. Peter suggested that I write this book and advised me to set my sights high. I will be happy if I have succeeded to his satisfaction.

I am very grateful to John Anderson Jr. and Howard Wolko, who helped me understand what aerodynamicists knew – or thought they knew – in the early days of military aviation. I also owe thanks to Dan Hagedorn, research team leader, and to

Melissa Keiser and Kristine Kaske-Martin, photo archivists, for they were especially helpful in ferreting out obscure information and imagery.

Fourteen NASM employees and volunteers worked on the five-year restoration of NASM's Nieuport 28; all deserve mention for their incredible collective skills, which are evident in the finished product. They are: Max Gainer, Kevin Govier, Jim Harrington, Restoration Team Leader Rich Horrigan, Curator Peter Jakab, Pete Johnson, Ed Mautner Jr., Dick Newhall, Bill Stevenson, Bob Taylor, Fran Tunstall, George Vencelov, Scott Wood ... and myself. Special thanks go to Bob and Max.

Mitchell Yockelson, military records archivist at the National Archives in College Park, Maryland, is listed in countless book acknowledgments, and rightly so. He has patiently guided many researchers, including me, through the voluminous Air Service and military records at the archives ... thank you, Mitch.

Key people at museums here in the United States and abroad offered hospitality and went out of their way to be helpful with my research; they include: Wes Henry, National Museum of the U.S. Air Force; Ron Newberg, Wings Over the Rockies Air and Space Museum; Tim Edwards, U.S. Army Aviation Museum; Dennis Parks, Museum of Flight; Ray Wagner, San Diego Air and Space Museum; Andrea Lareida, Fliegermuseum in Dübendorf, Switzerland; Henry Wydler and Wolf Christian Dingerdissen, Vehrkehrshaus der Schweiz in Lucerne, Switzerland; Comodoro Esteban Luis Correa and Eduardo Amores Oliver, Dirección de Estudios Históricos, Fuerza Aérea Argentina; and Fernando Benedetto, aviation historian in Buenos Aires, Argentina.

Many others have given encouragement, freely shared their expertise, or contributed rare photographs that added immeasurably to the text. They are: Charles Woolley; Roy Meyers, for his expert knowledge of cockpits and instrumentation; Willis Allen Jr.; James Ashenden Jr., Brian Hardesty, and Andy Parks, who made valuable information available from their fathers' archives on World War I aviation; Professor Bert Frandsen; Howard Whyte; Bill Nungesser; Dennis Gordon; Bernard Klaeyle, who is intimately acquainted with all things Nieuport; Art Kennedy; Ray Folsom; and Jane Renaud; also Greg VanWyngarden and Dan-San Abbott, for sharing their wealth of knowledge about the Imperial German Air Force; and Richard Allen and James Farmer, who contributed rare and colorful photographs.

Each of the following people, who has passed on, made important contributions to this book: Bob Cavanagh, Peter Grosz, Bob Rust Sr., Don Brady, Fred Dickey Jr., Dr. Jim Parks, Colonel Rick Glasebrook, H. Hugh Wynne, and Bergen Hardesty.

And not forgotten is Douglas Campbell, whom I met late in his life. Douglas Campbell, the first American-trained pilot to score a victory in aerial combat, inspired me and validated the reasons I had for writing a book about the Nieuport 28. Lieutenant Campbell, U.S. Air Service, was credited with six victories while flying this fighter in 1918.

It is customary to thank one's family, and my family is most deserving of this recognition. My wife, Saniya, our sons, Michael and Peter, and daughter, Claire, have helped in more ways than it is possible to acknowledge. I return their love tenfold.

FIRST COMBAT: 14 APRIL 1918

"I had him at a rare advantage, which was due to the greater speed and maneuverability of our wonderful machines." – Lt. Alan Winslow[1]

A solid overcast hung over Gengoult Aerodrome in the early morning of Sunday, 14 April 1918. Intermittent rain fell on the field, but visibility was good under the 300-meter ceiling and winds were moderate to gusting. One of the pilots noted that this was the "first day over the bloomin [*sic*] lines" but there was little to signify at the time that this "quite disagreeable" day, would be an illustrious one for the men of the 94th Aero Squadron and the Air Service, U.S. Army.[2]

Orders, posted the evening of 13 April, directed the 94th Aero Squadron to begin active operations the next morning at 6 a.m. with a patrol of the squadron's assigned sector, which ran in the shape of a fan from Pont-a-Mousson to St. Mihiel, to the north and west of Gengoult Aerodrome. The aerodrome was located about two and one-half kilometers northeast of Toul, France.

Captain David McKelvey Peterson, a former member of the Lafayette Escadrille and an experienced patrol leader, was designated flight commander, with two novice pilots, Lieutenants Eddie Rickenbacker and Reed Chambers, as the other members of the flight. Captain Peterson directed Rickenbacker to lead the flight should something happen to him.

Lieutenants Alan Winslow and Douglas Campbell were assigned to alert duty; they would keep vigil in the alert tent within the squadron's hangar, awaiting any developments that might send them quickly into the air in their Nieuport 28 fighters. The new Nieuport 28 fighter, with quick-starting Gnôme rotary engine and rapid rate of climb, was admirably suited to the task.

An outstanding leader and fighter pilot, David McKelvey Peterson excelled as a patrol leader in the Lafayette Escadrille. Peterson flew briefly with the 103rd Aero Squadron before transferring to the 94th, where he was to lead the first all-American patrol over the lines. Captain Peterson became commanding officer of the 95th Aero Squadron on 22 May 1918, and was promoted to major in August. R.L. Cavanagh

Rickenbacker and Chambers were circling the field early the next morning as Captain Peterson took off to join them. However, Peterson soon decided to return to the field because of poor weather and Rickenbacker, believing that Peterson had encountered engine trouble, took command of the patrol,

Nieuport 28s being serviced on the line at Gengoult Aerodrome. The aircraft in the foreground, sporting #12 on the fuselage, was flown by Lieutenant Eddie Rickenbacker as a member of the 94th Aero Squadron. R.L. Cavanagh

and he and Chambers set course for the front. After making several circuits along the front between Pont-a-Mousson and St. Mihiel, the two pilots decided to return to the aerodrome, but became separated on the way back as they descended through the overcast. Rickenbacker ultimately found his way back to Gengoult, while Chambers landed safely at another airfield.

Lieutenants Winslow and Campbell, in easy communication with the squadron's operations center, remained in the alert tent, playing a leisurely card game of Russian Bank. The operations center at Gengoult was linked by telephone to the observation post at nearby Mont St. Michel, which overlooked the aerodrome, and that station was in turn linked to antiaircraft sector control centers at Commercy, Lironville, and Dieulouard, running west to east along the battlefront. The early warning network in this sector was well-developed and quite efficient.

At 8:40 a.m., the squadron information officer received a report from the Lironville control center that two German fighters had been observed about fifteen miles away, flying in the direction of Gengoult Aerodrome. Winslow received the report moments later, and he and Campbell were immediately rushed in motorcycle sidecars to their waiting Nieuport 28s. The approaching German fighters were reported flying east towards the aerodrome at an altitude of 2,000 meters. These aircraft had apparently been alerted when Rickenbacker and Chambers had crossed the line not long before.

Lieutenant Campbell quickly took off to the west, and then banked left as he began a climbing circuit over the field to an altitude of 500 meters, where he would join up on Lieutenant Winslow, the alert leader. Alan Winslow picks up the story at this point:

> "Doug" started ahead of me, as I was to meet him above a certain point at five hundred meters, and then take the lead. I gave him about forty-five seconds' start, and then left myself, climbing steeply in a left-hand spiral, in order to save time. I had not made a complete half turn, and was at about two hundred and fifty meters, when straight above and ahead of me in the mist of the early morning, and not more than a hundred yards away, I saw a plane coming toward me with huge black crosses on its wings and tail. I was so furious to see a Hun directly over our Aviation field that I swore out loud and violently opened fire. At the same time, to avoid my bullets, he slipped into a left-hand renversement, and came down, firing on me. I climbed, however, in a right-hand spiral, and slipped off, coming down directly behind him and 'on his tail.' Again I violently opened fire. I had him at a rare advantage, which was due to the greater speed and maneuverability of our wonderful machines. I fired twenty to thirty rounds at him and could see my tracers entering his machine. Then, in another moment, his plane went straight down in an uncontrolled nose-dive – I had put his engine out-of-commission. I followed in a straight dive, firing all the way. At about six feet above the ground he tried to regain control of his machine, but could not, and he crashed to earth. I darted down near him, made a sharp turn by the wreck, to make sure he was

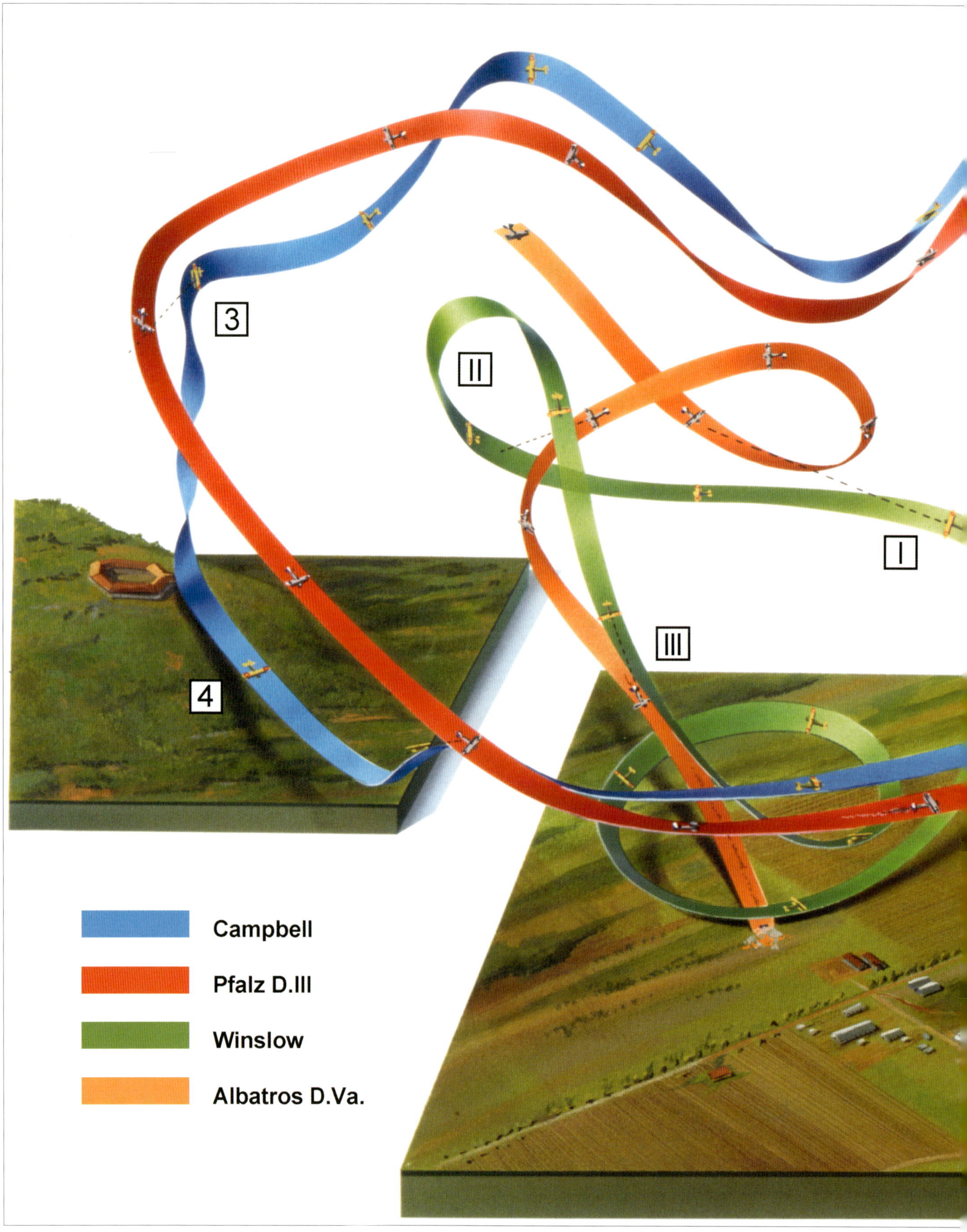
3
II
I
III
4
Campbell
Pfalz D.III
Winslow
Albatros D.Va.

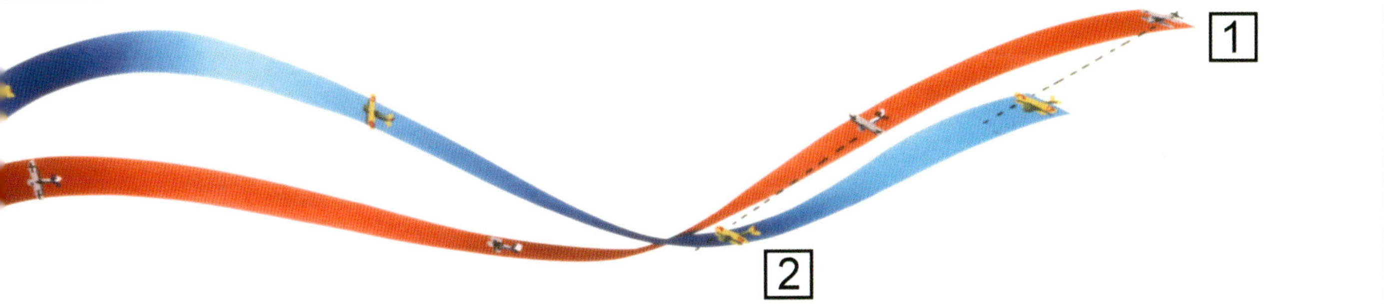

The first aerial victory scored by an American-trained pilot (Lt. Douglas Campbell), took place over the 94th Aero Squadron's aerodrome near Toul, France, on April 14, 1918. Lt. Campbell and Lt. Alan Winslow, flying in Nieuport 28 C.1s, downed two German planes in an engagement that lasted only four minutes. Here's how the action progressed:

1. Lieutenant Campbell takes off first and waits for Lieutenant Winslow to take off and assume lead of the formation.
2. Campbell banks right (in order to see Winslow, who has taken off and has already begun his engagement), when he is fired on by the pilot of a Pfalz D.III
3. Both pilots jockey for position and Campbell fires his first shots at the Pfalz from below and to the left.
4. Campbell's Nieuport stalls and drops to within 100 feet of the ground near the observation post atop Mount St. Michel. After recovering from the stall, Campbell climbs steeply and fires again at the Pfalz. The German plane catches fire.
5. Campbell fires about fifty rounds at the German, the Pfalz dives, and Campbell, now behind his foe, follows him down.
6. The Pfalz, now burning furiously, crashes 100 yards behind the 94th's hangars.

I. Lieutenant Winslow's portion of the battle begins immediately after he takes off. He fires at an Albatros D.Va. The German pilot reverses and comes out firing at Winslow.

II. Winslow climbs, enters a right-hand spiral, and comes down behind the German. Winslow opens fire and disables the engine of the Albatros. The German fighter goes into an uncontrollable dive.

III. The Albatros pilot tries to regain control near the ground, but cannot. He crashes in a field across the road from the 94th's aerodrome. Winslow makes a victory pass and then climbs to see if Lieutenant Campbell needs any help.

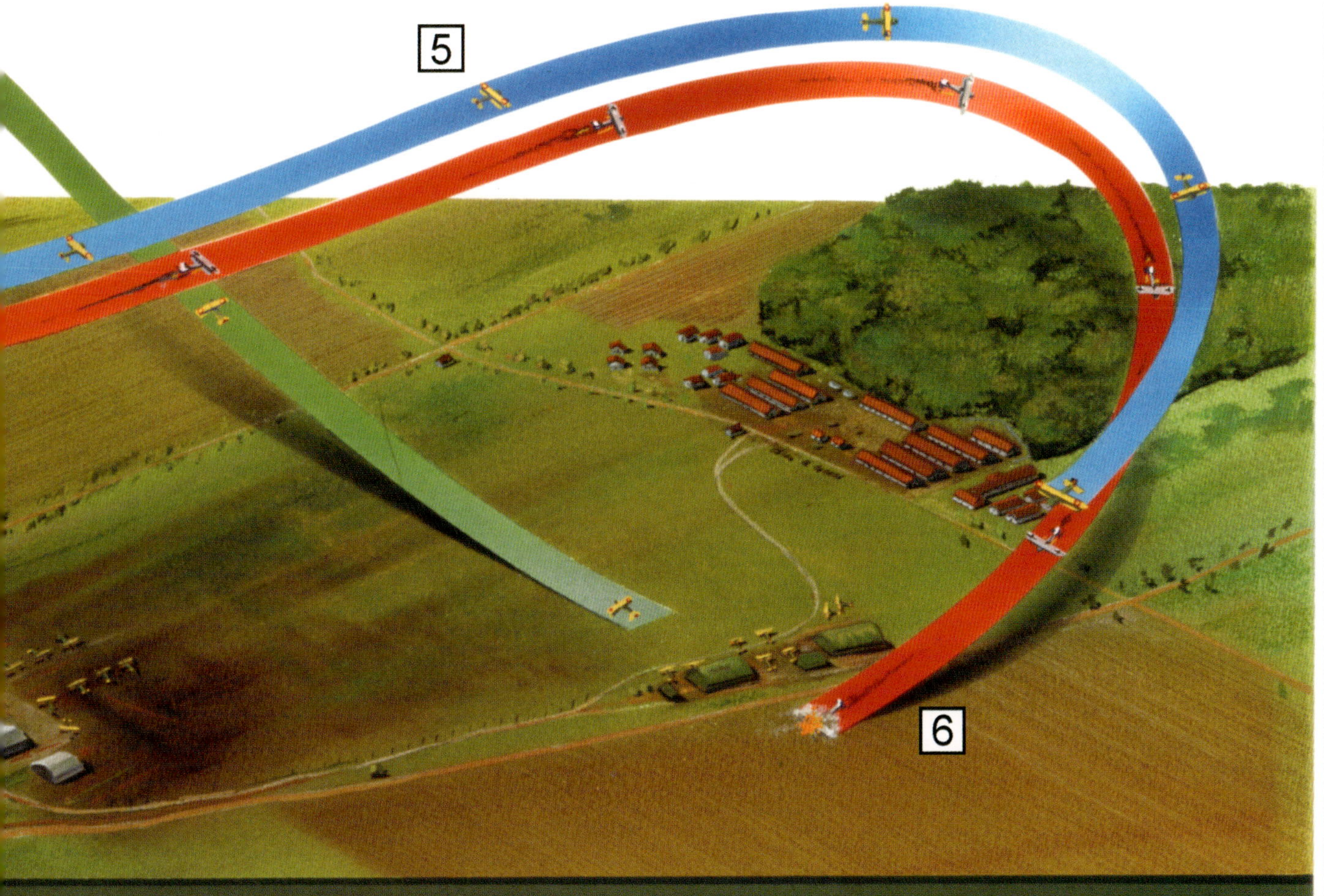

First Victories for the 94th Aero Squadron: artist Frank Wootton portrays the dramatic twin victories scored by the 94th on Sunday, 14 April 1918, the first day of combat operations for the squadron. Lieutenant Alan Winslow has downed his adversary and is seen climbing to assist his squadron mate, but Lieutenant Douglas Campbell has the situation well in hand. Painting by Frank Wootton, estate of Frank Wootton

> out of commission, then made a victorious sweep down over him, and climbed up again to see if "Doug" needed any help with the other Hun – for I had caught a glimpse of their combat out of the corner of my eye.[3]

Lieutenant Alan Winslow had downed an Albatros D.Va; the aircraft, sporting squadron markings of red and black stripes on the horizontal tail surfaces, had crashed and turned over across the road to the west of the field. Meanwhile, Lieutenant Douglas Campbell, in a letter written the next day to his parents, related his part in the air battle:

> Our squadron started regular patrols and alerts yesterday. Alan Winslow and I were on schedule to be on alert from 6:00 to 10:00 a.m. At 6:00, we had our planes wheeled out, and tested the motors to make sure they were running OK. The first two and a half hours were slow, but then things began to happen so quickly that we could hardly keep track of them.
>
> At 8:45, the telephone rang, and the message was that two Boche planes had been sighted some fifteen miles away, headed our way. At 8:50, I took off and had made a round of the field at 500 meters altitude when Winslow got into the air. He was to lead, and when he reached 200 meters, I was getting into position behind him. It was quite misty.
>
> All at once he turned, and I saw him chase a plane that wasn't more than 300 meters high. *It had black crosses on it!* I heard him shoot, and they both went out of sight under my wings. I banked up ninety degrees and turned, to get a view below so as to go help Winslow if necessary, and it was lucky I did, for just as I turned I heard the pop-pop-pop of a machine gun behind me, and there was another Boche shooting at me.
>
> For some reason I thought his tail was turned toward me as he shot, and the thought, 'Biplace [two-seater], keep under him,' flashed into my brain. He turned out afterward to be an Albatros [actually a Pfalz D.III] monoplace, but I had guessed wrong, and instead of getting above him, which would have been easier, I kept below him, maneuvering so as to try to get under his tail without letting him point toward me [i.e., a head-on pass], or get a shot at me from a broadside [i.e., from the rear-seat gunner].[4]

At this point, Lieutenant Campbell was to the left of the German aircraft while the enemy plane was in a turn. The American pulled up sharply to fire. Immediately, Lieutenant Campbell's aircraft stalled and fell to what he described as "within 100 feet of the ground." Lieutenant Campbell had "forgotten about the ground" during the excitement of combat.[5] As he recovered from the stall, he then found himself flying in the same direction as the German aircraft which was directly above him:

> It took over a minute to maneuver into a position behind and under his tail without exposing myself to his fire (I thought), but finally found myself right under him. Then I pulled my nose straight up into the air and let him have the bullets and I think he got some in his motor, for I saw some tracers hitting his nose.
>
> The next thing I knew, he was diving at about forty-five degrees, and I was behind and above him but behind his tail. Then I got a good aim, pulled the trigger, and held on to it. Two or three tracers hit him, and after about fifty rounds had been fired, a streak of flame came shooting out of his fuselage near the motor. I ceased firing, and watched him land and crash in a plowed field, his plane a mass of flame and wreckage.
>
> The pilot had had sense enough to unfasten his belt, and was thrown clear of the machine, escaping with some bad burns and broken bones.[6]

In this picture, taken in 1981, Douglas Campbell shows the author how he maneuvered to attack the Pfalz D.IIIa being flown by Unteroffizier Simon.

After observing the crash of his adversary's airplane (Campbell's adversary was flying a Pfalz D.IIIa, also sporting the colors of Jasta 64), Campbell made one complete circuit of the field – he needed to regain his composure – and then landed.

Pandemonium and joy reigned on the field. Lieutenant Winslow continues:

> Mind you, the fight took place only three hundred meters up, in full view of all on the ground and the near-by town; and it took place directly above our Aviation field. Furthermore, mine dropped about one hundred yards to the right, and "Doug's" one hundred yards to the left of our field. These are remarkable facts, for one of our Majors [Major Raoul Lufbery, highest-scoring member of the Lafayette Escadrille], who, with the French army since 1915, has shot down seventeen machines, never had one land in France – and here we go, right off the bat and stage a fight over our aerodrome and bring down two Huns right on it. It was an opportunity of a lifetime – a great chance.
>
> When we landed, only our respective mechanics were left in the "drome" to help us out of our flying clothes. The whole camp was pouring out, flying by on foot, bicycles, side cars, automobiles; soldiers, women, children, majors, colonels, French and American – all poured out of the city. In ten minutes several thousand people must have gathered. "Doug" and I congratulated each other, and my mechanic, no longer military, jumping up and down, waving his hat, pounded me on the back instead of saluting, and yelled: "Damn it! That's the stuff, old kid!" Then Campbell and I rushed to our respective Hun wrecks.
>
> On the way there, it was only half a mile, I ran into a huge crowd of soldiers – blue and khaki – pressing about one man. I pushed my way through the crowd, and

Unteroffizier Heinrich Simon's Pfalz D.IIIa crashed on the east side of Gengoult Aerodrome. Captain James Norman Hall managed to secure a large swatch of silver fabric before the aircraft burned up. Lieutenant Douglas Campbell had the fabric in his possession sixty-five years later. R.L. Cavanagh

The Albatros D.Va, flown by Vizefeldwebel Wroniecki, crashed and overturned (but did not burn) to the west of Gengoult Aerodrome. It has been righted and is being moved across the road on its way to the aerodrome. Via R.L. Cavanagh

Second Lieutenant Winslow in front of Wroniecki's Albatros D.Va. R.L. Cavanagh

heard somebody triumphantly say to the surrounded man in French, "There he is; now will you believe he is an American." I looked at the man – a scrawny, poorly clad, little devil, dressed in a rotten German uniform. It was the Hun pilot of the machine that I had shot down. Needless to say, I felt rather haughty to come face to face with my victim, now a prisoner, but did not know what to say. It seems that he would not believe that an American officer had brought him down. He looked me all over and then asked me in good French if I was an American. When I answered yes, he had no more to say.

A French and an American General blew up in a limousine to congratulate us – colonels, majors, all the pilots, all the French officers, mechanics – everybody, in the town and camp. All had seen the fight. One woman, an innkeeper, told me she could sleep well from now on, and held up her baby for me to kiss. I looked at the baby, and then felt grateful to my major, who pulled me away in the nick of time. I had mechanics take off everything available – the machine was a wreck – but I got some splendid souvenirs. The big black German crosses from the wings, his rudder, pieces of canvas with holes from my bullets in them, all his spark plugs, his magnetos, his mirror, clock, compass, altimeter, his clumsy signal revolver, etc. – It is a great collection.

"Doug" had set his Hun machine on fire at three hundred meters, and it had fallen in flames rolling over three times, and then completely burning up. There remained but charred wreckage, like the sacrifice of some huge animal. The Hun pilot [Unteroffizier Simon, Campbell's victim] had been thrown out and was badly off. His face, hands, feet, nostrils, and lungs were all burnt, while his leg was broken. He is now in the hospital and my Boche is probably commencing his job of ditch digging for the rest of the war. They got much valuable information from my man – the other couldn't speak. He was a Pole, said he had not been an officer because he was a Pole, although he had been an "aspirant" and a pilot at the front for two years. He said to me, with a sort of sigh of relief, throwing up his hands at the same time, "Alors, la guerre est finie pour moi."[7]

The Polish pilot, Vizefeldwebel Antoni Wroniecki, was indeed helpful to the Air Intelligence Section of the American Expeditionary Force (AEF), which promptly published his information in the daily *Summary of Air Information: Air Intelligence Bulletin*. The pilot reported that his unit, the 64th Pursuit Flight, was based at Mars-la-Tour and attached to German Army C. The squadron's zone of operations was from Étain, twelve miles east of Verdun, to Pont-a-Mousson. The pilot also reported that the squadron, composed of Albatros D.V and Pfalz fighters, had not yet achieved any victories. The *Bulletin* stated that the Albatros was "very much liked by the German aviators; [and],

Second Lieutenant Alan Winslow and his mechanic pose with Winslow's battered victim. R.L. Cavanagh

Winslow had his mechanics remove many souvenirs from his victim's aircraft including this "big black German cross," which is now in the collection of the National Air and Space Museum in Washington, DC.

although the Pfalz is probably faster and can rise with greater speed, it is not in favor because its maneuvering qualities are not so good."[8]

Lieutenant Winslow continues:

> That afternoon my wrecked Hun plane and the charred result of "Doug's" good work were exhibited in the public square of the town, surrounded by an armed guard, and overlooked by a French military band. It also was a great day for the town people, and has had a good moral effect. You can imagine it, when you realize it took place above their rooftops, at only three hundred meters, and that they were able to see the whole fight. The Americans are indeed welcome in the town now, and "Doug" and I can buy almost anything half price. An amusing incident was this; the fight was so near to the earth that bullets were flying dangerously all about the ground. No one was hurt, save a French worker in the field, who received a hole through his ear from one of my bullets, and is very proud of it.[9]

The day's excitement did not abate, but continued through the week. Journalists and photographers descended on the field the next day to write up the story and take pictures of the victorious pilots and their Nieuport 28s, as well as the remains of the German aircraft displayed in Toul's town square.

On 16 April 1918, an aide to General Gerard, Commander of the French Eighth Army, decorated Lieutenants Campbell and Winslow with the Croix de Guerre with Palm. An American movie crew showed up on the following Friday to take pictures of the squadron and "the heroes of Sunday." It was a fitting celebration for an event that was later described as the most spectacular battle in the history of the Air Service.

Obviously happy with their day's work, Lieutenants Winslow and Campbell pose with their squadron commander, Major John W.F.M. Huffer. Note that Campbell is not wearing an aviator's badge, as he had not been issued one. After achieving his first victory he felt that he had earned it, and promptly walked into Toul to buy one to affix to his uniform. R.L. Cavanagh

Below: The remains of Simon's Pfalz and Wroniecki's relatively intact Albatros are exhibited in the town square of nearby Toul. R.L. Cavanagh

This photograph of Lieutenant Douglas Campbell's Nieuport 28, taken several days after the eventful Sunday, was published in stateside papers weeks later. Note that Campbell's Nieuport is sporting the 94th Aero Squadron's "Hat in the Ring" insignia, but still carries the French cocardes. R.L. Cavanagh

Lieutenants Campbell and Winslow being decorated with the Croix de Guerre. R.L. Cavanagh

Campbell and Winslow after being decorated. Note that Lieutenant Campbell is now wearing his newly purchased aviator's badge. R.L. Cavanagh

The true significance of this dramatic first day was not lost on the leaders of the Air Service or their French allies. Colonel Corbiere, the Toul area troop commander, in his message to the 94th, stated that the squadron's success was due to "its immediate readiness, its initiative, its organization and the rapidity with which the pilots took the air … [with] brilliant results."[10] The 94th was also cited by the XXXII Army Corps of the French Eighth Army and commended by the American Chief of Air Service, with "congratulations to Lieut. Douglas Campbell [and] Lieut. Alan Winslow on their excellent work and their gallant conduct."[11]

First Army Air Service Commander Colonel Billy Mitchell best captured the significance for the American Air Service of this glorious event: "[This] bit of rare good fortune on the first day of independent operations on the front had a more important effect on American fighting aviation than any other single occurrence. It gave our men a confidence they could not have obtained any other way."[12]

Colonel Mitchell recognized another major factor that contributed to the success of the first day; the Nieuport 28 fighter that enabled Lieutenants Douglas Campbell and Alan Winslow to get into the air so quickly and maneuver so

Sunday, May 12, 1918

The New York Times

Rotogravure Picture Section, In Two Parts

8

Above: The caption appearing with this photograph in the Rotogravure section of The New York Times read: "German airplane in tatters and a total wreck except the engine, brought down by Douglas Campbell of Mt. Hamilton, Cal., who is said to be the first wholly American trained aviator to bring down a German flier." The New York Times, 12 May 1918

Right: Brigadier General Billy Mitchell, festooned with American and foreign decorations, is shown in a postwar photograph. Mitchell championed the continued production and use of the Nieuport 28 fighter by the U.S. Air Service.

effectively against the standard German fighters of the day, the Albatros D.Va and the Pfalz D.IIIa. In a communication dated 1 May 1918 to the Chief of the Air Service Mitchell suggested that: "The Nieuport twenty eight with Gnome motor, has proved very satisfactory as a pursuit [as fighters were then called] airplane," and Mitchell recommended that "its construction and that of the Gnome monosoupape [single valve] motor be continued with all speed for the use of the American Air Service in France."[13]

What follows is the story of the Nieuport 28 fighter, from its design inception in 1917, through its combat service with the fledgling American Air Service, and into the postwar era: the stunting and air races of the 1920s, the Hollywood years, and up to the present day, when many of the surviving examples of this elegant airplane have been restored to their former glory.

The Nieuport 28 will always be remembered as "America's First Fighter."

CHAPTER TWO

THE GREAT WAR IN THE AIR: 1914-1917

"This is a time for united effort for the country's welfare and so far as the aeroplane industry is concerned, it is good to learn that everyone is working admirably to produce the best possible machine in the quickest possible time." — C.G. Grey[1]

The French Take the Lead

France was preeminent in military aviation at the outset of the First World War. During the course of the four years that followed, France supplied the air forces of her allies with substantial numbers of airframes and aero engines, in addition to supplying her own air service. Engine development and supply were especially critical for the French and British because their air services relied "on engine power more than aircraft design to boost performance."[2] Fortunately, "the aero engine industry [would remain] French aviation's ultimate strength."[3] Significantly, in the fourth year of the war, the United States Air Service, AEF, would obtain the bulk of its aircraft engines and combat aircraft from the French aviation industry.

A number of factors contributed to France's dominant position in aviation among the warring powers. Prewar Europe was entranced by the feats of pioneer aviators, and no country more so than France, whose people had thrilled at the first successful Channel crossing by Louis Blériot in 1909. The Great Air Meet at Reims in 1909 drew enthusiastic thousands, young Roland Garros among them. Garros was inspired by what he saw: "Everyone was delirious ... I would have gambled my life to be like them."[4] Garros fulfilled his promise: he bought a plane, taught himself to fly, and proceeded to risk his life with thrilling exploits that captured the imagination of others. And there were many like Roland Garros – kindred spirits, who were inspired by the great aviation feats that took place in France and throughout Europe in the prewar period.

The French War Ministry was prescient about the coming war and the part that aviation might play in it. Supporters of military aviation realized that the quickest way to develop a strong air arm was to encourage interest in flying among the civilian population. The ministry established flight schools at Chalons and Vincennes in 1910 and the schools' graduate aviators were encouraged to enter the field of civilian competition, to "hone their skills and stoke the public's interest in aviation."[5]

The War Ministry also nurtured the infant aviation industry by staging competitions among airplane manufacturers, with the winners receiving lucrative contracts to build military airplanes. Three airframe companies, Nieuport, Bréguet and Deperdussin, received over 1 million francs in subsidies as a result of their successful performances in the fall 1911 competitions that were held near Reims.

At this time, French military aviation, newly organized under a permanent Inspectorate of Military Aviation, began to conceive its wartime mission, a mission that was soon perceived "as indispensable to the armies as cannon or rifles."[6] French military aviation, now referred to as "la Quatrième Arme Française" (the Fourth French Arm), and its industrial base would be quickly mobilized when the long-expected war began at last on 2 August 1914.

Among the French aviation companies that mobilized for war was the firm S. A. des Établissements Nieuport, located at Issy-les-Moulineaux, near Paris. A predecessor company founded by Edouard de Nieport, who had changed the spelling of his family name and that of his company to Nieuport, manufactured magnetos and starter motors, before venturing into aircraft design and construction in 1909.

The Nieuport Company enjoyed considerable success with its prewar designs; its Type IIN monoplane, powered by a modified and improved Darracq engine of Nieuport's own design, had enjoyed a creditable third-place showing in the 1910 trials. In 1911, however, the triumph of the Nieuport Type IVG, with first- and third-place showings in the Gordon Bennett Cup competition in July, was overshadowed by the fatal crash of Edouard Nieuport's airplane on 9 September. Charles Nieuport, a rated reserve military aviator like his late brother, succeeded Edouard.

In what was billed as a "Tournament of Aeronautical Champions," the Grande Semaine d'Aviation, held in August 1909 near Reims, was a great success for aviation. Over 500,000 people paid the attendance fee to watch the exciting aerial events and many thousands more observed from nearby hills. Willis Allen, Allen Airways Flying Museum

Edouard Nieuport, the illustrious founder of S.A. des Établissements Nieuport, was born in Blida, Algeria, in 1875. A champion cyclist in his youth, Edouard's mechanical skills and training as an electrical engineer led to the successful development of ignition systems for the emerging automobile industry. Edouard's passion and inventive genius turned to aviation in 1908; he is shown here standing before his first airplane. Edouard and Charles Nieuport Image Collection (Nie 13), National Air and Space Museum, Smithsonian Institution

Roland Garros' prewar exploits included an altitude record flight in 1912 and a risky first crossing of the Mediterranean in 1913. A military flyer at the start of the war, Garros was taken prisoner in 1915 when his aircraft was shot down. He escaped in 1918 and returned to combat, only to be killed in action at Vouziers on 5 October 1918. He was thirty-six years old at the time of his death. National Air and Space Museum, Smithsonian Institution (SI 73-6714)

Artist Gamy celebrates the emergence of La Quatrième Arme Française, "The Fourth French Arm." The aircraft depicted is a Nieuport Type IIG equipped with a 70 hp Gnôme rotary engine. This aircraft type placed first in the Coupe Michelin in 1911.

Charles Weyman prepares for takeoff in a Nieuport Type IVG, on his way to achieving victory at the Military Concours at Reims on 20 November 1911. His three-place aircraft was powered by a 100 hp Gnôme rotary engine. Edouard and Charles Nieuport Image Collection (Nie 166), National Air and Space Museum, Smithsonian Institution

Edouard Nieuport is pictured here in the cockpit of his first airplane at Issy-les-Moulineaux in December 1909. Weighing only 764 pounds, the lightweight airplane had a wingspan of 26 feet and was powered by a two-cylinder, 20 hp Darracq motor. Edouard and Charles Nieuport Image Collection (Nie 15), National Air and Space Museum, Smithsonian Institution

American pilot Charles T. Weyman crosses the finish line in a Nieuport Type IVG to win the Gordon Bennett Cup Race on 1 July 1911. An American flag is raised in his honor. Edouard and Charles Nieuport Image Collection (Nie 177), National Air and Space Museum, Smithsonian Institution

Left: Edouard and Charles Nieuport Image Collection (Nie 315), National Air and Space Museum, Smithsonian Institution

Gustave Delage joined the Nieuport Company in 1914 as technical director. Responsible for Nieuport's successful fighter plane designs, his success carried well into the postwar years with the widespread use of the Nieuport 29. After the firm merged with Astra Company in 1920, Delage remained as technical director and oversaw the construction of naval aircraft. Howard Whyte

Left: Charles Nieuport (1878-1913), in dark suit, is flanked on his right by Henri Deutsch de la Meurthe, Nieuport's financier, and on his left by A. Le Blanc and race pilot Jules Védrine. Edouard and Charles Nieuport Image Collection (Nie 176), National Air and Space Museum, Smithsonian Institution

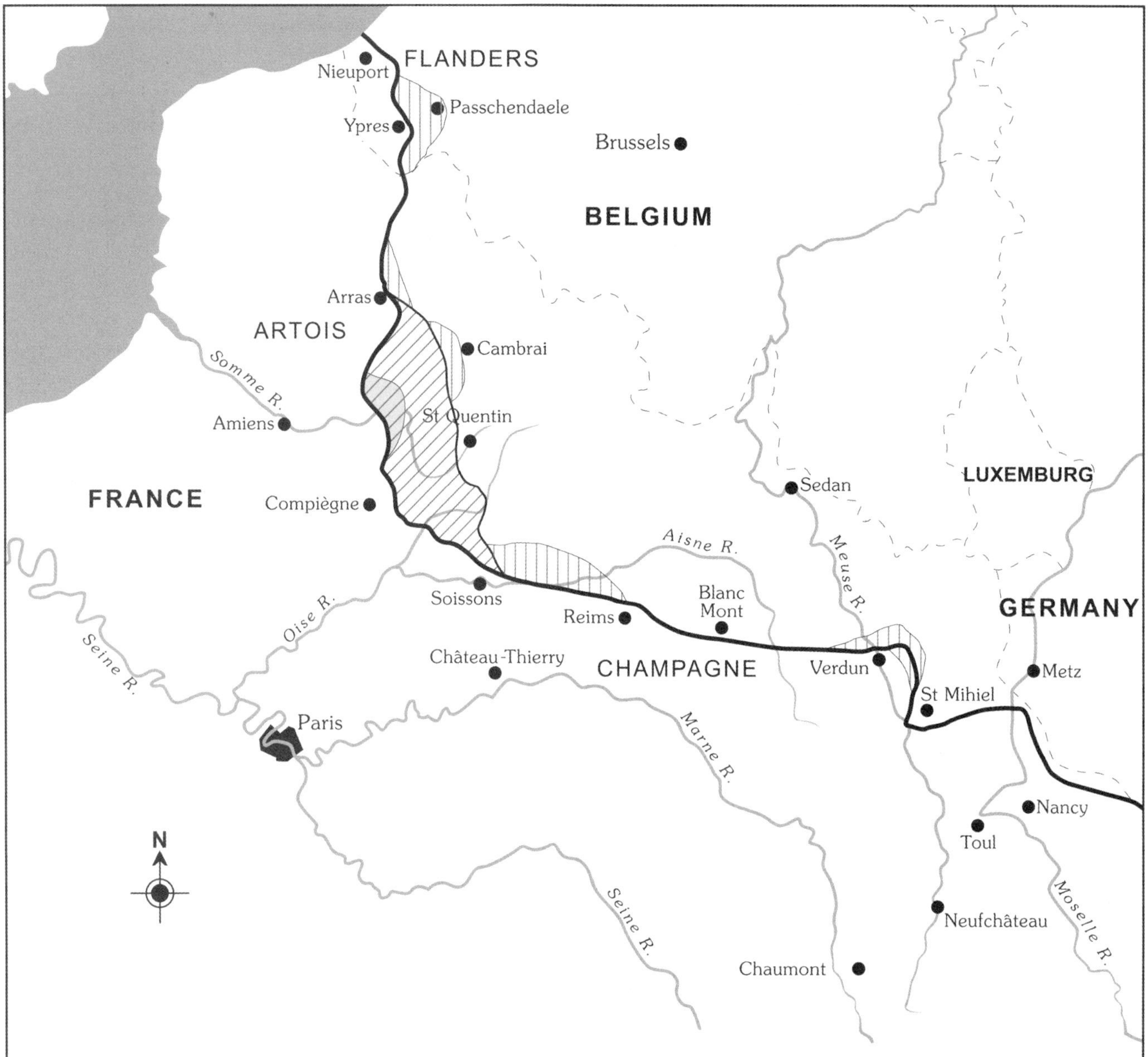

The Western Front

December 1914 to March 1918

After months of maneuver warfare, the Western Front stabilized at the end of 1914 with a trench line that ran from the Channel Coast to the border of Switzerland. Allied offensives in 1915 in the Artois and Champagne Regions and the second battle of Ypres, where poison gas was first used, produced over two million casualties with no appreciable change in the line.

The battles of Verdun (February 21 to December 18) and The Somme (June 24 to November 13) in 1916, the so-called "Year of Decision", took an enormous toll on both sides. After the failure of the French offensive at the Aisne River, British troops maintained the offensive spirit in 1917 with attacks at Arras, Flanders, and again, at Ypres (Passchendaele), ending the year with a limited success at Cambrai.

German armies withdrew earlier in 1917 to a more defensible line dubbed the "Hindenburg Line", that extended from Arras to Soissons. The combatants on the Western Front suffered over five million casualties during this three-year period with little to show for the horrendous price paid.

Scale in miles

0 25 50 75

Trench line, Dec 1914

Significant changes to the trench lines

Ground gained during The Somme Battle, 1916

German withdrawal to Hindenburg Line, Feb - Apr 1917

The company was stabilized and strengthened by the intervention of financier Henri Deutsch de la Meurthe, who purchased all of Nieuport's patents and established a capital fund of 1.2 million francs. The company's fortunes were further enhanced when a brilliant designer and aviator, naval Lieutenant Gustave Delage, became technical director. Delage's participation would ensure long-term success for the Nieuport Company.

The Nieuport Company's prewar fortunes peaked with the success of its Type IVG three-place monoplane at the Military Concours at Reims in the fall of 1911. The Type IVG proved to be the fastest airplane, with an average speed of 116.9 km/h over a 300 km course, and was also the strongest airplane among the entries. As a result of its success in the trials, Nieuport was rewarded with an order for ten monoplanes, newly designated as military Type IVM, plus a substantial bonus for having exceeded the announced specifications. Tragically, Charles Nieuport was killed in January 1913, while testing one of the new aircraft prior to delivery. However, with improved finances and management, the Nieuport Company would survive the loss of both of its illustrious founders.

Adopted by the French Air Force toward the end of 1915, the Caudron G.4 served as a bomber and reconnaissance aircraft. Powered by twin, 80 hp Le Rhône rotary engines or, alternatively, by twin 100 hp Anzani radials, the G.4 was reliable and possessed a good rate of climb. The G.4 served with every major Allied nation during the war. National Air and Space Museum, Smithsonian Institution (SI 2002-2589)

World War I

The Nieuport IVM equipped only one (Escadrille N.12) of the twenty-one squadrons that were operational when war was declared in August 1914. For a time, the Nieuport Company was content with building a competitor's design under license, but the fortunes of the company would change dramatically with the emergence of a brilliant new design in the second year of the war. By December 1914, the war of movement had ended on the Western Front. Exhausted Allied and German troops, unable to defeat or outmaneuver the other, dug in along a line across France from Nieuport on the Channel coast to the Swiss border near Belfort.

The prevailing tactical doctrine at the start of the war held that armies must "seize and maintain the initiative in battle."[7] However, existing frontal assault tactics, the use of weapons such as machine guns and masses of artillery, and the nature of the trench lines themselves favored the defense and ensured that continuance of the offensive doctrine would be extremely costly. The great offensives of 1915 to November 1917 – Artois and Champagne in 1915, Verdun and the Somme in 1916, and the abortive Chemin des Dames and Third Ypres in 1917 – resulted in appalling losses: over five million casualties suffered on both sides during this three-year period – with no appreciable change in the front line.

The war on the ground had stalemated, in contrast to the war in the air, which was beginning to be dynamic and fast-paced. Air fighting doctrine, established by both sides early in the war, held that "British and French air policy and overall military strategy was offensive, but the British pursued the air offensive more unrelentingly and inflexibly than the French. For much of the war, the Germans husbanded their resources, fought defensively, and planned to concentrate their aviation forces to seek an occasional mastery limited in time and space."[8]

Military aviation quickly proved its value to the ground armies in the opening weeks of the war. Aerial observations by French pilots enabled the British army to avoid encirclement by the German II Corps as British forces began their retreat from Mons, Belgium, into France in mid-August 1914.

On the Eastern Front, a German aviator, flying a prewar Taube, observed the movement of a Russian army into East Prussia. This observation allowed the German Eighth Army to encircle the Russian army and annihilate it at the Battle of Tannenberg. Ironically, the Russians, who possessed the second largest air fleet in Europe, failed to detect the enemy moves.

Days later, Paris and France were saved when pilot and aircraft designer Louis Bréguet observed the turn of von Kluck's army before Paris; this intelligence allowed the British and French armies to hit the exposed flank of the German army and drive it back, in a battle that would be known as the "Miracle of the Marne."

During the German retreat from the Marne to the Aisne River, a French aviator observed a large German artillery concentration near the village of Thiaucourt and dropped a note to a divisional artillery unit. The resulting barrage destroyed half the artillery of the German XVI Corps.

As a result of these initial successes, cooperation with army corps, observation, and artillery regulation became primary missions of the military air services.

The first recorded aerial victory on the Western Front occurred on 5 October 1914, when a French pilot and his observer downed a German airplane with machine-gun bullets. Shortly thereafter, a lone German plane crossed the

An innovative design entering service in 1916, the Sopwith 1 1/2 Strutter equipped the first strategic bombing air unit in 1916. The 1 1/2 Strutter was powered by a Clergêt 9Z, 110 hp rotary engine. Over 6,000 of these multipurpose aircraft were built in France and Great Britain. National Air and Space Museum, Smithsonian Institution (SI 82-3579)

The C class of aircraft (single-engined, armed two-seaters) was introduced in mid-1915. The Rumpler C.1 (shown here in the hands of French troops), was powered by a 160 hp Mercédès D.III in-line engine; it had an endurance of four hours and a ceiling of almost 16,405 feet. The stability of this aircraft made it an excellent platform for photo-reconnaissance. National Air and Space Museum, Smithsonian Institution (SI 84-14193)

Channel and bombed Dover before returning safely to base. German Zeppelins and Taubes had already visited Paris and other French cities and targets. The last months of 1914 saw the genesis and growing importance of several new missions for military aviation – tactical and strategic bombing, and air combat against opposing air forces.

Military aviation had begun to meet the prewar expectations of its ardent supporters. Rational measures, taken early in the war by the progressive chief of French aviation, Commandant Joseph Barés, doubled the number of French squadrons and these squadrons were tasked with specific missions (observation, artillery support, bombing, and fighting). In addition, the squadrons' aircraft, largely of prewar design, were becoming specialized, to more effectively meet their mission requirements. Standardization on fewer, specialized designs also brought greater production efficiency.

Prewar aircraft types included the Caudron G.3 for artillery ranging and corps observation, the Maurice Farman M.F. 11 pusher for general reconnaissance, the Voisin LA 5 pusher for bombing, and the Morane-Saulnier Type L fighting monoplane. The ubiquitous Le Rhône 80 hp rotary engine powered the Caudron and Morane, while the other aircraft were equipped with in-line, water-cooled engines. The year 1915 brought increased specialization of air missions, and a quest for new airframe designs and more powerful engines to meet the new requirements.

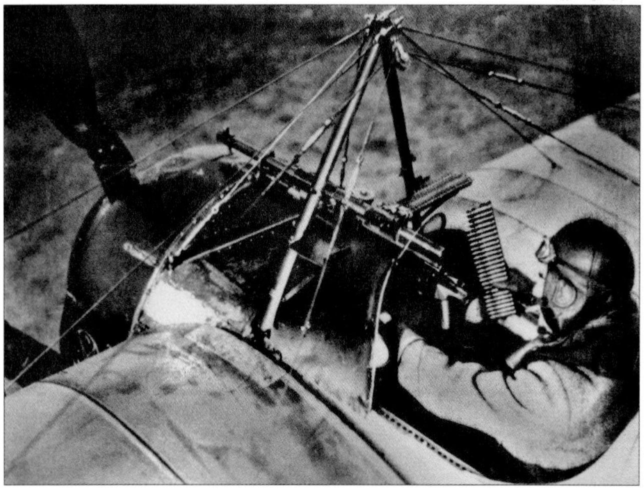

Roland Garros, seated in the cockpit of his Morane-Saulnier monoplane fighter, handles a clip of 8 mm cartridges for the lightweight "portative" Hotchkiss machine gun affixed to the cowl. Garros clamped two tempered steel pieces to the propeller. The sharp points of the triangular metal pieces, bore-sighted to the machine-gun bore, deflected the two percent of the machine-gun burst that would have otherwise holed the propeller. Ninety-eight percent of the burst passed harmlessly between the propeller blades. National Air and Space Museum, Smithsonian Institution (SI 90-4832)

This view of a crashed Fokker E.III offers an unusual look at the single Spandau LMG 08/15 machinegun. Powered by a Oberursel UL 9 cylinder rotary engine, the E.III had a maximum speed of 87.5 mph at sea level. Two synchronized machine guns could be mounted on the cowl. The aircraft remained a formidable weapon until the appearance of the Nieuport 11 in early 1916. National Air and Space Museum, Smithsonian Institution (SI 89-13098)

The following year, 1916, heralded the emergence of a truly military air arm, as a new generation of aircraft took to the air. These aircraft, designed with knowledge gained in wartime, included the French Caudron G.4 bomber and reconnaissance airplane, the British Sopwith 1 1/2 Strutter, also a reconnaissance and bombing airplane (powered by a French-designed, Clergêt rotary engine), and the German Albatros C.III reconnaissance airplane, powered by a 160 hp Mercédès D.III in-line engine. Useful load, range, ceiling, and speed of military airplanes increased markedly as these new designs were introduced. This year would also see the fighter mission finally come into its own.

Early attempts at air combat had been feeble, as aircraft, weapons (if carried), and tactics proved inadequate to the task. In 1915, Roland Garros, by now a seasoned member of France's Aviation Militaire, installed steel deflectors on the propeller blades of his aircraft, which enabled his machine gun to fire directly through the propeller arc. Now able to make direct attacks against surprised German aviators, Garros was wildly successful for a brief time, until he was downed by ground fire and taken prisoner.

After inspecting Garros' primitive device, noted designer Anthony Fokker fashioned a far more potent mechanism. Fokker's device, an interruptor gear that prevented the machine gun from firing when the propeller spun in front of the barrel, was quickly installed on Fokker E.I monoplanes and delivered to the front. German flyers Oswald Boelcke and Max Immelmann established their legendary reputations while flying the otherwise unremarkable Fokker Eindecker, or monoplane. It was the synchronizing device that made the Fokker Eindeckers deadly, and it would be a year before the Allies had a comparable device.

In a matter of weeks, Boelcke and Immelmann had become air heroes. Both airmen were awarded the coveted Pour le Mérite, the German Empire's highest honor, for having downed the then-required eight enemy airplanes. The more powerful Fokker E.III, some of which were armed with two synchronized machine guns, soon appeared, and continued the heavy toll of French and British bombers and observation planes. This period, lasting eight brutal months, became known as the "Fokker Scourge," but help was on the way.

The airplane that helped end the "Fokker Scourge" was a small fighter biplane, aptly named the Bébé (baby), or more correctly, the Nieuport 11. The Nieuport 11 had been inspired by Gustave Delage's prewar racing biplane, a design that had been intended to compete for the 1914 Gordon Bennett Cup.

The Nieuport 11 entered service on 5 January 1916. The plane's direct predecessor, the Nieuport 10, an underpowered two-seater observation plane, had found merit as a fighter plane when flown as a single-seater. A two-spar upper wing attached by V-struts to a single-spar lower wing of much smaller chord distinguished the Nieuport 11. This

Hauptmann Oswald Boelcke (fourth from left) and Oberleutnant Max Immelmann (sixth from left) stand proudly with their confreres. Both pilots wear the coveted Pour le Mérite.

feature, known as a sesquiplane, reflected Gustave Delage's compromise solution to the French air service's preference for a biplane's stability and Delage's own quest for greater speed. The smaller lower wing also afforded the pilot a better view below. Ailerons were attached to the 13-square-meter upper wing; the ailerons afforded far superior maneuverability compared to the cumbersome Fokker Eindecker, which relied on wing warping to control roll.

The performance and handling characteristics of this lightweight and highly maneuverable fighter were excellent for the time: 97 mph at sea level, a high rate of climb, and a ceiling of 15,000 feet, with flight duration of two hours. The Nieuport 11 was powered by an 80 hp Le Rhône rotary engine.

There were some drawbacks to this new design, however. The single, fixed Lewis machine gun, mounted on the top wing and firing over the propeller arc, was distracting for the pilot, who was required to change the 47-round Lewis magazine (later increased to 100 rounds) in the heat of combat. Of more concern to the pilot, however, was the apparent weakness of the sesquiplane (a design feature retained up to and including the Nieuport 27), believed to be caused by the annular fitting of the V-strut to the single spar of the lower wing. Heavy flight loads caused the relatively long-span lower wing to twist, or flutter, and break away.

The Nieuport 11 began to appear at the front in small numbers during the closing months of 1915 – a most propitious moment, as it would turn out.

The Allies and the Germans both sought to break the deadlock on the Western Front in 1916, and both sides, at relatively equal strength at this point in the war, planned major offensives to achieve this goal. Striking first at Verdun, the Germans were well-aware that France would make every effort to defend this vitally important and sacred sector. General Erich von Falkenhayn, chief of staff of the German Army, made this point crystal clear: "Within our reach behind the French sector of the Western Front, there are objectives for the retention of which the French General Staff would be compelled to throw in every man they have. If they do so, the forces of France will bleed to death – as there can be no question of a voluntary withdrawal – whether we reach our goal or not ... the objectives of which I am speaking now are Belfort and Verdun."[9]

The Germans assaulted the French defenses along an eight-mile front at Verdun on 21 February 1916. The small French garrison was surprised by the massive onslaught because German artillery had quickly destroyed French observation balloons along the narrow front, and concentrations of German fighters, mainly Fokker Eindeckers, had barred French reconnaissance and artillery planes from carrying out their vital missions. As a result, the French forces were blinded during the initial phases of the assault.

This photograph of a Nieuport 17 in flight illustrates the enhanced visibility downward due to the sesquiplane lower wing. The photograph also suggests the fragility of the single-spar lower wing. National Air and Space Museum, Smithsonian Institution (SI 88-16373)

Opposite
Top: The Nieuport 10 was one of the first projects that Gustave Delage undertook after joining the Nieuport Company in 1914. Entering service in 1915, the two-seater achieved some success as a single-seat fighter after the observer's position was covered over. Nieuport's distinctive sesquiplane design was introduced on the Nieuport 10 and was later copied by German designers on the Albatros D.III. The 80 hp Le Rhône rotary engine was the standard powerplant, and the standard armament, a single Lewis gun mounted on the top wing. Edouard and Charles Nieuport Image Collection (Nie 232), National Air and Space Museum, Smithsonian Institution

Center: A brilliant design, the diminutive Nieuport 11, or "Bébé," was in service with the French, British, Italian, Dutch, and Russian air services. It established the wartime reputations of the Nieuport Company and its designer, Gustave Delage. Powered by an 80 hp Le Rhône 9C rotary engine, the small, highly maneuverable fighter had a maximum speed of 97 mph and ceiling of 15,000 feet. It carried a single Lewis machine gun. Edouard and Charles Nieuport Image Collection (Nie 280), National Air and Space Museum, Smithsonian Institution

Bottom: Courtney Campbell, a member of the Lafayette Escadrille, managed to land his Nieuport 23 after losing his lower left wing on 7 July 1917. The cause was the inherent weakness of the annular fitting that secured the V-strut to the single-spar lower wing. Fortunately, the ailerons were on the top wing; this allowed some semblance of control in the event of loss of a lower wing induced by flutter. National Air and Space Museum, Smithsonian Institution (SI 2004-12845)

However, the French response in the air was swift and effective. Major Charles de Rose, Baron de Tricornot and a Marquis, who was acclaimed as the "father of the French fighter arm," was given authority to gather all available Morane and Nieuport 11 fighters (there were about 100 Nieuport 11 fighters on strength at this time) and the best pilots. With them, de Rose was able to form fifteen elite squadrons, with the objective of "sweeping the sky and driving the Germans out of it."[10] The Nieuport 11, in the hands of such skilled pilots as Navarre, Guynemer, and Nungesser, quickly overcame the obsolescent Eindeckers, and the French regained air superiority by April 1916. This concentration of elite French air units had in turn blinded the German forces, and greatly assisted the French infantry and artillery in stopping the German assault on Verdun. French ground forces, however, suffered 542,000 casualties in the process of stemming the German tide.

Above

Left: French General Franchet d'Esperey decorates Major Charles de Rose, "the father of the French fighter arm," with the Legion of Honor. Edouard and Charles Nieuport Image Collection (Nie 279), National Air and Space Museum, Smithsonian Institution

Center: Sous-Lieutenant Jean M.D. Navarre, acclaimed as the "Sentinel of Verdun," was credited with nine victories while flying with Escadrille N.67. Navarre ceased flying combat missions after being severely wounded on 17 June 1916. He was killed in a flying accident in 1919. Edouard and Charles Nieuport Image Collection (Nie 93), National Air and Space Museum, Smithsonian Institution

Right: Georges Guynemer, France's beloved military aviator, stands beside his Nieuport 10, nicknamed "Old Charles." Guynemer achieved fourteen victories while flying with Escadrille N.3, but most of his victories were scored after he transitioned to SPAD fighters. His Legion of Honor (Officer) citation read in part, "he has become for the enemy ... the most redoubtable adversary of all." Georges Guynemer was killed in combat on 11 September 1917. Edouard and Charles Nieuport Image Collection (Nie 288), National Air and Space Museum, Smithsonian Institution

Lieutenant Charles Nungesser is pictured with his cap reversed in the cockpit of his Nieuport 17. He scored twenty of his credited forty-three victories while flying with Escadrille N.65. Nungesser continued to fly in combat, despite having sustained numerous injuries, until he was retired in September 1918. Charles Nungesser was lost while attempting a transatlantic flight in 1927. Edouard and Charles Nieuport Image Collection (Nie 94), National Air and Space Museum, Smithsonian Institution

Opposite

Top: Interior of the Nieuport factory at Issy-les-Moulineaux, circa 1916. Edouard and Charles Nieuport Image Collection (Nie 100), National Air and Space Museum, Smithsonian Institution

Bottom: Neatly dressed women workers tack and stitch fabric on aircraft surfaces prior to doping the fabric. Edouard and Charles Nieuport Image Collection (Nie 234), National Air and Space Museum, Smithsonian Institution

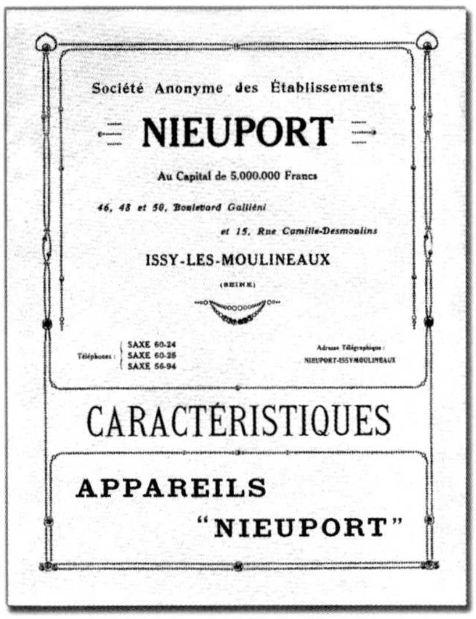

Société Anonyme des Établissements

NIEUPORT

Au Capital de 5.000.000 Francs

46, 48 et 50, Boulevard Galliéni

et 15, Rue Camille-Desmoulins

ISSY-LES-MOULINEAUX

(SEINE)

Téléphones: SAXE 60-24 / SAXE 60-28 / SAXE 56-94

CARACTÉRISTIQUES

APPAREILS

"NIEUPORT"

Front cover of a Nieuport Company catalog, circa 1918. National Archives

Through these efforts, Major de Rose had demonstrated the value of large and independent formations of fighters; these units were independent of their traditional role of providing close protection for observation and bombing planes. While some French fighter units continued in the army cooperation role, dispersed along the entire front line, the independent group, newly constituted as the Groupe de Chasse and under the command of GHQ, could be quickly concentrated at critical points along the line.

These were heady times for Gustave Delage and the Nieuport Company. Sales in 1916 were 26.4 million francs, a very substantial increase over the company's sales of 285,000 francs in 1914.[11] Nieuport's war effort was also reflected in a fivefold increase in employees over the number employed in spring 1915. The company had negotiated licensing agreements to build the Nieuport 11 with Italy, the Netherlands, and Russia, and had sold these tiny fighters to the UK (where they were used by the Royal Flying Corps and Royal Naval Air Service, along with their own D.H. 2s, to successfully combat Fokker Eindeckers on the British front), as well as a number of other countries.

Nieuport continued to mine the sesquiplane design with the addition of the Nieuport 16. This fighter featured an improved cowling, a headrest for the pilot, and provisions for four electrically fired Le Prieur rockets, which were effective against Drachen observation balloons. Most importantly, a more powerful Le Rhône rotary engine, rated at 110 hp, was installed. The airplane was nose-heavy, however, and Delage corrected this problem by increasing the wing area from 13 square meters to 15 square meters. The resulting design became the Nieuport 17, or "Superbébé," the most successful of all of Nieuport's sesquiplane designs.

Lafayette Escadrille pilot Norman Prince examines Le Prieur incendiary rockets that are installed on a Nieuport 11. The rockets, used by both the French and British air forces against hydrogen-filled observation balloons, were generally found on more powerful Nieuport 16s and 17s. Propelled by a small amount of ballestite, the Le Prieur rocket was accurate up to 400 yards. National Air and Space Museum, Smithsonian Institution (SI 2004-12846)

Below: Faster, heavier, and sturdier than the Nieuport 11, the Nieuport 17 entered service in March 1916. While the fighter was widely used by Allied air services, the Nieuport 17 pictured here was the personal mount of Canadian Ace Billy Bishop. The upper wing-mounted Lewis machine gun was replaced by, or used in conjunction with, a synchronized machine gun mounted on the cowl. Powered by a 110 hp Le Rhône rotary engine, the Nieuport 17 would be eclipsed by the slightly faster and more robust SPAD VII, powered by the revolutionary Hispano-Suiza engine. Edouard and Charles Nieuport Image Collection (Nie 326), National Air and Space Museum, Smithsonian Institution

The Nieuport 17, with greater speed (110 mph at 6,560 feet) and ceiling (17,400 feet) than the Nieuport 11 and fitted with a single fixed Vickers .303 machine gun (and/or a top-mounted Lewis), was well-received by Allied pilots, many of whom would make or enhance their reputations while flying the Nieuport 17. This illustrious group included Georges Guynemer, Charles Nungesser (who flew the Nieuport 17bis

fitted with a more powerful Clergêt 130 hp rotary engine), and Albert Ball and Billy Bishop of the RFC. The Nieuport 17 also equipped the American-volunteer Lafayette Escadrille, which had arrived at the Verdun front in May 1916. The Nieuport 17 was also in service with the air services of Italy, Russia, Finland, and Holland.

The Germans, having been bested by the Nieuport, directed several German companies to clone Nieuport's fighter design. The Siemens-Schuckert Werke ultimately produced ninety-four D.1 fighters (powered by a 110 hp Siemens-Halske rotary engine), and these aircraft saw service principally on the Russian front. Ironically, later German designs, including the Albatros D.III and the Pfalz D.III, incorporated a fatal flaw by adopting the narrow-chord, single-spar sesquiplane design. This flaw asserted itself as speed-induced flutter caused the wing to fail.[12]

On 1 July 1916, following an intense, weeklong artillery bombardment of German positions, the British Third and Fourth Armies began their long-awaited offensive on the Somme front. Twenty-six English and fourteen French divisions made the main effort, supported by French and British aircraft that outnumbered their air opponents by three-to-one. Allied mastery in the air, notwithstanding the carnage and ultimate failure of the ground offensive, continued throughout July, August, and into the middle of September. "The [aerial] Battle of the Somme was a glorious epoch for the Allies as well as for French aviation and, in particular, its fighter element,"[13] of which the vaunted Nieuport 17 formed a major part.

The tide of battle in the air would turn again in the fall of 1916, as Germany responded to the crisis with a number of effective measures.

Hauptmann Oswald Boelcke, arguably the most outstanding leader, teacher, and tactician of the air war, was recalled in late August from noncombat duties to form and lead Jasta 2, a squadron of expert pilots. Boelcke had been expressly forbidden to fly in combat by the Kaiser for fear of his loss to the nation, but his return was now required. Boelcke began to energetically implement reforms that were to change the nature of aerial warfare.

"He trained his handpicked fighters to understand that the squadron came first, that they had to stick together, and that the individual's victory tally did not matter, so long as the Jagdstaffel [Jasta for short, the new organization of fighter units, translated literally as "hunting echelon"] won. Before each unit flight, he issued instructions; afterward he gave a severe critique of the unit's performance. He emphasized the importance of thoroughly knowing the enemy aircraft's strengths and weaknesses. By formulating and teaching the rules of organized fighter aviation [which became known as Boelcke's Dicta], Boelcke set the pace in combat flight as he continued to score steadily, often having 'an Englishman for breakfast' in lone early-morning sorties."[14]

Oswald Boelcke codified the first set of air tactics with the dissemination of his "Dicta" in September 1916. He also demonstrated the benefits of formation flying and instilled the discipline required to do it successfully – something that opposing air forces would be required to learn. Boelcke was killed in a midair collision with a squadron mate on 28 October 1916. National Air and Space Museum, Smithsonian Institution (SI 76-13287)

Boelcke introduced the new Albatros D.II biplane fighter to combat, scoring the first victory, his twentieth, for his new unit on 2 September 1916. The Albatros D.II, powered by a 160 hp Mercédès D.III engine, flew at 108 mph and could climb to 17,000 feet. The fighter was armed with two synchronized machine guns, giving it a potent advantage in firepower. This fact was amply demonstrated on 23 November 1916, when Manfred von Richthofen downed Major Lanoe Hawker, VC, in a classic air battle that pitted the twin-gunned Albatros D.II against Hawker's slower D.H. 2 armed with a single Lewis machine gun. Hawker, even with consummate courage and skill, could not overcome the superior performance of his opponent's airplane, and he became von Richthofen's fifteenth victim.

The Albatros D.III soon replaced the Albatros D.II. The D.III, possessing greater range and ceiling, soon outclassed every opponent, much as the D.H. 2s and Nieuport 11s had earlier outclassed the Fokker Eindeckers. This new fighter was

German fighter pilots were once more ascendant, with the adoption of twin-gunned Albatros fighters. The Albatros D.III was favored by many of the best pilots, including Manfred von Richthofen, seen here taking off – or landing: it's hard to tell. Improvement over the Albatros D.II models in performance at altitude and rate of climb resulted from the use of a higher compression Mercédès D.IIIa engine and the Nieuport-inspired sesquiplane design. National Air and Space Museum, Smithsonian Institution (SI 92-1818)

especially effective when flown by the expert pilots of Jasta 2 opposing the Royal Flying Corps' obsolescent D.H. 2s.

In October, the Luftstreitskrafte (Imperial German Air Service) was organized under the leadership of Generalleutnant Ernst von Hoeppner, who reported directly to Field Marshal von Hindenburg, the new chief of staff. Von Hoeppner's staff now controlled all front-line air activities and also managed the aviation industry and supply. The implementation of these new strategies resulted in a substantial increase in the production of single-seat fighters and development of a new class of two-seater lightweight fighters that were designated CL. The Luftstreitskrafte, having lost air supremacy during the first months of 1916, had wrested it back by the end of the year.

Generalleutnant von Hoeppner redirected the major efforts of the German air service to the British front. As von Hoeppner later noted, "the British aviators evinced a keener spirit in combat, the French showed a lessening in this respect. For this reason, after the Somme Battle, the greater position of our pursuit aviation was opposed to the British."[15]

The redirection of German air efforts to the British front would prove costly to the Royal Flying Corps, for at this point in the war British pilots entered combat with largely inferior planes and inadequate and abbreviated training. There would be no lessening of the aggressive tactics of the RFC while awaiting the results of vastly improved training schemes and the fielding of more effective aircraft, however. The German air service would feel the full impact of these efforts in the last year of the war.

But the French were by no means out of the fighter air war, for the vaunted Nieuport sesquiplane fighters were now being replaced by a superior design. The SPAD VII, designed by Louis Béchéreau around the revolutionary Hispano-Suiza V-8 engine, began to appear at the front in August 1916, to the ready acclaim of the French pilots who received them: "We are delighted with the SPAD. It is much more flexible than the Nieuport [17], unbelievingly robust and its [machine gun] synchronization is noteworthy. But [its handling] requires some expertise. It is not yet the aircraft for Mister Everyone, like the B.B. [Bébé]."[16]

The story of the Hispano-Suiza engine merits attention because this engine, initially rated at 150 hp, and its progeny would dominate French fighter aviation throughout the balance of the war and well into the 1920s.

In 1914, rotary engines equipped 80 percent of all airplanes. These lightweight engines, unencumbered by a heavy cooling system, possessed the best power-to-weight ratio of the time and imparted little vibration to the light airframes that they powered. However, the limitations of the rotary engines were significant: they were notoriously inefficient in their use of both fuel and lubricant (castor oil), and required frequent overhaul. More importantly, there was an inherent design cap on their power output: attempts to increase power above 160 hp brought diminishing results (although the Bentley BR2 rotary, incorporating some features of the Hispano-Suiza in-line engine, was a notable exception), as proportionately greater energy was required to produce greater rpms. In addition, increased centrifugal forces acting on the spinning rotary engine risked the ultimate destruction of the engine.

Demands for greater aircraft performance, measured in speed and ceiling, continued unabated as the air war heated up. As the limitations of the rotary engine were already well-known, French authorities were most receptive to an engine design proposal submitted to them by a Swiss engineer, Marc Birkigt.

Birkigt, who was technical director of the Hispano-Suiza automobile firm in Barcelona, Spain, had designed an innovative water-cooled, aluminum monobloc, V-8 engine.

Paul Strähle, an Ace with Jasta 18, is shown with the trophy rudder from an RFC Nieuport 17 that he had downed almost fifty years earlier, on 25 May 1917. Strähle's adversary, Second Lieutenant John R. Anthony of RFC Squadron 1, fell over Tenbrielen, a victim of Strähle's Albatros D.III. Peter Kilduff

Marc Birkigt (1878-1953), seen here in a postwar photograph, is seated at his desk at the Hispano-Suiza Company in the Paris suburb of Levallois-Perret. Birkigt, Swiss by birth, started his career building automobiles in Barcelona, Spain.

Designed around the new Hispano-Suiza engine, the SPAD VII began to enter service in August 1916 and was widely adopted by the French and Allied air services. Armed with a single synchronized machine gun, the SPAD VII achieved a maximum speed of 119 mph when equipped with the 175 hp 8Ac Hispano-Suiza engine. National Air and Space Museum, Smithsonian Institution (SI 83-6839)

Above: Two variants of the Nieuport 24 shown here are from No. 1 "Cawnpore" Squadron, Royal Flying Corps. The squadron transitioned to S.E. 5 and S.E. 5A fighters in January 1918. Nieuport fighters equipped French, Italian, and Royal Flying Corps squadrons. The U.S. Air Service took delivery of 1,641 Nieuport fighters and training aircraft during the war. Edouard and Charles Nieuport Image Collection (Nie 332), National Air and Space Museum, Smithsonian Institution

Below: The first prototype of the Nieuport 28, N.4434, was tested at Villacoublay on 14 June 1917. The aircraft had provision for a main fuel tank and two reserve fuel tanks, one on either side of the pilot's seat, but carried only one machine gun. The design would go through several iterations before it emerged as a potent, two-gun fighter. S.H.A.A., via William Nungesser

The aluminum bloc, with steel cylinder sleeves screwed in, "saved weight, stiffened the crankcase," and contained all moving parts in "oil and dust free covers and lubricated from the engine's central pressure oiling system."[17] An immediate order for the new engines was recommended by French aviation authorities as a result of bench tests conducted during July 1915, in which the engine had run at full throttle for fifty hours.

The SPAD VII, equipped with this new 150 hp Hispano-Suiza engine, and possessing superior strength and greater speed in level flight and in dives, bested its contemporary, the Nieuport 17, but the Nieuport 17 retained the edge in climb rate and maneuverability. With the appearance of new German fighters, the performance of the SPAD VII was also improved, with the installation of a more powerful Hispano-Suiza engine rated at 180 hp. The growth potential of this engine was a key factor in its continued success.

Over the course of the next year, the Hispano-Suiza engine was successively up-rated to 200 hp, to 220 hp, and then to 235 hp, although these three variants required gearing to tame the additional power. This gearing requirement would prove immensely troublesome from both a manufacturing and a maintenance perspective. The new engine also tended to overheat, due to design and manufacturing defects, and this tendency was more prevalent with license-built engines. A new radiator design and more effective quality-control procedures gradually corrected the latter problems, but the reduction-gearing problem persisted.

By mid-1917, an enlarged and ungeared version of the engine, with an output of 300 hp, was already under development. The quest for ever-greater power from this engine would have a major impact on the early fortunes of members of the American Air Service, as they sought to equip their first combat fighter squadrons.

With the advent of heavier and more powerful fighters, the Nieuport Company was challenged to maintain a competitive position with its lightweight fighters. Teething problems with the geared Hispano-Suiza engine gave Nieuport some breathing space, and Gustave Delage responded with incremental airframe design changes incorporating more powerful rotary engines.

Delage clung stubbornly to the V-strut, sesquiplane configuration, however. The predictable result was an only marginal increase in aircraft performance. Delage also tested an experimental design utilizing the 150 hp Hispano-Suiza engine, but this design never got beyond the prototype stage.

The Nieuport 27 closely resembled the Nieuport 24 with additional refinements. Both fighters sported a fully faired fuselage and elegant tail, and were powered by a 120 hp Le Rhône rotary engine. Single fixed-gun Nieuport 24s and 27s were supplied to the air forces of Britain, France, and Italy.

In early 1917 Gustave Delage introduced a new fighter prototype. Equipped with a Gnôme 9N Monosoupape (single-valve) 160 hp rotary engine, this new model, designated the Nieuport 28C.1, was a radical departure from the now-obsolete sesquiplane design, and represented Nieuport's hope for the immediate future. France's Aviation Militaire took account of this new and elegant fighter and projected requirements for early 1918, "if the trials ... prove satisfactory."[18] Trials of the prototype Nieuport 28 commenced on 5 June 1917.

By mid-1917, French fighter squadrons were largely equipped with a mix of SPAD variants and Nieuport 17s, 24s, 24bis (produced before the 24, the bis reverted to a 17-type, steel-tube tail), and 27s. French authorities now directed that all 110 hp and 120 hp rotary-engined Nieuport fighters be replaced in combat squadrons by advanced designs that were under evaluation.

During the course of the war, dominance in the air shifted back and forth as many as eighteen times, sometimes for a period of days, before concentrations of enemy fighters at a critical point were neutralized, but more often for months at a time.[19]

As the war progressed, mastery in the air was increasingly achieved through a combination of factors: technological innovation, the introduction of superior airframes, engines and systems, and the industrial capacity to quickly put large numbers of these aircraft at the front. Competent leadership, well-trained and aggressive pilots, effective aerial tactics, and organizational support completed the equation. The United States, soon to become a belligerent in this war, would have much to learn from its allies.

CHAPTER THREE

FIGHTING MACHINES FOR THE AIR SERVICE, AEF

"We didn't know what a fighting machine was." — Colonel Benjamin D. Foulois, U.S. Air Service[1]

America's successful record of manpower mobilization during the First World War far outpaced the mobilization of American industry. Throughout the war, the American Expeditionary Force (AEF) remained largely dependent on its allies for the provision of tanks, artillery, machine guns, fighting planes, and many other necessities of modern warfare.

Postwar congressional and public scrutiny focused on the wartime production record of the U.S. aviation industry, for this industry and its proponents had raised the nation's expectations with visions of fleets of American-built fighting planes that would soon take to the air. Frederick Rentschler, president of Pratt & Whitney Aircraft Company during the 1920s, explained: "Immediately after our entry into the war, it was determined that one of our great contributions was to be in the air, and all generally accepted the idea that our great automotive companies, within a few months' time, could duplicate anything in quantity, and as Howard Coffin [president of Hudson Motor Car Company and chairman of the Air Production Board] put it, 'darken the skies over Europe'."[2]

These heady expectations would not be realized, for during the eighteen months of America's participation in the war, American factories failed to produce and ship a single fighter plane to fight in France. The much-modified British D.H. 4 bomber, the single type of fighting plane to be built and shipped from U.S. factories, was obsolescent by the time it reached France.[3] American trained pilots entered combat one chaotic year after war was declared by the U.S.; when they finally took to the air, they flew in foreign-built aircraft that were untested in combat or were in the process of being discarded by their new allies. What follows is a chronicle of events that led to this humiliating failure of America's aviation production efforts in World War I.

The Aviation Section of the Signal Corps, U.S. Army, possessed twenty-six qualified pilots and 142 airplanes when war with Germany was declared on 6 April 1917. These meager assets, dispersed across the United States, the Philippine Islands, and the Panama Canal Zone, were supported by a domestic aviation industry that had managed to deliver only eighty-three of the 366 airplanes ordered by the U.S. Army during 1916.

Prior to the declaration of war, American aviation factories had not produced a single modern combat plane capable of fighting and surviving on the Western Front. American aeronautical engineers and air officers had little concept of the function and design of modern combat aircraft. American air observers were not privy to developments in military aviation overseas, as Colonel Samuel Reber, former chief of the Aviation Section, U.S. Signal Corps, explained:

In that fog of war, no blanket was thicker than the one every army hung over its aircraft plans, and on no other single point was it so eager to learn the enemy's. Either could only examine the construction of enemy planes in use at the time, from the examples which fell in their lines; and foreign military attachés, who were never allowed permanently at the front, might, on visits, see the planes of the various armies at the aerodromes. But the new types that were in the process of manufacture were for no eyes except those of the experts in one's own army.[4]

By implementing President Woodrow Wilson's policy of strict neutrality, Secretary of War Newton D. Baker compounded the difficulties involved in acquiring vital intelligence regarding rapidly changing developments in military aviation.

Perhaps an even greater shortcoming of the Aviation Section at the beginning of the war was its lack of doctrine. Michael Doubler defined doctrine as "the fundamental, authoritative principles armies use to guide their mission accomplishment," and from doctrine, "an army derives its tactics, procedures, organization, equipment and training."[5] Once war was declared, the Aviation Section of the Signal Corps, reorganized in May 1918 as the Army Air Service, began to define its doctrine and organize the elements derived from it. The Aviation Section was clearly a start-up organization, and it would require all possible assistance that its new allies could offer.

Above

Left: Newton Diehl Baker, U.S. secretary of war from 1916 to 1921, was criticized by a Republican-controlled Congress after the war for failures in U.S. wartime-production efforts, particularly in the area of military aviation. National Air and Space Museum (NASM 00151233) Smithsonian Institution

Center: One of the first three U.S. military aviators, Benjamin D. Foulois participated in the Mexican Punitive Expedition as commander of the First Aero Squadron. Promoted in 1917 to the rank of brigadier general as chief of the Air Service, AEF, Foulois was under great pressure to equip and field the first American squadrons to support American troops. Major General Foulois was chief of the Air Corps when he retired in 1935, after thirty-seven years of service. National Archives

Right: Brigadier General George O. Squier (U.S. Military Academy, class of 1887), was chief of the Aviation Section, U.S. Army. National Air and Space Museum, Smithsonian Institution (SI 92-4093)

America Mobilizes

Organization and planning began in April 1917, with the creation of the Joint Army and Navy Technical Board. The board was charged with the responsibility for standardizing the designs and general specifications of aircraft to be procured by each of the services. Composed of three army and three navy aviation officers, the board reported jointly to the secretaries of the War Department and of the Navy. Among the army officers was Major Benjamin D. Foulois, who would become chief of the Air Service, AEF, eight months later, with the temporary rank of brigadier general.

The Chief of the U.S. Signal Corps (and immediate past chief of the Aviation Section), Brigadier General George O. Squier, gave an indication of the board's scope and authority when he stated that he "would not buy a stick of wood which this technical board of Army and Navy officers did not recommend."[6]

The Joint Technical Board began work in the absence of a policy directive that would have provided a basis for planning for numbers or proportions of observation, fighter, and bombing aircraft. With little information about how to proceed, the board was receptive to the ideas and proposals being offered by its new allies.

As British, French, and Italian military missions converged on Washington, DC, a cable was received from Premier Ribot of France. The cable, directed to the Joint Technical Board for review, read: "Two thousand planes should be constructed each month as well as 4,000 engines by the American factories. That is to say, in the first six months of 1918, 16,500 planes of the latest type, and 30,000 engines will have to be built. The French Government is anxious to know if the American Government accepts this proposition, which would allow the allies to win the supremacy of the air."[7]

Incredibly, Ribot's cable became the basis for establishing target numbers (but not types) of American combat aircraft and engines, with the requisite number of pilots and mechanics.

With Ribot's cable in hand, Major Foulois prepared the personnel and equipment requirements and appropriations legislation needed to meet these targets. Brigadier General Squier presented the plan to the secretaries of the War Department and of the Navy and quickly received their approval, followed by the approval of the General Staff.

On 14 July 1917, amidst a barrage of favorable press publicity, the House of Representatives voted on the enormous $640 million Aeronautic Appropriations Bill. The House passed the bill, authorizing a sum greater than the cost of the Panama Canal, without a single dissenting vote.

American and Allied media trumpeted the passage of the Aeronautic Appropriations Bill, and painted a fanciful picture of the accomplishments of American industry and aviators once the program got under way. A typical editorial, appearing in the *New York American*, boasted: "Fifty thousand American aviators in fifty thousand flying machines, each dropping one hundred dynamite bombs on German soil, would do the work."[8]

Official Washington also heralded the coming triumph of America's new air arm. Brigadier General Squier, who was also a member of the Air Production Board chaired by Howard E. Coffin, spoke of "winged cavalry sweeping across the German lines and smothering their trenches with a storm of lead, which would put the 'Yankee punch'... into the war, ... sweep the Germans from the sky, [and] ... blind the Prussian cannon." Squier continued: "The time will be ripe to release the enormous flock of flying fighters to raid and destroy military camps, ammunition depots, and military establishments of all kinds."[9]

These expectations seemed reasonable at the time because America, the most technologically advanced nation in the world, had pioneered mass production. Its vast automotive industry appeared fully capable of producing thousands of fighting planes.

Writing in *National Geographic* magazine, Major Joseph Tulasne, chief of the French Aviation Mission to the United States, proclaimed in a more restrained manner: "In America, the European types of airplanes and motors will be built, at first, to aid the English and French factories, in order that the Allies may have the largest possible number of battle planes at the earliest possible moment. Then the new airplanes, more powerful and better armed, will be built to be used during the summer of 1918. The unlimited resources of American industry will make it possible to carry out these two building programs." Tulasne continued, "The Allies are anxiously awaiting the aid

Right: "Uncle Sam's Fighting Face." This editorial cartoon appeared in the New York American; it reflected widespread expectations for U.S. military aviation when war was declared on Germany in April 1917. New York American, reproduced in Aerial Age Weekly

Below: Major Joseph Tulasne (third from left in front row), chief of the French Mission to the United States, poses with members of his mission on the steps of the National Geographic Society's headquarters in Washington, DC. National Geographic Society

Right: Generalleutnant Ernst von Hoeppner (1860–1922), chief of the Luftstreitskrafte (Imperial German Air Service), instituted the "Amerika Program" in order to meet the expected onslaught of American airpower. German fighter forces were greatly expanded as a result, and Germany deployed the vaunted Fokker D.VII fighter by mid-1918.

Far right: Major Raynal Bolling, prewar military flyer and chief counsel of the U.S. Steel Corporation, undertook a grueling three-month mission to Europe to report on the state of aviation affairs in France, England, and Italy. His commission's recommendations for aircraft types to be built in the United States were largely overtaken by the rapid changes in combat aviation technology in Europe. Promoted to colonel in August 1917, Bolling was killed in France in 1918, when he inadvertently crossed the front lines and was shot while attempting to evade capture. National Archives

of the American air fleet. If this fleet comes in time for the 1918 battle, it will be the deciding factor."[10]

General Ernst von Hoeppner, commander of the German air force (Luftstreitskrafte), observed that "the entry of America in the war was hailed in both countries [Britain and France] as offering the medium for the achievement of overwhelming air superiority through the use of her vast resources. The columns of the hostile press were filled with fantastic statements," he said. "In a short time, thousands of American planes were expected to swarm over Germany and force us to sue for peace."[11]

Although skeptical of the claims of America's industrial prowess, General von Hoeppner would not risk being unprepared for the onslaught of American airpower. His "Amerika Program," promulgated in June 1917, proposed doubling the number of fighter squadrons, creating new training schools, and increasing aircraft production. General von Hoeppner also directed that aviation technical superiority be maintained, and it was this momentous decision that ultimately led to the fielding of the Fokker D.VII, perhaps the finest fighter of the war.

The immediate order of business in Washington, however, was how to spend the funds appropriated to build the U.S. Air Service. Despite an influx of foreign military advisors, aeronautical engineers, brokers, and commission agents for foreign manufacturers, American aviation authorities soon realized that this group was not current with the latest developments in military aircraft overseas. As a result, Brigadier General Squier was urged to send a technical mission to Europe, to determine the best types of foreign designs to be built in the United States.

Major Raynal C. Bolling, an Aviation Section Reserve pilot who was also chief counsel for U.S. Steel Corporation, was named to head the commission, which included automobile and engine engineers, metallurgists, a banker, an efficiency expert, and an aluminum castings expert. In addition, ninety-eight men from the automobile industry were directed to visit foreign factories, to learn manufacturing procedures in order to effect an efficient technology transfer once they returned to the United States.

The Bolling Commission sailed from New York on 17 June 1917, and landed at Liverpool, England, on 26 June, in the thirty-fourth month of the war. The Bolling Commission soon found that aviation developments were proceeding at a frenetic pace, with Bolling reporting that the situation "must be watched daily in the light of developments which are taking place with a rapidity unequalled in any other branch of the military service."[12] Nowhere was this situation more apparent than in the ongoing development of fighter planes. *The mission of fighter aviation – to establish and maintain air superiority – underscored the critical importance of selecting the finest fighter plane to equip the Air Service, AEF.*

Following their arrival in Europe, members of the Bolling Commission began a whirlwind tour of England, France, and Italy, and then went back to France. They conferred with aviation authorities and manufacturers in each country about royalty payments and the training of U.S. pilots and mechanics in Europe, and investigated existing and contemplated airplane designs and the capacity of European factories to build them.

On 30 July 1917, Major Bolling cabled the following recommendations to Washington: 'Believe necessary [to] build both best fixed [engine] fighter and best rotary engine fighter now developed. These are SPAD with 200 [hp] Hispano and SPAD with 200 [Bolling erred, the Gnôme was 160 hp] Gnome Monosoupape [single valve]. Both may be superceded next year, but this is only a guess. Think Hispano 200 will probably be superceded after December 1918 by new, undeveloped engine.'[13] It is clear that Bolling's focus was on the status of engine development.

On 15 August 1917, newly promoted Colonel Bolling provided Brigadier General Squier with a comprehensive report relating the activities and achievements of his Aeronautical

Major Raynal Bolling and members of his commission on a visit to the Pomilio Factory in Italy in 1917. Bolling found the Italian aviation authorities particularly keen on providing training and materiel to the American Air Service. Aerial Age Weekly

Commission. Bolling discussed a wide range of issues, including resolution of the problem of royalty payments and the need to coordinate aircraft production from Europe rather than the United States, to minimize complications and achieve greater cooperation with the Allies.

Bolling noted the willingness of Britain, France, and Italy to provide training to U.S. aviators and mechanics, and the need for the United States to provide its allies with quantities of raw, semi-finished, and finished goods and materials. He reported that while the aeronautical industry in England was fully mobilized to meet the Royal Flying Corps' extensive program for 1918, French industry, at that time, possessed both the capacity and the experience to supply American aviation requirements.

Clarifying and expanding upon his earlier recommendation to build European designs in the United States, Colonel Bolling now advised building the following aircraft: the British Bristol biplace fighter and two French-built fighters, the SPAD XIII equipped with the 200 hp Hispano-Suiza in-line engine and the SPAD XV, powered by the 160 hp Gnôme rotary engine. The SPAD XV also differed from the SPAD XIII because of its lighter weight and monocoque construction. Bolling also recommended the British Airco D.H. 4 for day bombing and reconnaissance and the Italian Caproni Triplane for night bombing.

Colonel Bolling noted the difficulties, particularly from French sources, of providing sample airplanes to the United States and the "surprising lack of data covering articles of their manufacture." He added, "In most of the airplanes and engines factories, they are entirely without complete drawings, specifications and other tabulated information which we should consider essential in the [mass production] manufacture of airplanes and engines."[14]

In conclusion, Bolling recommended a program for the production of aircraft in the United States that would begin to supply the requisite number of airplanes at the front after 1 July 1918. It was evident to Bolling at that time that European production would have to take up the slack until American factories could gear up. Requirements for service and training aircraft in Europe prior to 1 July 1918 would have to be met with military aircraft built in Europe, principally in France.

On 30 August 1917, the United States and French governments signed a contract, with the French government agreeing to provide the U.S. Air Service, AEF, with 1,500 Bréguet 14 bombers and reconnaissance planes, 2,000 SPAD XIII fighters equipped with 200 hp Hispano-Suiza engines, and 1,500 SPAD XV or Nieuport 28 fighters, both types being equipped with 160 hp Gnôme 9N rotary engines.

The rotary-powered SPAD XV was soon dropped from contention for failing to meet performance requirements, but testing of several prototypes of the Nieuport 28 was still under way. Captain Herbert Hughes, a former official of the Packard Motor Car Company and an officer on Bolling's staff, paid a visit on 13 August 1917 to the Nieuport Company to receive a report on the ongoing tests of the Nieuport 28 fighter.[15] Gustave Delage, Nieuport designer and chief engineer, spoke enthusiastically about the Nieuport 28's climb rate of seventeen minutes to 5,000 meters, and its ability to achieve speeds of 205 km/h at that altitude.

Captain Hughes also inspected a monocoque version of the Nieuport 28 that was under development. This aircraft contained design elements that would later appear in the Nieuport 29, a highly successful postwar fighter powered by a 300 hp Hispano-Suiza in-line engine. Innovative and radically different from preceding Nieuport fighter designs, the Nieuport 29 would likely have entered combat had the war continued into 1919. (It was evident in mid-1917 that Delage and the Nieuport Company were already looking well beyond the Nieuport 28.)

The U.S. contract with the French government specified that aircraft delivery would commence in January 1918 and be completed by June 1918. The contract also provided for the substitution of later types of French-built aircraft if the new designs were deemed superior to the types specified in the contract. For its part, the U.S. government agreed to provide a large quantity of machine tools and raw materials, for delivery to a French port no later than 1 November 1917.

Bolling's projected requirements for the U.S. Air Service were clearly influenced by the French government's requirements for its own Aviation Militaire. French fighter projections for January 1918 foresaw a mix of SPAD XIIIs equipped with 200 hp Hispano-Suiza engines, Nieuport 28s with 160 hp Gnôme 9N rotary engines, and existing Nieuport 27s powered by the 120 hp Le Rhône rotary engine. Although the Nieuport 27 was still in service, French authorities had concluded that it was now inferior to current German fighters, and it was already in the process of being replaced by French squadrons. The French report also noted the importance of re-equipping bombing and observation squadrons, stating, 'it is indispensable that the greatest efforts be made to increase to the extreme limits, the fabrication of the Bréguet [14] and the Salmson [2].'[16]

The critical quest for a winning fighter-plane design remained unfulfilled, however, for during the fall of 1917 the Morane-Saulnier A1, another Gnôme 160 hp rotary-powered aircraft, appeared on the scene. Early tests of this monoplane fighter promised excellent maneuverability, speed, and rate of climb. Further tests of the Morane-Saulnier A1 and the Nieuport 28 would determine which of these Gnôme-powered fighters would prevail and equip French squadrons, along with the 200 hp SPAD XIII.

By mid-August 1917 Colonel Bolling's mission was fulfilled, and he was directed by General John Joseph Pershing, chief of the AEF, to remain in Paris to take command of aviation matters in the European Zone of the Interior, and continue monitoring aviation activities there. Most of the former members of the commission returned to the United States or to other duties in France or England, but Bolling retained the services of several officers, including Major Edgar Gorrell. Gorrell, who would later direct the Technical Section of the U.S. Air Service, would prove to be a highly influential Air Service officer in the months ahead.

Colonel Bolling had predicted earlier that it would take a year for the 200 hp Hispano-Suiza engine to be replaced by a more powerful engine, but Bolling and Gorrell were now concerned that it might be superseded sooner. They were also aware that a 300 hp scaled-up, ungeared version of the Hispano-Suiza engine was on the drawing board. Washington was informed of these facts by cable on 14 August 1917.

On 24 September 1917, Washington informed Bolling that the U.S. fighter-building program now included 1,500 SPAD XIIIs, powered by the 200 hp Hispano-Suiza engine. Colonel

The Morane-Saulnier A1 monoplane fighter, equipped with the Gnôme 9N rotary engine, showed great promise when first tested; its maneuverability, speed, and rate of climb were superior to those of the Nieuport 28. After it suffered several fatal crashes due to wing failure, its planned use as a first-line fighter ceased. U.S. Air Force (USAF-3030AC), via National Air and Space Museum, Smithsonian Institution

Bolling was also informed of a program to build 1,500 SPAD XIIIs powered by the newly developed V-8 Liberty engine. This program, which had been initiated without Bolling's knowledge, proved unsuccessful, as did another attempt to marry the Liberty engine to the successful British Bristol F.2B airframe. Largely politically motivated by a desire to standardize on the American Liberty engine, this effort resulted in several fatal crashes during testing: the up-rated, 400 hp, V-12 Liberty engine was much too heavy for the redesigned Bristol fighter.[17]

It was clear, both in the United States and in Europe, that engine development and performance were driving airframe design. As historian I. B. Holley observed, "As all designers knew, airframes are planned around engines" and "the power plant is the heart of the aircraft."[18] It was also becoming clear that those in charge of the U.S. building program were increasingly out of touch with events in Europe.

The program to initially equip the Air Service, AEF, with foreign fighting planes seemed reasonably well in hand by the late summer of 1917. The Air Service, however, would be heavily reliant on French production capabilities, as well as on the ability of American industry to meet its own obligations after tooling up. For a number of reasons, the aviation equipment program for the Air Service, AEF, would unravel during the months that followed.

On 15 October 1917, Major Gorrell, in his capacity as technical advisor to Colonel Bolling, recommended that "the United States be requested to build no more pursuit [fighter] aeroplanes of the types proposed at that date to be shipped to Europe for use on the Western Front."[19]

Gorrell's recommendation, a stunning reversal of policy, was prompted by several considerations, including the delay in provision of drawings for the 200 hp Hispano-Suiza engine and the resulting delay in getting the engine under production in the United States. Considering the timeframe required to get completed fighter aircraft from factories in the United States to the front, Gorrell concluded, "the United States could not build this [200 hp Hispano-Suiza-equipped] SPAD pursuit airplane in time for it to arrive in Europe before its effectiveness had practically ceased."[20] The principal factor motivating Gorrell's October 1917 recommendation was his judgment that the 200 hp Hispano-Suiza engine would soon become obsolete. Testifying in 1919 before a House subcommittee investigating war expen-

Top right: Major, later Colonel, Edgar Staley Gorrell graduated in 1912 from West Point. He served as a military aviator with the First Aero Squadron during the Mexican Punitive Expedition in 1916, and the following year went to Europe as a member of the Bolling Commission. Gorrell was instrumental in the policy determination to equip American squadrons with fighters built in Europe, rather than in the United States. After serving as technical director of the U.S. Air Service, Colonel Gorrell compiled the history of the Air Service in the months immediately following the Armistice. National Air and Space Museum (NASM 7B02796), Smithsonian Institution

"HONEST, GENERAL, I ORDERED AN EAGLE."
From the New York Herald.

Right: The realization that America's expectations for production supremacy would not be met is reflected in this editorial cartoon from the New York Herald. New York Herald, reproduced in Aerial Age Weekly ditures, Gorrell explained: "The German pursuit machine developed, and their two-place [reconnaissance] fighting machines were always above the French and made the 200-horsepower SPAD a worthless machine because of its lack of performance. Consequently the Allies had to get a better machine and they got that by increasing the horsepower of the 200 engine to 220 horsepower. The 220-horsepower engine ... was a failure for a long time, but afterwards they got it so it would run for an appreciable length of time."[21]

Gorrell's recommendation was approved, and effectively became policy for the remainder of the war, although this was not what Gorrell intended at the time. He believed that with sufficient foreknowledge, U.S. industry could build suitable fighter designs and get them to the front in time. Major Gorrell had the new 300 hp Hispano-Suiza engine specifically in mind for future use.

Attempts to produce other fighter designs in the United States for use overseas had failed, and the Air Service was now principally dependent on its French allies for fighters, bombers, and observation types. The timing had critical consequences for the U.S. Air Service.

During October 1917, the French accelerated their aircraft production in anticipation of the growing threat posed by the German "Amerika Program." French projections for aircraft at the front by April 1918, initially pegged at 2,665 aircraft, were increased to 2,870 aircraft and increased yet again, to 4,022 aircraft, with bombers and fighters given priority.

French fighter projections for April 1918 now included SPAD XIIIs equipped with 220 hp Hispano-Suiza engines and Nieuport 28s or Morane-Saulnier A1s, "if the trials of the latter prove satisfactory."[22] Efforts were well under way to increase production of Bréguet 14 and Salmson 2 bombing and observation planes, as well as the biplace SPAD XI that was also intended for the observation role.

In order to reach their production goals, the French sought to standardize on the best aircraft and engine designs. Problems persisted with the manufacture of the 220 hp Hispano-Suiza engine, and it would take time for subcontractors to build up their production runs on the SPAD XIII. These problems were finally resolved, but the production benefits would only be realized later in 1918. Ultimately, the SPAD XIII would be produced in greater numbers than any other wartime fighter.

Pressure was now building on Brigadier General Foulois to organize and equip the first American aviation units without delay. Foulois had prepared the original personnel and equipment projections for the U.S. Air Service, when he was a member of the Joint Army and Navy Technical Board. Newly promoted to brigadier general and installed as chief of the Air Service, AEF, in November 1917, Foulois promptly took charge of "all matters relating to the training, organization or equipment of the Air Service in France, England [and] Italy."[23] Foulois' approval was now required for plans and recommendations coming before the Joint Technical Board.

As part of the Foulois reorganization, Colonel Bolling was relieved as assistant chief of the U.S. Air Service and placed under Foulois' command, to act as the principal liaison officer of the Air Service, AEF, to the Allied Air Board.

Brigadier General Foulois had myriad problems, but the most pressing was the necessity to equip and quickly deploy American squadrons to support American infantry divisions that would soon enter combat. In response to a query from his new boss about the imminent supply of airplanes and engines from France, Colonel Bolling responded with some concern:

> The French have recognized what I feared might happen, namely, that our air program will develop more slowly than expected because of difficulties and delays in the establishment of airdromes, parks, depots, etc., and delays in our training program. Just now these are clearly the limiting factors rather than the provision of airplanes and engines ... Monsieur Lucher, Minister of Armament, who now controls airplane and engine production, told me that quite frankly the French would not be able to deliver to us the numbers of airplanes and engines promised by the dates agreed to. While he mentioned delays in deliveries of machine tools and raw materials [from the United States under the terms of the 30 August 1917 contract], *he did not conceal the fact that the cause of their decision is a large increase in their own air program.*[24] [author's italics]

France's inability to supply modern air equipment to the U.S. Air Service was caused by the rapid expansion of its own air service in response to the Amerika Program instituted by the German Luftstreitskrafte. Ironically, the Amerika Program was induced by the media prospect of American-built aircraft "flooding the skies over Germany." Brigadier General Foulois commented on the damage done by this unfortunate braggadocio in a letter to Dr. Charles D. Walcott, secretary of the Smithsonian Institution in Washington, DC: "The greatly exaggerated publicity, from the States, of our Air Service program, and what remarkable things we would do to the Germans this Spring, has been the worst thing that I have had to combat since my arrival as the English, French, and Italian publics fully expected us to do something wonderful, and the reaction has hurt us over here very much."[25]

On 30 November 1917, General Hageneau, chief of the French Mission attached to the American Army Headquarters, informed Foulois of the type of equipment that would be supplied initially by the French government to the U.S. Air Service for advanced training prior to entering front-line service. The communication read: "During this period of instruction, it suffices and is even advantageous to employ only airplanes of the most recent type. The squadrons can, therefore, be equipped at first with French airplanes of the present current type whilst waiting delivery of those ordered from the U.S."[26]

General Hageneau's statement appeared reasonable and reassuring, but each of the types proposed – Dorand A.R.s and/or Sopwith 1 1/2 Strutters for observation and day bombing, Voisin 8s and 10s for night bombing, and Nieuport 27s for fighter training – were obsolescent or obsolete, and all, with the exception of the Voisin 10, were then in the process of being removed from French squadrons.

General Pétain had decreed in October 1917 that the Nieuport 27 fighter was 'inferior to all contemporary enemy fighters.'[27] As Major Gorrell had observed that "we always give a flier training in the same type [of aircraft] he is going to use himself when he gets to the front," it now appeared that the first American-trained fighter squadrons would enter combat with the Nieuport 27 fighter.[28]

On 5 January 1918, General Pershing directed Brigadier General Foulois to expedite the development of the Air Service. Foulois promptly queried Bolling about the availability of the SPAD XIII fighter equipped with the 220 hp engine.

Bolling responded, "In reply to your inquiry regarding the SPAD, we are entitled under the [30 August 1917] agreement to demand the newer [220 hp] type of Hispano-Suiza engine, and I have dictated a letter to the Under-Secretary of State [for Air] telling him that is what we want. The question of deliveries of these machines depends entirely upon the arrival [from the United States] of raw materials."[29]

The raw materials and machine tools from the United States, however, and the supply of airplanes and engines from France were not forthcoming within the specified time. As a

The Nieuport 27, equipped with the 120 hp Le Rhône rotary engine, was clearly obsolete and being withdrawn from French fighter squadrons at the end of 1917. It might have equipped the first American fighter squadrons to enter combat, had not the untested (in combat) Nieuport 28 been substituted at the last moment. National Air and Space Museum (NASM 00074909), Smithsonian Institution

French squadrons were rapidly being equipped with the SPAD XIII when the first American-trained fighter squadrons were preparing for combat operations. The robust SPAD XIII could outrun all opponents in level flight or in a dive, but pilots found its 220 hp in-line Hispano-Suiza engine trouble-prone. American squadrons began to transition to the SPAD XIII in July 1918 when sufficient numbers became available. Alan Toelle

result, on 29 January 1918, General Pershing canceled the 30 August 1917 agreement.

The pressure on Foulois and the Air Service, AEF, to acquire airplanes to equip their rapidly forming squadrons was now intense.

On 16 February 1918, Brigadier General Foulois sent a formal request to the French government for a complement of airplanes for the Zone of Advance, as the front-line operational area was then called. Based on the French government's earlier offer, communicated on 30 November 1917 by General Hageneau, Foulois requested eighteen SPAD XIII fighters with Hispano-Suiza 220 hp engines to equip one squadron, thirty-six Nieuport 27 fighters with Le Rhône 120 hp engines to equip two squadrons, seventy-two Sopwith 1 1/2 Strutters (thirty-six were equipped with 120 hp Le Rhône rotary engines and the balance with 130 hp Clergêt rotary engines), and thirty-six Dorand A.R. 1 planes. The A.R. 1 and Sopwith aircraft were intended for the observation role.[30]

This request, formalized as Contract F-12 and dated 23 January 1918, specified that thirty-six fully equipped Nieuport 27s be delivered to Villeneuve by 1 February 1918. The SPAD XIIIs were intended for the American 103rd Aero Squadron, formerly called the Lafayette Escadrille and still under the direction of the French Army. The Nieuport 27s were intended for the newly formed, American-trained fighter squadrons that would shortly become operational.

Brigadier General Foulois was clearly unhappy with the prospect of equipping American squadrons with obsolete aircraft, and particularly so with the Nieuport 27 fighter. He directed his chief of supply to request sufficient SPAD XIIIs with 220 hp engines to be delivered by 15 March 1918 to equip two fighter squadrons for service use at the front. Foulois' rationale for this request was communicated to the French government: "To enable these squadrons to function to the best advantage, they will need first-class equipment. A further reason for furnishing the latest equipment is that these few squadrons will be the first ones in the American service to fly over the enemy's lines. Their performance will be watched by not only all the pilots in training, both in this country and in the United States, but by the entire American people. It is greatly to be desired that they should [not] be handicapped in any way as regards lack of up-to-date equipment."[31]

Foulois' plaintive appeal for the immediate supply of the same SPAD XIIIs then being supplied to French fighter squadrons appeared to fall on deaf ears.

Brigadier General Foulois communicated his lament to General Pershing in a memorandum dated 14 February 1918:

> These types of aeroplanes [the Dorand A.R. 1, Sopwith 1 1/2 Strutter, and Nieuport 27 fighter] are rated as 2nd class ... although a great number are being used by the French, at the present time, for frontline service. Although I fully disapprove of equipping any American Air Service squadrons with inferior types of aeroplanes, yet in view of the failure on the part of the United States to supply raw material as previously agreed upon, and further, in view of the fact that the French Air Service is, through necessity, [still] using a large number of these inferior types for front line service, I can offer no logical objection against equipping such number of our squadrons with these types of aeroplanes as the military necessity may demand."[32]

General John Joseph Pershing (1860-1948), shown here with Brigadier General B.D. Foulois, commanded the 2.5 million men of the American Expeditionary Force in France in 1918. General Pershing directed that the fledgling Air Service, AEF, be ready to support the growing numbers of US ground troops as they entered combat. National Archives

On 21 February 1918, M. Dumesnil, le Sous-Secrétaire d'État de l'Aéronautique Militaire et Maritime, informed Foulois that 'the two Nieuport [27] squadrons mentioned in your order of January 23 [Order F-12] and formed for purpose of training at the front, will be made up of planes, Type XXVIII [28], fitted with 150 [this should be 160] hp Gnome monosoupape engines.'[33]

The French government had not been entirely unresponsive to Foulois' plea in making a last-minute substitution of thirty-six untested (in combat) Nieuport 28 fighters in place of the outmoded Nieuport 27. However, no change was made in the observation and bombing types intended to initially equip American squadrons. Colonel Raynal Bolling indicated how the fighter substitution came about:

The Nieuport 28 equipped the four fighter squadrons of the First Pursuit Group, the first American-trained fighter unit to enter combat. This lightweight fighter, powered by a 160 hp Gnôme 9N rotary engine, was fast, highly maneuverable, and performed successfully during four months of combat operations. Many pilots were loath to give it up for the heavier – but more robust – SPAD XIII. The U.S. Air Service was the only air service to use the Nieuport 28 in combat.

> At the time that the [30 August 1917] contract was made, the SPAD [XV] monocoque and a new type of Nieuport [28] for this 150 Gnome Engine were about finished and were recommended by Lieutenant Colonel [Virginius] Clark, United States Army airplane expert [also a member of the Bolling Commission], as the best types of rotary engine fighters in the order mentioned. Although both Colonel Clark and the French experts were very sure of the success of both of these airplanes, neither of them proved successful. The largest measure of success attained by any airplane built for the 150 Gnome was attained by the new Morane [Morane-Saulnier A1 Parasol] monoplane ... About the 10th or 11th of January, in conversation with the Under-Secretary of State [M. Dumesnil was the Under-Secretary of Air], he informed me that the French had finally decided to adopt the Morane Monoplane in limited numbers as the rotary engine fighter for the Gnome Monosoupape Engine, and had placed an order for 600 of these airplanes and 1,000 of these engines, deliveries beginning March and to be completed by July 1, 1918.[34]

At the same time, the French government placed a tentative order for 600 Morane-Saulnier A1 Parasol fighters and 1,000 Gnôme 160 hp rotary engines for the U.S. Air Service, with a delivery schedule beginning midyear.

The Nieuport Company had failed in its bid to supply France's Aviation Militaire with its new Nieuport 28 fighter as a result of the superior performance of the Morane-Saulnier fighter. The French Air Service would now be equipped with the 160 hp Gnôme rotary-powered Morane-Saulnier MoS 29, the two-gun version of the A1, and the SPAD XIII with the 220 hp Hispano-Suiza engine. At this time, however, no one could have foreseen that the Morane-Saulnier fighter would be withdrawn from service and the American contract terminated as a result of fatal accidents several months later, which were due to structural failure of the wing.

Several prototypes of the single-gun Nieuport 28 had been built since the test flight of the first prototype in June 1917; the two-gun production version of the Nieuport 28 appeared at the end of the year. Anticipated contracts to supply the French air service had not materialized, but the Nieuport Company was tooled up and now ready to begin supplying the first American-trained fighter squadrons to take the field.

On 7 March 1918, eighteen Nieuport 28 fighters were flown to Villeneuve. Additional fighters began to trickle in after that, with some aircraft being destroyed along the way by storms or accidental fires before they could reach their destination.

The initial complement of Nieuport 28 fighters was delivered without full equipment or accessories, and there were only enough Vickers .303 machine guns (mostly used and worn) to supply each fighter with a single gun. American pilots were nonetheless overjoyed to receive their new fighters, with one pilot exclaiming: "New planes! ... we all had a hop. Planes are equal span bi-planes, equal chord, slight diheral top wing, 3 machine gun places [two cowl installations plus one midpoint atop the top wing], ailerons on bottom wing ... wonderfully wired, 2 vertical instead of 1 V strut, on each side. Maneuver[s] wonderfully."[35]

The Nieuport 28 fighter would serve creditably with four American squadrons (comprising the First Pursuit Group) for a total of four months in combat. During this brief period, American pilots such as Eddie Rickenbacker, David Peterson, and Douglas Campbell achieved Ace status; many other American pilots would learn the rudiments of air combat and achieve success while flying the elegant and nimble Nieuport 28.

Five American observation squadrons were initially equipped with a mix of Dorand A.R. 1s (nicknamed the "Antique Rattletrap" by American pilots), Sopwith 1 1/2 Strutters, and SPAD XIs, whose poor weight distribution made them difficult to fly. By August 1918, all five squadrons had been re-equipped with the outstanding Salmson 2.

The U.S. Air Service ultimately became familiar with all of the principal types of trainers, fighters, reconnaissance aircraft, and bombers manufactured in French factories. During the war, French industry supplied 73.5 percent of the 6,624 airplanes received by the U.S. Air Service in Europe. At war's end, the U.S. Air Service had forty-five bombing, observation, and fighter squadrons operational on the Western Front; all twenty of the fighter squadrons were equipped with foreign-built aircraft. The sole contribution of U.S. factories to air combat overseas consisted of license-built D.H. 4 bombing and observation aircraft equipped with the American Liberty 12-cylinder V-8 engine.

The dismal record of America's efforts to produce combat planes during the First World War became the focus of an acrimonious congressional investigation in the immediate postwar years. In his final report as Chief of the Air Service, AEF, Major General Mason M. Patrick (Patrick had relieved Brigadier General Foulois in May 1918) identified the underlying cause for many of the problems encountered by the Air Service during the war: "As we consider these errors with a view to avoidance in the future, one fact stands out most prominently, one common source of all our difficulties becomes apparent; these failures were the unavoidable result of our unpreparedness and of the necessity for actually preparing for war while hostilities were in progress."[36]

Major General Patrick's commentary may offer the best explanation for the abject failure of American industry to build fighting planes for the Air Service during the First World War. Fortunately, the humiliating lessons learned were not lost on a future generation of American civilian and military leaders, who wrought an aviation production miracle twenty-five years later during the Second World War.

Brigadier General Mason M. Patrick, a nonflyer, relieved Brigadier General Foulois of command of the Air Service, AEF, in May 1918. An able administrator, Brigadier General Patrick believed that unpreparedness was the root cause of many of the problems encountered by the Air Service during the war. Shown here as a major general, Patrick received his wings at age fifty-nine; he served as the first chief of the Air Corps before retiring in 1927.

Meanwhile ... the War on the Ground

During 1917, Germany remained on the defensive on the Western Front, while blunting the July offensives of the demoralized and ill-disciplined Russian armies in the east. The Germans launched offensives on the Eastern Front in July and September and, with the aid of the Bolshevik Revolution, defeated Russia before the end of the year.

On the Western Front, British forces assaulted the German Sixth Army at Arras in April 1917 in support of the disastrous French (General) Nivelle Offensive, which resulted in widespread mutiny in the French army. The assault occurred about the time the American Bolling Commission arrived in Europe, and when France's military fortunes were at their lowest ebb. The British army mounted offensives in Flanders and Messines to remove German pressure from the beleaguered French army.

From July to November 1917, British forces extended the Ypres salient by five miles, at a cost of 300,000 casualties. This battle would be known as Passchendaele, a name that evokes horror, as does the 1916 Battle of the Somme.

The last British offensive of 1917, employing 200 tanks in a surprise attack at Cambrai, was initially successful, before German counterattacks, greatly assisted by low-flying Halberstadt CL IV ground attack aircraft, regained much of the lost ground.

By the end of 1917, exhausted French and British armies awaited the massive spring offensives of a reinvigorated German army.

FOUR MONTHS OF COMBAT

"Your machine must be in the best of condition, as must be your guns. Live with your machine, get to know your mechanics and let them know that you are taking an interest in things. It is [up] to you to have that machine and its guns in the best of conditions.

"Upon your arrival at the front, get in touch with the older men and get their advice on how things are done. Keep your eyes and ears open and obey instructions, be keen to learn. Take things easy at first and finally, you will be a good pursuit pilot. If you think you know it all and refuse advice and do not do as told you by [your] flight commander and the older men in the squadron, you will most likely develop into a first class 'Daisy Pusher'.

"In combat your advantage lies in pressing the attack. Wait until you can see the man's head and then spray him with both guns. If you persist in shooting at long range, you will waste all of your ammunition, accomplish nothing, and find yourself out of luck when the time comes to save your own skin. Keep after the enemy. Do not give him a chance to fix his guns or to do anything else. However, remember, attack from the Front and 'Watch Your Tail'."[1]

Gearing Up

Tension mounted as excited pilots of the 94th and 95th Aero Squadrons prepared to collect their new fighters and begin final preparations for combat. After completing flight training at the Third Instruction Center at Issoudun, both squadrons entrained for Villeneuve-les-Vertus, the home of the First Pursuit Organization and Training Center. There they would receive the additional training and equipment necessary to become a fully functioning combat team.

The 95th arrived at Villeneuve on the morning of 18 February 1918, followed by the 94th on 5 March, with both units reporting to Major Bert M. Atkinson. Two other squadrons, the 27th and the 147th, still en route to France, would join the 94th and 95th on 1 June, and flesh out what would become the First Pursuit Group. All four squadrons would enter battle equipped with the Nieuport 28C.1 fighter.

Captain James E. Miller commanded the 95th Aero Squadron and a former Lafayette Flying Corps veteran, Major John W. F. M. Huffer, assumed command of the 94th. Miller, Huffer, and Major Gervais Raoul Lufbery, the distinguished Ace and former member of the Lafayette Escadrille, along with a sprinkling of other combat veterans, would instill the necessary skills and discipline of air fighting in the men as soon as the new Nieuport 28s were delivered and equipped for combat. The experienced members of the 81st Escadrille, a French fighter unit sharing the same aerodrome, would also assist the fledgling American pilots.

Captain Miller "raised a cheer" among his pilots with the news that "our new ships are ready."[2] Members of the 94th and 95th soon traveled to Villacoublay near Paris to collect fifteen Nieuport 28 fighters. Lieutenant Harold Buckley of the 95th described the journey:

> The weather broke on the sixth of March and we got away. Our pockets were empty but we had lovely circles under our eyes [some of the pilots had been living it up in Paris]. At Villacoublay, we hopped off, skimmed the broad terrain, saw with actual relief the outskirts of Paris glide by beneath our wings, and pointed our noses for Villeneuve, an hour or so away. Over our own aerodrome, we circled before landing, watching the swarm of tiny figures rushing out from the hangars and huts below at the unfamiliar screech of our 'Gnome' motors, then plumped down in the middle of the field and taxied back, each of us the center of a cluster of curious mechanics, those great boys who did all the work while we had all the fun. ... From this moment on, we began to live in a rose-colored fog of content. The camp began to hum. Mechanics were busy and important at last, tinkering, testing, polishing our little birds till they gleamed in the sun like birds of paradise, while we made dozens of excuses a day to sneak down to the hangars just to look at them and gloat.[3]

Not all of the fifteen planes had arrived safely at Villeneuve; several pilots experienced minor mechanical problems along the way and were forced to land, and others ran out of gas or simply got lost en route. Three of the ferry pilots turned over upon landing, having encountered a nasty habit of the Nieuport 28 to quickly go up on its nose. As Lieutenant Douglas Campbell of the 94th explained, "The tail was so light ... if you bounced too much or hit soft ground, there was nothing to stop it from going over on its back."[4] This would be one of several idiosyncrasies of the Nieuport 28 that the inexperienced pilots would have to master in the days ahead.

Above: Staff of the First Pursuit Organization and Training Center at Villeneuve-les-Vertus early in 1918. The group's commander, Major Bert M. Atkinson (center), would later command the First Pursuit Wing. The tall officer to Atkinson's right is Captain Philip Roosevelt; Roosevelt would become operations officer when the group was reorganized as the First Pursuit Group in May 1918. Charles Woolley

Right: Now with the American 94th Aero Squadron, Majors John W.F.M. Huffer and Gervais Raoul Lufbery had both served with the Aviation Militaire. Lufbery was credited with seventeen victories while flying with the Lafayette Escadrille. Huffer commanded the 94th Aero Squadron from 7 March to 7 June 1918. National Archives

Below: Lieutenant Hobart "Hobey" Baker stands before a pristine and unarmed Nieuport 28 fighter that he has just delivered. Baker served with the 94th Aero Squadron for several months before transferring to the 103rd in April 1918. Charles Woolley

Above: Novice pilots found that the tail-light Nieuport 28 nosed over readily. National Archives

Right: Personnel from the 94th Aero Squadron inspect the scant remains of a Nieuport 28 that was lost in the hangar fire at Villeneuve on 31 March 1918. Charles Woolley

Initial reaction to the new Nieuport 28 fighters appears to have been uniformly good. Lieutenant Waldo Heinrichs of the 95th extolled the virtues of the new fighters in a letter to a friend:

> Our new machines – type 28 Nieuport, are wonderful – maneuvers wonderfully. [They] don't vibrate on virage [a veering turn] and whip around fast. They vrille [tail spin] faster than a [Nieuport] 27 and dive much faster. Very stocky and lovely lines. We won't carry all the machine guns [the Vickers machine guns were then in short supply] – there are places for two Vickers and a Lewis. We have neither as yet. The motor [160 hp Gnôme rotary] is the only question. Will she stand up under weeks of combat? There's the question that only time will decide. Manufacturers claim fifty hours for it. We doubt it. Fuselage is splendidly streamlined and the whole ship is very sensitive.[5]

Other equally glowing observations were recorded after first flights in the Nieuport 28 were undertaken: "runs beautifully, easy & delicate as can be, …wonderfully wired [rigged],"[6] "maneuvers wonderfully,"[7] "made first flight with N-28 … . greatest things with wings I ever saw."[8] The consensus regarding the outstanding characteristics of the Nieuport 28 seemed to be the excellent maneuverability and flying ease of this elegant fighter.

Pilots were eager to see how the Nieuport 28 performed against other aircraft:

> We had a chance today to test our new Nieuport type 28 with a 180 H.P. Spad [VII] from the famous French 81st Squadron. Sewall and Jones from our Squadron took off just behind and climbed faster than the Spad [VII] up to 8000 feet, as high as the clouds were and found that with the Spad going full speed, our fellows could easily hold the pace. This puts much courage in our men. It is certain that our machines will outmaneuver the Spad. Our boys followed him down all the way too. We land slower than they, another advantage. They are stronger and more powerful machines, however.[9]

The men of the 95th could not contain their eagerness to begin patrolling the lines, guns or no guns. Their commander, Captain Miller, anxious to explore the front lines, had been killed in action on 9 March while flying a borrowed, fully armed SPAD. They had to overcome strong resistance to the idea of flying unarmed fighters over the lines – "a proposal so fantastic and unparalleled that our French comrades threw up their hands in horror at the mere suggestion," as Lieutenant

Harold Buckley recalled. The French 81st Escadrille agreed to provide one armed SPAD VII with an experienced pilot to escort three unarmed American Nieuport 28s over the lines, and Buckley dutifully recorded this auspicious event:

> Thus on the fifteenth of March, at eleven thirty a.m., the first American patrol hopped off and over the lines. For the first time we saw with our own eyes what we had been dreaming of for months. There was the battered countryside, honeycombed with shell holes as far as we could see, the erratic line of trenches zigzagging away in the distance, and the crumbled towns, desolate and abandoned, everything as we had pictured it a thousand times. The bursting anti-aircraft followed us up and down the line and occasionally bounced us around: we laughed to find this bogey considerably overrated. Our hawkeyed leader carefully avoided the German patrols, but the sight of them, sinister silhouettes in the offing, was sufficient to send the blood galloping madly through our veins. Two hours later when we wriggled our cramped limbs from our cockpits, there was a satisfaction in our souls that comes once in a lifetime.[10]

This was a bare portent of what was to come. The armed combat debut of the 95th would be delayed, however, for its pilots had not yet received gunnery instruction. As a result, the squadron received orders to proceed to the Gunnery Training Center at Cazeaux to gain the required proficiency, but not until after the pilots had transferred its complement of Nieuport 28 fighters to its sister squadron, the 94th.

Not to be outdone by the exploits of the 95th, Major Raoul Lufbery selected Lieutenants Eddie Rickenbacker and Douglas Campbell to accompany him on an unarmed patrol along the lines. Departing Villeneuve shortly after 8 a.m. on 19 March, the flight proceeded north of Reims along the Marne River, and close enough to German anti-aircraft batteries for Rickenbacker's plane to sustain slight damage. Upon landing at Villeneuve after the two-hour flight, Lufbery pointed out the presence of other aircraft in the air that his inexperienced flight mates had failed to see. The next day, Lufbery escorted two other fledgling pilots of the 94th along the lines. Major Lufbery and other experienced pilots continued to impart their combat wisdom to the neophytes, who would soon get their first taste of combat.

Flying time was at a premium during this period because the weather did not cooperate and, as one pilot noted, "[We] must save motors and only use them on actual patrol when machine guns come."[11] Additional Nieuport 28s were flown to Villeneuve in small numbers, and as these fighters were assigned, pilots began to take special interest in tuning up and personalizing their new mounts.

Lieutenant Douglas Campbell, a pilot with the 94th, was assigned Nieuport 28, serial number N.6164, on 23 March and

Shown here equipped with only one Vickers machine gun, this 94th Aero Squadron Nieuport 28 would wait several months before receiving its second gun. Lieutenant LeRoy Prinz sits happily in the cockpit. Bergen Hardesty

said, "since then I have spent most of my waking hours in the hangar."[12] Lieutenant Campbell had his mechanics install a compass, clock and altimeter, in addition to the Jaeger Paris-built tachometer that had already been installed. Campbell noted that the functionality of these instruments was rather limited:

> We had the following: A little glass bulb that had oil pulsating in it [oil pulsator] so you could tell if the oil was pumping or not. An altimeter, which was accurate within two hundred feet. It had no correction for atmospheric densities. In fact, we had no weather information at all. Then there was the tachometer, which was not of much use because it was generally out of order. The only really good instrument we had was one that was good because of several centuries of research and that was the clock. We used the clock hopefully as our fuel meter. We had fuel for 2 hours. This is how we judged whether or not we had enough fuel to continue combat operations. The turn and bank indicator wasn't invented until long after the war. We had a compass too but the needle was always spinning around and around and we never used it because it was so unreliable.[13]

The Nieuport 28 was sometimes subjected to drastic alterations to make the small cockpit more comfortable for oversized pilots. Lieutenant Bill Taylor, the youngest (at nineteen) and tallest (six feet, five inches), cut away some of the cockpit coaming to allow him to settle most of his body within the cramped cockpit.[14] Taylor also moved his windscreen forward six inches to prevent the air blast from hitting him in the face. Long-legged pilots found the rudder bars too close (Taylor moved his forward six inches), but any attempt to stretch out the legs led to increased discomfort from scorching heat due to the closer proximity of the engine.

On 1 April 1918, the pilots of the 94th flew their new fighters east to Epiez, an aerodrome situated on a hilltop in the valley of the Meuse approximately fifteen miles southwest of Toul. Epiez, described as "a vast sea of mud," was a dangerous spot for inexperienced pilots (Captain James Norman Hall flipped his aircraft upon landing on the field of mud), but fortunately, almost constant rain and fog kept flights to a minimum.[15] Prior to its departure from Villeneuve, the 94th had also lost two planes in a hangar fire that left seven other planes damaged.

The brief stay at Epiez was fortunate in one regard, for the logistical logjam seemed at last to break and the 94th began to receive spare parts, supplies, and flight clothing in abundance. Machine guns were still in short supply, however, and this meant that only one worn, but functional gun could be mounted on each airplane. It would be several months before the Nieuport 28 fighter would receive its full complement of two .303 Vickers machine guns.

To the Toul Sector ... and Combat

On 11 April, the 94th Aero Squadron left Epiez for Gengoult Aerodrome near Toul. Lieutenant Jimmy Meissner noted in his diary entry: "[Weather] cleared finally, so after breakfast in our room, got away about 9. Easy hop to Gengoult, 3 Km. from Toul, French observation field [the 94th would share the field with a French observation squadron]. Lufbery flew over French batteries to show them [the] new plane."[16] This was a prudent move, for anti-aircraft gunners were prone to shoot at unfamiliar – ergo enemy – aircraft.

The 94th was now only three days away from its first combat operation, and activity moved into high gear. Jimmy Meissner's diary entry for 12 April read, "All day getting 6195 [Nieuport 28 N.6195] in shape, taping gas & oil joints, remounting instruments, etc. Gun on in after, [and] insignia started." His entry for the 13th read, "In hangars all day. Finished painting insignia [the design had been suggested by the squadron's medical officer, Captain Paul Walters, and was rendered by a squadron pilot, Lieutenant John Wentworth] while mechs put on steel, copper wrapped plug wires & made sight brackets for gun. Machines are ready to start patrol and alert duty tomorrow."[17] Jimmy Meissner was slated to be on alert the next morning, along with Lieutenants Alan Winslow and Douglas Campbell, but Meissner was to be disappointed: "First day over the bloomin [sic] lines. Couldn't get sights mounted until noon, so missed out on alert and patrol from 6 – 10, 10 – 12. Campbell & Winslow, answering the alert call, met 2 Albatross [the aircraft that Campbell downed was a Pfalz D.IIIa] right over our field at 9:30 and got both by clever work."[18]

The Nieuport 28s of the 94th Aero Squadron that took to the air on Sunday, 14 April 1918, proudly bore the squadron's distinctive "Hat in the Ring" insignia. Most, if not all of the fighters, however, were still in French colors on the first day of battle.

These first American fighter combats took place on a quiet, almost dormant, sector of the front, at a time when the real air and ground war was flaring up to the northwest. Control of the 94th now passed from the First Pursuit Organization Center to the French Eighth Army, but the squadron continued to operate as an independent unit while under French control.

Aerial shot of the 95th Aero Squadron's Bessoneau hangar and Nieuport 28s at Gengoult Aerodrome just north of Toul. The aerodrome site is now a massive industrial park. Charles Woolley

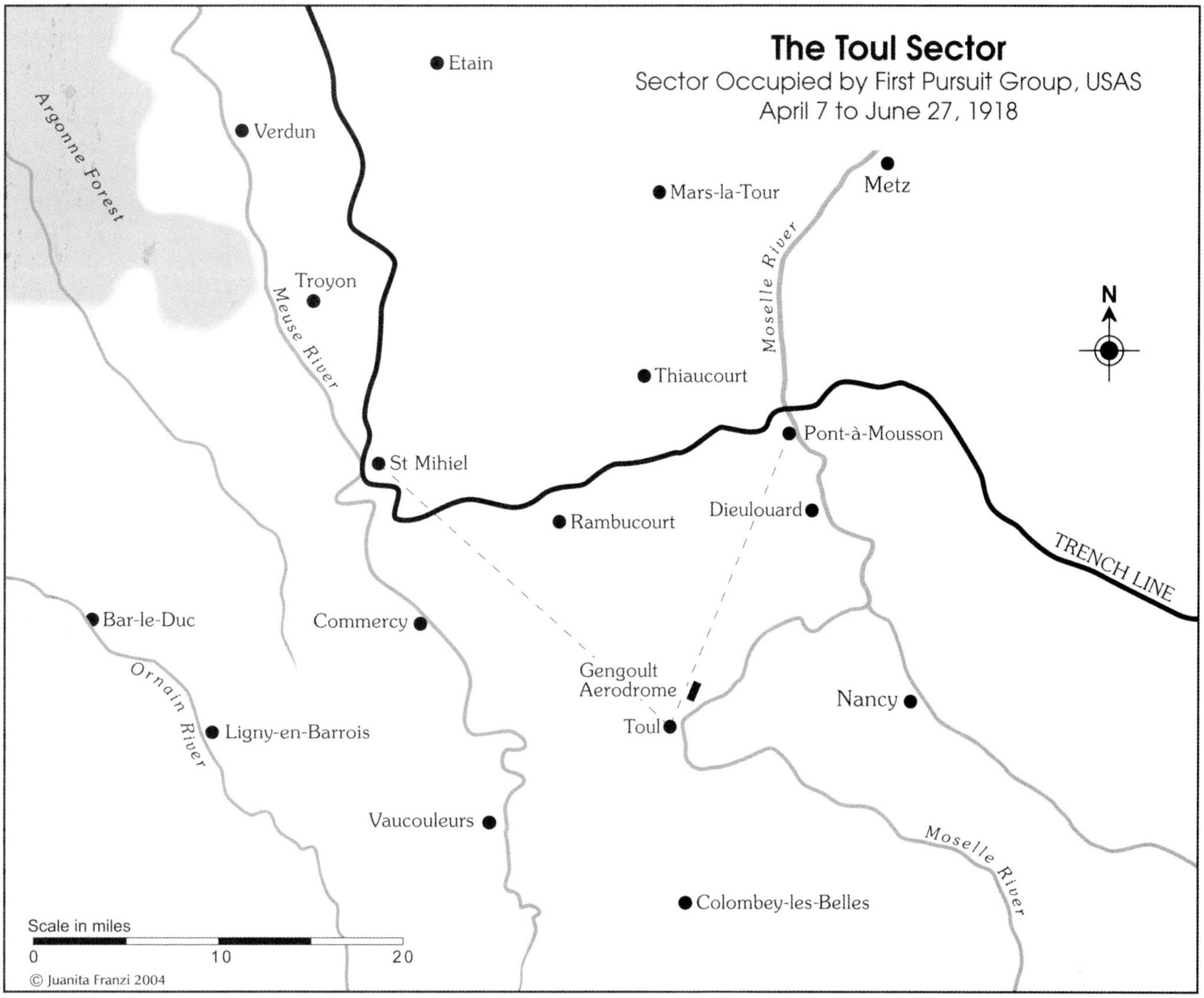

The Toul sector, bounded by St. Mihiel to the west and Pont-a-Mousson to the east, was ideal for the intended purpose of learning the rudiments of air combat with minimal risk. The front in this sector had been quiet and stable for almost three and one-half years, and liaison with the French anti-aircraft artillery units in the sector was superb. The early warning network contributed significantly to the successful combats of 14 April, and it would continue to get the Nieuport 28s quickly into the air in response to enemy air activity.

Operations on the Toul front from April through June 1918 enabled the First Pursuit Group to develop and practice flight tactics, command and control procedures, logistical and maintenance functions, and generally, to learn to function as an efficient and disciplined team. During this "grace period," all four squadrons of the group flew the Nieuport 28 fighter.

After beginning combat operations in mid-April, the members of the 94th Aero Squadron would have roughly ten weeks to learn their craft in the quiet Toul sector, before being transferred to what would be a very active and hostile front. The pilots of the 95th, and particularly those of the 27th and 147th Aero Squadrons, who came late to the Toul sector, would have far less time to prepare.

The 94th Aero Squadron carried the combat burden for the incipient First Pursuit Group during the month of April and much of May. Fog, rain, and low clouds kept pilots on the ground most days during this period but the pilots remained busy with their Nieuport 28s, completing the painting of American colors, squadron insignia and individual airplane numbers, and affixing custom designs on their cowls. Pilots sought also to improve the comfort, utility, and performance of their Nieuport 28s in a variety of ways. Lieutenant Jimmy Meissner added a map case to his cockpit and had a larger windshield installed; taller pilots who sat high in the seat needed added protection from the wind, and from gas and castor oil efflux from their rotary engines. Meissner, who had broken his landing gear on several occasions, had his mechanics install heavier gauge wire to strengthen the gear. This fix would later be made on all the Nieuport 28s.

James Norman Hall in #17, N.6153. Hall was downed in this airplane on 7 May 1918 and spent the rest of the war as a POW. Ray Folsom

Left: Natty Ned Buford (Lieutenant Edward Buford, Jr.) in front of his Nieuport 28, prominently marked with the insignia of the 95th Aero Squadron. Note that his fighter is equipped with two Vickers machine guns. National Archives Right: Ned Buford in flying gear. University of Texas at Dallas

Opposite
Top: Officers of the 94th Aero Squadron, with Nieuport 28 fighter in the background. In the front row, from left to right, are: Campbell, Meissner, Green, unidentified, Gude, unidentified, unidentified; in the rear row, from left to right, are: unidentified, Lufbery, unidentified, Huffer, Marr, unidentified, Rickenbacker, Chambers, Wentworth, Cook, Loomis, Winslow, and Smythe. National Archives

Bottom: A Nieuport 28 being moved out of the 94th Aero Squadron's Bessoneau hangar at Gengoult Aerodrome north of Toul. Beyond this aircraft is the 95th Aero Squadron's hangar and other Nieuport 28s belonging to the 94th and 95th Aero Squadrons. The Nieuport 28 on the right, with the concentric stripes on the cowl, is part of the 95th Aero Squadron's 3rd Flight. National Archives

Pilots were preoccupied with improving the performance of their single Vickers machine gun and rightly so, for machine-gun stoppages were among the most frequent causes of mission aborts.[19] Lieutenant Douglas Campbell, aware of the frequency of machine-gun jams, carried a small brass hammer tied to his wrist, ready to pound away on the cocking lever when an internal jam occurred. Lieutenant Eddie Rickenbacker took special pains to alleviate the problem by cutting away the left side of his windshield to gain better access to the machine gun in the event of the anticipated jam. Several pilots carefully honed the moving surfaces of their machine guns to improve performance and all, pilots and armorers alike, took extra care in adjusting the ammunition feed boxes, synchronizing interruptor gears, and loading ammunition belts. These efforts were deadly serious, as one pilot recalled, "Began to recalibrate my ammunition and found three bad cartridges in one belt of 300 shots. Awful! Could have been my death!"[20]

However, problems with the machine guns continued to recur and combat reports, letters, and diaries are replete with mentions of the problem: "I had miserable luck – I had my own man just where I wanted, was piquing [diving] down on him and pulled the trigger. My gun shot twice and then jammed. It was really awfully hard luck, for I couldn't fix it. The feed box had slipped, so she fired one shot at a time and then quit. I did everything I could, but finally had to give up and come home, as we were about fifteen kilometers their side of the line."[21]

The general inactivity along the Toul front allowed the pilots to practice their craft when weather permitted. They flew practice combats and patrols, honing their navigational skills, improving their gunnery skills by shooting ground targets, and enhancing situational awareness – learning to see the enemy before he saw you. Aerobatic practice was encouraged, but formation flying, a critical element on a more active front, was not. German pilots on this front were reticent about joining combat with large formations of Allied fighters, whereas the appearance of two or three Allied fighters might have the opposite effect.

Captain Ham Coolidge, a pilot with the 94th Aero Squadron, described the nature of combat missions on the Toul sector: "As chasse or fighting planes, our function is to patrol certain areas between certain times in search of Huns, and to offer protection to Allied reconnaissance, reglage [artillery cooperation] or photographic planes. We also do 'alert' duty, during which time we sit around waiting a telephone call reporting Boche planes over such and such a place, at a certain altitude and going in a certain direction. Then we hustle on up to meet them."[22]

The French early warning system on the Toul front was outstanding; messages identifying enemy air activity were given priority, and on the average took only four minutes from sighting to receipt of the information by the squadron's operations office. The Nieuport 28 was admirably suited to respond to the alert messages. Lieutenant Douglas Campbell

Below:
Ned Buford makes a low pass over a moving picture photographer. The wooden-framed Bessoneau hangars of the 94th and 95th Aero Squadrons are in the background. National Archives

Opposite
Top: A flight of the 95th Aero Squadron's Nieuport 28s prepares to take off. Aircraft with concentric, maroon and gold cowl markings are from the squadron's 2nd Flight. National Archives

Bottom: Getting into position for takeoff. National Archives

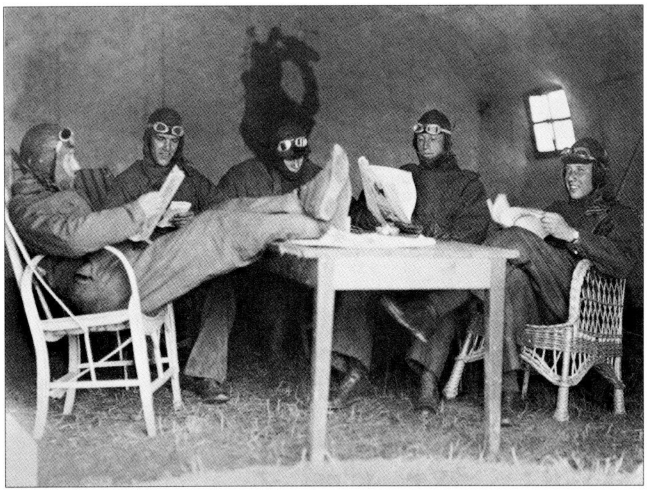

Pilots from the 95th Aero Squadron in the alert tent, relaxing while awaiting developments. National Archives

Nieuport 28s of the 147th Aero Squadron responding to an alert. National Archives

described the procedure that could get the fighter's rotary engine started and the airplane into the air within ninety seconds: "The mechanic would stand in front of the plane. He would shout 'Coupe' which would mean cut. The pilot would answer; 'Coupe' which would mean the switch was off. He would then turn the engine over two or three times and when he was ready to pull the prop, he would yell 'Contact' and the pilot would say 'Contact' and turn on the switch. The mechanic would give it a pull and off it would go. We had no warm-up period."[23]

Its quick-starting Gnôme rotary engine and excellent rate of climb enabled the Nieuport 28 to get up to altitude quickly; these factors were apparent on 29 April 1918 (as they had been on 14 April), when the 94th recorded its third victory:

> On this day, [Captain James Norman] Hall and [Lieutenant Eddie] Rickenbacker, sat on alert waiting for the weather to break in order to go after any Germans who ventured into their area. Three minutes before they were to go off alert at 6:00 P.M., a sighting was called in and they took to the air and within thirteen minutes they had located an Albatros between Montsec and Boussane at 6000 feet altitude. Both pilots dove to the attack and put several bursts into the German plane, which immediately headed for the ground with Rickenbacker close behind. When last seen at 2000 feet above the ground at Vignuelles, the plane still in a dive, pouring out black smoke. The victory, credited to Rickenbacker as well as Hall [this would later be amended to half credits for each pilot] was the future ace's first confirmed kill.[24]

The Competition in the Toul Sector

Flying was limited and combat was rare in April 1918, because of poor weather and little enemy opposition. German fighter pilots in the Toul sector at the time were flying the Pfalz D.IIIa and the Albatros D.Va. Comparing the performance of the two fighters, a British pilot said:

> The Albatros was a machine that, when manipulated skillfully, was good at heights at say up to about 10,000 feet, where it became heavy and clumsy on turns. It had no special qualities worth noting, being reasonably fast and fairly 'splitarse' [this contemporary term suggests that the aircraft maneuvered in a generally ragged fashion] at any height, and therefore, it was a nice machine to meet in combat as its tactics were limited to its comparatively mediocre performance. I fancy that the Germans clung to it for so long because it was such a nice machine to fly, unlikely to catch fire and having a fairly good gliding angle ... the Pfalz, unlike the Albatros, was not a popular machine with the Hun pilot ... and it was more or less regarded [by British pilots] as cold meat.[25]

The Nieuport 28 was clearly superior to both enemy fighters in speed, maneuverability, rate of climb and ceiling, but was underarmed, with only one machine gun fitted at the time. The Vickers also had fewer rounds (500) per gun than the German Spandau, which had a capacity of 800 rounds.

Jasta 64, based at Mars-la-Tour roughly fifty kilometers north of Toul, had contributed the first two victims of the 94th Aero Squadron on 14 April, and the German squadron had not scored a victory prior to that date. Jasta 64 (the Jasta would ultimately attain at least twenty victories, however, most of them were scored after the Jasta was equipped with the vaunted Fokker D.VII), later joined by Jasta 65 and equipped with Albatros and Pfalz fighters, patrolled the front between Verdun and Pont-a-Mousson in single aircraft or in flights of two or three. These small formations allowed the 94th and its sister squadrons to patrol with similar numbers of aircraft. American fighter pilots would also have occasional fateful

The Pfalz D.IIIa, equipped with the 180 hp Mercédès D.IIIa engine, was outclassed by newer Allied fighters. German pilots preferred the Albatros D.Va. National Air and Space Museum (NASM A-43638-K), Smithsonian Institution

A captured Albatros D.Va is shown here in British colors. Production of this widely used fighter ceased in February 1918, when Albatros Werke G.m.b.H. switched to licensed production of the Fokker D.VII. The Albatros D.Va was equipped with the 160 hp Mercédès engine. National Air and Space Museum, (NASM A-4330-B), Smithsonian Institution

encounters with other Jastas (60, 80, and K3) from adjoining sectors.[26] This generally unchallenging environment for training would prove detrimental several months later, when far larger, more aggressive and experienced formations of German fighters were encountered on another front.

In addition to the limited number of enemy fighters, the First Pursuit Group (so designated on 5 May, when the 95th Aero Squadron returned to combat) also encountered small numbers of German biplace reconnaissance and reglage (artillery cooperation) aircraft on the Toul front. These aircraft included the Rumpler, L.V.G., and Halberstadt. Climbing to an altitude of 20,000 feet to attack, the highflying reconnaissance planes was taxing for pilot (without oxygen) and plane alike, as Lieutenant Harold Buckley recalled: "We made endless climbs to 22,000 and 23,000 feet to intercept hostile photographers who were making our sector their playground and invariably found them a couple of thousand feet above us. We could almost see them thumbing their noses and laughing at us, while boiling with rage, but with frozen fingers and toes, we hung precariously at the absolute limit of our altitude … which invariably left us with an almost unbearable headache from the high altitude."[27]

Lieutenant Douglas Campbell remembered his frustration in attacking a Rumpler at altitude: "The Rumpler was, of course, excellent for its purpose because it could fly so high. I can remember chasing one up to 21,000 feet in a Nieuport one day. The Rumpler was about 1000 feet higher, I guess, and I would get under him and pull straight up, take a pot shot, but he was too far away for me to hurt him. I'd drop 2000 or 3000 feet before I'd catch myself. I tried this two or three times on the fellow, but I never did get close enough to him to hit him."[28] Lieutenant Campbell, however, persevered in attacking Rumplers when he could find them at a manageable altitude; Campbell achieved six victories during his brief combat career, four of them over the vaunted Rumpler.

By the end of April, the 94th Aero Squadron had scored three victories with no losses, and the pilots were generally pleased with their Nieuport 28 fighters. Colonel Billy Mitchell, commander of the First Army Air Service, took note of this in a communication to Major General Mason

Nieuport 28 pilots could down the high-flying Rumpler C.IV reconnaissance plane when they could catch it at lower altitudes. Equipped with a 260 hp Mercédès D.IVa in-line engine, the C.IV had a ceiling of 21,000 feet. National Air and Space Museum (NASM 00126464), Smithsonian Institution

Patrick, chief of the Air Service, AEF: "The Nieuport twenty eight with the Gnome motor has proved very satisfactory as a pursuit [fighter] airplane"; Mitchell recommended "that its construction and that of the Gnome monosoupape [single-valve] motor be continued with all speed for the use of the American Air Service in France."[29]

The following month of May, however, would bring greater intensity to the air war around Toul, and a dramatic reversal of fortune for the Nieuport 28 fighter.

Problems Develop

Lieutenant Jimmy Meissner was the first pilot to encounter the problem that became so closely associated with the Nieuport 28 fighter, and which ultimately rendered it hors-de-combat. The widely-held (but erroneous) explanation of the Nieuport 28's wing problem was that *the top wing shed its fabric during an abrupt pullout from a high-speed dive.*

Lieutenant Meissner picks up the narrative of his midday protection mission on 2 May 1918:

> Phil Davis was my partner as we flew along side by side towards Thiaucourt, searching constantly in all directions for anything with a hostile appearance in all that empty sky. I was trying to pick up the Salmson [the French aircraft to be escorted] somewhere below and, in looking forward again, I gave an instinctive start. Two planes were headed our way, between us and the lines just below our level, and they looked *Boche*. I'd never seen a German plane in the air in all my three weeks war flying, but these seemed darker in color than any French planes. This, coupled with an instinctive distrust acquired by all war fliers, made me dive and zoom quickly several times to tell Phil to come close and be ready. He drew up and together we watched the unknowns approaching.
>
> Just as the leader came past beneath me, I made a vertical bank climbing into the sun nearly over his head. A glance at the dashboard clock showed it to be five minutes to twelve as I turned, while the altimeter needle stood at 5300 meters, two necessary items if there was going to be

Right: Eddie Rickenbacker, Douglas Campbell, and Kenneth Marr. Rickenbacker infused the 94th Aero Squadron with new spirit, after he relieved Marr as commander on 25 September 1918. National Archives via David Ostrowski

Below: Mechanics pose in front of a flight of Nieuport 28s. Note that the second fighter still has a French cocarde displayed prominently under its left upper wing. Nieuport 28 fighters were later delivered in American colors. Ohio Historical Society

JIMMY MEISSNER'S CLOSE ENCOUNTER, 2 MAY 1918

(1)"Phil Davis was my partner as we flew along side by side towards Thiaucourt."

(2)"Just as the leader came beneath me, I made a vertical bank into the sun nearly over his head..."

(3)"With the vibration of my plane, I couldn't be sure, so I dove closer and – it was true! There were big black crosses..."

(4)"A quick dive until directly behind , and I slowly pulled the nose of my Nieuport up till the sights were in perfect line, I pulled the trigger..."

(5)"Diving with full motor in the excitement of the moment, that a lurch of the enemy made me dive almost vertically to avoid a crash."

(6)"The strain was too great, with a crack, my top wing seemed to break loose and whip back overhead at the instant that I shot under the Boche, so near that I thought that we had met."

All this page: Michael O'Neal

a combat to report. Then straightening out of the bank, I looked to see what the markings were on his wings. With the vibration of my plane, I couldn't be sure, so dove closer and – it was true! There were big black crosses and bird-like wing tips of the German Albatros [actually, a Hannover CL. II]. Instantly forgotten were Davis and the second *Boche*. I trusted him to dispose of that: my game was to get the leader. For he was so evidently so intent on stalking the Frenchman far below that as yet he sensed no danger from above.

A quick dive until directly behind, and I slowly pulled the nose of my Nieuport up till the sights were in perfect line with the Albatros [Hannover CL. II] fuselage only two hundred yards away. Very much excited, I pulled the trigger and held it while thirty rounds from my Vickers gun seemed to scatter all around the *Boche* without hitting him to judge from the tracers and his behavior. Jerking the plane into a spin, he dropped perhaps a thousand feet only to straighten right out and head North with me hot on his trail all the time.

A trail of black smoke it was now, but perhaps the same kind of camouflage that had fooled Doug Campbell a few days ago when a *Boche* got away from him by pretending fire. So I fired again till the gun jammed for the second time but luckily again it was only a miss-fire which two jerks of the charging handle fixed. The Albatros [Hannover CL. II] was going into a spiral when two tracer bullets went straight into its fuselage right back of the motor. Flames burst out from the cockpit instantly for I'd struck his tank, but to make sure that the pilot was not still alive and suffering, I kept up the shooting.

Diving with full motor in the excitement of the moment, I got so close that a lurch of the blazing enemy made me plunge almost vertically to avoid a crash. [Meissner had become fixated on his target and nearly collided with it, a common occurrence among inexperienced pilots.]

The strain was too great, with a crack, my top wing seemed to break loose and whip back overhead at the instant that I shot under the Boche, so near that I thought we had met. I wondered how soon the bottom wing would fold up to leave me in a wingless fuselage pointed toward Mother Earth 15,000 feet below: what beastly luck to die just as my first victory had been won, and myself to blame!

But, suddenly, I realized the top wing wasn't all gone, and the bottom wing hadn't folded up yet, the plane was still diving with motor cut off, still answering to the controls as I gently rocked the stick and pushed on the rudder. Surprised at still being alive, I looked up to see what really happened to the top wing. All the entering edge [leading edge] back to the main spar had torn off, taking the linen completely off the upper surface from wing tip to wing tip so that only about two thirds of the covering on the lower surface [of the top wing] was held against the ribs by wind pressure alone.[30]

Ground crewmen gaze at the tattered fabric and broken top wing on Lieutenant Jimmy Meissner's Nieuport 28, N.6144. Charles Woolley

Lieutenant Meissner, quite mystified by what had occurred, managed with skill – and a considerable amount of luck – to crash-land without injury to himself at an Allied aerodrome at Martincourt. His diary entry for that day noted "a collision on the way down ripped [the] top surface off [of the] upper wings."[31]

On 7 May 1918, Captain James Norman Hall, also of the 94th, had an even more dramatic escape when the leading edge on his right upper wing collapsed during dive recovery; moments later, his rotary engine received a direct hit from an anti-aircraft shell. Fortunately, the shell was a dud and Hall was able to crash-land in German-held territory, where he was promptly taken prisoner.

Ten days later, Lieutenant Eddie Rickenbacker, destined to become the Air Service's Ace of Aces, experienced the same terrifying wing failure. Although badly shaken by the experience, Rickenbacker returned safely to his aerodrome. (Details of Rickenbacker's experience and an in-depth analysis of the Nieuport 28's wing failure problem can be found in Appendix D.)

Lieutenant Wilfrid Casgrain of the 95th Aero Squadron was not so lucky on 30 May, when he was brought down between the trench lines after losing the leading edge of his upper right wing. Casgrain was taken prisoner by German troops occupying a nearby trench.

Lieutenant Jimmy Meissner had a repeat performance the same day that Casgrain was lost, this time losing the leading edge and fabric from his right upper wing during combat maneuvering. Flying the same Nieuport 28 (N.6144) that he had flown on 2 May, Meissner survived this incident as well, and returned safely to Gengoult Aerodrome.

Two days later, Lieutenant Waldo Heinrichs of the 95th Aero Squadron joined the select group of U.S. Air Service pilots who had experienced the failure of their Nieuport 28s' upper wings during combat maneuvers. Heinrichs survived this experience, but was severely wounded in a combat on 17 September. He spent the rest of the war as a prisoner of war (POW).

Jimmy Meissner in a sober mood, after his mishap following his first victory on 2 May 1918. Note the Liberty Bond poster doped to the lower wing. Bergen Hardesty

Bottom left: Hall's #17 in a photograph taken by a German pilot. The engine took a direct hit from a dud anti-aircraft shell moments after the leading edge of the fighter's right upper wing collapsed. Note that the drooping fabric, still largely intact, contains the broken leading edge. Alan Toelle Below: Captain Hall on the first leg of his journey to Karlsruhe POW Camp. Charles Woolley

Few American pilots experienced the terror of wing failure in flight, but it was enough to shake their confidence and that of their squadron mates in the Nieuport 28 fighter.

By early June, anxious pilots of the 94th and 95th squadrons, who had lauded the Nieuport 28 only weeks earlier, were clamoring for replacements. They were also at a loss to understand the phenomenon of upper wing failure,

Lieutenant Rickenbacker is smiling, having regained his composure after his experience with wing failure. The leading edge of the upper right wing he is holding has broken cleanly away from the front spar. R.L. Cavanagh

Lieutenant Wilfrid Casgrain, 95th Aero Squadron pilot. Charles Woolley

Jimmy Meissner after his second encounter with wing failure. National Archives

Lieutenant Waldo Heinrichs' Nieuport 28 under repair. Mechanics are preparing to remove the upper left wing. R.L. Cavanagh

and concerned because of what appeared to be a coverup: According to Buckley, "This had been immediately hushed up by the authorities as much as possible. No doubt they were afraid we would all get the 'wind up.' All inquiries were met by mysterious smiles. We knew something was wrong but exactly what we couldn't find out."[32] It was likely that the pilots could not get information because the authorities themselves had scant idea of the cause of the wing failures.

Lieutenant Rickenbacker contributed to the confusion regarding the rash of wing failures: "I knew I had not touched the Hun ... but I did not let the story get out for, fearing it might have an effect on the morale of the other boys if they knew that the machine was defective. I let the story go out that I had collided [with my adversary]. I told Maj. Atkinson [Major Bert M. Atkinson, commander of the First Pursuit Group] what I thought was the trouble, and he said that he would take it up and find out."[33]

Lieutenant William Plyler (center), 27th Aero Squadron pilot, in captivity at Karlsruhe. Plyler reported that he had experienced wing failure during an encounter with Pfalz fighters on 13 June 1918. Standing at Plyler's right is his squadron mate, Lieutenant Zenos R. Miller, who had been downed and taken prisoner on 20 July. David A. McElvain

Several Air Service officers weighed in with their analyses of the problem with the upper wings of the Nieuport 28. In a 9 June 1918 communication to the chief of the Air Service, First Army, AEF, Major Atkinson expressed his opinion that the "weak construction in [the] upper wing [was] due to both spars being too close to the middle," and he further noted that "upon redressing from a dive, the leading edge [would collapse,] carrying away the fabric from the upper surface of the wing." Major John Huffer, commander of the 94th Aero Squadron, attributed the problem to the thin plywood veneer on the upper leading edge of the upper wing. Huffer believed that exposure to the sun warped the veneer and loosened it from the spar underneath, which could cause the veneer to break away under the strain of a high-speed dive recovery. Captain Du Doré, a member of the Aeronautic Section of the French Army and a liaison officer at Gengoult Aerodrome, believed that the "wing [leading edge is] too weak; it gives way, the ribs between the [leading] edge and the central longeron [main spar] breaks the cloth, [which] tears off, and the wing loses the covering completely." Captain Du Doré urgently recommended that the leading edge of the upper wing be reinforced.[34]

Clearly, these officers had some understanding of the wing failure sequence and the circumstances under which it might occur. However, knowledge of why these failures occurred and what could be done about it would come only in the postwar years. In the meantime, pilots of the 94th and 95th Aero Squadrons would continue to fly the Nieuport 28 in combat, but with a much-reduced degree of confidence in their aircraft.

Pilots of the 27th and 147th squadrons did not share these concerns about the structural failure of the Nieuport 28's upper wings because these pilots believed they had been properly trained and disciplined to avoid such occurrences. One of their number, however, may have been the exception: Second Lieutenant William H. Plyler, a member of the 27th Aero Squadron, reported that he experienced wing failure (an official account declared that he had been driven down) in a harrowing combat with a flight of seven Pfalz fighters on 13 June 1918. After the wing's "leading edge gave way ... under the strain, and the wing fabric tore off ... Plyler's downward dash could not be halted. After tossing into three tailspins, his plane smashed into a thicket of four-foot [-thick] trees, wrecked."[35] Plyler survived the crash and was taken prisoner, with Flieger Bunning of K3 claiming the victory, his first.

An aircraft in-flight fire was an entirely different matter, for it is the nightmare of every air crewman. The Nieuport 28 had several fire-causing problems, some minor and easily corrected by training or quick fixes, but one that would only be corrected when a major redesign of the aircraft was undertaken later in the war.

Improper use of the coupé could cause a dramatic fireball explosion. The coupé, more commonly called a blip switch,

Little remains of Nieuport 28, N.6188, after a catastrophic fire. National Air and Space Museum, Smithsonian Institution (SI 83-16474)

was a button on top of the control stick that cut off ignition to all nine cylinders of the Gnôme rotary engine.

The Gnôme rotary engine had neither carburetor nor throttle, and engine rpm was controlled by a selector switch that varied the spark interval to the plugs, sparking each plug every two revolutions when the selector switch was set at full speed. The spark interval could be reduced to slow the engine or cut off ignition entirely. Because of the narrow rpm range of the engine, the blip switch was also required for intermittent fine adjustment of speed while taxiing or just prior to flaring out for landing.

The explosion problem resulted from novice pilots depressing the blip switch for too long a period without cutting off fuel flow to the engine, with the effect that the windmilling prop (the Nieuport 28's large prop was relatively unconstrained by a low-compression engine) continued to draw raw fuel into the cylinders and then flush it out the valves to puddle in the cowl, and then out again into the air or onto the ground. Releasing the blip switch resumed ignition and ignited the raw gas in the cowl, causing a spectacular fireball to occur. This problem was not always as serious as it looked, as the pilot could dive to put out the fire or the aircraft could be moved away from the fire if it occurred on the ground. The real solution, however, was judicious use of the blip switch. As one 94th pilot, Lieutenant Douglas Campbell, stated, "Nobody ever told us these things. We had to learn them ourselves."[36]

More serious fires were caused when the Nieuport 28's fuel lines began to break. On several occasions, copper tubing between the fuel tank and the engine broke in flight, due to engine vibration; the trouble was traced to improper annealing of the fuel lines and the lack of flexible coupling to protect against vibration. The Nieuport Company was unable to replace the defective tubing in a timely manner, so a squad of American mechanics was organized to quickly install new fuel-line connections (consisting of seven pieces of irregularly shaped line with flexible couplings) to ensure that the much-needed Nieuport 28 fighters could be kept in service.

The major fire hazard in the Nieuport 28 was the forty-liter reserve fuel tank, located immediately to the right of the pilot's seat. The death of Major Raoul Lufbery on 19 May 1918 brought this hazard home forcefully to the Nieuport 28 pilots of the First Pursuit Group.

The Death of Lufbery

Major Lufbery was a highly esteemed former member of the Lafayette Escadrille and a member of the American 94th Aero Squadron at the time of his death. His fatal combat with a Rumpler C.VII photoreconnaissance aircraft was witnessed from the ground by the citizens of Maron, a small village about eight miles east-southeast of Gengoult.

Lieutenant Eddie Rickenbacker reported after the war on the circumstances of Lufbery's death, saying, "the machine was in flames ... he jumped rather than stay in."[37] Rickenbacker's

Pensive Major Gervais Raoul Lufbery alongside a Nieuport 28 fighter. National Archives via R.L. Cavanagh

report appears to be the genesis for some of the confusion surrounding Lufbery's last combat: Did he jump or fall from his aircraft? The story bears closer scrutiny, and we begin as Lufbery returned from an early-morning patrol.

The 94th squadron's Alert Log shows that Major Lufbery landed his Nieuport 28, N.6193, at Gengoult Aerodrome at 8:41 a.m. after an early-morning tangle with an Albatros that had produced no results. He returned to the aerodrome only minutes before Lieutenant Oliver Jay Gude took off to attack a Rumpler C.VII that had overflown the field. Gude was embarking on his first combat, and it is likely that Lufbery watched with mounting exasperation as Gude failed to aggressively press home his attack against the Rumpler.

Lufbery immediately commandeered another Nieuport 28 (N.6178, assigned to Lieutenant Philip W. Davis), and he was airborne at 9 a.m. in pursuit of the Rumpler, which was then southwest of Nancy. Lufbery, in his haste to get away in the quick-starting Nieuport 28, may have failed to secure his safety belt, which would have involved adjusting four belt lengths (Davis was slighter in build than Lufbery) and then connecting the lap and shoulder belts to the central, quick-release latch at his waist. Lufbery's haste to get into the air might have been explained by the fact that he had not had a confirmed kill since he transferred to the 94th from the Lafayette Escadrille months earlier, and by his consternation with Gude's ineffectual performance in the air.

Major Lufbery caught up with the Rumpler at an altitude of 2,000 feet over the village of Maron and attacked, only to quickly break off in an apparent attempt to clear a gun jam. Lufbery quickly resumed his attack, but this time the German observer-gunner caught him with a short machine-gun burst.

Forty-four years later, Major Royal Frey, then director of the U.S. Air Force Museum, interviewed citizens of Maron who had witnessed Lufbery's last combat. Frey reported the following account of the battle, based on those interviews:

> Suddenly, the smaller airplane [Lufbery's Nieuport 28] flipped on its back and two objects fell from it – the pilot and a cushion [which proved to be a church kneeling cushion that Davis needed to sit higher and more comfortably on the seat]. The plane then headed in a slight dive toward the southwest from a point over the center of the village. A thin line of smoke began to trail from it, and a couple of seconds before it struck the ground, some flames appeared. It crashed to earth about a mile southwest of Maron, fifty feet northeast of the railroad track leading to Neuves-Maisons. When it struck the ground, it disintegrated in an explosion and was destroyed by fire. The pilot fell without making a sound.[38]

Two villagers reported to Major Frey that they had seen Lufbery's body "lying on its back with arms outstretched somewhat from its sides, completely dressed in a one-piece leather flying-suit." The witnesses were certain "that there was absolutely no blood on the pilot's face nor was he burnt on the hair or his face singed in the slightest. However, one of his thumbs was gone, on his right hand [the hand that controlled the stick] and he appeared to have a wound similar to a bullet hole in his left temple slightly back of and above his left eye."[39] Lieutenant Eddie Rickenbacker's postwar testimony that Lufbery's thumb had been severed by a bullet (which also penetrated the reserve tank of the Nieuport), corroborated the recollections of the villagers. Major Frey noted that "the autopsy report revealed that Lufbery died of a massive cranial fracture as he hit the ground."[40]

The evidence suggests that Lufbery fell from his Nieuport 28 when the airplane, apparently out of control, tipped over. It

Lieutenants Gude, Rickenbacker, and Winslow, and Major Lufbery smile for the camera. Bergen Hardesty

Somber citizens of Maron stand near the spot where Lufbery's body landed. Charles Woolley

Below: Major Lufbery's Nieuport 28, N.6193. Lieutenant Philip Davis would go down in flames in this airplane not long after Lufbery lost his life flying Davis' Nieuport 28.

is plausible that Lufbery's reaction to the severing of his right thumb and to the head wound reflexively caused him to snap roll the nimble Nieuport 28, throwing him, unfettered by the safety harness, and the cushion out of the airplane.

The pilots took special notice of the bullet-pierced reserve gasoline tank and ensuing fire that destroyed the airplane Major Lufbery had commandeered from Lieutenant Davis and flown to his death. Ironically, Lieutenant Philip Davis, flying Lufbery's Nieuport 28, N.6193, would be killed in action several days later on 2 June 1918. Lieutenant Davis also went down in flames after a bullet penetrated the reserve tank in his aircraft.

The position of the reserve gasoline tank in the Nieuport 28 did indeed pose a major hazard, and as one pilot noted, it "was put there as a special target for the enemy's incendiary bullets to get things over quickly."[41] Lieutenant Jimmy Meissner ("flying with side tank empty now to lessen fire danger"[42]) ceased filling the reserve tank in his Nieuport 28 as a result, and other pilots followed suit.

The reserve tank would be relocated to a safer position when the Nieuport 28 was later modified.

The Nieuport 28 Is Cashiered ... Temporarily

In a 12 June memorandum to Major General Mason M. Patrick, chief of the Air Service, AEF, Brigadier General Benjamin Foulois, chief of the Air Service, First Army, recommended that as "the defects in this type of aeroplane [Nieuport 28] are of such a serious nature that in my opinion they cannot be corrected sufficiently to authorize the use of this type of aeroplane on an active sector of the front, except at the risk of considerable unnecessary loss of life." Foulois further recommended that "immediate steps be taken to replace all aeroplanes of this type, by one place Spads, or an equally efficient and reliable British type."[43] Foulois' memorandum must have embarrassed Colonel Billy Mitchell, who had recommended only five weeks earlier that the construction of the Nieuport 28 "be continued with all speed for the use of the American Air Service in France."[44]

Pilots of the 94th and 95th Aero Squadrons registered their strong approval of Brigadier General Foulois' recommendation to speedily replace the Nieuport 28 with the SPAD XIII. Lieutenant Quentin Roosevelt of the 95th Aero Squadron commented in a letter, "At the moment every one is much pleased in our Squadron for we are getting new planes. We have been using Nieuports, which have the disadvantage of not being particularly reliable and being inclined to catch fire."[45]

The pilots of the 94th and 95th Aero Squadrons were looking forward with great expectation to receiving new SPAD XIIIs. However, the pilots of the 27th, and particularly those of the 147th, Aero Squadrons were adamant and vocal

Major Harold E. Hartney, Canadian-born commanding officer of the 27th Aero Squadron. Charles Woolley

Below: Officers of the 147th Aero Squadron stand proudly in front of one of their preferred mounts, the Nieuport 28 fighter. National Archives

Major Geoffrey Bonnell, 147th CO (with white dog), oversees a meeting of squadron mascots, to the delight of the pilots of the 147th, 27th and 95th Aero Squadrons of the First Pursuit Group. "Jake," the donkey, was the mascot of the 95th. National Archives

about retaining their nimble Nieuport 28s. Both of the latter squadrons, recent additions to the First Pursuit Group, had begun combat operations at the Toul sector on 2 June 1918.

Major Harold E. Hartney, a Canadian-born combat veteran of the Royal Flying Corps and now commander of the 27th Aero Squadron, recognized that while the location of the reserve gas tank in the Nieuport 28 posed "a particular hazard," the failure of the upper wing's leading edge during high-speed combat maneuvering was more the fault of an inadequately trained pilot: "Nobody told us about this weakness; nothing was done about it. We had to learn it ourselves. Early in my flying career I had observed that it was the weakest point in all these early airplanes, and I warned the boys about it. In fact, on one annoying occasion, I had to send to the rear a pilot who refused to believe that I knew what I was talking about in this matter and *crudely pulled back his stick at the end of a dive* [author's italics]. It broke his heart but it saved several valuable lives."[46]

Major Hartney's affinity for the Nieuport 28 was readily apparent when he later related the joy of his first flight in the aircraft: "I jumped into this first of our very own machines and spent a half hour sitting there studying the instruments. 'CONTACT!' And I was off. She climbed even better that the Camels at Gosport. For the first time in all my flying, I felt that the plane and I were really one. She maneuvered like a bird in flight, almost in response to my thoughts."[47]

Major Geoffrey Bonnell, like Hartney, had trained at Gosport as a member of the Royal Flying Corps and had experienced combat before being transferred to the U.S. Air Service. Assuming command of the 147th, Bonnell developed the squadron into a well-trained and cohesive unit before bringing it to the front in early June 1918.

Popular with his men, Major Bonnell became passionate in his defence of the Nieuport 28 and outspoken in expressing his distaste for the SPAD XIII fighter that was slated to replace it. Bonnell's actions in this regard were a factor in his being relieved from command of the 147th six weeks later, much to the consternation of his men. Before his departure, however, Bonnell would succeed in keeping the Nieuport 28 operational in his squadron for as long as possible by taking up the Nieuports of sister squadrons as they transitioned to SPAD XIIIs. Ultimately, the 147th would also make the much-resisted transition to the SPAD XIII, but not before the squadron succeeded in ensuring continued production of the Nieuport 28, albeit in modified form.

The Genesis of the Nieuport 28A

Early in 1918, the U.S. Air Service had planned initially to replace the Nieuport 28 with the highly touted ("it could maneuver around a clothes pin") and better-performing Morane-Saulnier MoS 29 monoplane equipped with the same Gnôme 9N rotary engine that powered the Nieuport 28. Deliveries to the Air Service were to begin in early June, but the French government canceled the production contract after finding the type to be unsafe: a French officer had been killed in February and an American pilot in the Lafayette Flying Corps had been killed in March when the wings of their airplanes folded up.[48]

As a consequence of the termination of the MoS 29 fighter contract, the U.S. Air Service decided to procure an additional 600 Nieuport 28s under contract A.S. 5365, dated 2 May 1918. This contract was now in jeopardy because of the design flaws, principally the upper wing defects, that had been found in the aircraft. But Foulois had yet to take into account the passionate desire of the 147th Aero Squadron's pilots to retain the Nieuport 28, and the fact that numerous modifications and improvements in design were already being planned. (The modifications made to the Nieuport 28 fighter, which emerged as the Nieuport 28A advanced trainer, are discussed in detail in Appendix C.)

Brigadier General Foulois would have canceled this contract if Lieutenant Colonel Halsey Dunwoody, assistant to the chief of the Air Service, AEF, for supply, had not made a convincing case on behalf of Major Geoffrey Bonnell and his pilots to stay the cancellation. In mid-June, Lieutenant Colonel Dunwoody sent the following telegram to Brigadier General Foulois: "It is requested that [you] get in touch with the pilots of the hundred and forty seventh squadron, all of whom state that they now prefer Nieuport 28 planes to SPADs. With regard to the cancellation of the contract for six hundred Nieuport 28 planes, in light of the twenty-three changes to be made in these planes, which we believe will greatly improve them and in view [of the] statements of pilots referred to, we advise withholding cancellation of the contract for the present. In the meantime we are making and will make every effort to obtain as many SPADs as possible."[49]

Brigadier General Foulois responded by telegram to Dunwoody on 19 June 1918. The telegram reads in part: "Regarding Nieuport 28 planes, [I] am familiar with views of pilots of hundred forty seventh squadron, also familiar with views of pilots of other squadrons who have had much more experience with Nieuport 28 planes. In view of present military emergencies and large number of changes contemplated in Nieuport 28, recommend you not cancel contract for six hundred Nieuport[s]. [I] insist, however, [that] you institute most rigid system of inspection of all planes and engines at factories and before planes and engines leave Orly [Orly Field was the aircraft distribution point for the Air Service]. Regardless of new changes contemplated in Nieuport 28 plane, this type can only be used effectively for certain classes of front line service, it is a very delicate machine and does not stand rough service."[50] In any case, the first deliveries of the modified Nieuport 28A advanced trainer would be made after the Armistice.

However, it would take weeks for each of the four squadrons of the First Pursuit Group to fully transition to the SPAD XIII. In the meantime, the Nieuport 28 fighter would have to soldier on through what was perhaps the most difficult period faced by the group during the First World War.

The German Spring Offensives

The last great German offensives of the war had begun several weeks before the First Pursuit Group deployed for combat to the quiet front around Toul. On 21 March 1918, Operation Michael, the long-awaited German offensive, opened with incredible intensity along a sixty-mile front between Arras and La Fère astride the Somme River. The objective was a breakthrough and roll-up of the British armies to the north, separating them in the process from their French and American allies to the south and east.

Three German armies hit the Third and Fifth British Armies using the Hutier tactics that had been developed by General Oscar von Hutier on the Eastern Front, and successfully demonstrated during the German counterattack at Cambrai on the Western Front in December 1917: "The weight of the [German] bombardment was now unprecedented, 6,500 guns fired on a forty-mile front, destroying all communications behind the lines and drenching the front line with gas and high explosive. Then 'storm troops', specialized assault-units carrying their own firepower in the shape of sled-borne light guns, light machine guns, grenades, mortars and flame-throwers, spear-headed the main infantry attack, destroying enemy strong points wherever possible and masking them when it was not. The infantry units that followed poured into the gaps they had opened, reserves being fed in to exploit [the initial] success."[51]

German ground and air preparations for the offensive had been kept secret, as German elite fighter, attack, bomber, and reconnaissance units were concentrated at the point of attack. German low-level strafing and bombing attacks, with fighters flying protection above, were very effective from the outset of the offensive. German units had been drawn from other points along the front, including the Toul sector, and the German Air Service briefly enjoyed a numerical superiority of 820 aircraft to 645 Allied aircraft (most of them obsolescent two-seaters), towards the end of March 1918.

The Royal Flying Corps, having made an intense effort to blunt the German offensive while suffering and inflicting high losses in planes and pilots, managed to regain air superiority by the beginning of April.[52] Operation Michael, after having gained a costly forty-mile-deep salient in the face of a determined British defense on the ground and in the air,

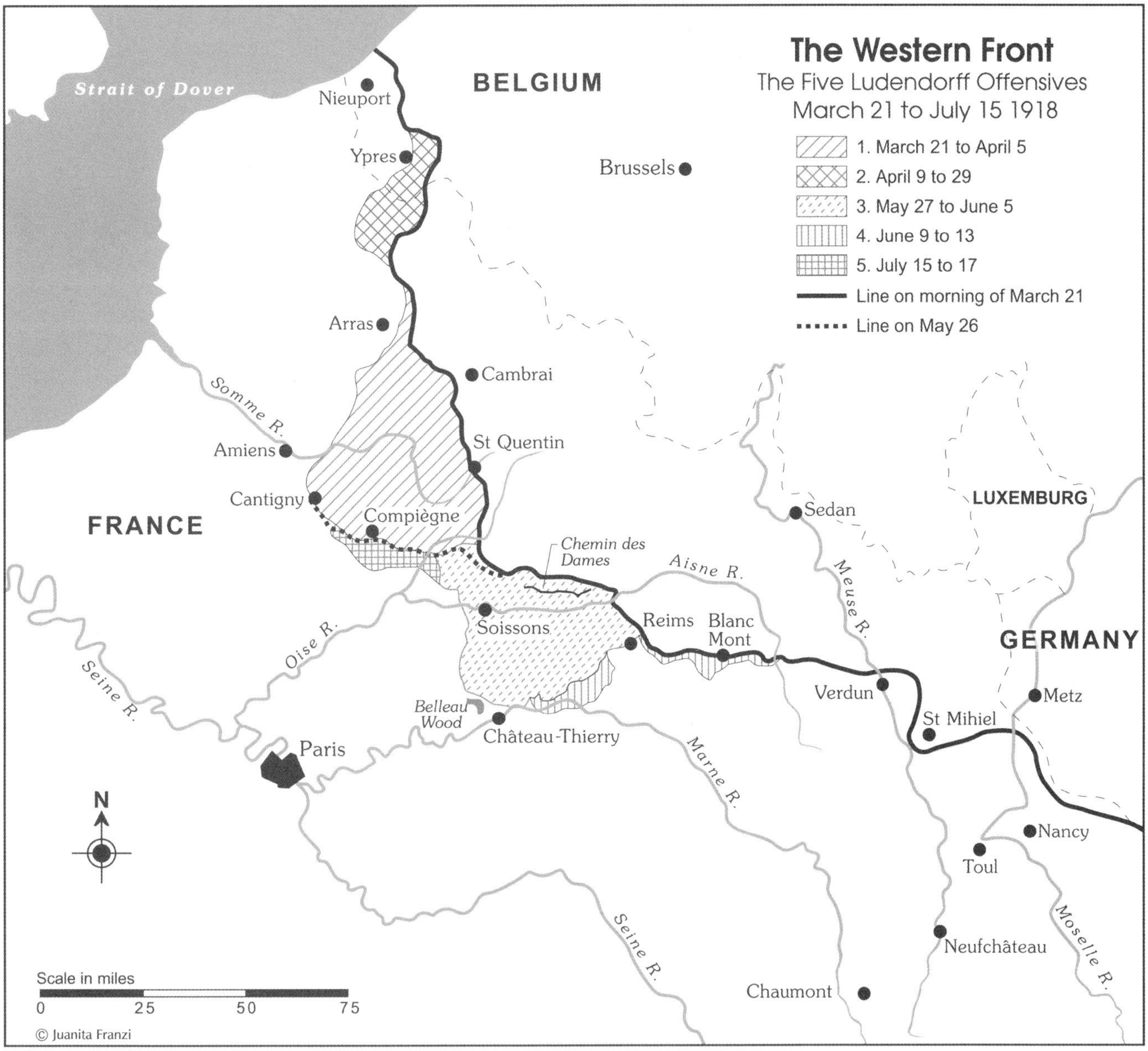

lost momentum after German forces outran their artillery and logistical support.

On 9 April 1918, the second German offensive broke against the British Fourth Army along the Lys River, and resulted in a penetration of ten miles before being checked, once again because the Germans had outrun their artillery and logistical support.

The third German offensive followed in late April, this time directed against the French Sixth Army along the Aisne River. The Germans struck along a thirty-mile front, penetrating as far as Château-Thierry along the Marne River, before the attack ground to a halt in early June. Growing American might was much in evidence, as elements of the U.S. 3rd Division withstood repeated German assaults at the Château-Thierry bridgeheads. American Marines of the 2nd Division cleared the Bois de Belleau and other positions nearby in a succession of frontal attacks that resulted in very heavy casualties on both sides.

Seven American infantry divisions were now at the front with eighteen more divisions in training or in reserve, and more American troops were arriving at French ports at a rate of 300,000 a month. The weight of these fresh American troops was beginning to be felt. In mid-June, Franco-American counterattacks stopped the fourth German offensive along the Noyons-Mondidier front. German gains were both miniscule and costly.

The Real War Looms for the First Pursuit Group

The First Pursuit Group received orders on 6 June 1918, to be prepared to move immediately, as the threat of an impending German offensive loomed nearby. Much work had been done on the group's Nieuport 28 fighters to prepare them for further combat. Additional Vickers machine guns were received and installed in early June, effectively doubling the fighters' firepower. Enterprising pilots directed their armorers to hone the working surfaces of their Vickers machine guns, substantially increasing the guns' reliability. The addition of unit sights (pictured in Appendix C) and ring and bead sights further enhanced the potency of the Nieuport 28.

Much to the surprise of the French technical representatives, squadron mechanics had found a way to increase the time between needed overhauls of the rotary engines: "Sergeant Albaugh [27th Aero Squadron], an expert on lubrication and cooling, had conceived the idea of drilling holes in the pistons and doctoring up the fragile little [Gnôme rotary] engine so that the oil circulation, for cooling the pistons ... was improved and the machine worked with much greater reliability than before."[53]

The squadrons were now practicing formation flying in preparation for meeting a far more numerous and disciplined enemy. However, the adequacy of their formation training prior to the move to the new front was being questioned, and events would prove that the criticism was entirely justified.

Lieutenant Eddie Rickenbacker's diary entry for 16 June read: "We had a squadron formation up for the first time today."[54] Formation training was begun since the First Pursuit Group would soon move from the quiet Toul sector to an active sector, with the town of Château-Thierry at its apex. No aspect of fighter combat would characterize the difference between the two sectors more than the large and aggressive formations of German aircraft that would soon be encountered on the more active Château-Thierry front.

The individual combats and small formations that had characterized the Toul sector, and their inadequate training in formation flying, left the pilots of the First Pursuit Group relatively unprepared to meet the best units of the German air force: "The training schools have not sent men to the front prepared for their work. They have not been taught to fly formation. The combat instruction given them has been based upon the wrong idea. They have been led to believe that their combat principles involved individual combat principally whereas individual combat [which had perhaps been inculcated in American pilots by their French instructors, who had a predilection and flair for individual combat] is a very rare occurrence."[55]

Nieuport 28 equipped with twin Vickers .303 machine guns, rearview mirror, and ring and post sight. Note adjustable safety-belt strap hanging over the edge of the fuselage. A four-point, quick-release clasp hangs from a chain on the end of the belt. Collection S.H.A.A., No B78 1506

Although the pilots of the First Pursuit Group still had much to learn, they had performed admirably in the Toul sector during their two and one-half months' combat deployment there. The group had established a better than 3-to-1 kill ratio against their opponents, with twenty-nine victories credited while incurring nine casualties, including six killed in action or in accidents. The majority of the victories (twenty-one) were credited to four pilots of the 94th: Captain Peterson and Lieutenants Rickenbacker, Campbell, and Meissner. Most of their victims were biplace observation aircraft.[56]

Toward the end of June 1918, the pilots and Nieuport 28 fighters of the First Pursuit Group transferred from the placid Toul sector to the Château-Thierry sector (officially known as the Aisne-Marne sector) in time for the fifth and final German offensive. The marked contrast of the Marne sector to what had been encountered at Toul was summed up by Lieutenant Harold Buckley of the 95th Aero Squadron in his postwar memoirs, "It was really a nice peaceful war we found there [at Toul] but at the time we were too dumb to appreciate it."[57]

A postwar Air Service history provides further detail about the operational risks that would be encountered in the new sector:

> From the point of view of tactical operations over the lines, the sizes of formations employed and methods of employing them, required almost as radical a change of methods by our pilots as was required by the big jump which all pilots had to make from the training schools to the front. At Toul, our pilots had been opposed by two squadrons of enemy pursuit [fighters] equipped with a rather inferior type of single-seat planes – Albatrosses [and Pfalzs]. At Château Thierry, the enemy had a large concentration of Fokker D. VII airplanes, whose crews showed a tenacity, aggressiveness, and persistence wholly new to our experience. While at Toul, our pilots had been able to achieve a remarkable success in attacks upon enemy two-seaters, and our Corps Observation aviation acted practically without interference. On the other hand, at Château Thierry, our pursuit was engaged practically daily with formations of the enemy as large in numbers as thirty and more and averaging about fifteen. In the Toul Sector, a single pursuit plane with a skillful pilot, if not very effective, was at least practically safe, and formations of between three and six did excellent and effective work. Flights in squadron formation had been practiced at Toul. From the first day at Château Thierry, they became the only method of operations employed.[58]

From Toul to Touquin

On 26 June 1918, elements of the First Pursuit Group began moving from Toul to Melun Field, their new aerodrome at Touquin, located approximately 140 miles due east by air from the environs of Paris. By 28 June all the elements of the group, including its complement of Nieuport 28 fighters, had arrived at Melun and were made ready for immediate action.

Lieutenant Edward Vernon Rickenbacker appears to be holding the brim of the squadron insignia, Uncle Sam's "Hat in the Ring." University of Texas at Dallas

A list of the various Jagdstaffeln (German fighter squadrons) arrayed on this front was provided to the American pilots immediately after their arrival. The list was lengthy and sobering, for it included the vaunted JG 1 (Jagdgeschwader Nr. 1, or Fighter Group 1, comprising Jastas 4, 6, 10, and 11), formerly under the command of Rittmeister Manfred von Richthofen (who had been killed in action on 21 April) and now commanded by Oberleutnant Hermann Goering, and JG 3 (comprising Jastas 2, 26, 27, and 36), under the command of Oberleutnant Bruno Loerzer. The pilots of the First Pursuit Group would soon become intimately acquainted with the colors and markings of these Jagdgeschwadern, as well as numerous other Jastas that were gathering in the Soissons-Reims area to support what would be Germany's final offensive of the war.

Another sobering bit of news, received from the French Sixth Army Intelligence, noted that the Fokker Dr.1 Triplane was "disappearing little by little" and being replaced by the Fokker D.VII: "The D. VII is reported by our pursuit pilots to be encountered frequently. It is an excellent machine, better than the 180 horsepower SPAD, equal to the 220 horsepower SPAD in horizontal speed, and is apparently able to climb faster, is extremely maneuverable and able to continue aerobacy at high altitudes of 5000 to 5500 meters."[59]

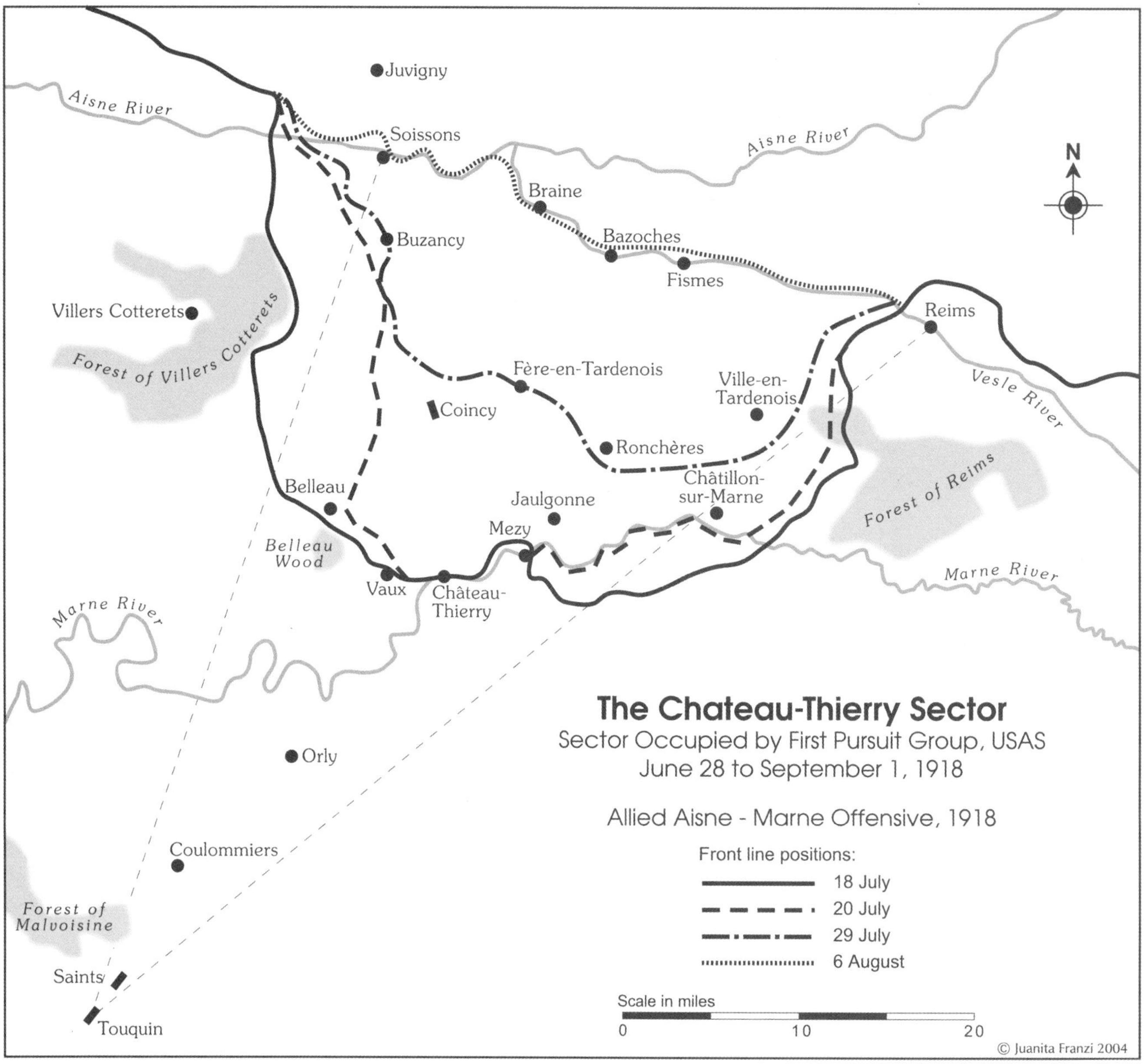

On 30 June the First Pursuit Group, now under the command of the French Sixth Army, was ordered to fly patrols over their new sector to familiarize themselves with the landmarks and terrain features: "Get into the air and look around. Gęt to know every foot of ground for thirty miles on every side of the aerodrome. You'll run into early morning ground haze but you must be able to get back even if you have to skim the treetops."[60]

This sector differed from the Toul sector in ways other than the much larger concentration of German fighter planes (it was estimated that the American units would be outnumbered four to one at times during the ensuing battle): the battle lines were fluid and the network of ground observation stations that had been so effective in the static area around Toul was lacking on this front.

The problem of acquiring essential intelligence about enemy front-line activity was compounded because the newly created aerodrome at Touquin was quite distant from the active front at Château-Thierry, the closest part of the twenty-mile-deep salient that had been created by the German army's third offensive. French army intelligence believed the next German assault was imminent and was fearful that an aerodrome closer to the front would be overrun. Gengoult Aerodrome at Toul was twenty kilometers from the front. Touquin, however, was forty-five kilometers from the front lines, and the combat zone extended a further five to fifteen kilometers beyond because that is where the German fighters usually sought to engage in combat.

The added distance to the front would tax the limits of the Nieuport 28's endurance, particularly for those fighters being flown with reserve tanks kept empty. The pilots, now flying

Leutnant Ernst Udet and his Fokker D.VIIF, "LO!" National Air and Space Museum, Smithsonian Institution (SI 88-1112)

Oberleutnant Hermann Goering, credited with twenty-two victories and the recipient of the Pour le Mérite, was the last commanding officer of JG 1. National Air and Space Museum, Smithsonian Institution (SI 87-15109)

Lieutenant Hamilton Coolidge, 94th Aero Squadron, pictured over Château-Thierry in June 1918. The photograph was taken by his squadron mate, Lieutenant Alden B. Sherry. Bergen Hardesty

three or more two-hour missions daily, would be taxed to the limits of their endurance as well. Under the circumstances, reconnaissance missions to ferret-out enemy activity on front lines and in the rear area were critical in this sector. Protection patrols (close protection of reconnaissance and photographic planes) by the fighter pilots of the First Pursuit Group would prove difficult and costly.

The Tide Turns

The battle raging on the Franco-American front from 1 July to 6 August 1918 has been characterized in three phases. The first phase involved preparation for the German offensive that commenced on 15 July 1918. Allied intelligence had pieced together General Erich Ludendorff's plan from German prisoners and deserters and Allied aerial reconnaissance reports. The second phase entailed the blunting of what would be the last German offensive of the war. The third phase encompassed the Allied Aisne-Marne Offensive, which immediately followed and erased the recent German gains, pushing the salient back to the Vesle River from Soissons to Reims. Seven American divisions and four French armies, supported by the American First Pursuit Group, three American Army Corps observation squadrons, three balloon companies, and other Allied air units, undertook this successful effort on 18 July 1918. This was a significant date: it marked the turning point of the war, as the initiative had now, finally and irrevocably, passed to the Allies.

The First Pursuit Group began operations on the new front on 1 July 1918, when a flight of six Nieuport 28s of the 94th Aero Squadron departed Touquin at 2:53 p.m. Reaching an altitude of 10,500 feet, the Nieuport 28s were bounced by an equal number of Fokkers of Jasta 66 over Bouresches, a short distance from Belleau Wood. Two enemy aircraft closed in and opened fire; Lieutenant Harold Tittman took a bullet near his heart, but managed to crash his airplane within the lines. Tittman sustained additional injuries, a concussion and two broken legs, in the crash; he survived, but never returned to combat.[61] Two Jasta 66 pilots, Leutnants Arthur Laumann and Werner Preuss, shared credit for downing Tittman; they would be credited with twenty-three and twenty-two victories, respectively, by the end of the war.

The following day two flights, totaling nine Nieuport 28s from the 27th Aero Squadron, met the "Richthofen Circus" in a melee that began at the upper limits of the Nieuport 28's service ceiling. German pilots attacked the lower flight of Nieuports, under the command of Lieutenant Donald Hudson, but failed to see the upper flight under Lieutenant Frederick Norton, which quickly fell on them. Six members of the 27th shared two victories in the ensuing combat, but the squadron

Lieutenant Fred Norton, "Jerry" the dog, and Nieuport 28, N.6234. Charles Woolley

lost two of its own. Two Jasta 10 pilots, Leutnants Lowenhardt (who had twenty-three aircraft and nine balloon victories at that point) and Friedrichs (twenty victories), shared a victory over Lieutenant Edward Elliott, who was killed in the action. Elliott's body was found after the Armistice. Lieutenant Walter Wanamaker was shot down by a noted Ace, Leutnant Ernst Udet of Jasta 4. (Wanamaker, who was wounded and taken prisoner, met Udet years later in Cleveland, Ohio, where Udet returned a trophy of his victory to Wanamaker – the rudder from Wanamaker's downed Nieuport 28, marked with N.6347.)

Major Harold Hartney, CO of the 27th Aero Squadron, recalled this particular combat in his memoirs, published in 1940: "It was an even fight – nine against nine – flyers of about equal skill but with greater experience on the side of the

Leutnant Udet inspects Wanamaker's downed Nieuport 28. Udet retrieved the rudder of Wanamaker's fighter as a trophy; the rudder was returned to Wanamaker in the USA fourteen years later. Greg VanWyngarden

Right: Lieutenant Walter B. Wanamaker was downed by Leutnant Ernst Udet of Jasta 4 on 2 July 1918. Greg VanWyngarden

Far right: Major Harold E. Hartney believed in the merits of the Nieuport 28 fighter. Charles Woolley

Bottom right: A Cairn terrier, the 147th Aero Squadron's mascot, proclaims, "Who Said Rats!" Lieutenants Wilbert White and Louis "Red" Simon, pose in front of a squadron Nieuport 28. National Air and Space Museum, Smithsonian Institution (SI 86-10364)

Germans. To offset this, we had the superior maneuverability of our faster and better climbing little Nieuports against the sluggishness of the Boche Fokker D. VIIs."[62] Hartney was correct as far as the superior maneuverability of the Nieuport 28 was concerned, however, the Fokker D.VII had comparable speed and ceiling, and a superior rate of climb. Rate of climb and ceiling would be considerably enhanced (fourteen minutes instead of thirty-eight minutes to reach an altitude of 5,000 meters, and ceiling increased from 5,000 meters to 6,000 meters) when the Fokker D.VIIF received the 185 hp BMW IIIa engine, in place of the 160 hp Mercédès D.III engine. The added horsepower and innovative high-altitude carburetor of the BMW IIIa gave it greater speed and superior rate of climb at higher altitude. The improved Fokker D.VIIF began to enter service in late July 1918, several weeks before the Nieuport 28 was completely withdrawn from combat.

Major Hartney also favorably compared the Nieuport 28 to the Sopwith Camel, a fighter that had brought laurels to the Royal Air Force – he preferred the Nieuport 28. Hartney had an occasion to test his theory when he challenged his old flying mate, Major Reginald Maxwell, RAF, to a mock combat. (Maxwell had flown with Hartney in 20th Squadron, RFC.) The combat and series of aerobatic maneuvers that followed demonstrated the skills of both pilots and thrilled the members of Hartney's squadron. Upon completing this important demonstration, which ended in a draw, Hartney was royally chewed out by his superior officer, Major Bert Atkinson, for "showing off."[63]

The 147th Aero Squadron was successful on 2 July 1918, when two flights of Nieuport 28s, one flight at 13,000 feet and the other above and slightly behind at 15,000 feet, encountered twelve Pfalz fighters that were also stacked in two echelons, seven aircraft above and five below. The 147th downed one Pfalz without loss in the dogfight that followed, and six American pilots shared credit for the single victory. That evening, Major Geoffrey Bonnell, CO of the 147th, and his squadron mates celebrated their first victory. Having achieved this victory, the pilots of the 147th were entitled to paint their squadron emblem on their Nieuport 28s. The distinctive insignia, depicting a Cairn Terrier dog with the legend "Who Said Rats!" dated back to the squadron's training days in Texas.

The 147th was credited with two more Pfalz fighters on 5 July and the 95th claimed one biplace but lost two pilots that day (Lieutenants Sidney Thompson, killed in action, and Carlyle Rhodes, POW), to two Jasta 2 pilots, Leutnants Karl Bolle and Hermann Frommhertz. It was Bolle's twentieth victory; Frommhertz's victory made him an Ace.

Two days later, three German pilots with twenty victories between them downed pilots from the 94th and 95th, and both were taken prisoner. However, the two American squadrons more than evened the score, with victories over two German fighters and two observation aircraft.

Rickenbacker Brings Home a SPAD XIII

Most of the pilots and men of the First Pursuit Group celebrated 4 July at Touquin with baseball games, joint dinners, and entertainment in the evening. Lieutenant Eddie Rickenbacker, however, and several fellow pilots from the 94th went to Paris where, as Rickenbacker's diary entry noted, "most of the boys had a big time," while he (Rickenbacker) "spent a peaceful afternoon and evening and then went to bed."[64]

Eddie Rickenbacker and his flight crew. Rickenbacker's own mechanical experience contributed to the enhanced performance and reliability of his SPAD XIII fighter. Ohio Historical Society

Rickenbacker had other ideas for the following morning, when he traveled to nearby Orly Field to inquire about the impending arrival of SPAD XIII fighters for his squadron. Lieutenant Rickenbacker was delighted to find three SPAD XIII fighters at Orly, awaiting delivery; he arranged to take possession of one of them (serial number S.4523) to fly back to Touquin on the following day. Pilots of the 94th and 95th were excited at the prospect of soon replacing their Nieuport 28s with the rugged and more powerful SPAD XIIIs. Lieutenant Quentin Roosevelt wrote, "At the moment, everyone is much pleased that we are getting new planes."[65]

However, as Lieutenant Rickenbacker noted in his diary entry for 9 July 1918, initial expectations for the SPAD XIII were somewhat misplaced: "Had my first trip over the lines today in the SPAD and am not quite as well pleased with same as I expected to be."[66] The airplane, specifically its geared, Hispano-Suiza in-line engine, would give frightful trouble to pilots and mechanics alike for the balance of the war. Its introduction at this crucial phase of the war would tax the First Pursuit Group, putting much of the burden on the less experienced 27th and 147th Aero Squadrons while the difficult transition from the Nieuport 28 to the SPAD XIII was undertaken by their sister squadrons.

Major Harold Hartney later expressed the prevailing attitudes of the pilots of the First Pursuit Group regarding replacement of the Nieuport 28s: "They took away our beloved little Nieuports and gave us 220-hp, gear driven SPADS. Both the 27th and the 147th were heartbroken; the 94th and 95th were delighted."[67]

During the early evening of 7 July, a squadron of RAF Sopwith Camels landed at Touquin Aerodrome. Additional Camels, Bristol fighters and a squadron of Handley Page bombers, contingents of the Royal Air Force's 5th and 9th Brigades, under the command of General Sir Hugh "Boom" Trenchard, soon followed. The American First Pursuit Group would soon be displaced to another, smaller aerodrome nearby. The arrival of the British contingent presaged the next German offensive, which was expected within days.[68]

Below: Pilots of the 27th Aero Squadron pose behind "Becky." This aircraft, flown by Lieutenant William Hoover, is the subject of a color profile in Appendix F. National Air and Space Museum, Smithsonian Institution (SI 2002-32399)

From Touquin to Saints for the Final German Offensive

At 9:30 a.m. on 9 July, the First Pursuit Group began to move to Saints, an aerodrome that would serve as home to the group during a period of some of the fiercest fighting it would encounter during the war.

On the evening of 14 July, German heavy artillery along the Ourcq and Marne rivers opened up, heralding the beginning of General Ludendorff's fifth offensive. The sound and flashes of the guns could be heard and seen ten miles to the west of Paris, which was fifty miles away. Ludendorff intended to pinch off the heavily fortified Reims area with an attack east of Reims by the German First and Third Armies, combined with an attack west of the area by the German Seventh Army.

Forewarned of the enemy's intentions by a variety of sources, which included aerial and ground reconnaissance and intelligence gathered from interrogation of prisoners and deserters, General Foch disrupted the attack east of Reims by ordering a "spoiling," or counter preparation artillery barrage. This action frustrated the efforts of the German shock troops about to begin their assault, and the French Fourth Army was able to halt the German attack within hours. However, conditions were far more dangerous west of Reims, where Allied defenses were weaker.

Fourteen divisions of the German Seventh Army crossed the Marne River at Dormans and established a bridgehead in depth. The American 3rd Division, fighting in three directions at once against the German assault, held its ground, and gained immortal fame in the process: the 38th Infantry Regiment of the 3rd Division became known as the "Rock of the Marne" as a result of its superlative defensive action.

Allied air activity was particularly effective and much in evidence during the days following the onset of the German offensive. This activity was reported in a French communiqué for 19 July 1918:

> The aviation [with the First Pursuit Group acting under the command of the French Sixth Army] continued to play a brilliant role in the battle during the days of July 16 [and] 17. On July 16, our bombing machines incessantly attacked the bridges over the Marne and hindered the passage of hostile troops. The latter, upon being attacked by machine guns and bombs as [they] were debouching on the N. and S. banks of the river, suffered severe losses and were, several times, dispersed. The bridge, which the enemy threw across opposite Dormans, collapsed after being heavily bombed. The transports of troops, which were crossing it, were hurled into the stream. Our bombing machines likewise carried out expeditions over the billets, railway stations, munition dumps and troop assembly points in the rear of the enemy front.[69]

With Allied air forces and artillery destroying the bridges, along with the stubborn defense by American troops, the Germans were unable to resupply their troops across the Marne River. General Ludendorff was forced to admit defeat, and began

A 27th Aero Squadron Nieuport 28 departs on an early morning mission. National Air and Space Museum, Smithsonian Institution (SI 2003-15273)

a general withdrawal from the Soissons–Château-Thierry–Reims salient just as General Foch, soon to be Marshal of France, was about to unleash his long-planned Aisne-Marne Offensive. The collapse of the last German offensive on 17 July 1918 marked the end of the Second Battle of the Marne, and also marked the strategic turn of the tide, as the initiative passed irretrievably to the Allies.

The First Pursuit Group was called upon to make heroic efforts from the first days of the German offensive, as Major Harold Hartney, CO of the 27th Aero Squadron, later recalled:

> I shall never forget July 15, 1918, as long as I live. It seemed as if the whole German Army, in desperation, simply hurled itself at our part of the lines around Château Thierry. Our boys were in the air practically all the time ... frantic orders came through asking us, high flying pursuit planes, to skim over the ground and try to fix the position and extent of the German advance, to try and determine how far over the Marne the Boche had reached. It was the ultimate of frenzied excitement. Allied troops of all kinds were rushing by us in both directions, French going back on relief, waves of Americans going forward. It was the climax of the war. None of my officers flew less than five hours that terrible day. In fact, the damage to our machines got so bad that I finally had to forbid them to go out any more because all of them had so many bullet holes in their wings and vital parts that I was afraid they would fall apart from bullet-hole fractures and we would be out of the battle entirely. We started work at 3:30 A.M. with 15 planes and the last machine landed after 9 P.M. [European summer days were long]. The boys were magnificent. I could not begin to put into words my admiration of the way they acted, that day, and for many days after.[70]

The First Pursuit Group helped blunt the final German offensive of the war, and then flew in support of the Allied offensive that immediately followed on 18 July 1918. French intelligence estimated that during this period, from 15 July to 5 August, the First Pursuit Group was outnumbered constantly, sometimes as much as four to one, by extremely aggressive and skillful German air forces arrayed against it. Lieutenant Harold Buckley, 95th Aero Squadron, recalled the group's intense combat during this period:

> [Our] halcyon days were over. No longer would we hunt in pairs deep in the enemy lines, delighted if the patrol produced a single enemy to chase. Gone were the days when we could dive into the fray with only a careless glance at our rear. There was trouble ahead. The action we craved was at hand; we could sense it in the air like an approaching storm. Beneath us, instead of the comparative calm of our old sector, its pastoral green complacency marred by a single ugly scar of brown and shell-torn ground, we now gazed appalled at a scene of utter chaos, while whole towns were blown off the map as we watched. The amount of artillery fire seemed incredible; we flew through clouds of dust and smoke at 12,000 feet. The sky around us was filled with Fokkers; instead of a lone two-seater or two, we counted the enemy in droves of twelve, eighteen and twenty.[71]

The First Pursuit Group faced its toughest trial during the three-week period from mid-July to early August 1918. Its primary mission during this time was the protection of Corps Observation planes during their reconnaissance and artillery regulation missions. The group was also directed to disrupt the work of German observation planes undertaking the same missions, and to inflict as many casualties and cause as much material damage as possible.[72] The latter objective usually meant low-level strafing of troops and horse-drawn transport, a risky mission that was becoming increasingly important.

Protecting Allied observation planes and attacking those of the enemy meant operating at altitudes of 3,500 to 4,000 meters, and this altitude rendered American fighters vulnerable to high-flying formations of German fighters, formations composed increasingly of the potent Fokker D.VII fighter. The vulnerability of American fighters was further increased because most of the ensuing combats took place miles behind the German lines, with persistent German pilots refusing to break off combat until Allied airplanes managed to cross back into friendly territory.

Outnumbered and Vulnerable

Several factors compounded the problem of the inferior numbers of fighters that the First Pursuit Group was able to put into the air. The biggest problem was the difficult transition from the Nieuport 28 to the SPAD XIII that was undertaken during this time. American mechanics were unfamiliar with the troublesome Hispano-Suiza geared engine, while the pilots had to learn the good and bad habits of the SPAD XIII ("it flew like a brick" was a common observation) after flying the nimble Nieuport 28.

The 94th Aero Squadron was the first squadron of the group to receive a large complement of SPAD XIIIs, taking possession of twelve SPADs on 13 July. The squadron's engineering officer, Lieutenant C. A. Rankin, had to go looking for mechanics capable of servicing and maintaining the new fighters in addition to preparing them for entry into combat.

The results were discouraging. At a time when operational readiness was of critical importance, the 94th was effectively out of service. The 94th mounted its first patrol of SPAD XIIIs on 17 July and continued to send up limited numbers of fighters after that, but the squadron's operational efficiency for the period fell. This was reflected in the scoring column: the 94th scored two victories on 7 July – it would not score again until 9 September, well after the difficult campaign in this sector had ended.

The strain of battle took its toll on pilots and airplanes alike and more minor problems, such as contaminated gasoline delivered to the 147th Aero Squadron and a general recall of .30 caliber armor-piercing ammunition, further eroded combat efficiency. Personnel of the 27th Squadron even experienced an outbreak of scabies, a contagious skin disease that caused severe itching.

As a result, inferior numbers of American fighters were in almost daily combat against superior numbers of German fighters, and the First Pursuit Group struggled to fulfill the mission assigned to it by the French Sixth Army.

As a protective measure, the French Sixth Army envisioned a double-tier barrage of fighters in the air throughout the daylight hours, and this required that all patrols flying through assigned areas position their flights at intermediate and high altitudes. The First Pursuit Group, however, lacked sufficient fighters to maintain formation strength at both altitudes. For a brief time, the group compromised its own protection in order to carry out missions that kept the fighters at lower altitudes, and therefore, rendered more vulnerable to German fighters:

> The unity of flight had to be interfered with as frequently, a flight [normally composed of six airplanes] did not have more than two or three planes available for duty. The mistake was therefore made for a short time, of utilizing squadron formations not echeloned by flight. These proved to be unwieldy, easily thrown into confusion by the enemy, unable to be controlled by a single leader and the more or less inexperienced pilots frequently became separated from them. They also had the disadvantage that they were forced to operate without top protection and, therefore, were frequently attacked by the enemy when he possessed the advantage in numbers, altitude and position in relation to the sun.[73]

This mistake was later rectified with the establishment of formations echeloned by flight, made practicable by increased numbers of serviceable fighters assigned to each squadron. However, during the height of the offensive and counteroffensive, a high toll of pilots and planes was taken, especially among the less skilled or disciplined American pilots. This was exemplified by the losses of Lieutenants Quentin Roosevelt of the 95th (Roosevelt's opponent, Unteroffizier Gräper of Jasta 50, thought him brave but inexperienced) and Max Parry of the 147th. Both pilots lost their formations and were attacked by superior numbers and killed. German fighters killed a 147th pilot, Lieutenant Daniel Cassard, on 16 July, after he dove on them in violation of squadron discipline; Cassard's flight commander was attempting to gain a more advantageous position against a formation of nine Fokkers

Lieutenant Charles A. Rankin (in cockpit), engineering officer of the 94th Aero Squadron, and Master Sergeant Victor Bertrandais. Bertrandais, an outstanding mechanic, was later commissioned. Ohio Historical Society

Lieutenant Quentin Roosevelt, President Theodore Roosevelt's favorite son, in a photograph taken while the lieutenant was in flight training at Issoudun. University of Texas at Dallas

Lieutenant Roosevelt's body lies alongside his crashed Nieuport 28, #14. The photograph was taken by a German photographer. Roosevelt's aircraft is the subject of a color profile in Appendix F.

Buried by the Germans near to where he crashed, Roosevelt's gravesite was later found and improved by advancing American forces. University of Texas at Dallas

Lieutenant Maxwell O. Parry of the 147th Aero Squadron, killed in action on 8 July 1918. Charles Woolley

Below: G-A-S Robertson of the 147th extolled the virtues of his Nieuport 28. Charles Woolley

when Cassard dove away. Cassard's decomposing body was found in a trench two weeks later, with the vertical stabilizer of his Nieuport nailed to a nearby tree.

The importance of formation flight and maintaining flight discipline were amply demonstrated during this period of intense fighting and, as combat progressed, it would be more strictly enforced. Only one month later, Second Lieutenant Frank Luke, soon to become one of the legendary pilots of the U.S. Air Service, was grounded for three days for making an unauthorized flight over the front lines without the protection of a formation.

While outnumbered and attacked from above by German fighters, the Nieuport 28 pulled more than one pilot out of an otherwise fatal encounter. This capability was clearly apparent in the combat reports written by two 147th pilots, Lieutenants George Albert Satello Robertson (nicknamed "G-A-S") and Thomas J. Abernethy, after their exploits on 15 July 1918. "G-A-S" Robertson, flying Nieuport 28, N.6232, and Abernethy, flying Nieuport 28, N.6206, departed their aerodrome at Saints together at 6 p.m. and flew into the thick of battle around Dormans where the Germans had crossed the Marne.

Robertson's combat report read:

> While on low patrol just coming out of a cloud south of Dormans, I saw a formation of 4 E.A. [enemy aircraft] diving towards me about 200 meters above and behind me. I put my nose slightly down and with all the speed I had, I pulled up, making a climbing bank to the left in almost a zoom up, meeting the first Hun almost dead on and getting a burst of perhaps 50 [shots] in him and he immediately dropped. The other E.A. had passed over me, I turned and was able to get one more burst into them but on account of clouds, I could not determine effects. My own machine, having some fifteen holes in it, five through the propeller, I went into a spin bringing it back under control in a thick cloud bank, through which I headed south and was able to land on [a] French aerodrome at Augers. The main occurring qualifications of the Nieuport type 28 were superior to that of the E.A. which I am sure helped me out of a tight corner.[74]

Abernethy had an even closer call, as his combat report related:

> While on low patrol, I was above the clouds in the vicinity of Dormans, when our formation dove through the clouds. I stayed above the clouds waiting to rejoin the formation through a gap in the clouds when I was attacked by one Fokker E.A. [enemy aircraft] from above. E.A. dove past me and I gave chase following to enemy line of balloons in neighborhood of Courmont firing about 100 rounds at 50 to 200 yards. Tracers observed to go straight into his fuselage. E.A. last seen about 50 feet from the ground. At the time, I was level with the line of balloons when 5 E.A. dove on me. My engine was shot through one magneto and one cylinder [note that the Gnôme rotary engine continued to function, however]. I made a running fight firing about 200 rounds at about 5 yds. to 20 yds. at different E.A. as opportunity presented itself. At this time, I was too busy to observe results of my fire. I landed N.W. of Courboin, just north of lake. I tried to save machine by flying her home but I was unable to get off the ground and regret to state I hit a shell hole, which put us on our nose, crashing machine beyond repair. Colonel Doree of the 4th U.S. Infantry advised me he would try and save machine guns and instruments of my machine. My success in combat and getting out of a very tight corner is partly due to the wonderful maneuvering qualifications of the Nieuport 28.[75]

A 147th Aero Squadron pilot, Lieutenant Thomas J. Abernethy. Charles Woolley

Leutnant Harry von Bülow-Bothkamp of Jasta 36 claimed this victory and became an Ace; fortunately, Second Lieutenant Abernethy came down in friendly territory.

The comments of these two American pilots reflect their strong, partisan views about the Nieuport 28 fighter, views

Above: Lieutenant Walter L. Avery, pictured here with his Nieuport 27 while serving as CO of Escadrille N.471. Escadrille N.471 was a French night fighter unit, and perhaps the last squadron to operate the Nieuport 27 in combat. Avery transferred to the 95th Aero Squadron on 23 July 1918, two days before he downed a German Ace, Oberleutnant Carl Menckhoff. Bette Applegate

Right: Lieutenant James Armand Meissner, new commander of the 147th Aero Squadron. Meissner had the difficult task of teaching his squadron pilots to appreciate the finer qualities of the SPAD XIII. National Air and Space Museum, Smithsonian Institution (SI 86-10370)

Below: Second Lieutenant Kenneth L. Porter, standing in front of a Nieuport 28 (believed to be N.6145, #10), flown by Second Lieutenant Ralph A. O'Neill of his squadron. Porter, a strong proponent of the Nieuport 28, deplored the relief of Major Geoffrey Bonnell as commander of the 147th Aero Squadron. National Air and Space Museum, Smithsonian Institution (SI 86-10367)

held by many of their 147th Squadron mates and by many of the pilots of the 27th Aero Squadron as well. As its sister squadrons made the transition to the SPAD XIII, the 147th took their discarded Nieuport 28s, with the intention of keeping them in service as long as possible.

Combats were plentiful during the middle of July, with the 95th gaining two victories on the 16th and three victories on the 25th, but losing three pilots taken prisoner and one pilot killed in action (KIA). Lieutenant Walter Avery was one of the squadron's victorious pilots on 25 July, when he conquered Oberleutnant Carl Menckhoff in a combat near Château-Thierry. Menckhoff, a recipient of the Pour le Mérite, had thirty-nine victories to his credit. Avery, who was flying a new SPAD XIII fighter, had joined the 95th only two days before. This was one of the few occurrences in this sector when an experienced, high-scoring German Ace did not prevail over an American pilot who was new to combat.

During the five-day peak of the German offensive and the Allied counteroffensive that followed, the 27th scored an impressive eleven victories, downing two observation planes and two balloons on the 16th, two more planes on the 17th, three on the 19th, and two more the next day. The 27th outscored its sister squadrons for the month of July by a healthy margin, but these victories were bought dearly, with the loss of three pilots KIA or DOW (died of wounds), two pilots downed and taken prisoner, and one pilot wounded. This last was Lieutenant Ralph Schmitt, whose poor eyesight – he had faked his eye exams – nearly got him killed. The depleted ranks of the 27th were filled within the week, but many of these green replacement pilots would suffer similar fates only days later.

The 147th scored one victory on the 16th but lost Lieutenant Daniel Cassard, who was shot down after he left his formation. A week later, the squadron was devastated when their respected and well-liked commander, Major Geoffrey Bonnell, was fired. The official record stated that Bonnell had been relieved of command and transferred to the American School of Aerial Gunnery at St. Jean De Mont. No doubt Bonnell's vigorous defense of the Nieuport 28 had been a major factor in his relief, in addition to a lingering poor relationship with his superior officer, Major Bert Atkinson. Major Bonnell's departure stunned the 147th, as Lieutenant Ken Porter recalled:

> Officers and men alike were shocked. Bonnell is the heart and soul of the 147th and as he bids his men farewell, most openly shed tears. The entire 147th stands down and not a propeller turns on this blackest day in the squadrons history. 1st Lt. John Hambleton, a veteran of the 95th Aero Squadron with two aerial victories, assumes command, but feeling is so intense in the 147th that he is transferred the next day to the 213th Aero Squadron. 1st Lt. Jimmy Meissner of the 94th with four victories – second only to Eddie Rickenbacker – assumes command the next day. [Ironically, Meissner's first task is to wean the 147th away from their beloved Nieuports.] An angry 147th starts flying at 0430 the morning of 24 July, bent on taking their wrath out on the only foe [with] whom they can come to grips.[76]

Second Lieutenant Wilbert White in flight gear. White was recommended posthumously for the Congressional Medal of Honor, for a combat that ended his life on 10 October 1918. However, the award was subsequently downgraded, and White posthumously received the Distinguished Service Cross instead. Charles Woolley

Piloting their Nieuport 28s, the 147th downed four enemy aircraft on 24 July, with Second Lieutenant Wilbert White scoring victories over two Albatros fighters while on an evening patrol over Château-Thierry. Five other pilots from the 147th shared two more victories that day – a fitting tribute to their former commander, as Lieutenant Brotherton noted in his diary that evening: "Everyone feeling good tonight because of a good day but we sure do grieve Major's loss & are pulling for him to get something better."[77]

The First Pursuit Group made an all-out effort on 20 July, sending up all available fighters, but did not experience a single combat. The retreating German forces had come to a temporary halt on the Vesle River, and this left the First Pursuit Group, based at Saints, seventy-five kilometers from the front. As a result, an advanced base closer to the front was established at Coincy. Supplied with gasoline and mechanics, the group was able to refuel and refit before returning from the front to their distant home base.

By late July the 95th and the 27th, in addition to the 94th Aero Squadron, were flying mixed formations of SPADs and Nieuports, a difficult proposition because of the different flight characteristics of the two fighters. SPAD XIIIs were being delivered with American-made, Marlin machine guns installed, and pilots encountered familiar jamming problems with the Marlins. Some replaced the troublesome Marlins with their tuned-up and familiar Vickers machine guns.

A large complement of new SPAD XIIIs arrived for the group on 28 July, but these aircraft were immediately put into storage, with orders that the group concentrate on Nieuport 28s until further notice. The following day, the 27th put up a patrol of twenty-one fighters to protect a single photoreconnaissance plane of the 91st Observation Squadron. That mission was uneventful.

On 31 July 1918, Lieutenant Alan Winslow, the first victor of the 94th Aero Squadron and the first to score while flying a Nieuport 28, was shot down by Leutnant der Reserve Emil Rolff of Jasta 6 and taken prisoner. Winslow, who was flying a SPAD XIII, S.15067, was severely wounded during the combat. Winslow was Rolff's second victory. The 95th and 147th squadrons each suffered a loss on the last day of July with no compensating victories.

The "Black Day of the 27th"

The events of 1 August 1918 bear close attention, because the day proved disastrous for the 27th Aero Squadron and would henceforth be referred to as "Jonah Day" or "the Black Day for the 27th."

The Operations Order for the 27th Aero Squadron for 1 August 1918 read:

Lieutenant William E. Brotherton. Brotherton was killed in action on 10 October 1918. Charles Woolley

Alan Winslow (at right) is seen after the war. German surgeons amputated his left arm after he was wounded and brought down on 31 July 1918. He died in 1935.

Below: Nieuport 28, N.6356. This was the last wartime-production fighter delivered to the U.S. Air Service, AEF. HISTAVIA 21, WW I Collection

Protection Patrol, 7h 05 to 9h 05; 18 planes, Lieutenants Grant, Dawson, Martin, Hunt, McElvain, Whiton, Vasconcells, Nevius, Beauchamp, Hudson, Polk, Rucker, Clapp, Roberts, Wehner, Sands, Luke,

to protect two Salmsons in Fere-en-Taredenois region [where Winslow had been downed the day before] *altitude, 3000 meters.*[78]

"Protection patrols became a synonym for sudden death,"[79] as one pilot correctly observed. The protection patrol flown by the 27th Aero Squadron on 1 August 1918 would take the lives of Lieutenants Beauchamp, Hunt, and Sands, as well as the lives of the two pilots and observers in the Salmsons of the 1st Observation Squadron – Lieutenants Sykes, Miller, Wold, and Wooten. In addition, three 27th pilots, Lieutenants Martin, Whiton, and McElvain, would be downed and taken prisoner.

A-Flight, under the command of Lieutenant Clifford McElvain, included Lieutenants Jason Hunt, Richard Martin, Arthur Whiton, and Leo Dawson, and all were believed to be flying Nieuport 28s. Lieutenant Dawson was believed to have aborted the mission early, while Lieutenant Donald Donaldson, thought to have been part of A-Flight on that day, appears to have been the sole member to return to Saints after the punishing combat had taken place.[80]

B-Flight, under the command of Lieutenant Jerry Vasconcells, included Lieutenants Oliver Beauchamp, Donald Hudson, Charles Sands, Ruliff Nevius, Ivan Roberts, and perhaps one other pilot. Vasconcells, Beauchamp, and Hudson were flying SPAD XIIIs that day, Sands was in a Nieuport 28, N.6275, and the others were believed to be piloting Nieuport 28s as well.

C-Flight did not engage in combat, apparently because of distance from the combats or aborts due to motor trouble, suggesting that these pilots were flying their new SPAD XIII fighters.

B-Flight, led by Lieutenant Vasconcells, met its escort, a Salmson photoreconnaissance plane, at 7:40 a.m. and flew north towards Oulchy-le-Château, near the Ourcq River. B-Flight had just accompanied the Salmson across the lines, when low-flying B-flight was bounced by eight Fokker D.VIIs from Jasta 6 that had risen to intercept them. Lieutenant Beauchamp, flying a SPAD XIII, was downed almost immediately; his body and crashed airplane were found several weeks later.

Lieutenant Charles Sands was in mortal combat with Leutnant der Reserve Emil Rolff, who had downed Lieutenant Alan Winslow of the 94th the day before. A Jasta 6 pilot, Leutnant Richard Wenzl, described the action:

I became aware that Rolff was in the middle of a real contest with an American [Sands]. As Rolff later told

A-Flight Leader Lieutenant Clifford McElvain of the 27th Aero Squadron with his Nieuport 28, #5. Note the Masonic emblem under the Vickers machine-gun emplacement. McElvain's aircraft is the subject of a color profile in Appendix F. Bergen Hardesty

Lieutenant Richard D. Martin (seated), 27th Aero Squadron, was wounded and taken prisoner on 1 August 1918. Charles Woolley

> me, this match had been going on for some time. The American climbed over Rolff with the help of his rotary engine, which has the advantage at low altitude – roughly 2,000 – meters! – and which I just wanted to watch – and then he attacked me too. But I couldn't allow that to happen and so I banked under him. Although he put up a desperate fight, I set him ablaze with my guns at an altitude of 1,500 meters. He fell in the forest north of Fere and burned to nothing.[81]

Lieutenant Donald Hudson's account of B-Flight's part in this first phase of the battle is of interest, because it reveals some of the characteristics of the SPAD XIII he was flying:

> Were attacked by 8 FOKKER biplane chasse machines east of Fere-en-Tardenois at 8h 10. I tried to bank to left and fell into a spin [and] when I came out of the spin, there were 4 E.A. [enemy aircraft] on my tail. I tried to turn again but fell into another spin, I was followed by the 4 E.A. down to 1000 meters. As I was coming out of spin, a machine was heading straight at me. I fired and he turned to the left, I turned a little to the left and turned back again being right on his tail, I fired about 20 rounds into him. He fell off slowly on his right wing and went into a spin, when I came out, the other machines were climbing up. Just as the fight began, I saw an E.A. fall on his right wing and spin in exactly the same manner as the machine I shot down. I saw something else fall in flames [possibly Sands]. A SPAD passed within 20 feet of my right wing, falling on its back [likely Beauchamp]. My engine was boiling and I could not climb as my nourrice [reserve tank] was empty, and by using the hand pump, I could just keep going.[82]

After extricating themselves from this first onslaught, Hudson and the other surviving members of B-Flight found retribution on the way home, when they encountered two Rumplers and promptly destroyed them. Hudson received credit for one victory and shared credit for two others, including one Fokker downed earlier, with his flight mates.

The battered remains of Lieutenant Oliver T. Beauchamp's crashed SPAD XIII fighter were found near Fere-en-Tardenois, another victim of the 1 August 1918 combat. Charles Woolley

A-Flight met almost total disaster, with only Lieutenant Donald Donaldson returning unscathed from combat. Donaldson's report of his first combat read in part: "Met SALMSON at 7h 50 and went with SALMSON into the lines going north. We made three circuits around Oulchy [Oulchy-le-Château], going into Germany [anywhere across the lines was referred to as "Germany"] and coming back over our lines in big circles [to allow the observer to change film]. As we went in for the fourth time, we were about 4000 when the fight started ... at about 8h 45 behind the German lines. The Huns came upon us at about 200 meters above us and to our left about that far, coming straight toward us head on. They turned and dove on our tails."[83]

Lieutenant James C. Wooten, an observer with the 1st Observation Squadron (photographed earlier, while a member of Escadrille Spa.140), was mortally wounded on 1 August 1918, while under the protection of A-Flight of the 27th Aero Squadron. Jane Wooten Renaud

A-Flight leader Lieutenant Clifford McElvain picks up the narrative at this point. His first combat that day was with members of Jasta 4, led by the eminent Leutnant Ernst Udet. His subsequent combat, with Leutnant Alfred Fleisher of Jasta 17, reveals much about the nature of the Nieuport 28 in close combat with a skilled German pilot flying the outstanding Fokker D.VII:

> As we got out of the truck, Jerry [Vasconcells, leader of B-Flight] and I agreed that if one of us were attacked, the other would go to his aid, if free to do so. Then we took off.
>
> There were no wide-angle lenses in those days. The cameras could shoot a strip about a mile wide, so the observation plane had to fly back and forth, in and out, for many trips, in order to map an area of any size. I joined our escort, a Salmson, over its field at the scheduled time and climbed with it to its mission altitude, around 18,000 feet. Things can happen so very fast in the air; one minute the sky will be empty, then, with the vigilance relaxed for just an instant, you can be surrounded by the enemy. It was standard practice to fly with necks swiveling constantly, systematically – scanning the sky – under, above, behind, below, on one side then the other – never stopping. I suppose you know that is why silk scarves came to be worn inside shirt collars. Necks would wear raw without them.
>
> At mission altitude, the pilot and observer, whose names I have never known, started taking their pictures. The area being photographed was well inside enemy territory and they flew in and out, back and forth; it seemed that they would never get through. I could see Jerry and his flight in the distance and somewhat lower than we, flying back and forth the same as we. Below us, I could see German formations rising to the attack. I would see them, lose them, then see them again, each time a little nearer. It was a long climb for them. I kept hoping that the Salmson would finish its picture taking before they reached us, but they kept coming and we kept going back and forth.
>
> Two German formations reached our level some distance away and climbed above us. A few minutes later, I saw that Jerry was engaged in combat. Now I was faced with a hard, hard, decision. If I didn't go to Jerry's aid and the Germans left me alone, I would never forgive myself. On the other hand, if I left my Salmson to help Jerry and the Germans then picked it off, I could never forgive myself. It was an agonizing moment of indecision. I couldn't tell for sure whether both German squadrons [Jastas 4 and 6] had ganged up on Jerry or not. A lot of them were there. My neck was still swiveling and suddenly the indecision ended. Toward the glare of the sun, I could see they were coming! I waggled my wings in warning (that was the only means of communication that we had). Then the fight was on. After that, all was confusion as it always was for me in combat. There are some who can describe every turn – everything that everybody did – in a dogfight. I never could.
>
> On escort missions, you don't chase targets but try to stay with your escort. You take every chance to fire a burst but you try to keep together. You keep your course in the direction your escort is going the best you can. You evade the airplane trying to shoot at you, but you try to keep them from shooting at your escort. You just do the best you can.
>
> At the start of this flight, our Salmson nosed down and headed for home. At that altitude, he was about as fast as the Fokkers and in the confusion that we kicked up, he shortly seemed to get away from them. I have heard that their plane was shot up and one or both of the men in it injured but they got back to our side of the lines with their film, their mission accomplished. I would like to know if that is true.[84]

A-Flight was apparently protecting a 1st Observation Squadron Salmson piloted by Lieutenant Ernest G. Wold, with Lieutenant James C. "Jimmy" Wooten observing. The Salmson was reported to have made three passes over the German lines, but was driven back each time before completing its work. The escorting fighters were now fully engaged, but Wold and Wooten persevered: "Jimmy decided to cross over alone and take the last magazine of pictures, which he did, several miles over the German lines, but on his return, was attacked by six Boches and a lively fight ensued."[85] The one-sided combat was brief; Lieutenant Wold, mortally wounded, died before the Salmson reached the ground. Lieutenant Wooten, grievously wounded, was rushed unconscious to a French dressing station; he died on the operating table before he could receive the Legion of Honor (which was not given posthumously) for his heroism.

Lieutenant McElvain continued:

> Well, even after they were gone, the fight went on. One by one, there were fewer Nieuports in the air; also fewer Germans. As I have said, the Nieuport 28s were more maneuverable than the German planes and so were hard to hit, but we could not readily break off combat, because, in a straightaway dive, the Germans were faster than we. Finally, there were no other Nieuports around. 'A' Flight was wiped out. I was alone with what was left of the German squadron. Being outnumbered by them was not the disadvantage it might sound, because they got in the way of each other as two or three at a time could try to aim at me. I could see whenever one was getting close to firing position, and then by a tighter turn than he could make, evade his aim and often get in a burst at another as I came out of my turn. There was a certain amount of exhilaration in being able to out-fly them, but there wasn't any future in it because how was I ever going to get away from them? All of a sudden, I found myself free. Apparently, the Germans had lost track of me in a turn. The observation plane had gone. I had had enough for one day and I headed for home, but still not quite able to believe that they wouldn't be on me again and so watched apprehensively behind me.[86]

McElvain's troubles, however, were just beginning:

> As I flew, looking behind me, forgetting to keep swiveling my neck, I discovered too late that I was on a collision course with a flight of five Fokker D-7s, coming at them out of the sun and they, apparently, did not see me. Here may have been another mistake. Maybe, I could have avoided them entirely, but, at the moment, it seemed to me that it was too late for me to do nothing but open fire, and my first burst went into the leader. I couldn't watch to see what happened to him, but I learned later … that he was wounded and crashed but survived. [Lieutenant McElvain had indeed downed a seven-victory Ace, Leutnant Gunther Schuster, but McElvain was never credited with the victory. Schuster, who was wounded, did not return to combat.]
>
> This outfit [Jasta 17, sporting dark painted fuselages and white radiators] didn't perform as the other squadron had, i.e., confusing each other by all trying to fire at once. The three others simply got out of the way and circled, leaving one man [Leutnant Alfred Fleisher] to deal with me by himself. This was the kind of combat that you trained for and read about but which seldom happened – a duel in the sky between two men armed with machine guns, alone and on their own, playing for keeps.
>
> I was very light in both fuel and ammunition by now, so my Nieuport was especially agile. Fleisher's Fokker D-7 [Fleisher was flying a Fokker D.VII equipped with a 185 hp BMW IIIa in-line engine] was faster and could out-climb me … . We met at about 13,000 feet and at that altitude, his supercharger gave him considerable advantage in climb and speed, but even so, our planes were pretty well matched. Each had its own superior characteristics; he could out-climb and out-dive, I could make tighter turns. It was a fair match, I think. It seemed that the fight would never end because we, and our airplanes, were so evenly matched that it was very hard for either of us to get a chance at a shot and any such chance was fleeting. [Fleisher later] said that I got a few holes in his plane and he scattered some splinters over me when one of his bullets hit a wooden longeron in my fuselage, but no real damage was done to either.
>
> Then, without any warning, my engine suddenly blooped and died and there I was, in combat, without power, and losing altitude fast. All I could do was maneuver the best I could, trading altitude for speed then pulling up and trying to fire back at Fleisher. The Nieuport was a low-compression engine, so my propeller continued to windmill and my guns would still fire, so Fleisher had no way to know the fight was over. All I could do was spar as best I could as he chased me right to the ground. Finally, when the time came that I had to straighten out for a crash landing, Fleisher moved behind me and I sat there waiting for the bullets from behind that would keep me from feeling it. It was only when I slowed down for the crash that my propeller slowed and stopped, and at that last instant, the Fokker dived past me and the pilot waved. He had seen my propeller stop and he knew I was through.
>
> Seconds later, I was upside down among small trees in a mess of twisted wreckage, struggling to get out before the fire started. But no fire started. I recalled later that no gasoline spilled. I thought at the moment that Fred had shot me down and I still give him credit for it, but I believe I was simply out of gas [which was very likely the case, as pilots continued to leave the Nieuport 28's

vulnerable reserve tank unfilled]. I tore myself loose and as I scrambled out, heavy boots were running toward me and I found myself surrounded by a ring of shiny bayonets in the hands of unfriendly Germans.[87]

Lieutenant Clifford McElvain's opponent, Leutnant Alfred Fleisher, left his own account of this combat:

It is the first of August 1918, cloudless sky, bright sunshine and unusual heat. When the order reached Jasta 17 to start in the direction of Soissons where formidable air forces were reported, we climbed into our FOKKERS with great joy in order to reach the cooler regions. The spirit in the squadron was good for we had shown excellent results during the last weeks without encountering any serious losses ourselves.

We flew five abreast and I had my place, as usual, to the left, next to our leader's plane, which, on this day was flown by Lt. [Leutnant] Schuster. Our regular leader, Lt. [Leutnant] Buckler, who had been decorated with the order of 'Pour le Merite'... had been wounded by a bullet through the heel.

From our quarters at Balatre, east of Roye, where aside from us, Jagdeschwader II was stationed, we advanced directly to the front and had almost reached an altitude of approximately 14,000 feet when something very surprising occurred. Suddenly, and entirely unnoticed by all of us – probably coming directly from the sun – a small enemy biplane of unknown type [McElvain's Nieuport 28] dashed with lightning speed upon our leader's plane and opened fire immediately at close range. An abrupt and instinctive glance backwards assured me that at the moment, there was no danger for me. My back was clear. Therefore, eyes front and aid to my hard-pressed comrade who had already been disabled and brought his smoking plane down in a sudden dive. The following impressions are still as clear in my mind as though this had only occurred yesterday.

I immediately directed the fire of my two guns at our adversary and thereby forced him away from my comrade. In order to escape my deadly barrage, my adversary climbed steeply so that he stood almost perpendicularly above me. This maneuver to gain safe altitude would have been achieved by him if my brave FOKKER had not shown an unusually marvelous performance. In great style, it followed this dash for altitude and *hung on its propeller* [author's italics] so that I could cover my adversary with a well-directed and continuous fire. In full recognition of this great danger, McElvain allowed his plane to glide down over the left wing and in this manner, escaped my fire. By this maneuver, he reached approximately the same altitude and now the advantage of my FOKKER were demonstrated which at the time – without boasting – flew to perfection.

Persistently and with resolute determination, McElvain attempted to fight me off again and again. Closely together, we circled around each other and often it seemed as though the world was standing on its head. The spirit of the chase had gripped me. However, because of

Leutnant Alfred Fleisher of Jasta 17 and his Fokker D.VII. Leutnant Fleisher's combat with Lieutenant Clifford McElvain resulted in his second victory; he finished the war with a total of six victories. Clifford McElvain and Alfred Fleisher, who later became lifelong friends, both attained the rank of colonel, in the U.S. Army Air Force and in the Luftwaffe, respectively, during World War II. Greg VanWyngarden

"HANGING ON THE PROP" – "The Fokker biplanes are said to be able to assume an attitude similar to that shown in this sketch, and to remain, apparently stationary for long periods." Flight Magazine, 21 November 1918

Daily life at Karlruhe POW Camp. Many POW Air Service pilots and observers were reunited here. David A. McElvain

Major Harold E. Hartney and his SPAD XIII, which is prominently marked with the insignia of the 27th Aero Squadron. National Air and Space Museum, Smithsonian Institution (SI 2003-15275)

the excellent maneuvering and, above all, my adversary's persistence to fight on, I succeeded in firing a few poorly directed series of shots. I believe McElvain had similar experiences. How long this circular battle continued, I do not know. This much, however, I can say, that throughout the battle, not one inch of altitude was given away.

At an altitude of approximately 1000 to 1500 feet, I was successful, after having completed a reverse ascending curve, to place several well-directed shots. Soon thereafter, McElvain exposed himself in a manner at first entirely incomprehensible to me [it was apparently at this point that McElvain's engine ran out of gas and stopped, and McElvain straightened out in preparation for landing]. I was able to gain a position 120 to 150 feet in back of him and had already aimed my machine guns upon him ready to pull the trigger in the fever of the chase. There I beheld, thank God, in the last moment, that the propeller of my adversary stood still and that the plane, completely out of control, prepared to land. For me, as for every other German soldier, there was now only one thing to do – to stop the battle immediately and to shake the hand of the defeated adversary in a chivalrous manner.[88]

Zenos R. Miller, Clifford A. McElvain, an unidentified man, and Arthur L. Whiton (seated) at Karlsruhe POW Camp. Miller, who was downed and taken prisoner on 20 July 1918, was a member of the 27th Aero Squadron, along with McElvain and Whiton. David A. McElvain

Lieutenant McElvain was indeed given a chivalrous hand by Leutnant Alfred Fleisher, the Jasta 17 pilot who believed he had shot McElvain down. Landing nearby, Fleisher approached McElvain, shook hands with him, and complimented him on his combat skills, before exchanging addresses in the hope that they might meet again and be friends after the war. This did in fact occur, and Fleisher and McElvain became lifelong friends.

The "Jonah Day" events of 1 August 1918 would never be forgotten by the 27th Aero Squadron's Commanding Officer, Major Harold Hartney, or his squadron mates who had survived the battle. Among the six pilots to be killed or taken prisoner on 1 August, three (Beauchamp, Sands, and Whiton) had been with the squadron only one week; the others (McElvain, Hunt, and Martin) were charter members, having joined the squadron in November 1917.

The balance of the month of August was peaceful in contrast to the five weeks prior. The squadron's CO, Major Hartney, characterized the period from the battle of 1 August to 21 August as one "of extreme quietude – testing those damned SPAD machines and testing new pilots."[89]

On 2 August, the SPAD XIIIs that had been stored earlier were distributed to the squadrons of the First Pursuit Group, and the Nieuport 28s were in the process of being ferried back to the training establishment at Issoudun. The 147th Aero Squadron would keep its Nieuport 28s a little longer.

By the end of the day on 8 August, the 94th Aero Squadron was fully equipped with SPAD XIIIs. The 95th scored two victories on 10 August, with the loss of one pilot killed and one wounded. The 95th lost another of its pilots the following day, and from this point on, the war in the air moved elsewhere and the First Pursuit Group would not score again until one month later. They would then be poised to support a major American offensive on another part of the front.

Elsewhere on 8 August, combined British and French armies hit the German Second and Eighteenth Armies in the first phase of the Amiens Offensive. Expecting an attack further north in Flanders, the Germans were unprepared for the Allied assault, which bagged 15,000 German prisoners. The second phase of the battle began on 21 August and ended with very substantial losses for the German army, with its forces retired to its final position behind the heavily fortified Hindenburg Line. General Erich Ludendorff, who referred to 8 August 1918 as "The Black Day" of the German army, concluded that "the war must be ended!"[90]

The 147th Aero Squadron flew an uneventful last patrol of Nieuport 28s on 13 August 1918, and stood down the following day to convert to SPAD XIIIs. Squadron CO Captain Jimmy Meissner noted in his diary that "the fellows [have begun] to believe more and more in SPADS,"[91] but this did not seem to be borne out by the vehement comments that some of the pilots wrote in the squadron's operational report or in their diaries. Among the comments were the following: "The best flying s - - - house I have ever tried," and "First and last flight for this - - - - - - - machine," and "tried out my bus today and found it to be rotten," etc., followed by a litany of engine problems and other inadequacies that would continue to plague the SPAD XIIIs in American service until the end of the war.[92]

On 14 August, the 147th squadron's beloved Nieuport 28s, the last of this type, which had been flown in combat by the First Pursuit Group since its first day, were ferried back to Orly and a new future with the training establishment at Issoudun. The war-weary Nieuport 28s had served faithfully and creditably for four months at the front.

The First Pursuit Group was commended by the commanding generals of the U.S. 26th Infantry Division and the French Sixth Army for its protection of Corps and Army observation planes during the Aisne-Marne Offensive. General Pershing, commander in chief of the AEF, commended the First Pursuit Group on 14 August 1918, stating, "With fine spirit and determination, [the group] has overcome obstacles and already achieved an enviable record."[93]

These commendations, especially Pershing's, were merited by the First Pursuit Group. The group, equipped principally with Nieuport 28 fighters during the Aisne-Marne campaign, successfully carried out its missions under the most difficult conditions. The group's record reveals the intensity of combat during this period: thirty-nine victory credits, two-thirds of which were fighters, while incurring thirty-one casualties, killed, wounded, or pilots downed and taken prisoner. Of this number, three squadrons, the 94th, 95th, and 27th, experienced close to a 1-to-1 ratio of victories to casualties incurred. The 147th Aero Squadron, which had clung to its Nieuport 28 fighters until the last, triumphed over ten opponents while losing three pilots KIA during this critical campaign.[94]

An ex-94th Aero Squadron Nieuport 28 undertakes new training duties at Issoudun.

Below: Nieuport 28, ex-147th Aero Squadron, at Issoudun.

Epilogue

On 30 August 1918, the First Pursuit Group was relieved of its assignment with the French Sixth Army and ordered to Rembercourt Aerodrome in the St. Mihiel-Verdun sector, in preparation for the major American offensive at St. Mihiel. The group would remain in combat at Rembercourt for the next ten weeks, until the Armistice took effect on 11 November 1918.

The group was assigned to the newly organized First Pursuit Wing, First Army, AEF, under the command of Major Bert Atkinson; Major Harold E. Hartney, formerly CO of the 27th Aero Squadron, assumed command of the First Pursuit Group.

Secrecy and vital intelligence information (including registration of artillery targets and information gleaned from visual and photo reconnaissance) contributed significantly to the success of the St. Mihiel operation. The objective of this operation was to pinch out the St. Mihiel salient and do it quickly, because the U.S. Army was committed to a major offensive within days on another part of the front. The Allies contributed to the air effort planned for the St. Mihiel Offensive by supplying additional fighter, artillery regulation, observation, and day- and night-bomber squadrons, and the total number of planes, all under the command of Brigadier General Billy Mitchell, chief of the Air Service, First Army, AEF, resulted in "the largest aggregation of air forces that had ever been engaged in one operation on the Western Front at any time during the entire progress of the war."[95]

The Allies' numerical advantage in the air over the German forces arrayed against them during the St. Mihiel operation was stunning: 1,481 Allied airplanes – of which 609 were American – versus 213 German aircraft, gave the American air commanders an almost 7-to-1 advantage. In spite of this numerical disadvantage, German fighter units, particularly JG 2, took a heavy toll of American bombers during this and the following campaign. Acquiring formation skills and discipline would improve the bombers' odds, as it had for their fighter counterparts.

SPAD XIII fighters were effective during the St. Mihiel operation by flying low-level visual observation missions in bad weather, spotting the movement of retreating German troops and the position of advancing American infantry. Low-flying fighters also attacked ground objectives, inflicting heavy losses on retreating German troops and transports caught out in the open.

The reduction of the St. Mihiel salient began at 5 a.m. on 12 September 1918, and by nightfall, converging attacks by the First Army had met at Hattonchâtel. The salient, which had been in German hands since 1914, had finally been eliminated.

The Meuse-Argonne Offensive quickly followed on 26 September, when the First Army, AEF, with the French Fourth Army on its left, assaulted heavily fortified German positions. Unlike the St. Mihiel drive, the terrain in the American zone left no room for maneuver, and this resulted in slow – and very costly – frontal attacks. The Germans continued to reinforce their positions in this sector because of a vitally important railhead at Mézières, approximately twenty miles west of Sedan.

At the outset of the Meuse-Argonne Offensive, the First Pursuit Wing was tasked with maintaining a barrage at medium and high altitudes and attacking enemy ground troops. The First Pursuit Group, acting as an independent unit, was given

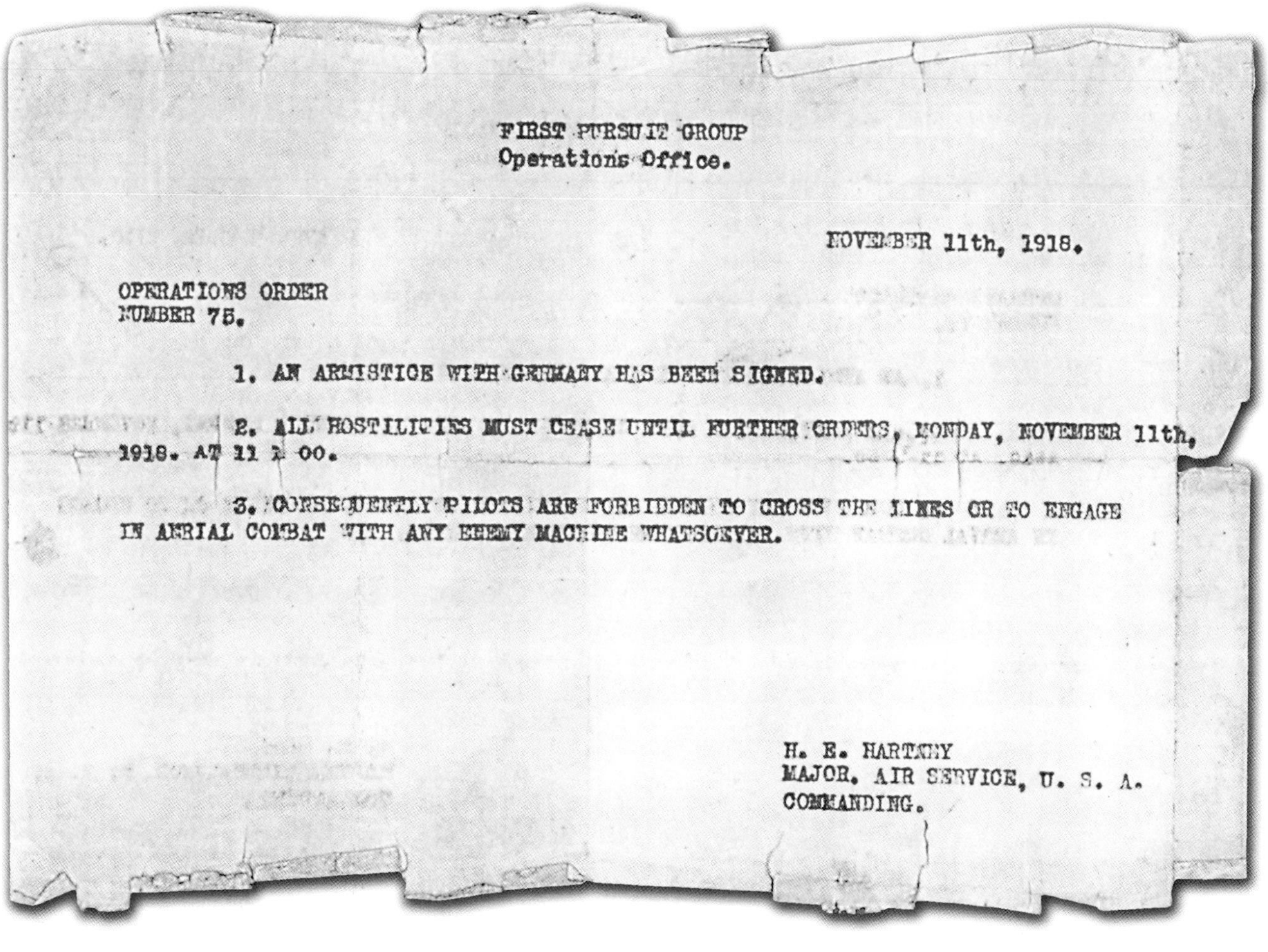

FIRST PURSUIT GROUP
Operations Office.

NOVEMBER 11th, 1918.

OPERATIONS ORDER
NUMBER 75.

1. AN ARMISTICE WITH GERMANY HAS BEEN SIGNED.

2. ALL HOSTILITIES MUST CEASE UNTIL FURTHER ORDERS, MONDAY, NOVEMBER 11th, 1918. AT 11 H 00.

3. CONSEQUENTLY PILOTS ARE FORBIDDEN TO CROSS THE LINES OR TO ENGAGE IN AERIAL COMBAT WITH ANY ENEMY MACHINE WHATSOEVER.

H. E. HARTNEY
MAJOR. AIR SERVICE, U. S. A.
COMMANDING.

the specialized task of combating low-flying German battle planes and observation balloons, and protecting infantry liaison and observation planes.[96] The Second and Third Pursuit Groups were tasked with the barrage.

On 1 November 1918, the First Army began the final phase of the Meuse-Argonne Offensive, and this time, broke through the last German positions. Now in open country, the American army raced up the Meuse Valley towards Sedan, only to be checked at the last moment to allow the French to take Sedan, the site of the French Army's 1870 humiliating loss in the Franco-Prussian War.

American fighter formations were perfected during this period, when concentrations of entire fighter groups flew sorties against outnumbered German air units; the ensuing combats proved costly to the Germans. At no time during the period from early September 1918 to the end of the war were American fighter units outnumbered by German fighters for extended periods, as they had been during the harsh combats of July and early August 1918.

Air Service Battle Order No. 46, dated 5 November 1918, read in part: "The enemy continues to retreat with his infantry in confusion. His artillery is gradually increasing its fire. The Air Service of the enemy wherever encountered has been destroyed or forced to withdraw by our own aviation."[97] By this time, American fighter squadrons had doubled in number since August, and had grown enormously in experience and effectiveness. The U.S. Air Service had just begun to flex its growing might when the Armistice ended the First World War, on 11 November 1918.

CHAPTER FIVE

AN ASSESSMENT OF THE NIEUPORT 28's COMBAT ROLE

Mr. Frear: *"The SPAD is better than the Nieuport, for a fighting machine?"*

Capt. Kindley: *"It is better for one type of fighting, that is, the diving, missing, and going home type; but for a fight which we call a dog fight – stay there and go round and round until you get him or he gets you – then for that kind of a fight, I say that the Nieuport is the best."*[1]

The Nieuport 28 elicited strong passions, both pro and con, among the American pilots who flew it in combat. Lieutenant Joe Eastman, 94th Aero Squadron, anticipating the replacement of his squadron's Nieuport 28 fighters remarked: " ... our squadron is to be supplied with SPADS in place of our present fire-trap wing shredders for which we are all going to journey to Paris for six or seven days SPAD instruction"[2] (there will be more from Lieutenant Eastman later in the chapter). Second Lieutenant Ken Porter, however, had a decidedly different view: Porter, a member of the 147th Aero Squadron, believed "the Nieuport 28 has repeatedly shown that in the hands of an alert, skilled, disciplined pilot, it is the match of any German pursuit machine on the Front."[3] Clearly, contemporary assessments of the Nieuport 28's fighting qualities ran the gamut.

The Air Service had preferred the SPAD XIII to equip the first American-trained fighter squadrons, but these fighters were not immediately available as France's expanding Aviation Militaire had prior claim on them. The Nieuport 28 was available, however, and by 15 June 1918 it had equipped all four squadrons of the First Pursuit Group. The Nieuport 28 served fledgling American pilots from early April in the quiet Toul sector, and through very difficult days during the Champagne-Marne Defensive and Aisne-Marne Offensive in July and early August 1918. By 14 August 1918, all four squadrons of the First Pursuit Group had transitioned to the SPAD XIII fighter, and by 1 November 1918 the U.S. Air Service had sixteen fighter squadrons, organized in three pursuit groups, in operation at the front. Fifteen of the sixteen squadrons were equipped with the SPAD XIII fighter.

In his final report as Chief of the Air Service, AEF, Major General Mason M. Patrick, stated, "the tactical history of the Air Service prior to the Meuse-Argonne offensive [commencing 26 September 1918] is largely concerned with its training. By the end of the St. Mihiel offensive [12–16 September 1918], however, it was felt, at last, that the American units then on the front had developed into trained combat organizations."[4] During much of what Major General Patrick referred to as the "training period," the Nieuport 28 was the U.S. Air Service's principal fighter.

In spite of the pilots' highly partisan comments, it is possible to make a fair and reasonable assessment of the Nieuport 28's role in combat and determine how well the aircraft served the U.S. Air Service, an organization that had essentially developed from scratch. And, ***with all other factors unchanged***, one might also determine how the First Pursuit Group would have fared if it had been equipped with the SPAD XIII at the outset of battle, as Brigadier General Foulois had wished. In order to answer these questions, we will compare the performance of the Nieuport 28 with that of the SPAD XIII, and also with the enemy fighters that were met in battle. There are additional important factors, however, that bear directly or indirectly on the Nieuport 28's effectiveness in battle. These factors include: mission capability (How well-suited was this fighter for its assigned mission?), operational readiness (maintainability in more modern parlance), and command and group effectiveness, for the Nieuport 28 fighter must be considered in the context of the growing effectiveness of the Air Service as a whole.

Performance

Comparing the performance of a combat aircraft with its peers and adversaries is the principal basis for judging its merits. Enemy fighters of special interest in our analysis were those encountered most frequently by the First Pursuit Group during their seven months in combat. Among these fighters were the Albatros D.Va and Pfalz D.IIIa. In May 1918, a total of 1,059 of both types were in operation at the front. Both types remained at the front in dwindling numbers while more potent fighters were being introduced.

In addition, there were some encounters with Fokker Dr.1 triplanes, which were in process of being removed from combat, and numerous encounters with two-seater, C class observation planes, such as the high-flying Rumpler. (As an aside, the fighter pilots of the First Pursuit Group were credited with victories over a greater number of two-seaters than over fighters at Toul. However, this ratio was reversed on the Château-Thierry front, when more than double the number of German fighters were claimed compared to two-seater aircraft.)

The Fokker D.VII, equipped with the relatively low-compression Mercédès D.IIIaü engine entered combat in May 1918. It was followed a month later by the superlative Fokker D.VIIF, equipped with the 185 hp BMW IIIa engine (both Fokker types are listed in the comparison chart below).

Elite German pilots were among the first to receive the Fokker D.VIIF. The Fokker D.VII, powered by the "over-compressed" Mercédès D.IIIaüv engine and offering performance comparable to the BMW engine, reached the front in September 1918. The SPAD XIII, which began replacing the Nieuport 28 in July 1918, clashed with German Jastas that were increasingly equipped with variants of the outstanding Fokker D.VII. Fokker D.VIIs were in service with fourteen Jastas by the end of May, forty-four Jastas by July, and seventy-eight Jastas by the end of October 1918.

The following performance specifications are derived principally from George Evans' study, entitled "World War I Aircraft Performance Chart."[5] Speeds and rates of climb are recorded for altitudes of 6,560 feet (2,000 meters) and 13,120 feet (4,000 meters):

Aircraft Type	*Speed @ 6,560'/13,120'*	*Rate of Climb to 6,560'/13,120'*	*Service Endurance*	*Ceiling*
Albatros D.Va	112 mph/96 mph	7 min./23 min.	2 hrs.	20,500'
Pfalz	107 mph/95 mph	7.5 min./24 min.	2 1/2 hrs.	17,000'
Fokker D.VII	114 mph/104 mph	8.24 min./18 min.	1 1/2 hrs.	19,000'
Fokker D.VIIF	119 mph/115 mph	6 min./12 min.	1 1/2 hrs.	22,900'
Nieuport 28	122 mph/115 mph	5.5 min./14 min.	1 1/2 hrs.	19,000'
SPAD XIII				
200 hp	126 mph/118 mph	6 min./15.5 min.	1 1/2 hrs.	22,500'
220 hp	130 mph/125 mph	5.25 min./13.25 min.	2 hrs.	23,000'
235 hp	135 mph/130 mph	4.75 min./12.25 min.	1 1/2 hrs.	23,000'

Although all of the aircraft listed carried two fixed, synchronized machine guns, the ammunition supply carried aboard varied greatly. The Fokker D.VIIF carried 1,000 rounds of 8 mm ammunition for its twin Spandau machine guns, and the Nieuport 28 carried only 500 rounds of .303 (7.7 mm) ammunition for its twin Vickers. The performance of the Nieuport 28 was further hamstrung for several months after it arrived at the front, until sufficient supplies allowed installation of a second Vickers machine gun. The SPAD XIII carried 800 rounds of .30 ammunition for its twin American-made Marlin machine guns, however, some American pilots preferred the Vickers and continued to use it.

George Evans noted an important omission in his presentation of facts and figures: "The biggest performance factor of all didn't seem possible to put into this chart: how a pilot melded with the best characteristics of any given aircraft."[6] This idea was eloquently addressed by Major Harold Hartney after taking his first flight in a Nieuport 28: "For the first time in all my flying, I felt that the plane and I were really one. She maneuvered like a bird in flight, almost in response to my thoughts."[7] Evans' admission also underscores Second Lieutenant Ken Porter's appraisal of the Nieuport 28 in the hands of an experienced American pilot who knew his airplane's capabilities intimately. Experienced German pilots flying aging Albatros and Pfalz fighters were able to defeat less-skilled Americans piloting superior fighters. Experience enabled a pilot to exploit the best characteristics of his fighter to the fullest.

Taking a different tack in a more recent study, Jack McCracken identified, weighted, and applied seven criteria to a list of eighteen candidate fighters in order to determine the best of the lot. McCracken gave the highest weight to speed and slightly less weight to snap turns – "the ability to perform very quick turns in combat."[8] McCracken noted that the Nieuport 28 and Fokker D.VIIF were comparable in speed, but the Nieuport 28 and the SPAD XIII could execute snap turns quicker than the Fokker D.VIIF. McCracken also considered rate of climb, armament, ceiling, steady state turns (the rate of turn without losing speed, an advantage in gaining a position on the enemy), and finally, endurance.

The rotary-powered Siemens-Schuckert D.IIIA biplane fighter emerged as the best fighter from McCracken's study; it is discounted for our purposes, however, because it appeared too late in the war to have had an impact in aerial combat. With the exclusion of the German Siemens IIIA fighter, the Fokker D.VIIF, equipped with the BMW D.IIIa engine, ranked as the best fighter in McCracken's study, with the SPAD XIII ranked fourth and the Nieuport 28 seventh on the list of top-ranked fighters.

German pilots also took note of the characteristics of opposing Allied fighters. A German intelligence document, prepared by Kofl.7 (7th Air Brigade, attached to the German Seventh Army) and dated 8 August 1918, reported on opposing air forces on its front at Soissons. Allied fighters encountered included the 140 hp and 180 hp (SPAD VIIs), the 200 hp supercharged (SPAD XIII), and the American 160 hp Monosoupape Nieuport (28). The German report noted that "the Fokker D. VII with the 160 hp supercharged Mercedes, is better in a turn [what McCracken referred to as a steady state turn] and more maneuverable than the SPAD 200 hp, but the SPAD is faster. The Fokker D.VII [F] with the 185 hp BMW is equally matched to the SPAD in every respect."[9] German pilots observed that the "SPADs [did] not enter into a turning fight [dogfight]"; they also reported that the "Nieuport [28] is a worthy opponent."[10]

American pilots remarked on the Nieuport 28's outstanding characteristics; these included excellent maneuverability and easy handling, good visibility, excellent glide ratio (expected of a lightweight fighter), and low landing speed. The Nieuport 28 had the ability to lose a cylinder or magneto and keep on flying, and the pilot could readily restart the engine if it stalled in flight.

Unlike the relatively simple Nieuport 28, the 235 hp SPAD XIII was a complex airplane, less maneuverable and inferior to the Nieuport 28 in the other qualities stated above. However, the SPAD XIII was rugged and fast: at 135 mph (at 6,560 feet), it was faster than all other fighters in level flight and in a dive. Veteran American pilots would make frequent use of these characteristics as the war progressed.

The Fokker D.VIIF merits special attention because it was a formidable opponent, made even more formidable when flown by an experienced and skilled German pilot.

Initially equipped with the Mercédès D.VIIaüv 180 hp engine, the Fokker D.VII's performance was improved with the installation of a higher compression Mercédès engine with an

Postwar view of a late-production Fokker D.VII, built under license by Ostdeutche Albatros Werke (OAW). Note thick, tapering top wing (see Appendix D) and square and rectangular air ducts in the radiator housing, designed to cool ammunition. Excessive heat sometimes caused inferior ammunition to "cook off." Below: A rear view of the clean line of the OAW-built Fokker D.VII.

Leutnant Ernst Udet prepares to demonstrate a Fokker-built D.VII to a postwar group of Allied officers and civilians. National Archives

output of 200 hp. However, the Fokker D.VIIF, equipped with the 185 hp BMW IIIa engine and an innovative, high-altitude carburetor, was the fighter most desired by German pilots. The Fokker D.VIIF appeared on the scene toward the end of the Nieuport 28's combat career; it outperformed the Nieuport 28 in rate of climb above 10,000 feet (the Nieuport 28 outperformed up to that altitude) and it could reach a higher ceiling of 22,900 feet. The outstanding features of the Fokker D.VIIF, however, were its superior handling and responsiveness at altitude.

Jack McCracken observed, "The [BMW] engine was designed for a compression ratio which was very high for that time, but was not designed structurally to withstand the resulting operational pressures of full power at sea level; but as the altitude increased, the throttle was opened to achieve increased RPM and thereby maintain a constant power with altitude – a very critical advantage. This feature transformed the Fokker D.VII from a run-of-the-mill fighter with good flying qualities into one that many claimed outperformed all others at altitude."[11] These features and the distinction between the Mercédès- and the BMW-powered Fokker D.VIIs, were noted in a postwar report written by Leutnant Ernst Udet. Udet was among the first Jasta pilots to receive the Fokker D.VIIF:

> The D.VII with the 160 hp motor [Udet likely was referring to the Mercédès D.IIIaü engine] was a technically outstanding aeroplane. However, its efficiency decreased considerably at altitudes above 13,000 ft.
>
> [The BMW] had the same weight as the Mercedes, but produced 185 hp and did not lose its efficiency at high altitudes ... During the first flights, I was amazed at the remarkable increase in power over the Mercedes. The engine was very smooth and throttled down easily ... On [30 June 1918] I used a BMW powered machine for the first time on line patrol, and noticed more than ever its tremendous advantage over the other Mercedes engined machines of my Staffel [Jasta 4]. In order to stay with them, I was forced to use half throttle only. My speed was much higher, particularly during powered descents, even at low altitudes, and at 16,500 feet, the machine was nicely balanced. There was ample power reserve, and in a fight, it is good to know that more power is available when desired. The rpm remained constant up to 18,000 ft. and with careful use of the altitude control, another 60-80 rpm were possible ... .
>
> There is no doubt that the BMW motor was the best aircraft engine used during the last period of the war. Its only fault was that it was born too late![12]

Captain Frank Burton, U.S. Air Service, reporting on combat airplanes at the front at the time of the Armistice, disparaged Allied fighter types: "The production of chasse [fighter] planes during the last year of the war was distinctly disappointing. Not one notable advance in this type of plane was made in this year in the Allied countries. On the other hand, the Fokker D7 [D.VII] was a distinct advance."[13] Historian John Morrow observed that the Fokker D.VII possessed "an apparent ability to make good pilots out of mediocre material," and this "was a tremendous asset with trained [German] fighter pilots in increasingly short supply. It was, and still is, widely regarded as the best fighter aircraft of the First World War."[14]

Mission Capability

As defined here, mission capability is a measure of an aircraft's ability to effectively carry out a specific assigned mission.

Clearly, a fighter may excel at one type of mission and fare poorly in another; this concept was implied in a postwar report on fighter aviation: "So much depends on the type of machine in pursuit work that one cannot express an opinion on pursuit operations without considering the type of machine. The SPAD machine was probably the fastest on the front, and as good as any at diving, but as all pursuit work is offensive, these two qualities should be coupled with the all important feature of maneuverability."[15]

During seven months of combat operations, the First Pursuit Group flew numerous types of missions: alerts, offensive patrols, protective missions, special missions that included close protection of Corps Observation airplanes, cooperation with bombing squadrons, attacks on observation balloons, and attacks on ground troops. On critical occasions, fighter pilots were also called upon to carry out low-level reconnaissance missions, usually in very bad weather.

Offensive patrols crossed "the enemy's lines in sufficient strength to cruise over his rear area, search out enemy aircraft, and attack them with the object of causing maximum casualties and inflicting the greatest possible damage to his air service."[16]

Protection missions were of two types: protecting Allied observation aircraft (day bombers were expected to provide their own protection), and preventing enemy aircraft from undertaking observation or artillery regulation missions or carrying out bombing attacks. Close protection missions were considered especially hazardous: "Perhaps the most disliked duty a Chasse patrol is called on to perform is to protect reconnaissance or photographic missions far into enemy territory, where they are at the mercy of any larger group of attacking fighting planes."[17]

As the air war progressed, First Pursuit Wing Headquarters directed that: "All tactical work ... will be performed in formation, the size of these formations, varying in accordance with the situation, the mission, and the enemy's dispositions. The formation of five or six planes, i.e. the flight, will be the basis of all tactical operations." In addition, all formations should "comprise a double echelon in depth and in altitude, the planes at the rear being highest up so that they can take advantage of their altitude to close in on the patrol leader by diving in case of necessity."[18] Altitude was considered a greater advantage in many cases than the number of fighters, and high protection was considered critical to mission success. This directive was promulgated toward the end of the war, when fighter squadrons had sufficient capabilities to meet it. Those capabilities meant sufficient numbers of serviceable fighters and pilots trained in formation work, conditions that did not exist in the Toul sector or in the harsh conditions that followed on the Château-Thierry front.

The Toul Sector

The Nieuport 28 was admirably suited to the conditions encountered in the Toul sector: with American pilots who were new to combat, the fighter was easy to fly and maintain, and it more than met the requirements for a fighter on this front. Possessing outstanding maneuverability, speed, and rate of climb, it outclassed enemy Pfalz and Albatros fighters unless they were flown by more skillful German pilots.

The quick-starting rotary engine of the Nieuport 28 enabled it to get very quickly – within 90 seconds – into the air. This feature, along with an excellent rate of climb up to medium altitude, enabled the fighter to perform well on alert missions, especially when used in conjunction with the excellent early warning system in operation in this sector. These factors were evident in the successful downing of an enemy observation plane by Captain James Norman Hall and Lieutenant Eddie Rickenbacker on 29 April 1918, thirteen minutes after they got the call from the early warning center.

The most compelling case for the Nieuport 28 may well have been made on the momentous first day of combat, 14 April 1918. Close scrutiny of the combat flight profile presented in Chapter 1 suggests that had Lieutenants Douglas Campbell and Alan Winslow been flying SPAD XIII fighters on that rainy Sunday morning, the outcome might have been far different.

As noted in Chapter 1, the air warning system in this sector was efficient and very quick. Early warning was a key to success on that first day, as two German fighters were rapidly approaching Gengoult Aerodrome. Another important factor was the quick-starting Gnôme rotary engine (coupled with the Nieuport 28's short takeoff roll and excellent climb rate), as was noted in the official history of the U.S. Air Service: 'The fact that the enemy pilots had blundered [over this aerodrome] could not, in all probability, have been turned to advantage had our liaison with the front have been less perfect or had the squadron been equipped with an airplane driven by a water cooled engine.'[19] If Lieutenant Winslow had answered the alert in a SPAD XIII, powered by the water-cooled Hispano-Suiza engine, he might well have been destroyed on the ground.

The third critical factor evident on that first day of combat operations was the superior maneuverability of the Nieuport 28, even at low altitude. Maneuvering the SPAD XIII at low altitude would have been a difficult and dangerous proposition, as one pilot remarked, "if you tried to roll a SPAD at even 50 feet, you'd never live through it."[20] The combat profile (pages 12-13) clearly shows that both German pilots were in a superior position when they opened fire on Lieutenants Winslow and Campbell (note that Lieutenant Winslow's Nieuport 28 was barely off the ground when it was fired on), but to no avail. The nimble Nieuport 28s in the hands of novice American pilots maneuvered quickly, but rather clumsily, to defeat the German pilots in combats that lasted less than ten minutes. The loss of one or both American pilots on the first day of combat would have had a disastrous effect on morale, both at the front and on the home front. The twin American victories that first day had exactly the opposite effect.

For the duration of the group's posting at Toul, patrols in large formation were counterproductive, because enemy fighters were few in number and not aggressive, and would not have been induced to combat by larger formations of American fighters. Protection missions were relatively safe in this sector for the same reasons. Perhaps for these reasons, formation flying was not practiced until a move to an active sector was imminent.

The Château-Thierry Sector

Toward the end of June, the First Pursuit Group moved from Gengoult Aerodrome near Toul, to an aerodrome relatively close to Château-Thierry. The Toul sector experience was summed up as follows: 'The aggressive spirit, which is a keystone of pursuit aviation, was developed to a high degree in the units of the 1st Pursuit Group – at the Toul sector. It is recognized that if the group had been forced to enter into active operations, such as were later encountered at Château-Thierry and in the St. Mihiel battle or in the operations west of the Meuse River, numerous grave shortcomings would have appeared.'[21]

German pilots were well-aware of the new fighters that the First Pursuit Group brought to this front, as a Jasta 6 Ace, Leutnant Richard Wenzl, observed: "On 1 July, the new Nieuport appeared for the first time at the Front and, indeed, it was flown by Americans. Apparently, they had two types of it, one with a weak engine and one with a strong engine. One could deal with the small type with the 160-hp Mercedes [equipped] Fokker, [but] the big type surpassed even the B.M.W. [powered Fokker D.VIIF]."[22] Wenzl may have confused a "weak-engined" Nieuport 28 with the Nieuport 27s of the American-led and -manned Escadrille N.471, which was still operational in the area. The commanding officer of Escadrille N.471 was Lieutenant Walter L. Avery, who would shortly transfer to the 95th Aero Squadron.

The Château-Thierry front, during the Champagne-Marne Defensive and the Aisne-Marne Offensive that immediately followed, was the crucible for the First Pursuit Group. During this time, the experienced 94th Aero Squadron transitioned to the SPAD XIII fighter, and was largely absent from combat during the height of the German assault and the Allied counteroffensive. As a result, the 27th, 95th, and 147th Aero Squadrons bore the burden during this very difficult period. The 95th and 27th began receiving SPAD XIIIs before the end of July, but the Nieuport 28 continued to predominate for the balance of the campaign.

Compared to the Toul sector, almost everything changed at Château-Thierry. Elite German pilots, many flying the new Fokker D.VII fighter, appeared in far greater numbers. American pilots had to fly a far greater distance in order to engage the enemy. Liaison with front-line troops was poor because of communications problems, and intelligence regarding enemy movements was crucial because of the fluidity of the battle lines. This last factor required that protective missions of Allied observation planes was the order of the day. Unfortunately, the First Pursuit Group had too few serviceable fighters to mount effective high and low formations, and as a consequence, Ace German pilots, principally from JG 1 and JG 3, took a heavy toll of American fighters.

Close protection of Allied observation planes meant sticking close – 100 to 200 meters above the observation plane – while flying at their altitude of roughly 4,500 feet (the same altitude required when attacking enemy observation planes bent on the same mission). Close protection work greatly inhibited the fighters' inherent offensive capabilities; it was also a dangerous proposition at this time, because there were too few Air Service fighters in operation to provide top cover. The unfortunate result was that American pilots were frequently bounced by enemy fighters and found themselves in a dogfight – if they survived the initial attack. Under the circumstances, the Nieuport 28's superior maneuverability, a quality highly valued by Major Harold Hartney, was a lifesaver. At the lower altitudes where the American pilots were forced to fly, the Nieuport 28 was also superior to opposing German fighters in climb rate and speed.

The St. Mihiel and the Meuse-Argonne Offensives

Fortunes improved for the First Pursuit Group after the very difficult days on the Château-Thierry front. From mid-August to early September, the group, which had now been joined by the Second and Third Pursuit Groups, stood down to complete integration and training with the SPAD XIII fighter and to prepare for the St. Mihiel Offensive. On 12 September, Brigadier General Billy Mitchell unleashed an overwhelming first strike of 1,476 Allied fighters, bombers, and observation aircraft against an estimated 295 enemy aircraft and targets well to the rear of the German lines. Mitchell assigned one-third of the fighter strength (the First Pursuit Group) to ground attack, destroying German observation balloons, and bombing and strafing German supply centers and troop concentrations.

Problems persisted with the troublesome Hispano-Suiza engines, and operational readiness of the fighter groups, all now equipped with SPAD XIIIs, remained low.

Costly close protection of observation planes had been largely abandoned by this time and American fighters now embarked on seek-and-destroy missions on enemy fighters.

The last and greatest American offensive in the Meuse-Argonne sector began on 26 September 1918. The First Pursuit Group, commanded by Major Harold Hartney, flew low-level patrols, performing reconnaissance and concentrating attacks against balloons, low-flying battle planes, and enemy troops. Combat operations reports now listed missions flown at 300 feet (and frequently much lower) to 1,000 feet, instead of 4,000 to 18,000 feet, as in prior missions. The morale effect of low-flying American fighters on American troops below was substantial, and the fast and rugged SPAD XIII fighters were well-suited to this role.

The Second and Third Pursuit Groups undertook medium- and high-cover flying in large formations along the ground troops' direction of attack, clearing the air space ahead for Corps Observation planes and protecting their wing mates below. The SPAD XIII was better-suited for formation flying than the Nieuport 28 because the SPAD had a throttle, which made formation flying easier and less tiresome compared to the rotary-engine-powered Nieuport 28, as one pilot observed: "...

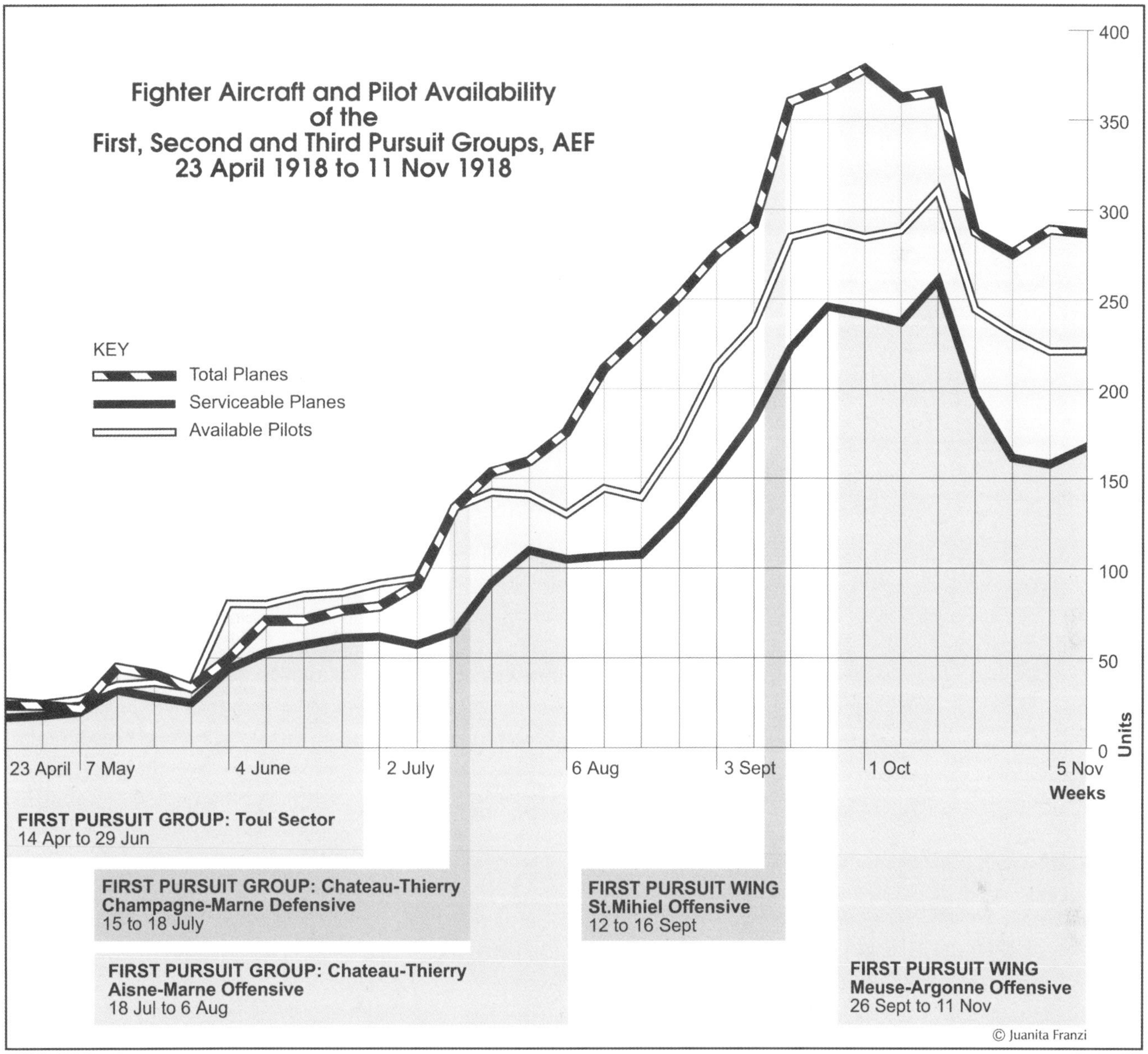

I spoke of the Nieuport 28 machine, because it has the rotary motor and is the hardest to fly in formation with, because you can't regulate your speed, but those with stationary motors, formation flying is easier … ."[23]

By this time, American fighter pilots had learned formation tactics and had developed the necessary discipline and leadership skills to make them effective. In addition, they had far greater numbers of SPAD XIII fighters in operation, fighters better suited by design than the Nieuport 28 to engage in formation work.

SPAD pilots used the speed advantage of their fighters to disengage and dive away if attacked from above, but they were admonished to use this tactic only as a last resort. When comparing how the SPAD XIII pilot and the Nieuport 28 pilot might react when attacked from above, some pilots made a clear, but derisive, distinction between the two fighters' modes of combat: "to dive is to run away, to maneuver is to stand and fight."[24]

The SPAD's speed advantage worked when one could safely disengage from combat, as Captain Hamilton Coolidge recalled in a letter to a friend:

> The Boches … sent a convoy of their prettiest little planes to escort me home [after Coolidge had flamed an enemy observation balloon]. The speed of a SPAD has been a matter of some discussion Dicky, but all I say is that I wish the doubters might have seen me on my way home this evening. Honestly, it was a funny sensation. After opening the motor wide and holding the head south, I knew there was nothing more I could do, so I sat there turned half around in my seat watching those boys and wondering whether or not they would catch me. For a while, they gained steadily, because their greater altitude gave them increased speed on the down slope, but after they once got on my level my old ship pulled gradually away from them

> and I couldn't resist putting my thumb to my nose when they turned and swung back chez eux [home].[25]

Diving attacks on enemy fighters, characterized as "hit and run" tactics, were utilized more often against Fokker D.VIIs, because pilots tended to rely more on the diving capability of their SPAD than its maneuverability. Captain Eddie Rickenbacker explained why when he was asked about the results of his combats with Fokker fighters: "[I got a] good many; but most of them were by surprise attack. I usually found that was the only way to get them. If I did not get him on my first attack, I would go off and come back later on ..."[26] Using these tactics, it is not surprising that the average American pilot was faulted for poor deflection-shooting skills; their record of success would have been greater if deflection-shooting skills, the mark of an accomplished pilot, had been practiced and employed more often in combat.

The campaign in the air was coming to an end, as German units were depleted by constant attacks all along the battle line. Generalleutnant Ernst von Hoeppner described the waning days of the Luftstreitskrafte: "Owing to the constant increase in the American units and the fact that our foes were delivering attacks simultaneously on almost all the fronts, it was impossible for us to [concentrate] our strength in one place as we had done in Flanders in 1917. We were far in the minority everywhere."[27]

Major Maxwell Kirby, 94th Aero Squadron, scored the last victory for the First Pursuit Group (and Wing) at 10:50 a.m. on 10 November 1918, almost twenty-four hours to the minute before World War I finally came to an end.

Operational Readiness

The critical importance of operational readiness, or maintainability, was readily acknowledged in the official history of the Air Service: "The number of machines in commission is probably as important a consideration as any in the operations of our pursuit units."[28]

Mechanical and supply problems and training deficiencies beset the Nieuport 28 at the beginning. Supply channels were poorly organized, and spare parts were difficult to obtain; the fighter operated for two months in combat with only a single machine gun installed. Field fixes of brittle fuel lines and weak landing gear were undertaken; they resulted in improved training and piloting proficiency, along with reduced engine fires and landing accidents. It took time to correct these problems, which were largely the result of an inexperienced organization new to combat.

Unlike the Nieuport 28 that had entered combat virtually untested, the SPAD XIII had been in combat for a year when American squadrons began to re-equip with it. The SPAD XIII was equipped with a more powerful Birkigt-designed, Hispano-Suiza engine than the ungeared 180 hp version installed on the SPAD VII.

Initially rated at 200 hp, and later increased to 220 hp and again to 235 hp, the new engine variant required reduction gearing in order to utilize the higher engine rpms and slow the larger propeller to its optimal rpm rate. The engine was difficult for licensed manufacturers to produce because "this [reduction] gearing was as demanding of nearly perfect metallurgy and heat treating as the rest of the engine was by other techniques."[29] Reduction gearing proved to be one of the costly weak links in this trouble-prone engine, as was observed after the battle of St. Mihiel: "It was impossible for our mechanics to keep more than 65% [of our fighters] serviceable, and pilots were not often able to do more than one mission each day, owing to the fact that the Hispano-Suiza motor, with reduction gear, was very difficult to keep in condition."[30]

The problems with the geared Hispano-Suiza engine were known, but the Air Service did not initially appreciate their full effect on operational readiness; this lesson, however, was soon learned. An instructional memorandum circulated to pilots and mechanics stated: "In comparison with a Nieuport, there is a great deal of work required to keep a SPAD in running order, and pilots must aid their mechanics as much as possible by explaining clearly and intelligently any faults that may show up while in the air."[31]

American pilots quickly found that myriad problems – overheating, oil leaks, faulty pumps, carburetors, magnetos, gauges, and generally poor workmanship, in addition to the faulty gearing – plagued the trouble-prone Hispano-Suiza engine. Lieutenant Joseph Eastman recorded his thoughts on the subject in his diary entry for 24 July 1918:

> My Spad, after five changes of oil pumps, was again given me to make a practice flight this morning in preparation for the regular patrol at 15h this afternoon. I no more than cleared it off the field when something – a connecting rod – broke, smoke blew into the pit, the entire plane shook with vibration, and I was barely able to regain the field without accident. This was my lot after nearly a week fussing with the tub. Rankin [engineering officer of the 94th Aero Squadron] at luncheon, told me to take number 10, which he said was in good condition. Later I learned it was the machine that Coolidge and Sherry had unsuccessfully attempted to use. I went out to it and found it still in the process of repair. I waited until time for the patrol and learned in that time further of its disquieting departure from a machine in good condition. The motor is an unheard-of-make [likely license-built], the throttles are offset and require a new technique in manipulation; its gas thumb lever needed a pair of pliers to move, and neither guns nor sights have been tested. Although my habitual appearance is one of cow-like docility and temperamental imperviousness, I left the ground in a state of mind that jumps out of the chair when a door is closed above a whisper. After two minutes in the air, I began to gather the evidence

> of my switchboard. Both the air and oil pressure were less than half the normal figure – and the important little temperature hand was doing a comedy skit in the region of 105 degrees or 25 degrees hotter than is conducive to successful flying. A few minutes spent hopefully in pursuit of the patrol failed to influence the gauges for the better. I piqued [dived] for the field and instead of the temperature cooling, it continued to augment in its own cheery fashion. The motor stopped firing over Coulommiers, struggled to life, coughed, missed, and revolved feebly by turns letting me down nearer and nearer to an unpromising landscape – which by the grace of God, I was enabled to clear.[32]

Several days later, Eastman's SPAD was still beset with problems: "I took it for a tour of the field but was drenched by the over-heated water as before. The mechanics, with whose business I'm daily growing more acquainted, are changing the radiator. These planes are certainly causing a lot of trouble as compared to the [Nieuport] 28s which were at least simple to keep on the line."[33]

Lieutenant Eastman's problems with his SPAD XIII were widespread, and his squadron's operational readiness was severely degraded as a result. Historian Alan Toelle analyzed the effect in a study undertaken in 2001. The objective of Toelle's study was to "compare the [sortie] readiness of the airplanes [SPAD XIII and Nieuport 28] and also relate the pilot's ability to complete a mission [sortie efficiency] with both types of aircraft."[34] After careful analysis of the 94th Aero Squadron's daily reports, which included condition of planes, flight logs, and daily operations reports, for the period 15 April through 11 November 1918, Toelle concluded that the Nieuport 28 had a sortie readiness of 86 percent, compared to the SPAD XIII's sortie readiness of 70 percent. The Nieuport 28 was also superior to the SPAD XIII in mission completion – 92 percent for the Nieuport 28 and 80 percent for the SPAD XIII. Overall efficiency, therefore, was 79 percent for the Nieuport 28 and a rather dismal 56 percent for the SPAD XIII.

When one enters the number of the squadron's fighters into the equation, the 94th fielded an average of fourteen Nieuport 28s for a mission and thirteen SPAD XIIIs, and this despite the fact that the complement of planes in Air Service fighter squadrons had been increased from eighteen to twenty-three in July. Toelle also considered the ability of "journeyman pilots" (basically, the average pilots of the 94th) to carry out the assigned mission; he found that "the Nieuport 28 still [had] a significantly better chance of completing a sortie than the SPAD XIII."[35]

Engine maintenance and reparability (replacement of wing and tail assemblies, etc.) of the Nieuport 28 were far easier and less time consuming than of the SPAD XIII. It took roughly four hours to change the Gnôme rotary engine on the Nieuport 28; replacement of the Hispano-Suiza engine on the SPAD XIII could take up to four days. It was evident from the long list of instructions given to pilots and mechanics that the SPAD XIII, particularly the engine, had to be babied: "When doing aerobacy, it is best to not throttle your motor lower than about 600 R.P.M., otherwise it may stall. If a steep dive does not start the stick [propeller] turning, pulling up slightly and at the same time turning (to the left with the 180 h.p. [engine] and to the right with the 220 h.p. [engine]) may give the needed additional impetus to start the stick revolving." The penalties for not following the rules were clear: "These rules must be observed at all times and particular attention paid to the proper speed of your motor, especially in cold weather. If you do not watch these things carefully, the motor will soon burn out due to lack of oil. A cold motor is also very apt to fail just as you are leaving the ground."[36]

The relative ease of servicing this 95th Aero Squadron Nieuport 28 is apparent in this photograph. Bergen Hardesty

During the height of the Meuse-Argonne Offensive in October 1918, American pursuit squadrons were suffering high attrition of airplanes and pilots alike. Replacement of SPAD XIII fighters at this time was becoming a real problem. The Air Service had instituted a very rigorous inspection system, and as a result, many aircraft were rejected that French squadrons would have happily accepted. In addition, the production of the geared Hispano-Suiza engine was being curtailed, as production was being switched to a larger, 300 hp ungeared engine. This new engine was intended for the Mark III Sopwith Dolphin as well as the Nieuport 29, which were then under development and intended as possible replacements for the SPAD XIII. Under these tight circumstances, Major General Mason Patrick, chief of Air Service, AEF, promulgated a strict rationing policy: "under no condition, will any squadron, no matter what the reason is, be allowed to obtain more than 9 pursuit machines ... per month."[37]

Considering "our great shortage of chasse planes and also the natural difficulties with water-cooled engines in the winter time ... [the Gnôme rotary was] especially suited to winter use," Major A. D. Butterfield, executive officer of the Technical Section, said, in recommending that the modified Nieuport 28A (600 of which were under order as advanced trainers) be returned to combat service.[38] Conceivably, the modified and improved Nieuport 28 could have returned to combat, but this did not happen, for the war ended one month later.

Major Harold Hartney and Lieutenant Alfred Cunningham, respectively commanding officer and operations officer of the First Pursuit Group, in a photograph taken one day after the Armistice. R.L. Cavanagh

Command Effectiveness

Major General Mason Patrick believed that the Air Service had become a trained combat force only after the end of the St. Mihiel Offensive in mid-September 1918. This section explores the many factors that brought the Air Service to this level of maturity.

Shortly before the St. Mihiel Offensive, the command structure of the Air Service, AEF, was strengthened at every level. Direction at the top improved when General Pershing prevailed upon his U.S. Military Academy classmate, Major General Mason M. Patrick, to become chief of Air Service, AEF, relieving Brigadier General Benjamin Foulois. Major General Patrick brought much needed calm and administrative skills to the Air Service. Foulois ultimately became Patrick's deputy, where Foulois found his level as an able administrator, after briefly serving as chief of Air Service, First Army. Brigadier General William "Billy" Mitchell, who had feuded with Foulois, relieved him as chief of Air Service, First Army.

Mitchell, a very demanding taskmaster, infused his organization with his drive and determination. "Not particularly skilled as a combat pilot ... he was a superb air tactician. He wrote clear concise battle plans for his pilots and watched meticulously to make sure that they carried them out [to] the letter. It was a commander's fault if a unit did not follow his orders."[39] These were the qualities of an able and effective commanding officer, and were evident in Mitchell's planning and execution of the massive air assault at St. Mihiel, the largest assemblage of combat aircraft up to that point.

With the expansion of the fighter forces, Major Bert M. Atkinson was promoted to head the newly organized First Pursuit Wing, comprising the First, Second, and Third Pursuit Groups. Some of the pilots of the 94th and 95th Aero Squadrons, First Pursuit Group, were transferred to the newly operational squadrons, adding their leadership skills and combat experience to the newly formed groups. Historian Bert Frandsen described Atkinson's contribution in the development of the First Pursuit Group as follows: "he saw [his mission] largely in terms of logistics – the final assembly of pilots, mechanics, airplanes, vehicles, and other unit equipment into pursuit squadrons. He may have been an aviator, but his mission, as he saw it was [as] a manager, not a combat leader."[40]

Major Harold E. Hartney, formerly commander of the 27th Aero Squadron and now CO of the First Pursuit Group, was in every sense a combat commander. Hartney, a Canadian by birth, had seen extensive service with the Royal Flying Corps, before being tasked with the organization and training of the American 27th Aero Squadron. His rigorous training of flying cadets: "forced landings, outside landings, aerial combat, aerobacy of all types and, most important of all, the approach for a landing without an engine," elicited criticism of "stunting" or "showing off" from other officers, many of them nonflyers or pilots with little or no combat experience.[41] Hartney would be plagued by this "desk-bound mentality" for the balance of the war.

The 27th and 147th squadrons, commanded respectively by Majors Hartney and Geoffrey Bonnell, experienced fewer problems with Nieuport 28 engine fires and wing failures (notwithstanding Lieutenant Plyler's experience, described in Chapter 4) than the 94th and 95th, as a result of the rigorous training that the 27th and 147th had received. (Ironically, Hartney himself once experienced an embarrassing engine fire after improper use of the coupé button.)

Hartney and Bonnell, both combat veterans of the Royal Flying Corps, were appreciative of the Nieuport 28's handling and maneuverability (particularly the latter feature, so successfully manifested by the British Sopwith Camel), and were among the Nieuport 28 fighter's strongest advocates. Majors Hartney and Bonnell brought a different culture to the First Pursuit Group. German pilots accurately perceived the cultural differences, with these observations made in August 1918: "The French show up when they are in large groups and superior numbers, and are willing to attack; otherwise they are timid and will only attack two-seaters. When attacked, they go home. The Americans show the same aggressive spirit as the Englanders, but they are inexperienced."[42] In fairness, Allied pilots leveled the same criticism of timidity at their German adversaries.

The 27th and the 147th Aero Squadrons joined their sister squadrons, the 94th and 95th, at Toul in late May 1918. The initial reaction of the veteran flyers to their new associates was unwelcoming, even unfriendly, for the new arrivals were perceived to be cocky and arrogant, and they overcrowded the barracks area. The newly arrived squadrons were referred to scornfully as the "Canadian Circus," as both squadrons had trained under the British system in Canada. However, the differences were more deeply rooted in their respective approaches to air combat as practiced by the French and British air forces.

The real problem was a lack of doctrine. Throughout the war, the U.S. Air Service borrowed heavily from both of its principal allies, but as the war progressed, the Air Service adhered more closely to British doctrine. This was true for several reasons: one was the elevation of British-trained Major Harold Hartney to command of the First Pursuit Group; another was an increasing infusion of RFC- and RAF-trained American pilots, and also, the full realization of the vital necessity of disciplined formation work.[43]

The British standard for fighter combat was very aggressive and demanded formation discipline and strict adherence to the flight commander's directives, the flight commander being considered the most important element in fighter combat. The French view questioned the value of large formations. In a treatise written in 1917 (but published in the *Bulletin of the Information Section, Air Service*, in August 1918), a renowned French fighter pilot wrote: "A squadron of pursuit machines nearly always creates an empty sky before it. Its use is advantageous to insure the mastery of a certain place during a given time but not for bringing down the Boches. The group of two or the solitary hunter has up to the present time given the best results."[44] This doctrine, dating to 1915, was appropriate for the conditions encountered in the Toul sector, but inappropriate

An aggressive looking Lieutenant Eddie Rickenbacker is strapped in his Nieuport 28 fighter and ready for a mission from Gengoult Aerodrome at Toul. Rickenbacker became an Ace while flying the Nieuport 28. National Archives

once the First Pursuit Group moved to the Château-Thierry sector. In 1918, the Aviation Militaire, in the face of larger German formations, increased formation size to four fighters, however, the penchant for individual combat remained ingrained among some of the French Aces.

Upon assuming command of the First Pursuit Group, Major Hartney began to put his personal touch on the group – moving the group closer to the British doctrine of fighter combat, and instituting more rigorous training in gunnery and formation work. His style of leadership was described in his memoirs:

> By far the most important thing I did was to keep in constant personal touch with the officers and men of every squadron. I was among them all hours, learning their thoughts, their methods and their capabilities. I don't believe any commander ever kept in closer contact with his organization. We had frequent conferences of officers, in different groups for different purposes – interpretation of orders, explicit plans of attack and, especially, the free exchange of new ideas. ... I realized I could no longer take part in all patrols. I was, however, determined to do even more actual flying but only on new and untried equipment or in the testing of experimental air tactics before making them part of our regular setup.[45]

Major Hartney promoted the most able and aggressive men into positions of flight and squadron leadership and, unlike his predecessor, he expected his squadron commanders to fly and to lead. With his background and training, Hartney recognized the value of patrol leadership, for patrol leadership had become "the most important factor in determining air supremacy."[46] Captain Edward V. Rickenbacker, promoted on 25 September to the command of the 94th Aero Squadron, was perhaps the most shining example of Hartney's policy of promoting through meritocracy. James Meissner, a former squadron mate, commented after the war on Rickenbacker's qualities of leadership: "He was regarded very highly: they all admired him because he had so much enthusiasm and tried to keep up the spirits of everybody else as well as his own and he always did everything he could to get everything for the group. While a squadron commander was not obliged to fly with his group [this was true under Major Atkinson's command], he did ... Rickenbacker felt it was his responsibility to protect the greener men. He flew above, and if he saw any Germans coming, he was there to warn them."[47]

Under Hartney's tutelage, the cultural divide between the squadrons of the First Pursuit Group disappeared. The unaggressive, ill-disciplined, and infirm pilots (those who had memorized the eye chart or had other maladies that made them unfit to fly) had mostly been shunted aside or had not survived in combat. What emerged was a more aggressive, better trained, and competent organization with a uniquely American character. Reflecting the high degree of confidence gained by the end of the war, one highly placed American officer stated that the U.S. Air Service as a whole now possessed a personality "incomparably better than the British, French, or Boche."[48]

Conclusion

Pilots of the First Pursuit Group began learning their craft on the quiet Toul Front after their dramatic debut on the first day of combat operations – the outcome on this day might have been far different had they been equipped with the Spad XIII instead of the nimble Nieuport 28. Easy to fly and maintain, the Nieuport 28 fighter was well-suited for the Toul sector; its speed and maneuverability were more than a match for the types of enemy fighters it encountered. Its quick-starting rotary engine and short takeoff roll, coupled with an excellent rate of climb, made it an effective fighter for the alert missions that were common on this front. Machine-gun stoppages, the cause of most of the aborted missions in this sector, diminished the Nieuport 28's success, as did the fact that for several months only one worn machine gun could be supplied for each aircraft. The SPAD XIII, with its trouble-prone engine (the cause of most of its aborted missions), would have fared quite poorly at Toul with only one machine gun installed.

The First Pursuit Group's claims of a roughly 3-to-1 victory ratio at Toul, achieved against German two-seater observation planes and admittedly inferior German fighter pilots and planes, gave confidence to the fledgling American fighter pilots. That confidence, however, would be severely tested after the move to the active Château-Thierry front.

The group's claims of 1-to-1 victories and losses in July and August reflected the intensity of operations at Château-Thierry. Formation flying, which had proven counterproductive at Toul, was vital on this front, but the group lacked both the numbers of aircraft and the tactical skills necessary to combat large formations of from fifteen to as many as thirty German aircraft. Elite German pilots, some with victory claims of fifteen or more kills, took a toll, mostly of the least-experienced or ill-disciplined American pilots – those who would straggle or break away from formations. Compounding these difficulties were the frequent close protection missions flown at lower altitudes and without top cover. Under these circumstances, however, the Nieuport 28 proved its worth in a way that the SPAD XIII could not: if a pilot was forced into combat when attacked from above, the superior maneuverability of the Nieuport 28 and its superior performance at the lower altitudes flown enabled the pilot to stay and fight, and hopefully stay alive.

Problems with engine fires and wing failure brought an end to the Nieuport 28's combat career. This decision was made in spite of the fact that the causes of engine fires were being corrected with field fixes of defective fuel lines and proper pilot training. It should also be noted that in spite of the intensity of operations at Château-Thierry, no incidents of wing failure were recorded during that campaign. The problem that had caused such consternation on the Toul front may have been resolved because pilots had learned to operate the Nieuport 28 with finesse – without overstressing the wings.

The SPAD XIII began supplanting the Nieuport 28, first in the 95th and then in the 27th Aero Squadrons (the 94th transitioned to the SPAD XIII earlier in July), but the pilots of the 147th clung to their beloved Nieuport 28s until the campaign at Château-Thierry was over in August.

The SPAD XIII fighter performed well in the final months of the war. Three pursuit groups were in operation under U.S. command prior to the St. Mihiel Offensive. Formations now became effective, with greater numbers of SPAD XIII fighters in service (the number of Air Service fighters at the front more than doubled from mid-August to mid-September), and with experienced flight leaders now in command. SPAD XIII fighters flew top-cover and low-level strafing missions, even dropping anti-personnel bombs, for some fighters were now equipped with bomb racks. American pilots had become proficient in using the best features of their SPAD XIII fighters to successfully combat the potent Fokker D.VIIs. While these "hit and run" tactics were generally effective, they were disparaged by those pilots who preferred the maneuverability of fighters like the Nieuport 28.

Although the problems with the geared Hispano-Suiza engine were never completely resolved, the SPAD XIII remained in service until the end of the war. Had the war continued, the Nieuport 28A would have been operational as an advanced fighter trainer, and it is likely that a direct drive, 300 hp Hispano-Suiza equipped fighter, possibly the Nieuport 29, would have replaced the SPAD XIII in American fighter squadrons.

Overall, the record achieved by the First Pursuit Group and the Air Service in the last three months of the war was remarkable, considering all the factors that had coalesced in the prior four months to make it happen. During this brief period, American pilots learned to function as a skilled and disciplined team. Meritocracy reigned, as proven men were promoted to a level of command, from chief of Air Service, AEF, to squadron flight commander, where they would excel. Administrative, logistical, and maintenance support functions, sorely lacking at the beginning, were now generally well-established and effective.

Combat experience was the single most important factor that molded Air Service fighter squadrons into an effective fighting force: tactical lessons and basic skills had been learned at Toul and honed during harsh days at Château-Thierry, leadership and organizational capabilities were developed – and amply demonstrated during the massive Allied air offensive at St. Mihiel. In late September, aggressive – and experienced – American fighter pilots began the final great American offensive on the Meuse-Argonne front, where they would continue to sharpen their skills.

To a significant degree, the Nieuport 28 fighter enabled the Air Service to achieve this level of effectiveness, but the benefits and accolades would accrue to the SPAD XIII fighter that replaced it in combat. In the final analysis, however, it was providential that the first American-trained fighter squadrons to enter combat were equipped with the nimble Nieuport 28C.1 fighter.

CHAPTER SIX

THE NIEUPORT 28 IN POSTWAR SERVICE

With the end of what was then the most destructive war in history, the victorious Allies were faced with a glut of war materiel, including weapons stripped from Germany under the terms of the Versailles Treaty. While this proved a boon to lesser countries, which were now able to equip their forces with the most modern equipment at bargain-basement prices, much of the war materiel produced by Great Britain, France, and the United States was retained for future use. Surplus uniforms and accoutrements were carefully packed and stored, ordnance conserved in Cosmoline, and surplus ships mothballed. However, because of their fragility, high maintenance requirements, and rapid obsolescence, military aircraft could not be put into long-term storage: they would remain in operation until salvaged, destroyed, or disposed of on the civilian market.

Among the many types of military aircraft brought from France to the United States after the war for brief military use was the Nieuport 28A advanced trainer. This type was also later supplied, in small numbers, to the Swiss Fliegertruppe. In addition, the Fuerza Aérea Argentina operated several wartime-production Nieuport 28s, having received them as a gift from a French military sales commission that visited Argentina in 1919.

The U.S. Air Service, AEF: Winding Down

Anticipating the end of the war, Assistant Chief of the Air Service Colonel Halsey Dunwoody informed the French undersecretary of state for aeronautics that "in the event of an armistice, the United States would probably cancel all orders and stop activities, and [Dunwoody] requested that a statement be prepared showing our total liabilities to the French Government."[1] The U.S. military services, which were now moving with a clear purpose and alacrity not seen at the beginning of the war, duly canceled all contracts with the French government for aviation material "not necessary for the maintenance of our present air forces" within days after the Armistice.[2] At the same time, cancellations and stop-delivery directives were issued on all orders placed with England, Italy, Switzerland, and Spain.

Colonel Dunwoody, now head of the Air Service Liquidation Board, began to deal with problems associated with the cancellation of orders and also with the status of aircraft and aviation material at Air Service schools and air stations. It was decided that aircraft and aviation material at the schools and stations would be collected at a central point (Romorantin was the central collecting station in France, with Issoudun as a backup) and put back into inventory for continued use in France, packed for shipment to the United States, salvaged, or disposed of as directed.

In all, 208 wartime-production Nieuport 28 fighters had been delivered to the AEF between March and August 1918, and most of these aircraft were lost through combat or accidents, or subsequently salvaged and sold. A total of 909 aircraft, of all types, in Air Service inventory were salvaged (after engines, engine parts, instruments, and instrument parts had been removed) and sold between 11 November 1918 and 30 August 1919, and proceeds from the sale amounted to 34,000 French francs, or roughly $5,800.[3] Among the 909 airplanes salvaged and sold were 64 Nieuport 28 airframes.

A policy for settling outstanding production-contract claims by the French government was recommended by the Air Service Liquidation Board and subsequently approved. "It was agreed ... that the Air Service would only accept delivery for, or pay indemnity on material made especially for the Air Service and that could not be used by the French Government. It was further agreed that if complete quantities of the items selected could not be delivered, the above amount would be reduced by the value of the undelivered quantities."[4] To establish the amount due the French government, a team of American and French officers undertook an inspection of all French factories producing airplanes for the U.S. Air Service. This group submitted its final report to Major General Mason Patrick, chief of the Air Service, AEF, in late December 1918.

Among the factories inspected were Niepce & Fetterer, Savary et de la Fresnaye, and Lioré et Olivier. The first two firms were building Nieuport 21 training planes for the French and American air services; Nieuport 27 trainers for the French, American and Belgian air services; and Nieuport 80, 82, and 83 training planes for the U.S. Air Service.[5] Lioré et Olivier was then utilizing its entire production capacity in building the Nieuport 28A trainer for the U.S. Air Service.[6] All three companies were building Nieuport designs under license, as the Nieuport Company was then concentrating on development of the promising Nieuport 29 fighter.

Lioré et Olivier had received an order for 600 Nieuport 28A advanced trainers in autumn 1918, with delivery of the first fifty airplanes promised to the Air Service by 1 November 1918. The company, however, was unable to deliver any aircraft before 11 November 1918, due to problems incorporating required design modifications of the wartime production fighter.

The first test of a reconstructed Nieuport 28 that incorporated the design modifications began at Orly in mid-October 1918; by 5 November, the first of the production series was ready for flight testing.[7] With the signing of the Armistice six days later, the program was subject to immediate cancellation.

After inspecting the Lioré et Olivier facilities on 17 November, Air Service officers calculated that the company could complete 170 Nieuport 28A trainers and supply parts for 100 additional aircraft. This estimate became the initial basis for settlement negotiations with the French government. Six months later, this projection had been pared down to production of 100 airplanes.[8] The aircraft, equipped with 160 hp Gnôme engines, ultimately cost 31,300 French francs each, spares extra. With the value of the franc dropping from 5.80 francs to the

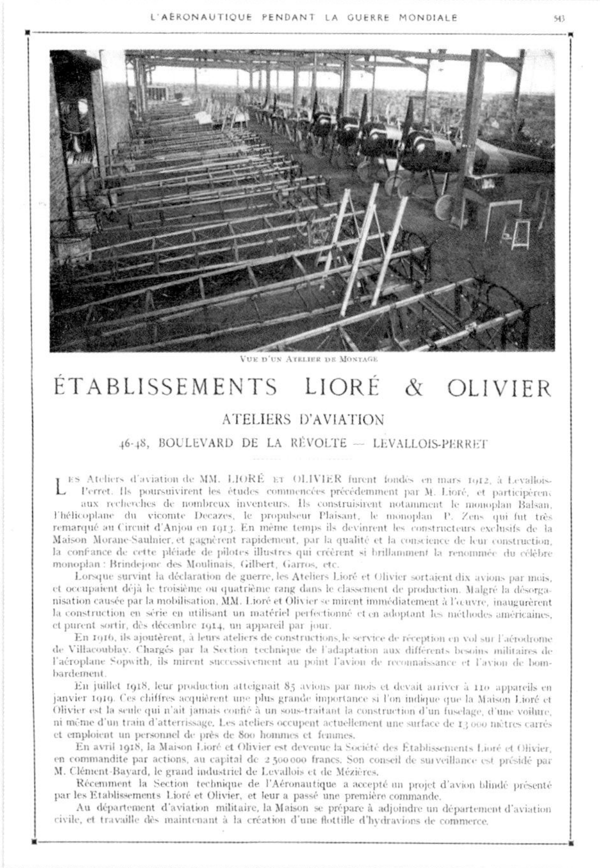
L'AÉRONAUTIQUE PENDANT LA GUERRE MONDIALE

VUE D'UN ATELIER DE MONTAGE

ÉTABLISSEMENTS LIORÉ & OLIVIER

ATELIERS D'AVIATION

46-48, BOULEVARD DE LA RÉVOLTE — LEVALLOIS-PERRET

Les Ateliers d'aviation de MM. LIORÉ ET OLIVIER furent fondés en mars 1912, à Levallois-Perret. Ils poursuivirent les études commencées précédemment par M. Lioré, et participèrent aux recherches de nombreux inventeurs. Ils construisirent notamment le monoplan Balsan, l'hélicoplane du vicomte Decazes, le propulseur Plaisant, le monoplan P. Zens qui fut très remarqué au Circuit d'Anjou en 1913. En même temps ils devinrent les constructeurs exclusifs de la Maison Morane-Saulnier, et gagnèrent rapidement, par la qualité et la conscience de leur construction, la confiance de cette pléiade de pilotes illustres qui créèrent si brillamment la renommée du célèbre monoplan : Brindejonc des Moulinais, Gilbert, Garros, etc.

Lorsque survint la déclaration de guerre, les Ateliers Lioré et Olivier sortaient dix avions par mois, et occupaient déjà le troisième ou quatrième rang dans le classement de production. Malgré la désorganisation causée par la mobilisation, MM. Lioré et Olivier se mirent immédiatement à l'œuvre, inaugurèrent la construction en série en utilisant un matériel perfectionné et en adoptant les méthodes américaines, et purent sortir, dès décembre 1914, un appareil par jour.

En 1916, ils ajoutèrent, à leurs ateliers de constructions, le service de réception en vol sur l'aérodrome de Villacoublay. Chargés par la Section technique de l'adaptation aux différents besoins militaires de l'aéroplane Sopwith, ils mirent successivement au point l'avion de reconnaissance et l'avion de bombardement.

En juillet 1918, leur production atteignait 85 avions par mois et devait arriver à 110 appareils en janvier 1919. Ces chiffres acquièrent une plus grande importance si l'on indique que la Maison Lioré et Olivier est la seule qui n'ait jamais confié à un sous-traitant la construction d'un fuselage, d'une voilure, ni même d'un train d'atterrissage. Les ateliers occupent actuellement une surface de 13 000 mètres carrés et emploient un personnel de près de 800 hommes et femmes.

En avril 1918, la Maison Lioré et Olivier est devenue la Société des Établissements Lioré et Olivier, en commandite par actions, au capital de 2 500 000 francs. Son conseil de surveillance est présidé par M. Clément-Bayard, le grand industriel de Levallois et de Mézières.

Récemment la Section technique de l'Aéronautique a accepté un projet d'avion blindé présenté par les Etablissements Lioré et Olivier, et leur a passé une première commande.

Au département d'aviation militaire, la Maison se prépare à adjoindre un département d'aviation civile, et travaille dès maintenant à la création d'une flottille d'hydravions de commerce.

The interior of the Lioré et Olivier factory, showing a batch of Nieuport 28As in various stages of production. Note that the fuselages are in wartime-standard French camouflage; this would later be changed to OD (olive drab) as directed by the U.S. Air Service in October 1918.

Below: "Hello Joe" decorates the fuselage of this wartime-production Nieuport 28. This fighter, shown in a postwar photograph, had been disarmed prior to use as a trainer in France; it most likely was salvaged or scrapped, and was not among the aircraft shipped from France to the United States in 1919. Greg VanWyngarden

F-CGT-A
F

6373

dollar in April to 6.45 francs to the dollar in July, each aircraft cost the U.S. government close to $4,800.[9]

The AEF accepted eighty-nine new Nieuport 28A trainers at Romorantin as part of the final Liquidation Settlement and eighty-eight of these aircraft were carefully packed in tongued-grooved crates lined with tar paper and strapped with iron, and

Opposite
Top: A postwar courier Nieuport 28A operated by Compagnie Générale Transaérienne. This aircraft, likely surplus from the Air Service contract with Lioré et Olivier, was one of many ex-military planes that flooded the civilian market after the war. S.H.A.A. via William Nungesser

Middle: This Nieuport 28A, N.6373, was photographed at Bolling Field, Washington, DC, in 1919. It is one of eighty-eight Nieuport 28As that were shipped to the USA from France after the war. National Air and Space Museum, Smithsonian Institution (SI 88-14941)

Bottom: Most of the Nieuport 28As received in the United States after the war were transferred to training bases at March Field in California or to Carlstrom Field in Florida. Carlstrom Field is seen in this aerial photo. Florida State Archives

Below: A Nieuport 28A trainer, repainted in gaudy red, white, and blue, at Carlstrom Field, circa 1920. Greg VanWyngarden

Bottom: This Nieuport 28A at Carlstrom Field is painted in postwar OD (olive drab); it is one of the aircraft featured in the color profile section in Appendix F. Greg VanWyngarden

marked for shipment to the United States.[10] This was part of a total of 1,551 Allied aircraft, including 612 U.S.-produced D.H. 4s, that were shipped to the USA, including the final shipment on 20 August 1919.

The U.S. Air Service Stateside

By 19 June 1920, fifty-three Nieuport 28As were inventoried at Air Service bases located across the United States. Twelve aircraft had been transferred earlier from the Air Service to the U.S. Navy, to be modified for service as shipboard fighters. No accounting has been found for the balance of the aircraft received in the United States.

Most of the Air Service Nieuports were based at Aviation General Supply or Repair Depots in Fairfield, Ohio, Middletown, Pennsylvania, and Montgomery, Alabama. Several airplanes were based at Bolling and Mitchel Fields, and one wartime-production Nieuport 28 (listed as serial number N.6298 and marked P-38, it was destroyed in a crash on 30 May 1920) was among many types of aircraft being flight-tested at McCook Field in Ohio.[11]

The Nieuport 28A now entered its principal, but very brief, postwar Air Service role as a training airplane. During the war, primary flight training had been provided at fifteen fields across

Above: A group of Carlstrom pilots with their Nieuport 28As in the background. Greg VanWyngarden

Below: Lieutenant Grey crashed this Nieuport 28A at Carlstrom Field. Florida State Archives

the country, but soon after the war ended training was consolidated at two pilot schools: March Field in Riverside, California, and Carlstrom Field in Arcadia, Florida. The Nieuport 28A, in addition to other wartime American and Allied aircraft, was used for flight instruction of both army and navy officers, the latter being trained on land-type planes for later service aboard ships. At the time, five Nieuport 28As were on the roster at March Field and thirteen were serving at Carlstrom Field.

The following excerpt from an issue of *Air Service Newsletter*, provides a vignette of the small-scale, army and navy peacetime operations then going on at Carlstrom Field:

> The naval officers detailed to Carlstrom Field for instruction on land type planes, are doing excellent work in aerial gunnery, formation flying and combat practice. Patrol flights are being made under conditions approaching as closely as possible to those which would influence an actual offensive. The handling of the formation as a whole and of each plane by the individual, are carefully checked by accompanying instructors. A photographic plane flying at an altitude of ten thousand feet was sent over a line between Carlstrom Field, Punta Gorda, North Labelle, and the home station with a protection of Thomas Morse scouts being close at hand, the skies in the region of sixteen thousand feet being scoured by five Nieuport single seaters. Punta Gorda and Fort Myers were passed and Labelle had been reached without incident but just as the formation was turning for home, the two rear Nieuports were pounced by two SPADS, which had approached in the sun at a great altitude. Beating off the assailants, the flight returned to the field, but one pilot failed to appear. Lt. Anthony Fehr, embroiled in the melee following the sudden descent of the SPADS, was carried into an area of clouds and lost sight of his adversary. In the minute or two which elapsed before he again obtained a clear field of vision, the rest of the planes had disappeared, the visibility being none too clear. Lt. Fehr dropped down to look the terrain over for landmarks. Nothing familiar was in sight so he picked a road which he thought would lead him home, but after following it for a short distance, he realized that he was heading in almost the opposite direction from the field near the town of Bigler, twenty miles from Carlstrom, with his gas tank almost dry. Upon telephoning in, a De Haviland, with a supply of gasoline, was sent to replenish

> the Nieuport's tank and start it home. The field with its activities and bustling about below, the perpetual drone of motors from above, brings one back to the rattling days of nineteen seventeen and eighteen.[12]

By 1920, the immense stock of aircraft, engines and spare parts, including the 1,551 Allied and 347 German airplanes returned to the USA after the war, was posing a problem for the Air Service, as well as for the U.S. aeronautical industry. Many of the airplanes had become obsolete or unserviceable, and the rapidly demobilizing Air Service lacked the personnel (95 percent of all officers commissioned during wartime had been discharged) and facilities to maintain the remaining aircraft in safe operating condition. The glut of wartime aircraft impeded the postwar recovery of the U.S. aircraft industry, which was still reeling from production cutbacks at the end of the war. As a result of these conditions, the Air Service wasted no time in disposing of vast quantities of aviation material.

The positive effects of the disposal of hundreds of surplus aircraft, acquired by civilians at rock-bottom prices, were immediately felt, as the 'Barnstorming Era' and the ensuing aviation craze got under way across the country. Many of these aircraft were Curtiss JN-4 or Standard J-1 trainers offered at several hundred dollars – engines extra. Surplus Nieuport 28 trainers that had cost $5,400 when new could now be ordered, fob, point of storage, in 'as is' condition, and without warranty for as little as $200 in 'need of general repairs throughout,' or $300 in need of 'new fabric and wiring and repairs to landing gear.' Engines were extra; the price of Gnôme 9N rotary engines in 'A' condition was $200 ($75 in 'C' condition) and propellers went for a song, at $2 each.[13]

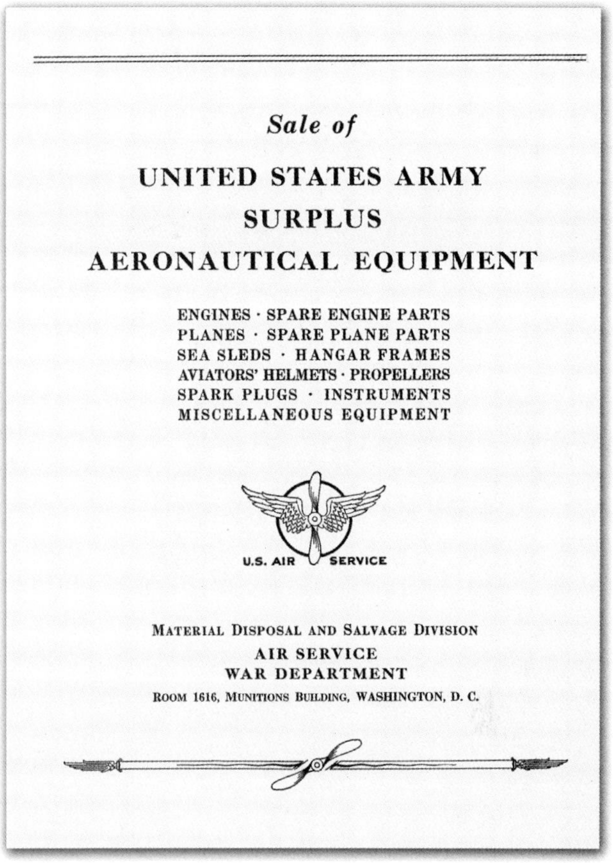

Sale of

UNITED STATES ARMY
SURPLUS
AERONAUTICAL EQUIPMENT

ENGINES · SPARE ENGINE PARTS
PLANES · SPARE PLANE PARTS
SEA SLEDS · HANGAR FRAMES
AVIATORS' HELMETS · PROPELLERS
SPARK PLUGS · INSTRUMENTS
MISCELLANEOUS EQUIPMENT

U.S. AIR SERVICE

MATERIAL DISPOSAL AND SALVAGE DIVISION
AIR SERVICE
WAR DEPARTMENT
ROOM 1616, MUNITIONS BUILDING, WASHINGTON, D. C.

This Air Service War Department catalog listed a fantastic array of surplus airplanes and aeronautical equipment at bargain-basement prices. Bob Repich

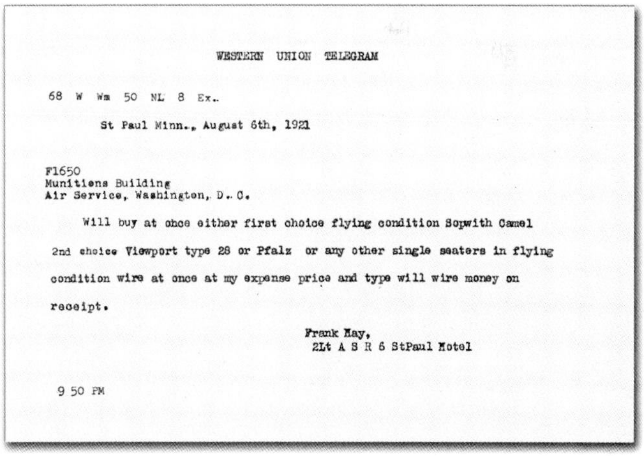

WESTERN UNION TELEGRAM

68 W Wm 50 NL 8 Ex..

St Paul Minn.., August 6th, 1921

F1650
Munitiens Building
Air Service, Washington, D.. C.

Will buy at ohce either first choice flying condition Sopwith Camel 2nd choice Viewport type 28 or Pfalz or any other single seaters in flying condition wire at once at my expense price and type will wire money on receipt.

Frank May,
2Lt A S R 6 StPaul Hotel

9 50 PM

Civilians took full advantage of the "as is, where is" surplus aeronautical material. Failure to inspect was not an allowable condition for rejection of the order once the shipment was made. National Archives

Scouting for the Fleet

In his annual report for 1920 on the state of the U.S. Navy, Secretary Josephus Daniels described some new developments just getting under way in naval aviation:

> Development of ship planes, rugged yet handy, light but dependable; capable of flying from ships, of conveying personnel to observe, and to battle with the enemy, and to assist in controlling the fire of the ship's artillery, is proceeding. Though the operation of such machines is filled with complications, we confidently look forward to the day when aircraft will be transported by all classes of naval vessels. Four battleships of the Atlantic Fleet are each equipped with two flying-off platforms; each ship being supplied with two ship planes. At Guantanamo, the department has proceeded with preparation of a flying field for land planes, and is arranging for the handling at this base of the different types of aircraft operating with the fleet.[14]

The concept of flying light scouting aircraft off of battleship turrets was not new to the U.S. Navy, as they had been monitoring similar operations by the British and French navies since October 1917, when a Sopwith Camel made the first flight from a wooden platform atop a turret of the HMS *Repulse*. In November 1918, the U.S. Navy began experimenting with the use of land planes flying from ships, with platforms being built on the No. 2 and No. 3 turrets of the USS *Texas*.

The *Texas* joined the annual fleet maneuvers in the Caribbean in March 1920. On 9 March 1919, Lieutenant Commander

Edward O. McDonnell, senior pilot of the Ship-Plane Unit, made the first flight off the No. 2 turret of the *Texas,* which was anchored off Guantanamo Bay Naval Base. McDonnell piloted a Sopwith Camel on this momentous occasion. Also aboard the *Texas* was a Sopwith 1 1/2 Strutter, equipped with a radio unit that "used both voice and CW transmission very successfully while conducting gunnery spotting for the *Texas* long range gunnery records."[15] This was the first practical use of voice radio in the U.S. Navy for gunnery spotting. Not long afterward, the USS *Mississippi* joined the fleet at Guantanamo and participated in launching trials of its Hanriot HD-1 fighter.

A second Ship-plane Unit formed in May 1919 and trained in land-plane operation with the Air Service at Langley Field, Virginia. Three months later, this unit was demobilized and the group of budding pilots returned to their ships or other stations and the planes and aviation materiel went to the nearby Naval Air Station Hampton Roads. However, this was a temporary hiatus, for many of these pilots would later reconvene at Carlstrom Field in Arcadia, Florida, when the Atlantic Fleet Ship-Plane Unit was formed there in October.

The Navy pilots were eager to learn from their Air Service counterparts, as this contemporary account of their activities related: "Besides the [Air Service] cadets, there are 16 Naval officers at Carlstrom who are receiving instruction in the operation of army land planes. These officers have taken to land machines like ducks to water. They are busily engaged in combat practice with Nieuport 28's and are given a thorough course of instruction in the operation and manipulation of this type of machine. The Nieuport or a similar type of plane will be the one eventually used by these officers to fly from gun turret platforms or decks of airplane carriers."[16]

The Navy had already decided on the three aircraft types that would equip the Ship-Plane Unit, once the aircraft had been modified for shipboard use at the Naval Aircraft Factory (NAF) in Philadelphia. The three types, all relatively lightweight aircraft, were the Sopwith 1 1/2 Strutter, Sopwith

This 1920 view of the interior of the Naval Aircraft Factory at the Navy Yard in Philadelphia shows seven Nieuport 28As undergoing modification for shipboard use. Note that the fuselage of the closest aircraft is still in wartime French standard camouflage, while all of the other aircraft are in postwar OD (olive drab). All will be repainted in Aluminum Enamel before entering service with the fleet. National Archives

A close-up of the cockpit of an aircraft undergoing modification at the Naval Aircraft Factory. National Archives

The twin air bags on the underside of the cowl, in addition to the air bag contained in the fuselage, would help keep the aircraft afloat if it went into the water. Much depended on full and timely inflation of the air bags. San Diego Air & Space Museum

Camel, and the Nieuport 28A. On 5 January 1920, the director of the Air Service directed the commanding officer at the Aviation General Supply Center, Middletown, Pennsylvania, to deliver twelve Nieuport 28A airplanes and twelve Gnôme 160 hp rotary engines to the NAF.[17] NAF began modifications of the Nieuport 28As, after assigning U.S. Navy Bureau Numbers (5794 to 5805) to the aircraft.

The modifications required for shipboard use were extensive, and also imposed a weight penalty. Each of the Nieuport 28As, in addition to two Marlin machine guns and 250 rounds of ammunition, received a telescopic sight, tachometer, altimeter, a reconnaissance system (radio set), and emergency flotation gear. The latter two systems contributed close to 150 pounds to the aircraft's gross weight of 1,625 pounds.[18] The Camels and 1 1/2 Strutters received essentially the same modifications as the Nieuports.

The water landing and flotation system would prove to be complex and troublesome. A wooden hydrovane, reinforced with fabric and intended to prevent nose-overs, was installed on the landing gear and on the landing skid; it was assumed that the pilot would make a tail-low landing in the water. Three rubberized-fabric air bags were installed, to prevent the aircraft from sinking – two bags on either side of the landing gear under the lower wings and one bag installed in the fuselage closest to the tail to achieve the required buoyancy. Bicycle valves protruded through the fabric, allowing full inflation of the tail bag to be maintained at all times.

Air bottles and a hand pump provided security against slow leaks in the two front air bags. However, the rolled-up bags required two manual operations before they could be properly deployed and inflated: the wheels had to be dropped off first (as the bags could not inflate with the wheels in place) and then the bags would be released, to inflate evenly to a streamlined shape. This procedure did not always work as planned.

Pristine Nieuport 28As, Sopwith Camels and 1 1/2 Strutters emerged from the Naval Aircraft Factory, repainted in postwar U.S. Navy colors: Aluminum Enamel on wings and fuselage, with red, white, and blue vertical stripes of equal width on the rudder, and the traditional national insignia of a white star within a circle emblazoned on the wings. The aircraft were distributed to the Naval Air Station San Diego for the Pacific Fleet (for naval pilots who were then training at March Field), and to the Atlantic Fleet at Hampton Roads, just in time for the fleet's departure for the Caribbean for the 1920 naval maneuvers.

Alfred Melville "Mel" Pride was a twenty-two-year-old reserve lieutenant (junior grade), when he was ordered to Arcadia, Florida, in October 1919 to train on land planes. Lieutenant (junior grade) Pride was one of the pilots who had begun training at Langley Field, and he now rejoined some of his former classmates at Arcadia under the command of Lieu-

A lineup of navy aircraft at San Diego Naval Air Station. Among the aircraft in the center are Nieuport 28As, Sopwith Camels and Sopwith 1 1/2 Strutters of the Pacific Fleet Ship-plane Unit. San Diego Air & Space Museum

Close-up of a Nieuport 28A modified for shipboard operation. San Diego Air & Space Museum

An intrepid group of pilots, many of them members of the navy's Ship-plane Unit. Among them are Lieutenant (junior grade) E.A. Letzkus (at left in upper row), Lieutenant Commander Godfrey de C. Chevalier (middle in upper row), Lieutenant (junior grade) A.M. Pride (second from right in upper row), and Lieutenant (junior grade) Jacob Wolfer, seated in front of Pride. Seated directly in front of Chevalier is Lieutenant Commander Willis Haviland, a former member of the Lafayette Escadrille. This photograph was taken aboard the seaplane tender USS Shawmut. Fred Dickey Jr.

A disassembled Nieuport 28A being hauled up onto the dock at Guantanamo, Cuba, in January 1920. Fred Dickey Jr.

Nieuport 28A and Sopwith 1 1/2 Strutter. Fred Dickey Jr.

Up the bluff to an assembly point on level ground. Fred Dickey Jr.

Nieuport and Sopwith scouts await final assembly. Fred Dickey Jr.

A Nieuport 28A is carefully hoisted aboard. Fred Dickey Jr.

A Sopwith 1 1/2 Strutter is hoisted aboard ship. Note the Nieuport 28A in the foreground; the device atop the Nieuport's upper wing is a generator. Dennis Gordon

The Nieuport 28A is seated atop the USS Arizona's turret No.3. This aircraft is the subject of a color profile in Appendix F. Fred Dickey Jr.

Left: Looking down on the USS Arizona's No.3 turret. This photograph was taken from a tethered kite balloon. Fred Dickey Jr.

Frontal view of a Nieuport 28A atop turret No.3 of the USS Arizona. The hydrovane forward of the landing gear and the twin air bags underneath the cowl are clearly shown. Fred Dickey Jr.

The USS Arizona's Nieuport 28A. Fred Dickey Jr.

Another view of the Arizona's Nieuport 28A. Fred Dickey Jr.

The Arizona's Nieuport 28A scout is secure atop the No.3 turret. The holes in the rear of the fuselage allow access to the air bag within. Fred Dickey Jr.

Lieutenant (junior grade) Alfred "Mel" Pride takes off from the fifty-three-foot platform atop the Arizona's No.3 turret. The time is 9:06 a.m. on 17 March 1920. Pride's engine cut out before he could land ashore, and he was forced to ditch. Pride was rescued by a flying boat and his Nieuport 28 was recovered, but in heavily damaged condition. Fred Dickey Jr.

The fuselage of Mel Pride's Nieuport 28A (ex-N.6461 and BuNo A-5794) is brought aboard the USS Shawmut. The aircraft sustained water and structural damage and was promptly surveyed. Fred Dickey Jr.

Lieutenant (junior grade) Jacob Wolfer attempted a cross-wind takeoff in a Sopwith 1 1/2 Strutter and did not make it, crashing onto the rear deck instead and killing one of the crew. Fred Dickey Jr.

tenant Commander Godfrey de C. Chevalier. Upon completion of his training, Pride, along with Lieutenant (junior grade) Jacob Wolfer, was assigned to the USS *Arizona* just prior to its departure for Guantanamo Bay, Cuba, in January 1920. Joining the *Arizona* were sister ships *Nevada*, *Oklahoma*, and *Pennsylvania*, all equipped with turret-mounted platforms and a complement of planes, pilots, and mechanics.

The principal mission for the Atlantic Fleet Ship-Plane Unit was spotting ship's artillery fall of shot, and scouting was their secondary mission. Fifty-three-foot platforms, approximately twenty feet in width, had been built on the No. 2 turret of each battleship and forty-eight-foot platforms were built on their No. 3 turrets. The heavier Sopwith 1 1/2 Strutters, at a gross weight of 2,283 pounds each, were positioned on the forward high turret and the Nieuport, at 1,625 pounds gross weight, sat atop the rear high turret.[19]

Flight operations commenced when an aircraft began its takeoff roll on the short platform, gaining speed both under its own power and with the assistance of the battleship, which was steaming at top speed with the turret trained into the wind. Prior to takeoff, a sailor stood nearby holding a hand-held anemometer to determine the speed of the wind over the ship's turret – a speed of twenty-two knots was required before the airplane could be safely released – and even then, after it left the platform the airplane was expected to drop precipitously almost to the sea, before slowly gaining altitude.[20] Once safely airborne, the plane would carry out its assigned mission, relaying information on artillery correction by Morse code back to the ship, before flying back to land on the flats west of Guantanamo Bay. The aircraft were then trucked back to the dock and hoisted aboard a lighter for return to their base atop a battleship turret.

Lieutenant (junior grade) Pride related the procedure for a turret takeoff:

> Before being released, the plane's tail was supported in a trough about four feet long and high enough so that the fuselage was level. It was restrained from going forward by a release hook until full power and wind were proper. We tried ordinary pelican hooks at first, but they were erratic and hard to operate and so we made up release hooks of our own in the ship's machine shop, which worked much like a bomb shackle. The turret was trained so that the apparent wind was right down its centerline. With the battleship's slow speed, this usually put the ship almost across the wind for launchings from No. 3 turret. We found from experience, that we had to have at least twenty-two knots of relative wind down the turret, and, at that, we sank until our wheels just cleared the water.[21]

On 17 March 1920, Pride took off from turret No. 3 at 9:06 a.m., and circled for about fifteen minutes above the ships while he worked on the balky radio, finally heading north for Santa Cruz del Sur. At the time, the battleships were engaged in target practice south of the Cuban keys of Jardines de la Reina.

Pride had reached the first of the keys when his Gnôme rotary engine began to cut out. Pride picks up the narrative at this point:

> The Nieuport had been pretty well loaded down with radio and floatation gear which our Navy had added to it, and it was necessary to cut the ignition every few minutes and let the engine 'coast' and cool itself. This I did, but it was not enough and first one, and then others, of the cylinders cut out until there was not enough power to keep the plane flying. I had to land just off the first, or outer keys. There was a little chop, which probably tripped the hydrovane which was supposed to keep the plane from nosing over, it went over slowly but the tail remained awash, and I stayed with it for a while. When this seemed to be getting me nowhere, and it looked like the plane might sink at any moment [Pride had been unable to drop the wheels because of insufficient altitude, and as a consequence the exterior flotation bags could not be fully inflated], I thought about swimming for land. I was sighted from a flying boat, Murphy piloting, which had been sent out to look for me.
>
> They took me aboard and we returned to the SHAWMUT [seaplane tender], which sent a party to recover the plane. They found it still afloat, recovered it and we thought of trying to fix it up, but the immersion had done it no good, and there was some structural damage, and it was not thought worth it. The engine was found to have three of the piston heads burnt through.[22]

Accidents, sometimes caused by pilot error, were frequent and sometimes fatal. In early March, Lieutenant (junior grade) Jacob Wolfer, Pride's fellow pilot aboard the *Arizona*, attempted a flight in a Sopwith 1 1/2 Strutter from the No. 2 turret, as Pride later recalled: "On this particular day, the combination of turret angle and ship's course produced a slight crosswind. Since the plane was so light, it was easily susceptible to such winds. The right wing lifted up a bit, the left wheel rolled off the platform, and the plane bounced off one of the guns of turret one before coming to rest on the forecastle. The crash killed a man on the forecastle, Seaman G. H. Hall, and injured Apprentice Seaman R. T. Blankenship."[23]

On 1 April 1920, Lieutenant (junior grade) Hardendorf, flying a Nieuport off the *Nevada*, got lost and crashed into the water after running out of fuel. His navigation error was attributed to the compass that had been made for wartime patrol planes. Affixed to the Nieuport's cowl close to the rotary engine, "the predictable result was that they spun with the engines." Hardendorf came down in the water one hundred yards from the shore of one of the outlying islands, but he was unable to swim the short distance to shore because of sharks circling his downed Nieuport. After the sharks left the area, Hardendorf managed to get ashore and began constructing a still from his plane's tubing (to distill sea water, as no emergency equipment was provided for the Ship-Plane Units), when he was spotted from the air and rescued.[24]

Lieutenant Eckhout was the only fatality among the unit's complement of pilots. Piloting a Nieuport 28, Eckhout apparently lost control on takeoff from a field at Guantanamo, and crashed.

Ship-plane Unit operations soon came to an end, but pilots continued spotting missions for the fleet during its second cruise. However, this time they flew from a land base at Hacacal Beach, Guantanamo, and operated completely different aircraft than had been flown from the ship turrets. These types included the Vought VE-7, the deHavilland D.H. 4B, and the Loening M-80.

By August 1922, all surviving Nieuport 28A scouts had been stricken from Navy lists or sold to civilians, most of the planes coming from the complement of six Nieuports assigned to the Pacific Fleet (the only known turret-based operations on the West Coast were off the USS *Mississippi*).

The operations of the Ship-plane Units were exciting, risky, and brief, and were undertaken at a time when far more portentous events were about to impact U.S. Naval Aviation. In 1924, trials of airplane catapults aboard ship got under way, and perhaps as a result of these successful tests, the platforms that had been built atop the battleship turrets were finally removed.

Secretary of the Navy Josephus Daniels, after describing the development of ship planes in his 1920 report, briefly mentioned "the former collier *Jupiter* is being converted into an aircraft carrier and will be ready for commissioning during the winter. This craft, renamed the *Langley*, will give the fleet an opportunity to develop the usefulness of vessels of this character."[25] Secretary Daniels had little inkling of what was getting under way, and it would take the "battleship Navy" many years to accept and fully appreciate the immense striking power of this new weapon.

Soon after the dissolution of the Ship-plane Unit, many of its pilots, including Lieutenant (junior grade) Pride, were assigned to the aviation detachment of the USS *Langley* at Hampton Roads. The unit and its mission had been a minor footnote in the history of U.S. Navy operations, and Pride felt that his Naval career took an important turn when he went aboard *CV-1*, the Navy's first flattop.[26] In 1959, Admiral Alfred M. Pride, who had flown a Nieuport 28 off the USS *Arizona*'s No. 3 turret in 1920, retired after a forty-one-year career in naval aviation.

In Swiss Colors

The U.S. 147th Aero Squadron mounted an escort mission very early on the morning of 25 June 1918. Departing Gengoult Aerodrome at 4:30 a.m., the squadron set off approximately 50 miles to the northeast to rendezvous with a single Salmson reconnaissance plane over Lorry at 5:00 a.m. The ensuing mission proved a disaster for the five-man A-Flight, for the

Chevalier, Haviland, and Eckhout. Lieutenant Eckhout was killed not long after this photograph was taken. Fred Dickey Jr.

Eckhout's fatal crash in a Nieuport 28A. Fred Dickey Jr.

The Ship-plane Unit experiment did not last long. The U.S. Navy soon perfected shipboard airplane catapults, and the USS Langley, the first of the navy's long line of aircraft carriers, became operational within a short time. Lieutenant Commander Godfrey de C. Chevalier made the first landing on the Langley. Fred Dickey Jr.

Second Lieutenant James Ashenden, 147th Aero Squadron, seated on the turtle deck of his Nieuport 28 at Toul. Ashenden named his plane "Helen M.", after his fiancée, Helen Mathews. James F. Ashenden Jr.

CHICAGO FLYER INTERNED

Lieut. James Ashenden and his damaged plane in which he was forced to descend in Switzerland.

Knowledge that he has nobly done his part in winning the war must content Lieut. James Ashenden, Chicago aviator, whose air battles came to an end when he was forced to descend in his damaged airplane in Switzerland and was interned by that little spot of neutrality in the maelstrom of warring nations.

The Journal received a picture of the wrecked machine, showing its condition when it landed in Switzerland.

Lieut. Ashenden is the son of Mr. and Mrs. Edward Ashenden, 1323 Albion avenue, and at the time of his misfortune was a member of a French air squadron. He is a graduate of Loyola college and enlisted in the aviation service in June, 1917. He received his preliminary training in Canada and at Fort Worth, Tex., going to France in March of last year. He is 22 years old.

Early last spring the engagement was announced of Lieut. Ashenden and Miss Helen Matthews, daughter of Mr. and Mrs. William Matthews of 1452 Pratt boulevard. They will be married when peace comes and the young airman can be released by his Swiss guardians.

The Chicago Journal reported that Second Lieutenant Ashenden was interned after landing his damaged plane in Switzerland. James F. Ashenden Jr.

Salmson, from French Escadrille N.122, failed to appear – its pilot having determined that the mission was too far over the lines. A-Flight spent thirty fruitless minutes searching for the errant Salmson before deciding to return to Gengoult, but only Lieutenant Thomas Abernethy managed to return safely, although almost out of gas. The rest of A-flight, Lieutenants Charles "Pip" Porter, George Robertson, William Brotherton, and James Ashenden, after evading intense anti-aircraft fire and negotiating a freakish windstorm and heavy cloud cover, crash-landed miles from their base. The result of the abortive mission was one pilot and four Nieuport 28 fighters lost.[27] No enemy aircraft had been sighted.

The lost American pilot was Second Lieutenant James F. Ashenden; Ashenden had inadvertently strayed into Switzerland before crashing at Derendingen, 20 miles north of Bern and 130 miles southwest of his aerodrome at Toul. Second Lieutenant Ashenden was arrested by a Swiss dental unit, as was reported to the chief of staff in Bern: "This morning, an American pilot landed near Derendingen. He was arrested by the Dental care unit [Zahnkrankenkompanie] and was reported to the army physician. We gave orders to transport the pilot here; the plane is being recovered under supervision of an officer from the Jura regional office. Jura states that the pilot flew into heavy fire over Upper Alsace, flew into Switzerland, and was observed over Deleberg."[28]

The American Attaché in Bern arranged Ashenden's repatriation months later, after the chief of staff of the Swiss Armed Forces suggested an exchange with a German pilot officer (Leutnant der Reserve Tatje), who had been interned in Switzerland since 17 June 1917. Second Lieutenant Ashenden subsequently departed Switzerland on 28 November 1918, but his aircraft was retained by the Swiss authorities.[29]

Ashenden's Nieuport 28, serial number N.6212, was new, having been ferried by Second Lieutenant Kenneth Porter from

Second Lieutenant Ashenden's Nieuport 28 in the process of being meticulously rebuilt by the Fliegertruppe (Swiss Air Force). Bergen Hardesty

Colombey-les-Belles to Gengoult Aerodrome on 10 June 1918, only fifteen days before the ill-fated flight. After being assigned the aircraft and re-rigging it, Second Lieutenant Ashenden made several flights to test its flight characteristics and machine guns before flying a fifty-four-minute protection patrol on 18 June. The aircraft had accumulated only five flight hours during its brief time with the 147th Aero Squadron before it crashed in Swiss territory on 25 June 1918.[30]

It would appear that the Swiss Air Force (Fliegertruppe) was the sole beneficiary of A-Flight's abortive mission. Impressed with the modern (by their standards) two-gun Nieuport 28, they promptly began a careful reconstruction of the damaged, low-time, fighter. After being rebuilt, it was painted in Swiss colors and given the Swiss number 607 and the nickname 'Bébé', because it was thought to be a cute design. The aircraft's official Swiss designation was Nieuport-Bébé-Jagdeinsitzer (Nieuport baby, single-seat fighter).

Leutnant Robert Ackermann test-flew the repaired fighter in 1919, and pronounced the Nieuport's control qualities "gut."[31] Ackermann also ably and dramatically demonstrated the Nieuport's handling qualities several years later when he won an aerobatic competition, besting twenty-two competitors from five different countries. The occasion was the First International Flight Meeting, held in 1922 at Dübendorf, Fliegertruppe's first permanent air base.

Without an extensive aeronautical industry of its own, Switzerland relied heavily on foreign aircraft designs, but insisted that its pilots be trained at home. The success of Leutnant Ackermann's feat induced the Fliegertruppe to acquire fourteen more Nieuport 28s from French surplus stocks, to be used as advanced pilot trainers. These aircraft were the unarmed, modified A version of the Nieuport 28, and were still being marketed by Nieuport Astra (so named after Nieuport's merger in 1921 with Société Astra et Compagnie Générale Transaérienne) as late as 1924.[32] Acquired in 1923 and 1924, the new Nieuport 28As, renumbered 685–698, joined the Fliegertruppe's stable of fighters and fighter trainers that included the Fokker D.VII and Hanriot HD-1 (the Swiss Air Force would also hedge its bet during WW II by equipping its fighter force with German Messerschmitt Me-109 and French Morane 405 and 406 fighters). Nieuport Swiss number 607 was upgraded to the standards of the newly received Nieuport 28A fighters, and all became part of the complement of training planes at Thun, an airbase situated 17 miles southeast of Bern.

During Swiss number 607's operational life with the Fliegertruppe, routine maintenance dealt with the usual engine problems and several propellers had to be replaced along the way. However, fuselage stress fatigue was detected in August 1925, and this necessitated retirement of the aircraft. After

Below: Nieuport 28, N.6212, is rebuilt, painted in glossy red, and ready for international aerobatic competition. After a brief but successful career in competition, it entered service as a Fliegertruppe training aircraft, redesignated aircraft number 607, Nieuport "Bébé" (baby), Jagdeinsitzer (single-seat fighter). Bergen Hardesty

Opposite
Top: The Fliegertruppe was pleased with the performance of the Nieuport 28 and acquired fourteen more in 1923 and 1924. This aircraft is number 688 in a range of numbers, 685-698, assigned to the newly acquired aircraft. This aircraft is the subject of a color profile in Appendix F. S.H.A.A. via William Nungesser

Left center: The Fliegertruppe hedged its bet by equipping with both French and German aircraft. Here is a Fokker D.VII fighter in Swiss colors.

Right center: The Fliegertruppe also had French-built Hanriot HD-1s.

Bottom: Here is number 607 during its third career, now in Fliegertruppe colors of the period. This aircraft (N.6212) was upgraded to Nieuport 28A standards. R.L. Cavanagh

688

640

653

607

serving as a static exhibit, number 607 was given long-term storage in a military hangar at Thun, after the airfield there had been deactivated.

The remaining Nieuport 28As soldiered on for a number of years, being used to train pilot cadets and exciting crowds at air displays with demonstrations of aerobatic prowess.

By 1930, the high-time aircraft in the batch had reached 600 flight hours and were stripped in preparation for a total overhaul. Substantial structural damage was revealed, and as a result, all of the surviving Nieuport 28s were decommissioned and put on the block. The principal of Dietikon Trade School near Zurich acquired number 688 for his students at the subsequent sale:

> Mr. Ernst Meier [the principal] announces, that after obtaining consent from the president of the federal airport agency in Dübendorf, he was able to purchase a complete airplane along with several demonstration materials for our school at a very favorable price. Although the plane was in use until very recently, the price, including materials was only 160 Swiss Francs. The trade school had to agree in writing not to use the plane for aviation. Herr Lips [a member of the school board] fully appreciates the worth of this acquisition; however, he voices his wish that in the future, purchases of this kind should be discussed in the school board meeting beforehand. The school board approves the purchase retroactively.[33]

After brief use at the trade school, number 688 spent a thirty-four-year sojourn in several local barns and attics. In 1964, Doctor Dollfuss, an elderly Swiss pilot who had formerly flown the Nieuport 28, rediscovered number 688; he prevailed upon the officials of Dietikon Trade School to have the aircraft restored and put in a place of honor.

Fliegertruppe's Nieuport Bébés were a favorite with the crowd attending military air shows at Dübendorf in the 1920s.

Two examples of the Nieuport 28 are exhibited today in Switzerland's premier aviation museums: number 688 in the Vehrkehrshaus der Schweiz in Lucerne, and number 607, formerly of the American 147th Aero Squadron, in the Fliegermuseum in Dübendorf. Number 607 is the only surviving Nieuport 28 to have seen action in the Great War.

A lineup of Nieuport Bébés at Thun. R.L. Cavanagh

A Swiss pilot is photographed standing next to his Nieuport Bébé trainer. Note the nonstandard, replacement short cowl on his aircraft. R.L. Cavanagh

A cockpit shot of a Swiss Nieuport Bébé trainer, looking down at the foot rests and rudder bar, a portion of the control stick, and the reserve fuel tank, located in the belly. The relocation of the reserve tank from the right of the pilot to the belly of the aircraft was a principal characteristic of the modified Nieuport 28A. Note fuel shutoff valve at lower left.

Below: Number 686, one of fourteen Nieuport Bébé trainers acquired from Nieuport Astra in 1923-1924. R.L. Cavanagh

Fliegertruppe had a clever means of breaking the Nieuport Bébé down for truck transport. R.L. Cavanagh

Swiss pilots and number 698. R.L. Cavanagh

Number 698 is destroyed in a crash. All surviving Swiss Nieuport Bébés were decommissioned in 1930. R.L. Cavanagh

After years of attic and barn storage at the Dietikon Trade School near Zurich, number 688 was restored, and is now on permanent exhibit at the Vehrkehrshaus der Schweiz in Lucerne, Switzerland.

The only surviving Nieuport 28 combat veteran of World War I, Second Lieutenant James Ashenden's N.6212 metamorphosed into a Swiss aerobatic champion, and then served the Fliegertruppe for several years as a training aircraft, number 607. Retired from service in 1925, this historic aircraft is now prominently displayed at the Fliegermuseum in Dübendorf.

Fuerza Aérea Argentina

The genesis of the Fuerza Aérea Argentina (Argentine Air Force) may have been the successful 1907 flight of the balloon, *Pampero*, from Buenos Aires to Las Conchillas in Uruguay.[34] The excitement generated by this international event inspired the establishment of the Argentine Aero Club, which included military personnel among its members.

The Aero Club and the public at large enthusiastically supported the creation of la Escuela de Aviación Militar (the Military Aviation School) in 1912, by funding the purchase of training planes from Europe. The mix of aircraft seemed to reflect the ethnic mix of Argentina itself (and would continue to do so for the next several decades) with the acquisition of French aircraft (including two Nieuports, a Blériot, a Farman, and a Morane-Saulnier Parasol) and a German Taube, subscribed to by the local German community. The Jockey Club funded the purchase of a Santos-Dumont 'Demoiselle.'

The onset of World War I had a severe impact on the Military Aviation School, for new aircraft and technology, as well as spare parts for prewar types, were now unobtainable. Total flights and hours flown dropped significantly as a result, and by 1918 the school's diminished complement of training aircraft were all antiquated.

The high point of 1918, however, was a historic airplane crossing on 13 April of the Andes Mountains by Teniente Luis C. Candelaria. Teniente Candelaria made the 120-mile crossing in a Morane-Saulnier Parasol, reaching an altitude of 13,000 feet and navigating through the lowest passes of Neuquen. Chilean pilots replicated Candelaria's feat in December 1918, and again in April 1919, but each time they crossed the Andes at the most difficult point, the Cordillera Real, between Mendoza and Santiago de Chile. Argentine pilots were now challenged to match the feat of the two Chilean pilots, however they would have to wait until the arrival of newer aircraft before undertaking this risky mission.[35]

The former warring powers wasted no time in sending air missions to South and Central America to dispose of surplus aircraft and equipment. In 1919, Argentine military aviation was rejuvenated as a result of new material obtained from visiting French, Italian, and British air missions. Among the aircraft received from the French mission in early February were two Nieuport 28 fighters (serial numbers N.6338 and N.6339) and one SPAD VII. All three aircraft were believed to have been a gift from the French government. Both Nieuport 28s, which arrived in their wartime camouflage, were subsequently painted, with Argentine national markings added on wings and rudder: N.6338 was designated number 1 and N.6339 was designated number 2. The SPAD VII was painted gray, and being the only one of its type it did not receive a number.

After receiving the sanction of the minister of war, three Argentine pilots, Primer Tenientes Antonio Parodi and Pedro Zanni (who had failed in an earlier solo attempt to make the crossing), and Teniente Benjamin Matienzo, proceeded to Mendoza in May (which is late fall in Argentina) to begin training for the difficult mission. The three pilots had planned to attempt the overflight in a formation of two Nieuport 28s and the SPAD VII, their motto being: "*¡insistir, insistir, hasta cruzar; pero cruzar todos o ninguno!* [Onward, onward, until we cross, but cross all three, or not at all!]." Teniente Matienzo, however, had resolved to press on alone if the others turned back.[36]

An eyewitness remembered the three pilots participating in a military parade shortly before their attempted crossing:

Fuerza Aérea Argentina receives new military aircraft, including two wartime-production Nieuport 28s, from a French mission in 1919. Dirección de Estudios Históricos

Lineup of aircraft at the Military Aviation School at El Palomar, Argentina. Dirección de Estudios Históricos

Bearing Argentine national colors, but with the sun not yet painted on the tail, this Nieuport 28 still sports wartime-standard French camouflage. Both Nieuport 28s supplied to the Fuerza Aérea Argentina were equipped with ailerons on the top and bottom wings. These aircraft had obviously been part of a Nieuport test project to improve the roll efficiency of the aircraft. Pushrods (seen directly behind the interplane struts), which were connected to the lower ailerons, activated the upper ailerons. This aircraft is the subject of a color profile in Appendix F. Dirección de Estudios Históricos

Another photograph of a Nieuport 28 at El Palomar. This shot clearly shows the pushrod arrangement and the slight droop of the portside set of ailerons. Both Nieuport 28s were likely modified for tests undertaken in mid-1918 to improve roll moment. This was part of the ongoing refinement of the design of the Nieuport 29, which culminated in short-chord, long-span ailerons on the lower wings only. Dirección de Estudios Históricos

"That year, there were three new participants in the parade who crossed over our provincial capital [Mendoza] every day. Part of their flight was made in formation, while the other part consisted in their making individual passes at different altitudes. We ended up being able to recognize them even without seeing them. Parodi's Nieuport usually went by practically grazing the roofs of the rather low buildings. At a midway altitude, between 700 and 1,000 meters, Matienzo would pass by with the other Nieuport, the red no. 1. [Matienzo's plane had purportedly been repainted red by this time, in preparation for the record flight.] And at a higher altitude, although very close to that of Matienzo's plane, Zanni's gray SPAD would pass by. The SPAD's engine made a very different sound from the other two planes."[37]

Argentine Nieuport 28 with other aircraft at El Palomar. Fernando Benedetto via Dan Hagedorn

The prospects for a successful crossing at the Cordillera Real were harrowing; the pilots made a number of attempts, but continued to encounter high winds blowing against them as they reached higher altitudes. They were not deterred from attempting a final flight, however: Departing Los Tamarindos airport on 28 May 1919, the planes "formed a closed 'V' pattern as they made toward Chile, flying at an altitude of roughly 2,000 meters over the city of Mendoza. As they made their way toward the Cordillera over the Rio Mendoza Valley, they had already reached 5,000 meters and the intensity of the wind was such that the planes practically made no forward progress. Parodi was the first to call off the flight, who, after thirty-four minutes from when he took off, landed back at Los Tamarindos. Zanni followed him, landing one hour and twenty-nine minutes after having taken off."[38] Matienzo, true to his word, continued the flight; he was observed for a brief time from Punta de Vaca and Punta del Inca before disappearing from view.

Teniente Benjamin Matienzo's body was found six months later in a mountain valley – that now bears his name – at an altitude of 4,000 meters. It was later ascertained that he had survived the crash of his Nieuport 28 after it ran out of fuel. Attempting to walk through heavy snow towards the village of Las Cuevas, he had succumbed to exposure, not knowing that a miner's camp stocked with provisions was only 300 meters away. Teniente Matienzo's body was returned home, where he was given a funeral worthy of a great hero.[39]

The following year, now-Capitán Antonio Parodi, flying a S.V.A. 5, made a double, non-stop crossing of the Cordillera. Parodi and Zanni were later lauded for their epic feats, in a manner that clearly conveyed the reverence in which these early aviation pioneers were held:

Here we are all gathered together, all of Buenos Aires, with open arms to receive this triumphal pair of

Teniente Benjamin Matienzo, piloting Nieuport 28, N.6338, made a valiant attempt to cross the Andes in May 1919.

A recovery team collected Teniente Matienzo's body six months after he succumbed to exposure. His body was found at an altitude of 4,000 meters. Teniente Benjamin Matienzo was given a hero's state funeral in Buenos Áires.

Wrecked engine and landing gear of Teniente Matienzo's Nieuport 28, collected from the crash site thirty-one years later.

Captains, who have returned as if painted with the blue of the sky and the Argentine flag, as they say, and whose aviator jackets even appear to shine with a new light, as if these men had touched the very heavens with the crests of their kepis ...

How full these young men's eyes must be with the sight of the greatness they have seen! They saw beneath them, from the vantage point of those temperamental beasts that they piloted, the line of the eternally snow-crested peaks, raised there by some primeval explosion of whiteness, as if they desired to paint the white stripe of our beloved flag on the firmament; they have seen, in a small corner still warm from the martyrdom it witnessed in spite of the surrounding snow and ice, the tragic spot where Matienzo had taken his last breath, alone in the immensity, with his face turned toward the heavens and pecked by the condors, whether because those birds saw in him a rival of the sky or as an object of prey... . They also have seen, over the crest of the mountain which that warrior of the stars, Almonacid, would later cross in the middle of the night, the future path by which our own army would one day fill the valleys with liberty.[40]

Nieuport 28, N.6339, remained at la Escuela de Aviación Militar until transferred in 1924 to Air Group 1. The airplane was retired from service two years later, when it became impossible to maintain.

In February 1950, almost thirty-one years after Teniente Matienzo crashed in the Andes, the remains of his Nieuport 28, N.6338, were recovered from a slope on the Cordillera Real. The few components that survived the harsh elements are now on permanent display in a place of honor in the Museo Nacional de Aeronáutica in Buenos Aires.

IN CIVILIAN HANDS

Barnstorming and Airshows

Southern California was a mecca for aviation enthusiasts throughout much of the 1920s; flying weather was glorious and small airfields dotted Los Angeles, Riverside, and Orange counties at a time when urban sprawl was only just beginning to encroach.

Interest in aviation was at its peak during the decade, and people flocked to local grass fields to watch Earl Daugherty, Emery Rogers, Eddie Martin, and others compete in air races and perform aerobatics, parachute jumps, wing walking, and other exciting feats. Aerial services in the area were widely available for flight instruction, aircraft sales and service, aerial surveying, and photography. A budding aviation and motion picture industry would solidify the area's preeminence in aviation activities and draw national attention to it.

The proximity of military and naval airfields at March Field in Riverside and San Diego Naval Air Station, ninety miles due south, added immeasurably to the local civilian aviation scene. Many Curtiss JN-4D "Jennies", "Tommy Morse" Scouts, S.E. 5s, SPADs, deHavilland D.H. 4s, and even Fokker D.VIIs, formerly in military hands, soon found civilian pilots at the controls. Among the aircraft types disposed of not long after the war were a small number of Nieuport 28A trainers.

According to U.S. Navy Aircraft Records, only six of the original twelve Navy Nieuport 28As survived the rigors of active operations, and these were stricken from the records before being offered for sale to the public. Earl S. Daugherty, a Long Beach flight school operator, bought one (USN Bureau Number 5805) from the sale at San Diego Naval Air Station in August 1921, and Emery Rogers bought two (Bureau Numbers 5801 and 5804) at the same sale. Earle Ovington also purchased a Nieuport 28 trainer, possibly one of the aircraft sold at March Field around the same time.[1] All surviving Nieuport 28 trainers were now being disposed of around the country, for the brief postwar U.S. military career of the Nieuport 28A had come to an end.

Twenty-four-year-old Earl S. Daugherty received Aero Club F.A.I. license number 87 in 1911, after instruction on a Curtiss pusher. Prior to America's entry into World War I, Daugherty flew as an exhibition pilot in the Midwest before returning to southern California. After wartime service as a flight instructor at March Field, Daugherty established "Chateau-Thierry" Airport at Long Beach. By 1925, Daugherty had moved to a larger, twenty-acre field nearby, where he operated twelve aircraft while doing business as the Earl S. Daugherty School of Aviation.

Daugherty and his Nieuport 28 were a familiar sight at air races and air meets in the Los Angeles area. The Air Rodeo at Pasadena in December 1921 featured a five-lap race between Daugherty and Bert Creeth, both flying Nieuport 28s (Creeth's Nieuport belonged to Emery Rogers), and two other pilots flying Catron and Fisk triplanes. Among the exhibitors at the event was twenty-four-year-old Amelia Earhart, who had taken her first flying lesson in January. Earhart's secondhand Kinner "Airster" was entered in the Pacific Coast Ladies Derby. A double wing-walking exhibition also featured a parachute jump by "Fearless Freddie," with a "parachute furnished and packed by Ed Unger."[2]

The dedication of Clover Field on 15 April 1923 drew Chief of the Air Service Major General Mason M. Patrick and every available airplane in Southern California.

The Memorial Day Air Meet at Long Beach Municipal in 1925 drew many of the area pilots, including Daugherty, and attracted over 25,000 spectators. Earl Daugherty was tragically killed three years later, when the wing of his Laird biplane collapsed; Daugherty was remembered in the area for many years after his death as the "Earl of Long Beach."[3]

Emery H. Rogers returned to the Los Angeles area after commanding flight operations at Souther Field in Americus, Georgia, during the war. Rogers briefly operated a small airline in partnership with Sydney Chaplin, brother of comic actor Charlie Chaplin, but ended the business relationship after a

Earl S. Daugherty's School of Aviation at Chateau-Thierry Airport in Long Beach, California. Daugherty stands at left, in front of the tail of his Standard J-1. David Hatfield Collection at the Museum of Flight

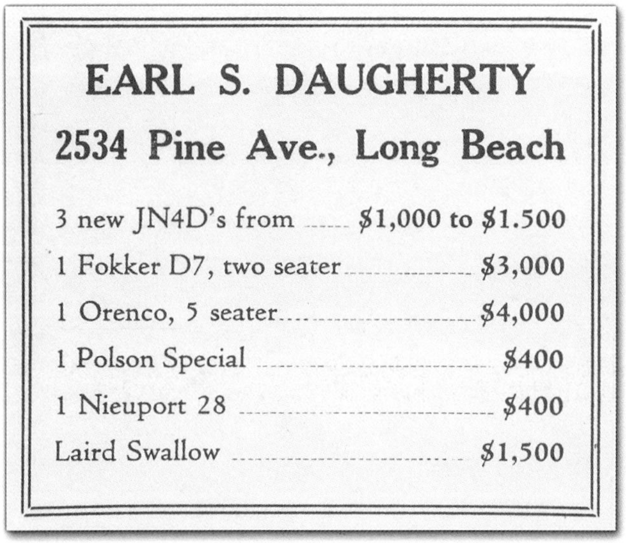

EARL S. DAUGHERTY

2534 Pine Ave., Long Beach

3 new JN4D's from	$1,000 to $1.500
1 Fokker D7, two seater	$3,000
1 Orenco, 5 seater	$4,000
1 Polson Special	$400
1 Nieuport 28	$400
Laird Swallow	$1,500

Daugherty's advertisement in Western Flying Magazine. Western Flying Magazine

Daugherty and his Nieuport 28 in flight. Note that his aircraft has full-span wings. Peter Bowers

Earl Daugherty favored his Nieuport 28 as a backdrop for his Christmas cards. Frank Kirkman

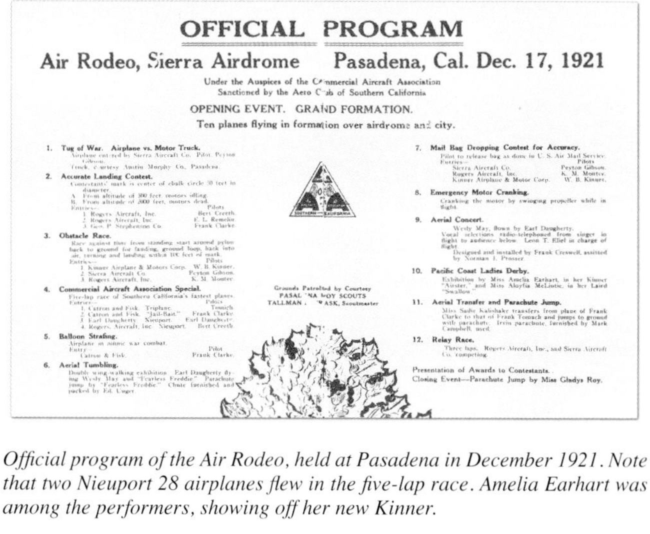

OFFICIAL PROGRAM

Air Rodeo, Sierra Airdrome Pasadena, Cal. Dec. 17, 1921

Under the Auspices of the Commercial Aircraft Association
Sanctioned by the Aero Club of Southern California

OPENING EVENT. GRAND FORMATION.
Ten planes flying in formation over airdrome and city.

1. **Tug of War. Airplane vs. Motor Truck.**
2. **Accurate Landing Contest.**
3. **Obstacle Race.**
4. **Commercial Aircraft Association Special.** Five-lap race of Southern California's fastest planes.
5. **Balloon Strafing.**
6. **Aerial Tumbling.**
7. **Mail Bag Dropping Contest for Accuracy.**
8. **Emergency Motor Cranking.**
9. **Aerial Concert.**
10. **Pacific Coast Ladies Derby.** Exhibition by Miss Amelia Earhart, in her Kinner "Airster," and Miss Aloyfia McLintic, in her Laird "Swallow."
11. **Aerial Transfer and Parachute Jump.**
12. **Relay Race.**

Presentation of Awards to Contestants.
Closing Event—Parachute Jump by Miss Gladys Roy.

Grounds Patrolled by Courtesy
PASADENA BOY SCOUTS

Official program of the Air Rodeo, held at Pasadena in December 1921. Note that two Nieuport 28 airplanes flew in the five-lap race. Amelia Earhart was among the performers, showing off her new Kinner.

disagreement. Rogers subsequently took over Chaplin Field (located on Wilshire Boulevard in Los Angeles), changed the name to Rogers Airport, and began operating an aviation sales and manufacturing business on the site.

Rogers supplemented his fleet of Standard J-1 trainers with the acquisition of two ex-Navy Nieuport 28As in August 1921. Rogers, now piloting one of his speedy Nieuports, challenged another pilot to a pylon race, the other pilot flying a monoplane based at DeMille Field (owned by Cecil B. DeMille), across Wiltshire Boulevard. Rogers triumphed in successive races, until he suggested to the losing pilot that he would exchange planes and still come out on top.[4] This proved to be a fatal mistake; Rogers was killed when he apparently blacked out on a turn and crashed his opponent's monoplane. After his death on 27 November 1921, Emery Rogers' widow continued to operate Rogers Airport for several years, before selling out to developers.

Aviation pioneer and airmail pilot Earle L. Ovington (credited with making the first U.S. airmail flight on 11 September 1911) purchased a surplus Nieuport 28A. Ovington was Commodore of the Santa Barbara Aero Club and flew from Las Turas Lake Airport. The grand opening of Las Turas Airport in June 1924 drew over fifty airplanes and pilots from the Los Angeles and Santa Barbara areas. Ovington later sold his Nieuport 28A to airplane pilot and designer Joe York of Long Beach.

Joe York kept his Nieuport 28A at Earl Daugherty's field in Long Beach. His Nieuport got an unintended makeover when the airplane was involved in a freakish accident.

York had his airplane parked in the street while he worked on the engine. A storage battery, placed temporarily on the top wing, provided ignition in place of the magnetos. After starting, the engine went flat out, and promptly jumped the chocks and sped down the street before crashing and badly damaging one wing tip. Rather than rebuild the wing tip, York reduced the span of each wing by two feet and three inches and put in I-struts, which made the ship quite a bit faster and more solid. The airplane could fly up to 155 mph, and for the next three years was believed to be the fastest civilian plane on the West

Top left: Winning pilots and parachutists at the Memorial Day 1925 Air Meet in Long Beach include (from left to right): E.C. Davis, Ray Freeman, Art Goebel, Earl Daugherty, Jack Frye, Eddie Martin, and W.B. Kinner. David Hatfield Collection at the Museum of Flight

Above: Emery Rogers and Jim Webster in front of Rogers' Standard J-1. Rogers bought two Nieuport 28As from the U.S. Navy in 1921. David Hatfield Collection at the Museum of Flight

Below: The dedication of Clover Field in 1923 drew airplanes from all over Southern California.

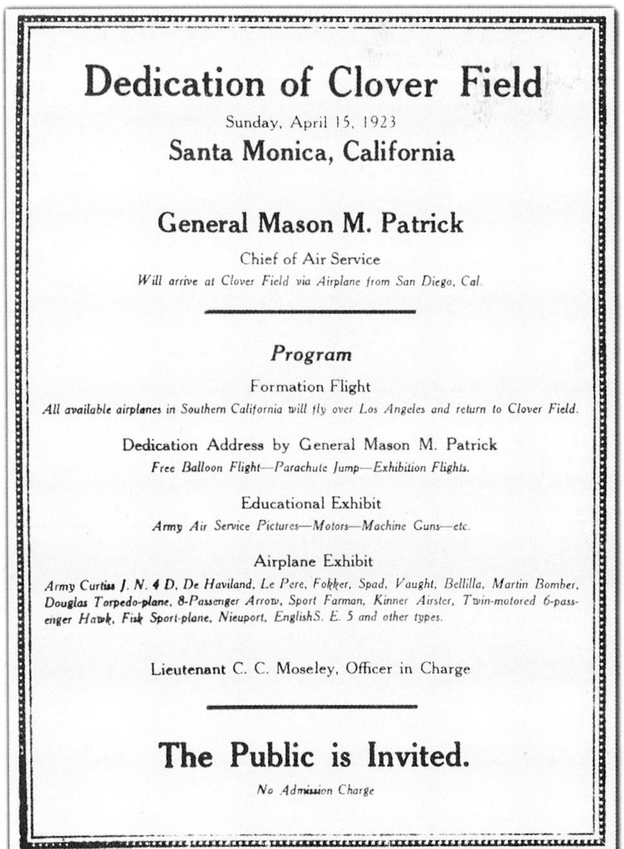

Dedication of Clover Field

Sunday, April 15, 1923

Santa Monica, California

General Mason M. Patrick

Chief of Air Service

Will arrive at Clover Field via Airplane from San Diego, Cal.

Program

Formation Flight

All available airplanes in Southern California will fly over Los Angeles and return to Clover Field.

Dedication Address by General Mason M. Patrick

Free Balloon Flight—Parachute Jump—Exhibition Flights.

Educational Exhibit

Army Air Service Pictures—Motors—Machine Guns—etc.

Airplane Exhibit

Army Curtiss J. N. 4 D, De Haviland, Le Pere, Fokker, Spad, Vaught, Bellilla, Martin Bomber, Douglas Torpedo-plane, 8-Passenger Arrow, Sport Farman, Kinner Airster, Twin-motored 6-passenger Hawk, Fisk Sport-plane, Nieuport, EnglishS. E. 5 and other types.

Lieutenant C. C. Moseley, Officer in Charge

The Public is Invited.

No Admission Charge

Coast. Enamored of the modified Nieuport 28's performance, York's friend Eddie Martin purchased the clipped-wing Nieuport for $650, later stating, "it was a beautiful ship and I just had to have it."[5]

Right: Aviation pioneer and airmail pilot Earle Ovington.

Below: Eddie Martin's advertisement in Western Flying Magazine.

Bottom: Eddie Martin with his beloved clipped-wing Nieuport 28A. Vi Smith, author of From Jennies to Jets: The Aviation History of Orange County

Eddie Martin had received flight training in a Standard J-1 purchased from Emery Rogers. He and his brother, John, later organized a business in Santa Ana, offering flight instruction, sales, and service, and advertising an established reputation for service and good workmanship. Eddie drew crowds to his Sunday air shows while flying his favorite airplane:

> Whenever I wanted to get a crowd out to the airport, I'd wait until Sunday church services were getting out and I'd fire up the Nieuport. You could hear it for at least 10 miles when it was just on the ground. Once you got it in the air, you could be heard for at least 15 miles, especially in those days when everything was so wide open. The rotary engine was a two-cycle affair so it was pretty noisy anyway plus you had that exhaust coming out of the bottom of the cowling. I would fly over town and do a few stunts and go back toward the airport. Pretty soon, there was a string of cars heading toward the airport to see what was going on. I tell you that plane was my pride and joy all the time I had it. Even today, looking at a photo of it does something to me.[6]

Eddie Martin and his modified Nieuport 28A were invited to Clover Field in 1928 to honor the "Round the World" U.S. Army flyers. The California Air National Guard patrons were interested in offering the public a comparison between the Nieuport 28 of 1918 and the newest Curtiss Hawk fighter, and Eddie Martin was the only civilian pilot to participate. Martin put on a stunning exhibition: "On takeoff, I held it just off the ground surface until the end of the runway then pulled the stick back. When I was about 20 feet in the air, I did two snap climbing rolls. I figured after that, that even C.C. Moseley, who was the big boss at Western Air Express and also head of the Air National Guard, would have to admit that I could fly pretty darn well."[7]

Eddie Martin rebuilt the tail assembly after discovering structural problems during a major inspection. He sold his cherished Nieuport 28A in the early 1930s, reportedly to a young flier in Pomona, California.

The Barnstorming Era waned across the country as the 1920s drew to a close. Most of the once plentiful and inexpensive military-surplus aircraft had been junked or were sitting idle in need of spare parts. Federal regulations now governed the maturing aviation industry: the Air Commerce Act, passed in 1927, regulated interstate air traffic, required federal examination and licensing of pilots, and mandated air safety, including the wearing of parachutes by stunt pilots. Airplanes were now familiar sights around the country and the public was being stimulated by far more spectacular achievements in aviation, such as Charles Lindbergh's epic crossing of the Atlantic Ocean.

Southern California experienced rampant growth during this period and the small airfields that once dotted the area were being sold off to developers. Army pilots at Clover Field complained that "golf links, tennis courts, archery ranges, picnic grounds and wading pools" were chipping away at the field's boundaries and making the field unsafe.[8] Brigadier General James Fechet, assistant chief of the Air Corps, ground looped at Clover Field and ended up in a bunker on an adjoining golf course. Furious, Fechet demanded that the bunker be removed or the Army would vacate the field. The City of Santa Monica removed the bunker, but Clover Field's days as an Air Corps base were numbered.

Ironically, famed pilot turned developer Earle Ovington contributed to the problem. Ovington bragged to a friend, "Things have gone wonderfully for me. My subdivision was a great success. Lots that I sold for $1,295 are now $2,195 and some higher. Fine homes are going up on my Casa Loma and it is acknowledged one of highest class residential sections in the city."[9]

Several factors, however, would sustain Southern California's preeminence in aviation activities for decades to come. These factors included the burgeoning aircraft industry, the unchanging gentle weather … and the movies.

The Hollywood Years

Early in 1930, First National Properties Inc. contracted with Garland Lincoln to provide a Nieuport 28 (registered as 2538, but more likely 2539) and "2 others not as yet identified" for the film production of *The Dawn Patrol*.[10] Lincoln, a movie stunt pilot, had assembled a small group of original World War I airplanes in anticipation of their use in this film.

Eddie Martin and his Nieuport 28A in flight. "Once you got it in the air, you could be heard for at least 15 miles"; it was a great way for gathering the crowds after Sunday church services." Ray Folsom

The Dawn Patrol was based on a short story entitled *Flight Commander,* by former Rhodes Scholar and World War I pilot John Monk Saunders. Saunders had also written the story for the 1927 production *Wings,* the first movie – and the only silent film – to win a "Best Picture" Oscar. He would win another Oscar several years later for *The Dawn Patrol*, and continued his association as story or screenplay writer for many of the aviation films that followed in the 1930s.

Garland Lincoln's contract with First National called for his airplanes to be delivered to the "English Field Location," a British airfield set constructed at Triunfo, near Thousand Oaks, California, by 30 March 1930. Lincoln's three Nieuport 28s would command $45 per hour while the engines were running, or $30 per day if the engines were not run. The studio had the right to "alter, paint and/or decorate said airplane so that it may resemble and represent airplanes of a type similar to those used in warfare in accordance with the story upon

Garland Lincoln's collection of original military aircraft met the needs of Hollywood studios, in quest of authenticity for films portraying World War I aerial combat. Lincoln had been employed as a pilot by Howard Hughes during the filming of the 1930 production of Hell's Angels. Academy of Motion Picture Arts and Sciences

which the photoplay, *The Dawn Patrol,* is based."[11] This latter clause reflected Director Howard Hawks' objective of reproducing "with the utmost attainable authenticity, the actual conditions of air warfare between the British and German flying services."[12] Hawks's quest for authenticity resulted in an intensive search for guns, uniforms, and equipment, including combat airplanes, that would have been found on the Western Front in 1915. This may well have been the principal business motivation for Garland Lincoln to collect and maintain examples of rapidly diminishing numbers of original World War I airplanes.

Garland Lincoln's aviation experience predated World War I. At age twelve, Lincoln was assisting pioneer aviators like Lincoln Beachey at Ascot and Dominguez Field near Los Angeles. On 22 March 1918, Signal Corps cadet Lincoln soloed a Curtiss JN at North Island near San Diego, later serving as a flight instructor after receiving his wings. After discharge from military service, Lincoln held myriad aviation jobs in the Southern California area: as a pilot for Cecil B. DeMille, and as a barnstormer, aerial surveyor, flight instructor, designer and builder of several aircraft, corporate pilot, and chief test pilot for Joseph Kreutzer, Los Angeles-based manufacturer of the six-place, tri-motor "Air Coach." In 1928, Garland Lincoln found his real calling when he signed on to fly for Howard Hughes in his production of *Hell's Angels*. This assignment would employ Lincoln for two years and seven months.

Inspired by the epic *Wings,* Howard Hughes resolved to create an even more spectacular film. His insistence on verity and dramatic effect in aerial combat scenes proved costly in terms of time and money (over twice the $2 million cost and production time of *Wings*), crashed airplanes, and three lives lost. Hughes was also obliged to reshoot much of the film in order to make it a "talking picture." But in the end, Hughes succeeded gloriously; nearly 1.3 million people mobbed Hollywood Boulevard on 27 May 1930, to watch the celebrities arriving for *Hell's Angels* premiere at Grauman's Chinese Theater. The film grossed well over $7 million, gaining a substantial profit for Hughes' risky venture.

Hell's Angels premiered just as shooting for *The Dawn Patrol* was getting under way. Garland Lincoln had assembled three Nieuport 28s and a Swallow, and all four aircraft were to serve as part of the British squadron featured in the film. The Nieuport 28s served principally as static displays, with occasional engine run-ups, taxiing, and one takeoff shot. Other aircraft, such as disguised Travel Airs (which flew for both sides in the air fighting sequences), Thomas-Morse S4C Scouts, and Standard J-1s, were used during the filming. Jennies and Canucks were employed as German types, in addition to several Pfalz D.XIIs, all of which remained on the ground.

The Dawn Patrol premiered at the Winter Garden Theater in July 1930, receiving critical acclaim for its dramatic portrayal of combat stress and the authenticity that Hawks had

Garland Lincoln's Nieuport 28s were featured as static displays and in flying sequences in the 1930 film production of The Dawn Patrol. Richard Allen

sought and brilliantly achieved. The film, a financial success, influenced many aviation films that followed. (Howard Hughes had tried and failed to stop its production, rightly fearing competition with *Hell's Angels*.)

The following year, the Fox Film Corporation made *Heartbreak,* a film featuring air combat on the Italian front with a slight variation on the standard love-triangle plot: American pilot (Charles Farrell), falls in love with an Austrian countess (Madge Evans), shortly before killing her brother in aerial combat. Fox contracted for Garland Lincoln's three Nieuport 28s and referenced the aircraft's registration numbers as 2539, 10415, and 75W. These registration numbers, assigned by the Aeronautics Branch of the U.S. Department of Commerce, bore no correlation to the aircraft's original French serial numbers. This made it difficult, but not impossible, to determine at least part of the chain of ownership for each of Lincoln's three Nieuport 28s.

Garland Lincoln's Nieuport 28, registered as 2539 and intended "for motion picture work," was purchased from Rogers Aircraft Inc. on 18 December 1929. This aircraft

Above: Front view of a modified Nieuport 28, with clipped wings, N-struts, and a Thomas-Morse cowl. This particular Nieuport 28 was given the registration number 2539; it was one of three Nieuport 28s that Garland Lincoln provided for the filming of The Dawn Patrol in 1930. H. Hugh Wynne Below: Side view of Number 2539. Note the ill-fitting Thomas-Morse cowl. H. Hugh Wynne

Another of Lincoln's Nieuport 28s, fitted with a Thomas-Morse cowl. This aircraft also appeared in the 1930 film production of The Dawn Patrol. Lincoln purchased this aircraft from Johnny Vickers in 1929. Gordon Williams Collection at the Museum of Flight

Lincoln's third Nieuport 28, with I-struts and the unattractive Thomas-Morse cowl. H. Hugh Wynne

Garland and Pauline Lincoln (at left and center) with a Union Oil representative and Lincoln's stable of rental aircraft, at Metropolitan Airport in Van Nuys, California. H. Hugh Wynne

was very likely one of the two Nieuport 28As that the late Emery Rogers had acquired from the U.S. Navy in August 1921. Records show that Rogers had installed a 110 hp Le Rhône rotary engine, and that the aircraft was later used for skywriting and "smoke and cloud effects" for movies in the late 1920s.[13] Lincoln reinstalled a 160 hp Gnôme engine, standard for the Nieuport 28, in January 1930.

Johnny Vickers of Pomona, California, sold his Nieuport 28 to Garland Lincoln on 23 December 1929. Lincoln's registration application on 3 February 1930 noted that the airplane had a new motor installed and was intended for moving picture work at Howard Hughes' Caddo Pictures Corporation. This aircraft, initially registered as 10415, received a restricted airplane license (R10415) and was approved only for a "specially designated purpose," in this case, "motion picture work".[14]

Lincoln purchased a third Nieuport 28 on 5 February 1930 from Ivan R. "Ole" Olsen, who guaranteed that the property was "clear of all debt" and offered "as is."[15] Olsen's bill of sale noted that the ship consisted of "Nieuport fuselage, landing gear and motor, 3 wings, uncovered and a fourth wing, not complete, 1 pr. wheels, tires and tubes, miscellaneous motor parts and control surfaces complete."[16] After rebuilding the aircraft and substituting a 160 hp Gnôme for the 110 hp Le Rhône that Olsen had installed, Lincoln's reconstituted Nieuport 28 received registration number 75W on 4 April 1930.

Although the planes were used primarily as static displays, Garland Lincoln was increasingly concerned with the wear and tear on his trio of Nieuport 28s; a taxiing accident during the filming of *The Dawn Patrol* had upended one of them, after it ran into a gopher hole. Torn between preserving his small fleet of valuable aircraft on the ground and supplying the film industry with authentic aircraft for aerial work, Lincoln decided to design and build replicas of the Nieuport 28 that could take the stresses of aerial combat scenes.

Lincoln's first replica Nieuport 28 was completed in 1932, and duly named the LF 1 or "Lincoln Fighter 1." The aircraft bore an external resemblance to the wartime Nieuport 28, but there were significant design differences, evidence of both Lincoln's skill as a aircraft designer and of his quest for a high performing and safe aircraft. LF 1 had a steel tube fuselage, N-struts, one-piece upper wing with no dihedral, and ailerons across most of the full trailing edge of the lower wings. Powered by a Gnôme rotary engine (the distinctive sound of the rotary engine could hardly be simulated), LF 1 was restricted to stunting and movie work, and registered as NR 12237.[17]

LF 2, built in 1935, incorporated some further improvements such as a fixed pitch Hamilton steel propeller and a Wright J-4-B radial engine and fuel injection system. Lincoln claimed a top speed of over 200 mph and a docile landing speed of only 58 mph for this aircraft. LF 2 was registered as R75W.[18]

Above: Garland Lincoln's LF 1 – Lincoln Fighter 1 – resembled the Nieuport 28 and undertook the flying sequences when the aging Nieuports were relegated to static display. Fitted with what appears to be an original Nieuport 28 cowl, LF 1 has an authentic appearance. H. Hugh Wynne

Right: Actor Richard Dix, festooned like a bandit, stands in front of Lincoln's LF 1 in a promotional photograph for the film Ace of Aces. H. Hugh Wynne

Right: Another view of Lincoln's LF 1. David Ostrowski

Richard Allen

Richard Allen

A promotional shot for Paramount's The Eagle and the Hawk. H. Hugh Wynne

Rob Krehbiel remembers helping build LF 3 in 1937–38, as a student at Curtiss-Wright Tech in Glendale, California, Garland Lincoln's hometown. Students and faculty at the school built the fuselage, empennage, landing gear, engine mount and other parts, but Lincoln, as Krehbiel recalled, "built the wings in his living room."[19] LF 3 was also powered by a Wright J-4-B engine. The registration number of this aircraft and its subsequent history are unknown, although it was quite likely intended for movie work and stunting like its sister ships.

Fox Film Corporation contracted with Garland Lincoln once again to supply airplanes for the 1934 production, *Hell in the Heavens* starring Warner Baxter as a British flyer. Baxter's love interest was played by Conchita Montenegro, with Arno Frey as the fearsome German baron.

Lincoln's company, Garland Lincoln Air Service, supplied four Nieuport 28s, five Travel Airs and one "Baby" Travel Air (equipped with a 110 hp Warner Scarab engine), three Wacos, a Liberty-powered D.H. 9, and Lincoln's LF 1. In addition to his air fleet, Lincoln furnished four pilot/actors, mechanics, and arranged for insurance to cover all contingencies. Lincoln's pilots would receive $66 per week plus $50 per hour of flying time.[20] A question remains as to where Lincoln acquired his fourth Nieuport 28, listed as Nieuport #4 on the contract. In any case, all four Nieuport 28s were to be used as static displays, with only LF 1 engaged in actual aerial filming, along with the other types of aircraft listed. Before filming began in August, Lincoln declared that two of his airplanes (2539 and 75W) had been salvaged, and federal registrations had subsequently been cancelled for both aircraft. (This may explain how Lincoln was able to obtain a similar registration – R75W – for his second LF, which would be completed the following year.)

Hell in the Heavens may have been the peak of Garland Lincoln's business activity as a supplier of aircraft to the movie industry, for another young, aggressive, and skilled pilot-businessman appeared on the scene – his name was Paul Mantz.

Albert Paul Mantz was born in 1903 in Alameda, California, several blocks from where his close friend Jimmy Doolittle had grown up. Paul took his first flying lesson shortly after the end of World War I, and in 1927 he joined the U.S. Army Air Corps as a flying cadet at March Field near Los Angeles. While Mantz's Army flight instructors recognized his exceptional flying skills, his Army career abruptly ended one day before graduation, when Mantz was discharged as a result of a "buzz job" on a train and nearby railroad station crowded with passengers waiting to board. Heeding advice from his flight instructor to find his future in commercial

Several of Lincoln's Nieuport 28s appear in this shot, on location for Fox's 1934 production of Hell in the Heavens*. The Nieuport 28 in the foreground has an unorthodox tail. H. Hugh Wynne*

Above: Garland Lincoln's LF 1 did the flying sequences for Hell in the Heavens. H. Hugh Wynne Below: The studio's attempt at re-creating an authentic World War I aerodrome. California mountains appear in the background in this location at Triunfo, near Thousand Oaks, where many of the aviation films were shot during the 1930s. H. Hugh Wynne

Above: Another view of Lincoln's stable of aircraft, assembled for Hell in the Heavens. H. Hugh Wynne Below: One of Lincoln's Nieuports appears in this photograph, along with his D.H. 9, parked in front of the hangar. Two Waco Fs and an Orenco are seen in the background. H. Hugh Wynne

Above: Cast members and crew of Hell in the Heavens pose for the still camera. H. Hugh Wynne Below: Ted Parsons, former member of the Lafayette Escadrille (in German uniform, center), looks at Warner Baxter, star of the film Hell in the Heavens. Lincoln's I-strut Nieuport 28 is in the background. Garland Lincoln, in French uniform, stands second from right. H. Hugh Wynne

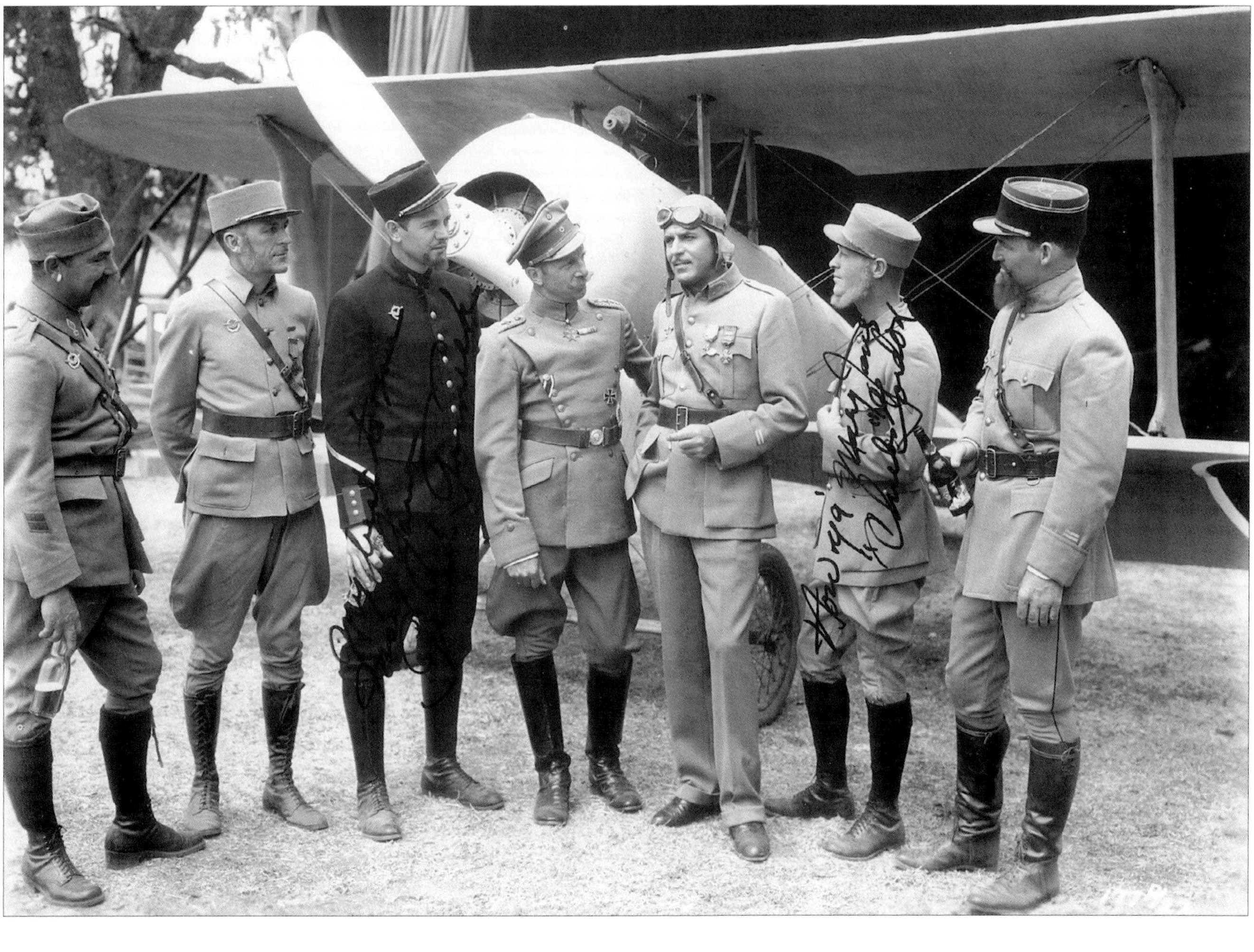

aviation, Mantz headed for nearby Hollywood to become a movie pilot.

Paul Mantz found himself an outsider in the movie industry. In 1932, movie pilots had organized the Associated Motion Picture Pilots, or AMPP, after receiving a charter from an affiliate of the American Federation of Labor. Many of the pilots felt that it "was high time they organized themselves and placed certain monetary values on their individual and collective talents."[21] The best pilots and aerial photographers, including Garland Lincoln, became charter members of the AMPP. This august group rejected Paul Mantz because he was intensely competitive, attempting to undercut their bids for movie contracts as a non-union shop. However, they and the movie studios soon learned to respect him for his flying skills and business acumen.

After establishing United Air Services Limited at Burbank Airport in the early 1930s, Mantz received his first movie credit for *Air Mail*, a 1932 Universal production, starring Ralph Bellamy and Pat O'Brien. The film received high marks for its aerial sequences and special effects, the high point being Mantz's flight in a Stearman C-3 through a small hangar at Bishop Airport in Bishop, California. Mantz was paid $100 for this risky stunt, which few other pilots wanted to attempt. After having established his reputation as a movie stunt pilot, Paul Mantz was finally invited to join as a card-carrying member of the AMPP; many of his competitors had concluded that it was better to have him as an insider.

The 1930s were great days for the movie pilots, as the studios produced over 100 aviation films during the decade – the genre was second only to westerns. Fixed base operators like Garland Lincoln at Metropolitan Airport, Paul Mantz at Burbank, and Howard Batt (a contemporary of Lincoln's and a seasoned stunt pilot in his own right) at Clover Field, obtained most of the studio contracts, but with Mantz's United Air Services taking an increasingly larger share of the business. By 1937, Garland Lincoln was beginning to dispose of his stable of airplanes, including the Nieuport 28s that he had acquired and carefully preserved.

In 1938, Paramount Pictures gathered cast, crew, and equipment for what was to be the largest aerial film production since *Hell's Angels*. Directed by a World War I Lafayette Flying Corps pilot, William Wellman, *Men with Wings* was billed as "Paramount's All-Technicolor Cavalcade of American Aviation," a celebration of its twenty-five-year history. The film traced developments in American civil and military aviation through the characters of two pilots, played by Fred MacMurray and Ray Milland, while Louise Campbell played the romantic interest and Andy Devine played the mechanic and pal.

Paul Mantz (standing at right, with hat in hand), with a group of United Air Services' charter customers at Burbank Airport. Carter/Mantz Collection via Jim Appleby

Above: Two LFs, built by Garland Lincoln but now belonging to Paramount Pictures, are on their way to work in Paramount's 1938 production, Men with Wings. H. Hugh Wynne

Right: Paul Mantz, by this time the premier Hollywood movie pilot, sits in a Nieuport 28 that will star in Men with Wings. This aircraft has unoriginal N-struts, Thomas-Morse cowl, and metal cowl panels, and is further distinguished by the lack of fairing on the cabane struts, the wheel cover, and clipped wings. Carter/Mantz Collection via Jim Appleby

Below: Another view of the Nieuport 28 spruced up for Men with Wings. Carter/Mantz Collection via Jim Appleby

Number 5246 is pictured from another angle. Carter/Mantz Collection via Jim Appleby

A lineup of Nieuport 28s awaiting new livery, for use in The Dawn Patrol. Carter/Mantz Collection via Jim Appleby

A rear shot of the same lineup, showing a number of other World War I aircraft or look-alikes. Carter/Mantz Collection via Jim Appleby

Paul Mantz received the principal contract to supply planes, pilots, and technical expertise (his own) for *Men with Wings*. In addition to three camera planes, Mantz assembled over thirty vintage and modern aircraft representing the twenty-five-year spectrum of aeronautical development. These aircraft included: a 1910 Curtiss pusher replica, six Travel Airs (which had stood in for Fokker D.VIIs in many prior movies and were commonly referred to as "Wichita Forkkers"), one original Fokker D.VII, a SPAD VII, two Thomas-Morse Scouts, three D.H. 4s, two Boeing 100s (a favorite of Mantz's for aerobatics), a Stearman C-3, two Boeing 247s, an NA-50, and several Curtiss JN-4s and Buhl Pups, in addition to three Nieuport 28s and two LFs.[22] Paramount now owned or controlled the Nieuport 28s that had formerly belonged to Garland Lincoln.

Men with Wings was released on 16 July 1938 with much fanfare. However, like too many of the aerial films of the 1930s, while the colorful aerial scenes were thrilling and memorable, the storyline was trite and uninspiring. As a consequence, this big-budget film had little staying power, and it is largely forgotten today. A remake of *The Dawn Patrol* would follow shortly.

The 1938 production of *The Dawn Patrol* utilized essentially the same script and aerial scenes as the 1930 production, but assembled an entirely different, and more effective, cast of experienced movie actors. Errol Flynn played the leading role, with supporting roles played by David Niven and Basil Rathbone. The film's location changed from Triunfo, now developed, to the Warner Brothers ranch at Calabasas. The familiar lineup of Nieuport 28s sported the

Below: This often-seen promotional photograph for the 1938 production of The Dawn Patrol shows a lineup of four Nieuport 28s; film stars Errol Flynn and David Niven are seated in the first and second airplanes, respectively. At this point in time, these aircraft constituted four-fifths of the Nieuport 28s known to exist in the U.S. – all that remained of those shipped from France to the U.S. in 1919. Numerous modifications to these Nieuport 28s (all are of postwar vintage) have been noted in prior captions, but these aircraft also have nonstandard Marlin machine guns above the wings and bogus tail numbers, applied by Hollywood to confound future aviation historians. H. Hugh Wynne

same colors and markings as in the earlier film, but this time there were four of them.[23]

The Dawn Patrol differed from other films of the genre, as one historian observed: "*The Dawn Patrol* represents the turning point in the World War I air combat film genre [starting with *Wings*], shifting the emphasis away from spectacle to the psychological examination of characters' motivations and emotions."[24] Devoid of any romantic diversions, the film's focus remained on individual pilots' reactions to combat stress and in the case of Flynn, and then Niven, the fundamental change manifested by their manner and outlook after each assumed command of the squadron.

The 1930 production of *The Dawn Patrol* (whose title was changed to *Flight Commander* when the 1938 version appeared in theaters) premiered when pacifism was at its peak in the USA; it was the same year that *All Quiet on the Western Front*, possibly the greatest and most pacifistic of all war films, appeared on the screen. The 1938 production, with a slight variation in the script, heralded the coming war when Courtney (played by Flynn), consoles a young pilot: "Then one day [the World War] will end as suddenly as it began and we'll go home. *Till some other bunch of criminal idiots sitting around a large table shoves us into another war.*"[25] Warner Brothers' publicity reflected this sentiment when the movie premiered on 12 December 1938.

The 1938 rendition of *The Dawn Patrol* ended the era that had begun with *Wings* in 1927. The remake was later lauded by a film historian as "perhaps the most thoroughly competent screen dramatization of the genre [and] a wholly fitting tribute to the man [John Monk Saunders] who had written the vast majority of the original World War I air stories reaching the screen in the late 1920 and early 1930s."[26]

As the decade ended, the American movie industry began to raise public awareness of the growing turmoil in Europe and the Pacific, and of the incipient war. The Associated Motion Picture Pilots (AMPP) would be adversely – and permanently – affected by this trend. The U.S. military services were beginning to mobilize, and they were well-aware that movies could be a very effective recruitment tool. The War Department was now eager to cooperate with the studios, and this meant provision of military planes, pilots, equipment, and locales if the movie story was deemed appropriate to the preparedness effort. The small fleets of World War I airplanes sat idle as attention turned elsewhere.

The AMPP protested the War Department's policy but failed, for national defense was more important than securing

the livelihood of the movie pilots, and the public was clamoring for more contemporary military films. Paul Mantz, however, divined opportunity for his company; he could supply the needed camera planes, pilots, and expert cameramen to the military. Mantz's acumen paid off again, and what followed was a spate of movies that fit the bill for the flying services of the Navy (*Wings of the Navy*, 1939, *Flight Command*, 1940, *Dive Bomber,* 1941), U.S. Army Air Force, (*Flying Cadets* and *I Wanted Wings*, 1941, *Air Force,* 1943), U.S. Coast Guard (*Coast Guard*, 1939) and the Royal Air Force (*International Squadron* and *A Yank in the RAF*, 1941). Mantz had the contract for all of these films. Paul Mantz would continue to monopolize the aerial film business for the next twenty years.

One film that Mantz had no part of was *Captains of the Clouds*, a 1942 Warner Brothers production starring James Cagney, Dennis Morgan, Alan Hale and others, all with roles as Canadian bush pilots who attempt to transfer their skills to the Royal Canadian Air Force. This was to be Garland Lincoln's last film, and also the last film that AMPP pilots worked on as a team. Lincoln was shortly recalled to active duty in the Army Air Force, where he served as a flight instructor and staff pilot for the duration of World War II, separating from the service in 1946 as a lieutenant colonel. He died in 1986.

Paul Mantz was commissioned a major in the Army Air Force in 1942, fifteen years after he had been discharged from the Air Corps one day short of getting his wings. Lieutenant Colonel Mantz would ultimately command the Army Air Force's First Motion Picture Unit, and produce a string of highly successful training films. Mantz returned to civilian life in 1944, becoming actively involved in air racing for several years while becoming re-established in the movie business.

Paul Mantz had acquired a collection of antique aircraft, including Garland Lincoln's Nieuport 28s, from Paramount Pictures in 1941. Garland Lincoln was disgusted when he found out what Mantz had done, because he had intended to buy them back after the war. In 1961 Mantz partnered with competitor Frank Tallman, merging their joint collection in a venture called Tallmantz Aviation Inc., which operated the Movieland of the Air Museum. Albert Paul Mantz was killed in a flying accident in 1965 while making the film *The Flight of the Phoenix*.

The thrills of the Golden Age of Aviation, fueled by many of the aviation movies produced during the 1920s and '30s, will likely never be experienced again. And many years would pass before interest in World War I aircraft was rekindled. The credit for preserving the few remaining examples of the elegant Nieuport 28 must go to Garland Lincoln, and thence to Paul Mantz and Frank Tallman, who subsequently collected and owned at one time, all of the original Nieuport 28s that exist in the United States today.

Nieuport 28s and/or Garland Lincoln's LFs appeared in aerial scenes or ground settings in the following movies: ***The Dawn Patrol*** (First National, 1930), ***Heartbreak*** (Fox, 1931), ***The Last Flight*** (Warner Brothers, 1931), ***Lost Squadron*** (RKO, 1932), ***Ace of Aces*** (RKO, 1933), ***The Eagle and the Hawk*** (Paramount, 1933), ***Life is Cheap*** (Columbia, n.d.), ***Hell in the Heavens*** (Fox, 1934), ***Devil's Squadron*** (Columbia, 1936), ***Roaming Lady*** (Columbia, 1936), ***Suzy*** (MGM, 1936), ***Men with Wings*** (Paramount, 1938), ***The Dawn Patrol*** (remake, Warner Brothers, 1938), ***The Story of Vernon and Irene Castle*** (RKO, 1939), ***Stunt Pilot*** (Monogram, 1939), ***Captain Eddie*** (Fox, 1945).[27]

THE SURVIVORS

NASM Restores a Nieuport 28

In April 1995, restoration technicians at the National Air and Space Museum's Paul E. Garber Facility in Suitland, Maryland, removed a Nieuport 28 biplane fighter from among a jumble of airplanes stored in Building 21. As it was now on the restoration schedule, the Nieuport 28 fighter's fuselage and engine, wings and tail section, along with all other associated parts, were moved across the way to Building 10, where a complete teardown would begin.

On 2 May 1995, technicians began removing fabric from the airplane; by the end of the month the engine, fuel and oil tanks, magnetos, rudder bars, cabane struts, crossbracing wires, stringers, firewall, landing gear, and all metal parts had been carefully removed, labeled, and stored. A thorough inspection of the Nieuport 28's many components revealed several significant surprises about the airplane's origin.

NASM's Nieuport 28 had been received from James H. "Cole" Palen, founder of the Old Rhinebeck Aerodrome in New York, in trade for a Nieuport 10 trainer. At the time that the airplane was accessioned in 1986, it was believed that it had originally served as a U.S. Navy battleship-based scout in the early 1920s – at least that was the unfounded story that came with the airplane. Subsequent teardown raised doubts about the airplane's origin, and further research determined conclusively that NASM's airplane was not one of the twelve Nieuport 28s that had been specially modified to fly off of a battleship turret. The keys to discovery were the serial numbers that were revealed once the fabric had been stripped from the wings and the oil tank had been removed.

The manufacturer's four-digit serial number and date of manufacture (month and year) were clearly stamped on the rear spar of each wing section. The upper wing panels had a manufacturing date of February 1919 and were serial numbered 7103 (left panel) and 7226 (right panel); the lower left wing panel was numbered 6465, fabricated in November 1918, and lower right panel numbered 6432, made in October 1918. The number 6497, found etched on the face of the firewall, indicated the serial number of the airplane's fuselage.

The U.S. Navy had assigned Bureau Numbers, or BuNos, to each of the twelve Nieuport 28s that it received in 1919-20 from the Air Service, and NASM's restoration team members knew these numbers. A key document, located at the National Archives, listed the corresponding French serial numbers for the twelve Navy aircraft; a quick scan of those numbers showed that none of them matched any of the serial numbers found on NASM's airplane.

At this juncture, several things about the Nieuport 28's origin had been established: (a) it was not an ex-navy scout (in addition to the results of the serial number examination, no evidence had been found of any of the modifications that were

The serial numbers and dates, stamped on the upper and lower wings (the serial number and date 7226 2 19 were found on the upper right wing) and etched on the front of the firewall, confirmed that the Nieuport 28 in the collection of the National Air and Space Museum (NASM) was built after the war as a Nieuport 28A. None of the serial numbers matched, and this demonstrated that NASM's Nieuport 28A had been assembled from components of several different aircraft.

made to the navy's Nieuport 28 aircraft at the Naval Aircraft Factory); (b) the airplane was a postwar Nieuport 28A, given the dates of manufacture associated with all of the serial numbers; and (c) the airplane was a composite of original parts from more than one aircraft, and also contained parts and fabrications that were not to original specifications. In addition, many of the components associated with the Nieuport 28A, such as the Marlin machine guns, synchronization system, and belly fuel tank, had long since been removed.

With this new knowledge and considering the known operational uses of the type, several restoration options were discussed. These options included restoring the aircraft as an U.S. Air Service trainer, as this was the principal postwar use of this type. Or it could be restored as one of the Nieuport 28s from Garland Lincoln's stable of movie airplanes, for the fuselage, mated with clipped wings, was known to have been used in *The Dawn Patrol*, although NASM's aircraft had been received with a set of full-span wings. The airplane could also be restored in navy colors. Although it was now known that NASM's Nieuport 28 never saw navy service, twelve of this type had interesting, though brief, careers as U.S. Navy scouts flying off battleship turrets.

However, each of these options were eliminated in favor of one that was most consistent with the rationale for having the Nieuport 28 in the national collection: "The main reason we have a Nieuport 28 in the collection is to document the aircraft type first used by organized American units under American colors in combat."[1] The decision was thus made to restore NASM's Nieuport 28, an amalgam of several postwar airplanes, as one of the wartime U.S. Air Service Nieuport 28s. The question now was: Which one of the many Nieuport 28s that served in combat should be selected?

The following guidelines were established for determining which specific Nieuport 28 fighter would be selected as the model for NASM's restoration project: the aircraft and pilot would have an interesting and highly commendable combat history, and the aircraft would be well-documented, in order to ensure the highest degree of accuracy in the restoration process.

It was decided that the restored Nieuport 28 would have the markings of the 94th Aero Squadron, as this was the first American unit to achieve victories while operating this type, and it was the most successful of all Air Service fighter squadrons during the war. In addition, its aircraft were the best documented among the four squadrons that had operated Nieuport 28s.

Among the 94th Aero Squadron's Nieuport 28s to be considered was N.6144, flown by Lieutenant James A. Meissner in two successful combats, for which he received the Distinguished Service Cross and Oak Leaf Cluster. French-trained Lieutenant Alan Winslow scored the first victory with the type (N.6184) on 14 April 1918. On the same day, while piloting N.6164, Lieutenant Douglas Campbell became the first American-trained pilot to score a victory. Also on the short list was N.6159, flown by Lieutenant Eddie Rickenbacker when he scored his first victories, and N.6283, with which he scored his fifth, thus becoming the first American-trained Ace. Another aircraft, N.6158, was also considered, for this fighter, which was piloted by both Captain David McKelvey Peterson and Lieutenant Douglas Campbell, had the highest tally of victory claims.

Ultimately, Lieutenant Meissner's Nieuport 28, serial number N.6144, was chosen to represent the type, as first flown by the U.S. Air Service in early combat operations. This aircraft was chosen, rather than one of the more famous ones such as either of Eddie Rickenbacker's two aircraft, Douglas Campbell's N.6164 (several Nieuport 28 reproductions already honor this particular aircraft and its pilot), or Alan Winslow's N.6184, "because it is representative of the famous 'hat in the ring' " period of the 94th Aero Squadron, without misleading museum visitors into thinking that the NASM aircraft actually is one of the especially well-known American Nieuport 28s.[2] The very worthy Peterson-Campbell Nieuport 28 (N.6158) was dismissed from contention because it lacked sufficient photographic documentation.

Lieutenant Meissner's N.6144 proved to be a valid choice. Meissner had scored two victories with this particular fighter. He twice experienced wing failure, but Meissner and N.6144 survived both episodes. Meissner's Nieuport 28 was later destroyed, however, after he turned it over to a less-experienced pilot.

James Armand Meissner ended the war as a major, in command of the 147th Aero Squadron. While he was initially credited with eight victories, this tally was later reduced to five and two-thirds victories, after the U.S. Air Force Historical Division recalculated all credits awarded to Air Service pilots. (Prior to this, a full credit had been given to each pilot who shared in any confirmed victory.) For his exploits, Meissner received the French Croix de Guerre and twice received the Distinguished Service Cross, the second highest award for valor given by the United States Army.

Once the decision was made to restore NASM's Nieuport 28 as Lieutenant Meissner's Nieuport 28 fighter, N.6144, members of the restoration team assembled a wealth of data about the aircraft type from sources throughout the United States, Canada, and Europe. The data, which included photographs, blueprints, plans, drawings, systems manuals, and articles; operational, unit, and personal histories; and specifications for fabric, tires, dope, Vickers .303 machine guns, camouflage, and markings; was used extensively during the restoration process to ensure the utmost accuracy in the fully restored aircraft. The gathered material filled seven curatorial boxes, which are now stored in the curatorial files at the Aeronautics Department of the National Air and Space Museum.

During the course of the restoration process, team members sourced original Nieuport 28 components and maintained frequent contact with a network of consultants, curators, and

Restoration technicians used this photograph as the guide to ensure that NASM's Nieuport 28 was accurately painted in the colors and markings of Lieutenant Jimmy Meissner's fighter, as it appeared on 15 May 1918. R.L. Cavanagh

restorers at other museums; these people made substantial contributions to the success of the project.

Ultimately, it was a largely volunteer team of multitalented restoration technicians and conservators, under the direction of Curator Peter L. Jakab, who expertly restored NASM's Nieuport 28 to pristine condition. The Nieuport 28 fighter, proudly sporting the colors of Lieutenant James Meissner's N.6144 as it appeared on 15 May 1918, is now on permanent display at NASM's Steven R. Udvar-Hazy Center at Washington Dulles International Airport.

Photo Essay of NASM's Nieuport 28 Restoration

The photo sequence on the following pages documents the highlights of the five-year restoration of NASM's Nieuport 28:

1. The Nieuport 28 fuselage, with red and black cowl, is spotted in a jumble of stored aircraft awaiting restoration
2. The fuselage fabric is removed, revealing original, replacement, broken, and missing components, numerous repairs, and years of accumulated grime
3. The lattice wood pilot's seat will be replaced, after details of an original seat have been carefully studied
4. The metal plate nailed on the rear spar brackets the wing panel's four-digit serial number and date of manufacture
5. The curator inspects the detail of the lower left wing
6. Technicians remove cylinders from the Gnôme 9N rotary engine
7. The Gnôme engine awaits cleaning and conservation
8. The nonoriginal JN-4 wheels will be replaced and correctly sized tires will be sourced
9. New wood: a newly fabricated former is joined to original longerons. NASM restoration guidelines specify that every replacement part be stamped with NASM and the date of fabrication. Every effort is made to preserve original components, including grafting a new piece on to an original, but broken, fragment
10. Bomb carrier lugs, not found on the wartime production Nieuport 28, are removed
11. This photo shows cabane strut attachment points and control wire detail
12. The fuselage is complete, with wood and metal components cleaned and conserved with varnish or paint
13. An original cowl replaces the unsightly and nonoriginal "Tommy Morse" cowl

14. A NASM technician (a former P-38 pilot) experiences the Nieuport 28's cramped cockpit while testing the fit of the shoulder harness

15. Technicians fit engine accessories

16. A pristine Gnôme rotary engine is secured forward of a newly constructed oil tank

17. Laying up of two-ply fuselage panels. These were correct for the wartime production fighter, but were replaced by compressed paper panels in the Nieuport 28A

18–20. Fitting the two-ply panels

21–23. Detail of newly built vertical and horizontal stabilizers, elevators and rudder

24. Attaching the tail fairing

25. Fabric is fitted on to the upper left wing panel

26. Fabric tape is doped on top of each fabric-covered wing rib

27. The fine art of stitching doped tape and fabric to the wing ribs

28. The elevator is doped

29. The U.S. Air Service cocarde (roundel) is painted on the upper wing panel

30. Technicians inspect the fuselage fabric

31. The propeller awaits painting after being balanced, varnished, and having the tips protected with fabric

32. A visitor to the paint room inspects the newly painted fuselage

33. Braiding bracing wire

34. Fashioning the venturi used to pressurize the fuel tank

35. Constructing ammunition box for use with inner Vickers machine gun

36. Test fit of ammunition box for outer machine gun installation

37. Cleaning and calibrating tachometer

38. Routing interplane struts

39. Removing small dents from an original cowl that had been purchased from another museum. This turned out to be one of the amusing highlights of the restoration process, as the badly dented cowl had been obtained for use only as a study guide. The restoration team manager, however, upended the cowl, and after stepping into it, found that the large dents could be judiciously removed by careful application of his heavy boots. Further attention to the remaining small dents restored the cowl to its original contour.

40. The cowl is painted with Lieutenant James Meissner's distinctive red and silver lightning pattern

41. Lieutenant Meissner's squadron number 8 is painted on

42. Fabric wheel covers are cut for the correctly sized wheels

43. Installing cockpit coaming

44. Final detailing: painting the wood segments separating the flying wires

45. Final detail in the restoration process: installing the ID plate in the cockpit

46–47. The great day arrives! The rollout of NASM's restored Nieuport 28 fighter from Building 10

48. Preparing for the official rollout photographs

49. NASM's multitalented restoration team poses proudly beside their completed project

1
N13Y
PENN AIRWAYS
EXPERIMENTAL

2

3

4

5

6

7

8

9

10

11

12

13

14

15

16

17

18

19

20

21

22

23

24

25

26

27

28

29

30

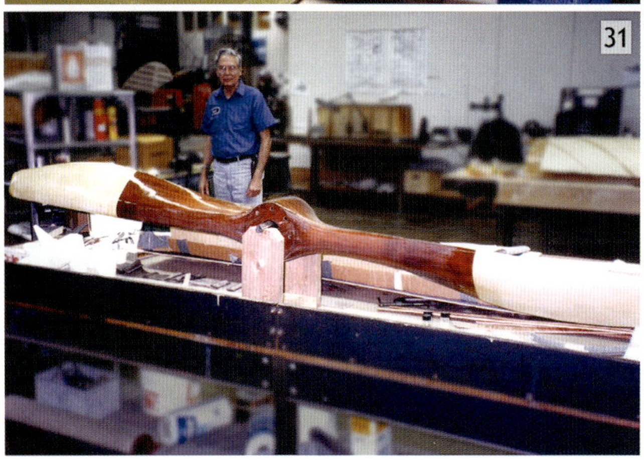
31

32

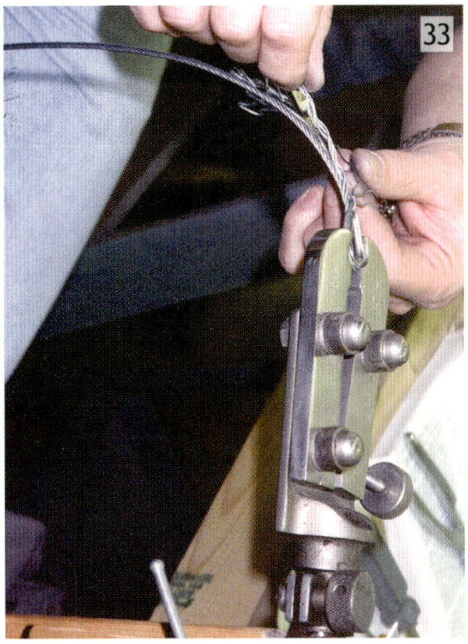
33

34

35

36

37

38

39

40

41

42

43

44

45

46

47

48

49

The Survivors

Don Brady, a Nieuport 28 aficionado from Hayward, California, recalled seeing and photographing a "number of N.28 airframes at Orange County Airport" sometime in 1955.[3] This was the first of several visits he made to Orange County Airport, and at the time, these aircraft belonged to Paul Mantz. Brady photographed two of the airframes, which were stored inside a galvanized hangar; the others were photographed with parts of other aircraft that were piled chock-a-block outside the hangar.

Brady remembered, "four stripped down, non-flying fuselages, three with sheet metal side cowl panels, and one with plywood cowls covered with fabric. All had Thomas Morse S4C engine cowls [and] 160 hp Gnôme monosoupape engines installed. None of the airframes had fabric behind [the] cockpit, and [each had] stringers and formers broken and missing [with] some in better shape than others – all had sheet metal [mounted] to lower longerons from cockpit to tailskid."[4]

According to Brady, some of the fuselages had metal bucket seats (which were not original to the Nieuport 28) and one had a wooden seat, possibly the remains of an original seat. He saw numerous spare airplane parts throughout the hangar, and several sets of wings resting on the rafters above. He noted that all of the aircraft "appeared to be similar in basic modifications," including one that was in flying condition and "painted sky silvery blue, with a Thomas Morse cowl, bobbed wings [and] N type interplane struts."[5]

Don Brady had ventured to Orange County Airport to take measurements of one of the Nieuport 28s stored there before preparing a set of accurate drawings. However, Bergen Hardesty, another fan of the type, completed this task before Brady could finish his exhaustive measurements. Hardesty's drawings, derived from his measurements of a Nieuport 28 belonging to Frank Tallman (this aircraft was ex-Jarrett collection, and had never been used as a movie prop), provide the best technical documentation of the Nieuport 28 available today.

The five Nieuport 28s (essentially five fuselages and a mélange of wings and parts) encountered by Brady and Hardesty are, collectively, the remnants of the original shipment, sent to the United States in 1919. These aircraft have subsequently been restored or preserved, and are found in the United States in museums and in a private collection. Additional examples of restored or conserved Nieuport 28s exist in the United States and in Europe. For a variety of reasons, it is difficult to accurately establish the degree of originality of each of the surviving Nieuport 28s.

Restored aircraft are classified depending on their degree of originality, between a *Restored Original aircraft,* "an artifact composed of at least 50 percent original components [by surface area or volume], and the remainder returned to accurate early condition with the same materials, components and accessories", and a *Reproduction,* "a reasonable facsimile in appearance and construction of an aircraft made with similar materials, and having substantially the same type of engine and operating system."[6]

Don Brady photographed these derelict airplanes at Orange County Airport in 1955-1957. In the foreground is the stripped fuselage of a Nieuport 28A. Don Brady

Another jumble of airplane components in outdoor storage at Orange County Airport. Don Brady

This upended Nieuport 28 fuselage is safely stored within a hangar. Don Brady

The principal difficulty in tracing the lineage of Nieuport 28 survivors in the United States is the absence of documentation linking each aircraft to the original shipment of Nieuport 28A trainers brought here in 1919. Compounding this difficulty is the fact that all of these aircraft were modified along the way,

Above: This Nieuport 28 is being restored to flying condition. Don Brady Below: After being restored to flying condition, it was flown by Colonel Kimbrough Brown, USAF, on exhibition flights in commemoration of fifty years of U.S. military aviation. The aircraft was later sold at auction to James E. Hall. Don Brady

with original parts removed and/or mixed with those from other airframes. Hollywood confused the matter further by painting bogus numbers on the tails of the aircraft. However, we are able to partially establish the provenance of some of these aircraft by examining Federal Aviation Administration records. Fortunately, no such problems exist outside the U.S., as there is sufficient documentation available to provide clear provenance for each of the surviving Nieuport 28s in Europe.

What follows is the location and known genealogy of surviving Nieuport 28s – those with at least a modicum of original parts – around the world.

Ex-Movie Stars

National Air and Space Museum: Steven F. Udvar-Hazy Center, Chantilly, Virginia

Movie stunt pilot Paul Mantz, then operating as United Air Services Ltd., obtained "various and sundry antique airplanes and parts of airplanes" from Paramount Pictures in 1941.[7] Included among the lot he acquired were four Nieuport 28s, all in nonflying condition. Mantz was banking on the future of aviation films, but the country was soon to enter World War II, while Mantz himself would be commissioned in the U.S. Army Air Force the following year.

One of these Nieuport 28s, later registered by the FAA as N4123A when it was restored to flying condition, *may have* belonged to Garland Lincoln before he disposed of his stable of aircraft to Paramount Pictures in 1937–38. While it appears in the lineup of Nieuport 28s in publicity shots for the 1938 production of *The Dawn Patrol*, there is no clear documentation to substantiate Lincoln's ownership prior to Mantz's acquisition of the aircraft from Paramount in 1941.[8] What *is* known is that Mantz transferred title of this particular aircraft to himself (Mantz's United Air Services was dormant during the war) after he returned from active duty in August 1944. Mantz had reorganized his operation as Paul Mantz Air Services and began buying many of the World War II fighters and bombers that were made surplus at the end of the war; he was also getting heavily involved in air racing. In the meantime, his collection of earlier vintage aircraft sat idle, much of it in outside storage.

In 1957, Paul Mantz traded this Nieuport 28, along with a set of full-span wings, to Cole Palen, founder of Old Rhinebeck Aerodrome in Rhinebeck, New York. Mantz received a Standard J-1 in trade, which he required as a backup aircraft for the filming of *The Spirit of St. Louis*. What was to have been an even-up trade dissolved when Palen saw the poor condition of the Nieuport 28, once it had arrived at his aerodrome. Palen valued the Nieuport 28, however, so he closed the deal with Mantz by negotiating an additional consideration of $200.

Cole Palen returned the aircraft to flying condition and applied to the FAA for certification in 1958. Registered as N4123A, the Nieuport 28 flew regularly in air shows at Old Rhinebeck Aerodrome, with occasional visits elsewhere, until Palen retired it in 1972. After being on static display at the aerodrome, it was transferred to the Intrepid Sea, Air, and Space Museum in New York City harbor, where it was exhibited until 1986. In that year, the National Air and Space Museum obtained it in trade for a Nieuport 10 trainer that had once belonged to French Ace Charles Nungesser.

The restoration of NASM's Nieuport 28 was completed in 2000, and it was moved into storage pending completion of the new museum at Dulles Airport. The aircraft was installed in the Steven R. Udvar-Hazy Center prior to the museum's grand opening in December 2003.

A search of FAA records determined that Paul Mantz had once owned the Nieuport 28 that later became part of NASM's collection. This close-up photograph from the film The Dawn Patrol shows four Nieuport 28s. The fourth aircraft in line, with full-span wings, may be NASM's aircraft, now restored in the colors of Jimmy Meissner's fighter. R.L. Cavanagh

Top: Here is Cole Palen's Nieuport 28 as it appeared in an early visit to Wright-Patterson Air Force Base on 25 June 1961. The occasion was a reunion of World War I pilots. Palen acquired the aircraft from Paul Mantz in 1957. R.L. Cavanagh

Above: Palen's Nieuport 28 is best remembered in this paint scheme – the colors of Lieutenant Douglas Campbell's N.6164, #10. R.L. Cavanagh

Left: After Cole Palen grounded his Nieuport 28 in 1972, the aircraft was displayed in New York Harbor aboard the USS Intrepid. It is seen here being removed from the Intrepid's exhibit by NASM technicians in 1986. It is on its way to long-term storage at NASM's Paul Garber Facility in Maryland where, nine years later, NASM began restoring it.

Opposite: After a meticulous five-year restoration, NASM's Nieuport 28 is hoisted aloft, for permanent display at the new Steven R. Udvar-Hazy Center at Dulles Airport. Photo by Dane Penland, National Air and Space Museum, Smithsonian Institution (SI 2006-22799)

James E. Hall, Midland, Texas

This aircraft can be traced back to Johnny Vickers, who sold it to Garland Lincoln in December 1929. The aircraft was initially registered as R10415 (later as NX10415) and restricted to motion picture work. As reported in the last chapter, this aircraft flew in the 1931 production of *Heartbreak*, and may also have flown a year earlier in the 1930 production of *The Dawn Patrol*. Garland Lincoln sold this aircraft to Paramount Pictures Inc. in February 1938, and it was among the four Nieuport 28s acquired from Paramount by Mantz's United Air Services in February 1941.

In 1954, this aircraft was registered as N4728V. After being restored to flying condition, it was subsequently flown for four months by Colonel Kimbrough S. Brown on exhibition flights to Bolling and Andrews Air Force bases, in commemoration of the 50th anniversary of military aviation. This is the aircraft that Don Brady had seen earlier (possibly in 1956 or 1957) being restored at Orange County (now John Wayne) Airport, painted "sky silvery blue."

Tallmantz Aviation Inc., a partnership formed in 1961 between Paul Mantz and movie stunt pilot Frank Gifford Tallman III, acquired the airplane that same year. Repainted, and with an original Nieuport 28 cowl installed (but still with N-struts and clipped wings), it was flown by Tallman and movie pilot Jim Appleby for several years, until it was sold to the Rosen-Novak Auto Company of Omaha, Nebraska, and Morrison Quirk Grain Corporation of Hastings, Nebraska, in February 1966.

In 1968, Parke-Bernet Galleries Inc. of New York City managed the major sale of vintage aircraft that had been assembled by Frank Tallman and the late Paul Mantz (Mantz had been killed in 1965 during the filming of *The Flight of the Phoenix*). The auction took place at the Movieland of the Air Museum at Orange County Airport on 29 May 1968. James E. Hall of Midland, Texas, acquired the Nieuport 28, registered as N4728V, at this auction. At this writing, it is believed that Mr. Hall, a former race driver, still has possession of this aircraft.

Above: Number 5246 (registered as NX10415) in another photograph, taken during the filming of Men with Wings in 1938. H. Hugh Wynne

Opposite

Top: Number 5246 as it appeared sometime in the early 1950s. It shows the faded colors of a static-display Nieuport 28 used in the 1945 production of Captain Eddie. R.L. Cavanagh

Center: The same aircraft, in a new set of colors and sprayed silver all over.

Bottom: A recent photograph of Jim Hall's clipped-wing Nieuport 28A, now fitted with an authentic cowl.

N
5246

National Museum of the U.S. Air Force, Wright-Patterson AFB, Dayton, Ohio
Ray Folsom, presently of Paso Robles, California, made a deal with Frank Tallman in the early 1960s to acquire a Tiger Moth biplane in exchange for building up two complete Nieuport 28s from parts that Tallman would provide. The parts provided included a set of clipped wings, a full wing panel, fuselage, Gnôme rotary engine, and landing gear, and Folsom supplemented this with a spun cowl and an additional landing gear. Folsom also purchased additional miscellaneous parts from Neal Sorensen in Minneapolis, Minnesota.[9]

Folsom was soon joined by George Hunt, a retired machinist who had an interest in obtaining the Tiger Moth. Folsom and Hunt parted ways shortly thereafter, when Folsom left for South America, and George Hunt completed one Nieuport 28, which Frank Tallman then registered as N8539. After Tallman's death, the aircraft was transferred to Tallmantz Aviation Inc. in 1978, and later sold to Kermit Weeks, founder of the Fantasy of Flight Museum in Polk City, Florida. On 8 November 1985, the National Museum of the United States Air Force acquired this Nieuport 28 via an exchange with Kermit Weeks.

It is possible that N8539 was previously registered as N2539, when it was owned by Garland Lincoln. If so, it is one of the two U.S. Navy Nieuport 28s that Emery Rogers purchased in 1921 and was sold to Lincoln in 1929 by Rogers Aircraft Inc. According to NASM records, this aircraft was sold in dismantled condition by Lincoln to Ed Erickson at Mines Field, California, on 2 October 1937, and to Paramount Pictures Inc. three days later.[10] Paul Mantz's United Air Services acquired it from Paramount in 1941, along with the other three Nieuport 28s that Paramount owned.

Now in the collection of the National Museum of the United States Air Force, this Nieuport 28 reproduction is painted in the colors of a 95th Aero Squadron fighter. Wes Henry, National Museum of the US Air Force

U.S. Army Aviation Museum, Fort Rucker, Alabama

A Christie's catalog described this Nieuport 28 as "a true basket case"[11] when the contents of the Wings and Wheels Museum were auctioned on 6 December 1981.

This Nieuport 28 was among the aircraft that Paul Mantz had originally acquired from Paramount Pictures, and later became part of the Tallmantz collection. Frank Tallman later traded it to Aeroflex in New Jersey for a Morane A1, and Aeroflex subsequently sold it to Dolph Overton's Wings and Wheels Museum in Florida.

Guy Black, under the auspices of the Historic Aircraft Collection (HAC) in England, purchased the components and had them shipped to England. Mike Tate bought and briefly owned the collection of Nieuport 28 parts, but HAC reacquired the parts once it was determined that restoration of the aircraft was economically viable.

Tim Moore of Skysport Engineering Ltd. restored the aircraft to flying condition for the Historic Aircraft Collection, and the Nieuport 28 made several flights on the UK flying circuit before it was traded to the U.S. Army Aviation Museum at Fort Rucker, Alabama. This Nieuport 28, bedecked in the colors of the 95th Aero Squadron, is now on static display at that museum.

Acquired from the Historic Aircraft Collection in the UK, this Nieuport 28 reproduction is now on display in the U.S. Army Aviation Museum at Fort Rucker, Alabama.

Brent Moné, Santa Rosa, California

Although clearly not an original aircraft, Garland Lincoln's LF belongs in this section because of its extensive experience in movies, as a stand-in for aging Nieuport 28s. Built by Garland Lincoln in 1932, and registered in 1933 as NR 12237, this aircraft was used for flying sequences when Lincoln's original Nieuport 28s had been consigned to static shots on the ground.

The second LF, registered in 1935 as 75W, changed to NX-75W in 1939 and was sold to Harry McClure in 1941 for private flying. However, the Civil Aviation Administration denied approval for the Experimental or Restricted license renewal in 1942, and the aircraft was sold for junk in 1945. The whereabouts of the third LF, built at Curtiss-Wright Tech in 1938, is unknown – presumably, it did not survive.

Below: Here is Garland Lincoln's original LF 1 in later life. This aircraft accumulated a lengthy list of screen credits, dating back to the early 1930s. Jim Appleby

Frank Tallman purchased the Garland Lincoln LF 1, NR 12237, from Perry Boswell in Florida in August 1956 (its use during the intervening period is not known), and later moved it to Orange County Airport in Santa Ana, California. In 1972, Tallman received a Special Airworthiness Certificate for N 12237, for the purpose of "Exhibition and Filming Motion Pictures."

The aircraft was used extensively for movie work until the aircraft crashed on 15 January 1974 at the Getty Oil Ranch at Piru, California, during the filming of *The Great Waldo Pepper*. The aircraft was under way from Orange County (John Wayne) Airport to the film site, a two-hour ferry flight. Upon arrival at the location, the ferry pilot misjudged his altitude, stalled the aircraft, and cartwheeled after hitting the ground. The plane was severely damaged, but the ferry pilot was unhurt.[12]

Frank Tallman sold LF 1 to Kip Moné on 13 November 1975 for $2,500. Kip's son, Brent, of Santa Rosa, California, current owner of LF 1, is restoring it to flying condition.

A ferry pilot crashed the LF 1 in 1974 en route to the film location of The Great Waldo Pepper. Movie stunt pilot Jim Appleby is seen standing behind the heavily damaged aircraft. Jim Appleby

Brent Moné, the current owner of Garland Lincoln's LF 1, has begun a long-term restoration of this historic airplane. Brent, standing at left in this photograph, is overseeing the installation of the engine on the metal-framed aircraft. Brent Moné

Others in Museums and Works in Progress

Museum of Flight, Seattle, Washington

George Burling Jarrett began collecting militaria in 1915 at age seventeen. His passion grew unabated, until it was reported that by 1935 he had amassed 7,000 pieces, much of that gathered during his numerous trips to Europe. In 1930, the Steel Pier amusement center in Atlantic City, New Jersey, provided space for his collection, and there it remained until 1933, when Jarrett moved his "Museum of World War History" to his father-in-law's farm at Moorestown, New Jersey. Jarrett's special interest was World War I military airplanes, and his collection soon included a Fokker D.VII, Thomas-Morse S4C, SPAD VII, D.H. 4, Sopwith Camel, Pfalz D.XII, and a Nieuport 28.

George Jarrett acquired his Nieuport 28 in 1935 from R. F. Coody in Lakeland, Florida, where he found it "standing on its nose," a plaything for neighborhood children.[13] Jarrett restored it in the colors of Edwin C. Parsons' Nieuport 17: silver, with a black cowl, and with Parsons' initials painted on the fuselage. His Nieuport 28 remained in Parsons' livery until it was repainted in 1938 as a publicity tie-in for the film *Men with Wings* (it was repainted as an exact match of Nieuport #4, which was prominently featured in the film) and was displayed briefly at the Steel Pier.

After he was called to active service in the U.S. Army Ordnance Corps in 1939, Jarrett's aircraft collection remained, mostly in outside storage, at the Moorestown, New Jersey, farm. In 1947, Colonel Jarrett moved the collection to a farm near Aberdeen, Maryland, but by then most of the airplanes had badly deteriorated. Recognizing the enormous cost of repair and maintenance, Colonel Jarrett began disposing of his collection. In 1949, Frank Tallman offered George Jarrett $500 for the SPAD VII, Pfalz D.XII, Sopwith Camel, and the Nieuport 28. According to Jarrett that was a fair price, considering the dreadful condition of the airplanes.

Frank Tallman stored the hulk of his newly purchased Nieuport 28 outside a building at the Boston Mechanics School at Boston Airport (now Logan Airport), where it continued to deteriorate until Tallman transferred it to Ned Kensinger, in exchange for Kensinger's restoration of Tallman's Sopwith Camel. Robert Rust Sr. of Fayetteville, Georgia, obtained Tallman's SPAD VII in exchange for restoring Tallman's Pfalz D.XII. All of these aircraft had once been part of Colonel Jarrett's collection.

Having coveted the Nieuport 28 more than the SPAD VII, Robert Rust sold the SPAD VII to Jim Petty to finance the purchase of the Nieuport 28 from Ned Kensinger. Rust also received a number of Nieuport 28 spare parts in the deal. Rust then began a very slow, but meticulous restoration of the Nieuport 28.

In April 1990, Douglas Champlin purchased the still-unfinished Nieuport 28 from Robert Rust Sr. for the Champlin Fighter Museum in Mesa, Arizona. Jim Appleby collected the unfinished aircraft from Robert Rust's hangar in 1996 and transported it to his own facility in California, where he continued the restoration process. Roger Freeman of Vintage Aviation in Texas ultimately completed the restoration of this Nieuport 28 for the Champlin Fighter Museum. Champlin's entire collection, including the beautifully restored Nieuport 28, was acquired shortly thereafter by the Museum of Flight in Seattle, Washington.

Colonel George Jarrett's "Museum of World War History" included this Nieuport 28A. This late 1930s photograph was taken at Jarrett's farm in Moorestown, New Jersey. Art Kennedy

14
14

Opposite
Top: The shed provided minimal protection from the elements. Colonel Jarrett's collection deteriorated during World War II, when Jarrett was on active duty with the U.S. Army Ordnance Corps. Art Kennedy

Left center: Now owned by Frank Tallman, Jarrett's old Nieuport 28A lies derelict alongside a shed at Boston (now Logan) Airport. William Nungesser

Right center: Another shot taken at Boston Airport. Note the compressed-paper cowl panels that identify this Nieuport 28 as a modified 'A' variant. William Nungesser

Bottom: This beautifully restored Nieuport 28, which had once belonged to Colonel Jarrett and Frank Tallman, was acquired from the Champlin Fighter Museum, and is now on display at the Museum of Flight in Seattle. Roger Freeman

San Diego Air & Space Museum, San Diego, California

This Nieuport 28 full-scale reproduction originated with Ray Folsom's agreement with Frank Tallman in the early 1960s. Although George Hunt undertook the restoration, Hunt and Folsom later agreed to evenly split the $30,000 purchase price paid by the San Diego Air & Space Museum when the airplane was acquired by the museum in June 1978. This aircraft was registered as N28GH in June 1976.

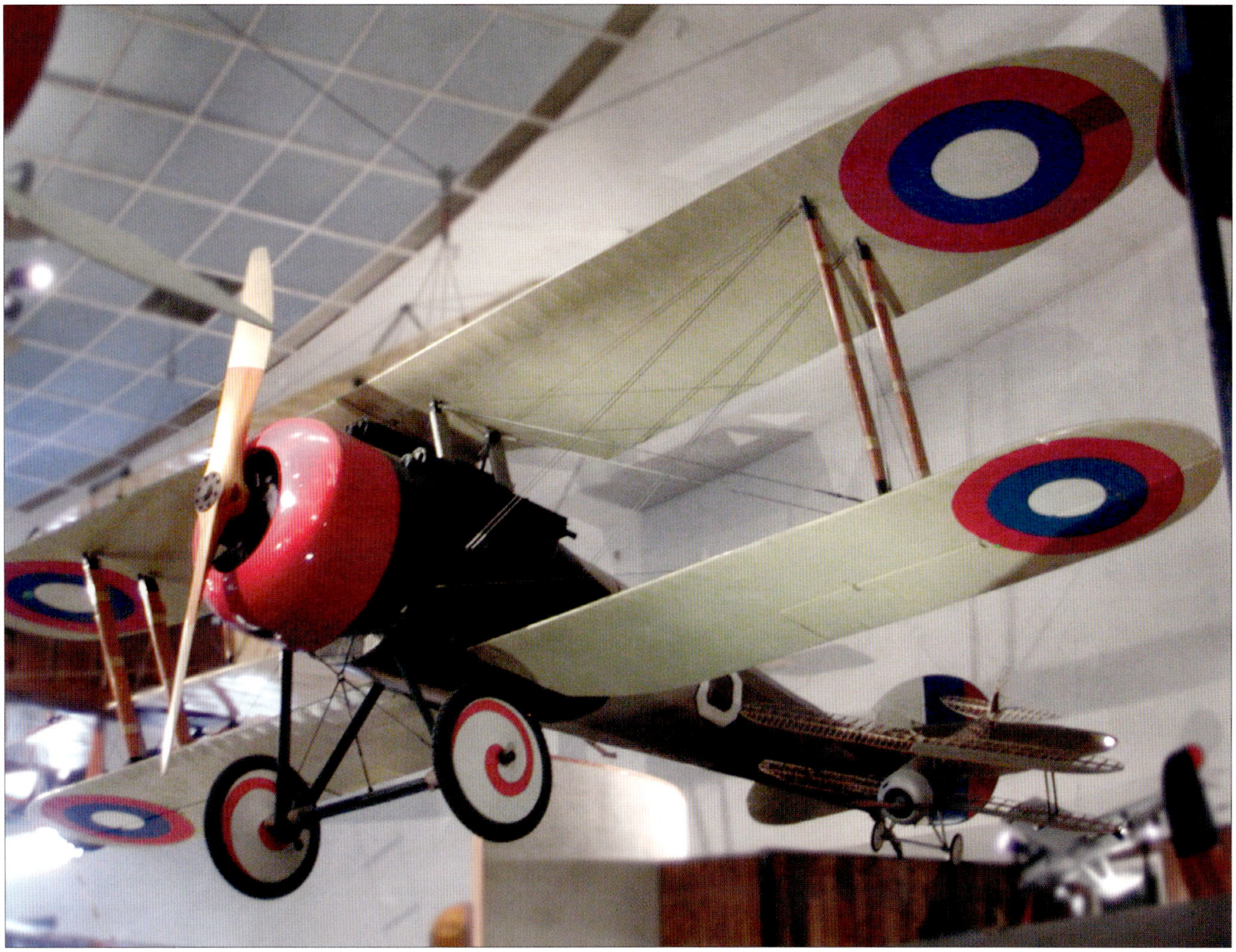

George Hunt's full-scale reproduction Nieuport 28, on display at the San Diego Air & Space Museum. San Diego Air & Space Museum

National Museum of Naval Aviation, Pensacola, Florida
Art Quinney of British Columbia, Canada, assembled the airframe of his reproduction Nieuport 28 in 1978, using Bergen Hardesty's plans and many photographs of the type that Quinney had gathered. Howard Wells, of Sepulveda, California, purchased the unfinished airplane from Quinney's estate after his death, and finished it in the colors of the U.S. Navy's BuNo 5796, a Nieuport 28A scout that had been assigned to the USS *Nevada* in the early 1920s. According to museum records, the airplane is now on loan to the National Museum of Naval Aviation in Pensacola, Florida.

Art Quinney's craftsmanship is evident in this photograph taken at his home in British Columbia, Canada. Unfortunately, Quinney died before he could complete his project.

Howard Wells finished this Nieuport 28, started by Art Quinney. Painted as a U.S. Navy Ship-plane Unit scout, it is now on loan to the National Museum of Naval Aviation in Pensacola, Florida.

Robert Rust Jr., a Work in Progress, Fayetteville, Georgia
Prior to his passing in 2003, Robert Rust Sr. began building another Nieuport 28, utilizing some original parts that he had obtained from Frank Tallman in exchange for having overhauled a 180 hp Mercédès engine for a Fokker D.VII. His son, Robert Rust Jr., a pilot and restorer like his father, intends to finish the project his father started.

Fliegermuseum, Dübendorf, Switzerland
Although modified to Swiss Air Force postwar standards, this aircraft is the most original and historically significant of all extant Nieuport 28 fighters. Its history is traced to Lieutenant James Ashenden's flight on 25 June 1918, which resulted in his internment in Switzerland and the subsequent rebuilding of his crashed aircraft (Nieuport 28, serial number N.6212) by the Swiss Air Force.

Leutnant Robert Ackermann's success with the refurbished airplane in international aerobatic competition prompted the Swiss Air Force to obtain fourteen more of the type, for use as advanced trainers. These aircraft were all Nieuport 28As, built after the war. Ashenden's N.6212 is the only wartime-manufactured Nieuport 28 fighter remaining in existence.

This aircraft, renumbered 607 after entering Swiss service, remained operational in the Fliegertruppe until it was retired in 1925. It is exhibited today in a place of honor at the Fliegermuseum in Dübendorf.

Right: A former Eastern Airlines pilot, the late Bob Rust Sr. was a real aficionado of the Nieuport 28.

Swiss Bébé number 607 (formerly USAS N.6212) at the Fliegermuseum in Dübendorf, Switzerland. R.L. Cavanagh

Vehrkehrshaus der Schweiz, Lucerne, Switzerland

This Nieuport 28A, number 688, one of fourteen purchased by the Swiss Air Force after the war, was operational as a training aircraft until 1930. It was purchased by the Dietikon Trade School and used briefly by the school, before being put in long-term storage. In 1964, an elderly Swiss former pilot who had once flown the type prevailed upon the Dietikon School to restore the aircraft. The Vehrkehrshaus der Schweiz later acquired the restored aircraft.

Museo Nacional de Aeronáutica, Buenos Áires, Argentina

This museum houses the remains of Nieuport 28, serial number N.6338, the aircraft flown by Teniente Benjamin Matienzo in his failed attempt to cross the Andes in 1919. Matienzo's body was recovered not long after the crash; the remnants of his airplane were recovered thirty-one years later, in 1950, and brought back to be housed in the museum.

Swiss Bébé number 688 on display at the Vehrkehrshaus der Schweiz in Lucerne, Switzerland. R.L. Cavanagh

Nieuport 28s of the Fuerza Aérea Argentina. Fernando Benedetto

The remains of Teniente Matienzo's Nieuport 28, collected from his crash site thirty-one years after his death, occupy a place of honor at the Museo Nacional de Aeronáutica in Buenos Áires. The gentleman standing to the right is Comodoro Esteban Luis Correa, then director of the museum.

Flying Reproductions: Past, Present ... and Future

Owls Head Transportation Museum, Owls Head, Maine
Carl Swanson, who also built the museum's SPAD XIII, built this flying Nieuport 28 reproduction. The aircraft is equipped with a 160 hp Lycoming radial engine.

Great War Flying Museum, Cheltenham, Ontario, Canada
This museum's flying reproduction is painted in the colors and markings of Lieutenant Eddie Rickenbacker's Nieuport 28, #12.

Musée Stampe & Vertongen, Antwerp, Belgium
This flying reproduction Nieuport 28 originated in the United States in 1972. Started by Clarence J. "Jim" Pawkett of Riverside, California, this project was completed by Jim Robertson after he acquired it in 1978. The late Frank Ryder obtained the aircraft in 1990, and moved it from its familiar habitat in Yucca Valley, California, to Guntersville, Alabama, where it was flown in Aerodrome '92. Frank Ryder combined the names of Lieutenant Robertson and Harry Wooldridge, who rebuilt the aircraft, and painted the name Robertson Wooldridge on the side of the aircraft. The aircraft is powered by a 220 hp Continental radial engine. The Musée Stampe & Vertongen Museum, which opened in 2001, apparently acquired the aircraft from the Frank Ryder estate.[14]

Carl Swanson's reproduction Nieuport 28 at Owls Head Transportation Museum in Maine. Owls Head Transportation Museum

Jim Appleby, California

Movie pilot Jim Appleby set the standard for flying reproductions of the elegant Nieuport 28. Among those now flying is Appleby's #5, in the colors of the 94th Aero Squadron. Built for Jim Osborne of Riverside, California, in 1976, #5 (tail number 6190) is now owned by Javier Arango, and flown by Chuck Wentworth of Antique Aero at Paso Robles, California. Javier Arango's airplane is now powered by a 160 hp Gnôme rotary engine. Another Nieuport 28 reproduction (also #5, but with tail number 6187) built by Jim in 1979, is owned by Ed Doyle of Hampton, Iowa.

Jim Appleby designed and built his reproduction Nieuport 28s for motion picture and air show work. His aircraft, incorporating modifications to enhance performance and safety, feature a re-engineered steel tube fuselage with added thickness on the fuselage walls, a steerable tail wheel, and a Warner 145 or 165 hp radial engine. The wings are strengthened (with minimal weight penalty) by installation of cap strips on the top of each rib from trailing edge to leading edge, unlike the production version, which carried the top cap strip only to the main spar. Jim changed the false ribs (see Appendix D for further detail) and stitched each rib and fabric all the way from trailing to leading edge. The substitution of Dacron for linen added further strength to each wing.

The late Robert Schuler made production plans of Jim Appleby's Nieuport 28, and several other pilots have used these plans in constructing their reproduction aircraft. Among them are Jim Pawkett, Press Womack, Howard Whyte, and Andrew King.

Above: Jim Appleby is about to undertake a film sequence, during the 1978 production of the TV series Salvage 1, starring Andy Griffith. Jim Appleby

Below: Jim Appleby (kneeling) and Zona Appleby (in cockpit) with their reproduction Nieuport 28. Jim Appleby

Jim Pawkett, Riverside, California

Jim Pawkett built at least three Nieuport 28 reproductions. The present whereabouts of the aircraft pictured below is not known, and the second aircraft, leased by Frank Tallman during the production of *The Great Waldo Pepper*, was destroyed when Tallman crashed into power lines while on a ferry flight. Tallman was injured, but survived this crash. The third reproduction, as reported earlier, is now found in the Musée Stampe & Vertongen in Antwerp, Belgium.

Press Womack, Selma, California

Press Womack, a crop duster from Selma, California, is several years away from completing his Nieuport 28 reproduction, which he began building in 1992. Womack will install a 165 hp Warner radial engine for test flying, but has configured the aircraft firewall to accept a freshly overhauled 160 hp Gnôme rotary engine once the testing is completed. His aircraft has a steel tube fuselage and empennage, and will have brakes and a steerable, wooden tailskid.

Below: Jim Pawkett's reproduction Nieuport 28; this was one of at least three reproduction Nieuport 28s built by Pawkett. H. Hugh Wynne

Right: Howard Whyte's reproduction Nieuport 28 in flight, with Andrew King at the controls. Howard Whyte

Howard Whyte, Douglassville, Pennsylvania

Howard Whyte's reproduction Nieuport 28, painted in the colors of the 27th Aero Squadron, was first test-flown in August 2005. On 30 September 2005, while attending the World War I Fly-In at Dayton, Ohio, Whyte experienced engine failure shortly after takeoff and crashed, with Howard sustaining some injuries. The aircraft was seriously damaged, but it is being rebuilt.

Andrew King, Virginia

Andrew King grew up not far from Old Rhinebeck Aerodrome, where his father, Bill, and uncle Dick volunteered their piloting skills. Among his first memories, at age four or five, is the very distinctive and very loud sound of the Gnôme rotary engine of Cole Palen's Nieuport 28. His visual memory is of "two or three guys on each wing" of the Nieuport 28 as it was swung into position for takeoff, likely with his uncle Dick at the controls.[15] King also remembers conversations with Douglas Campbell, who visited the Aerodrome on several occasions

At this writing, King has completed the wings, fuselage, tail, and gear of his reproduction Nieuport 28. The aircraft will be powered by a Gnôme rotary engine that he obtained through an eBay auction. The finished aircraft will be painted in the 94th Aero Squadron colors of Douglas Campbell's Nieuport 28, serial number N.6164.

Other Nieuport 28 reproductions were under way at the time of this writing.

Movie pilot and airplane builder Andrew King at his place of business in Virginia. Andrew is building a reproduction Nieuport 28 that will be painted in the colors of Douglas Campbell's N.6164. Andrew's father and uncle were associated for many years with Cole Palen's Old Rhinebeck Aerodrome in Rhinebeck, New York.

APPENDICES

Appendix A
Flying the Nieuport 28

Certainly the loveliest racehorse lines of all the World War I aircraft belonged to the French Nieuport 28, and like the beautiful thoroughbred it resembles, it also had real speed and agility. I share the feeling of others lucky enough to fly the "28" that it certainly is the epitome of World War I flying. After you have flown this beauty, you are ready to throw old rusty water-cooled engines at other much better publicized Allied and German aircraft. — Frank Gifford Tallman III[1]

Several present-day pilots became intimately acquainted with the Nieuport 28 while flying original, rotary-engine-powered aircraft during air shows or while filming movies. Among these latter-day pilots were the late Frank Tallman, a former US Navy pilot and partner of Paul Mantz, and Dick King, an Old Rhinebeck Aerodrome pilot. Jim Appleby, a former US Air Force pilot, acquired exceptional knowledge of the Nieuport 28, having extensively flown Tallman's clipped-wing Nieuport 28. He also designed and built several widely copied Nieuport 28 reproductions, and restored numerous 160 hp Gnôme rotary engines for himself and others.

A report prepared by pilots of the Historic Aircraft Collection (HAC) in the UK offers additional insights into the flying characteristics of the Nieuport 28. Guy Black purchased HAC's example at a Christie's auction on 6 December 1981 from Dolph Overton's Wings and Wheels Museum. Formerly part of Frank Tallman's collection of Nieuport 28s, this aircraft was acquired in trade by Aeroflex, who then sold it to Overton. Skysport Engineering Ltd. restored the aircraft to flying condition and it was flown at Old Warden Aerodrome in England in 1991 and 1992.

The following accounts, taken from these pilots' reports, would be familiar to First Pursuit Group pilots who flew the Nieuport 28 fighter in 1918.

I. Preflight

A. Inspection

Absent an Air Service crew chief, the pilot faces a demanding task in preflighting an antique Nieuport 28. Walk-around starts at the cockpit, by first making certain that the shutoff valves are in the proper position. If an oil shutoff valve is installed, it must be turned on, and fuel and both master and selector switches turned off. The fuel control valve on the quadrant must be in the off position and the control stick in neutral position, and not tied back to lock the controls. After removing the inspection panels, check for evidence of oil leaks. Turn on the fuel selector and drain the fuel drain-strainer before checking for fuel contaminants. Turn off the fuel selector after completing this procedure. Check for leaks from main oil line to the oil pump, and be certain that the oil and fuel tanks are properly filled.

The Gnôme rotary engine and cowl requires special attention. The condition of the propeller and propeller bolts are examined and the cowl is inspected to see if it is securely attached. Oil puddling in the bottom of the cowl is examined for evidence of metallic flaking, a sign of a serious engine problem. The compression of each cylinder is checked. Evidence of darkening discoloration on the cylinder heads reveals cylinder burning, caused by the use of too rich or too lean a mixture.

The valve rocker should be freshly lubricated. Circlips, holding the push rod and rocker pin at the top of each push rod, and the jam nut, locking the cup end of the tappet rod at the bottom of the push rod, must be checked to see that they are secure.

Since oil tends to settle in a rotary engine's lower cylinder, the single cylinder valve is pushed open, and oil trickling out into the hand is examined for evidence of metal flaking. External oiling of valve stems and pins, etc., is done as required.

Airframe inspection is equally demanding: Fabric tears have to be repaired, while fabric wrinkles might reveal a broken longeron or former. Wings are inspected and all cables checked for proper tension. A visual check of the tires quickly tells if there is a problem with tire inflation. A wing tip is pushed down to reveal the soundness of the bungee cords on the landing gear. All control surfaces must move freely and the tailskid, with steel shoe attached, is checked for damage. When everything is in order, it's time to climb into the cockpit. Prudence dictates that there be someone with a fire extinguisher standing by.[2]

B. Getting In

Without the help of a convenient stepladder, the procedure for entering the Nieuport 28's tiny cockpit requires both strength and agility. Grabbing hold of the leather cockpit coaming with the right hand (the leather coaming around the cockpit opening protects the pilot's head from the sharp metal edge of the fuselage panels), the pilot steps up off the ground with his left foot; simultaneously reaching forward for the left center section strut with the left hand; at this time, his left foot is on the (7.5" x 4.5") aluminum wing step. He transfers his right hand from the leather cockpit coaming to the right center section strut, carefully raises his right leg over the coaming (so as to not kick in the side of the fuselage) and into the cockpit before stepping onto the seat. He now raises his body to line up with the cockpit, bringing his left leg from the step into the cockpit, and is now standing with both feet on the tufted seat. With right and left hand firmly grasping the coaming, the pilot slowly lowers his body, while at the same time sliding his feet forward and then placing them on the rudder bar. The lap and shoulder safety belts are then secured.

C. Engine Run Up

Remove ground extinguisher safety pin. Never start the aircraft without large chocks and ground personnel on the tailplane. The switch is turned on, both cocks and the mixture set to rich, with all ignition switches off or zero; also the blip switch is depressed as an added measure while the engine is turned over 2–3 times. Fuel should be seen to flow out of the lower valve on the bottom cylinder. Turn the mixture off and then switch all ignition switches on and the selector to [position] 4. The engine usually fires with 2–3 blades [rotations] and, of course, then starts at full power. When the engine fires, the mixture should be opened slowly [via the fuel adjustment quadrant] to the 2/3 forward position, and selector then turned to position 3, contributing to a short warm-up period at reduced power.

The engine will run on setting one after about 20 seconds, following checks on both magnetos. With a 'reduced' ignition selected, a reduction in [fuel] mixture is advised.

When the engine is running too rich, a deep 'clanking' metallic sound can be heard and reduced by a leaner mixture setting. If you reduce the mixture too much, the engine will fade and then the aggressive use of the mixture lever is needed to recover the engine.[3]

Ground crewmen turn the Nieuport 28 into the wind and chock each wheel. With fuel/air lever retarded and coupé button depressed for safety, the propeller is pulled through several times (priming may or may not have been necessary, for the engine will generally run either way) before "switch on" is yelled by the crewman about to pull the seven-foot prop to start. With a "switch on" response from the pilot (in

Dick King pilots Cole Palen's Nieuport 28A at Old Rhinebeck Aerodrome in New York. This photograph dates back to the 1960s. Dick King

this case, Dick King): "the engine roared to life, and when I say roared to life, it really roared. Because of the one valve arrangement and the high horsepower of the engine, the noise was deafening. I held back on the control stick and other mechanics were holding the wings, but even then, the little Nieuport was straining at the chocks."[4]

II. Flight

A. Takeoff

Full power is used for take off with directional control being very good. The aircraft has a strong tendency to swing to the left so considerable right rudder is required. Forward view is poor and view to the left of nose even worse due to [the] Vickers gun installation.

The take off run is approximately 150 yards in still air and lift off speed [is] 45 mph. RPM [is] 1350 and climb out [is] made at 60 mph.

Take off with an aft C[enter] of G[ravity] produces a strong nose up tendency held with approximately 4–5 lbs. push. An aft C of G can only be produced by having little fuel in the forward tank, so for demonstration flights, it is suggested that the fuel tank is to be full.[5]

Jim Appleby recalled his first flight in Tallman's Nieuport 28: "I worked out a signal with the [equally new to the Nieuport] ground crew, to pull the chocks with long ropes as soon as I nodded my head. ... I ran up the engine to full power, and called the tower, and then looked down at the tach to check the rpm ... [seeing that,] the crew immediately pulled the chocks and the next thing I knew, I was airborne! You had to have a fighter pilot mentality to prepare for takeoff behind this very powerful engine."[6]

B. Climb

During full power operation, right rudder is required to keep the slip ball [an air speed indicator was fitted to the forward port interplane strut] central at 55–60 mph. With a forward C of G, there is still a tendency for slight pitch up.[7]

Frank Tallman's observation about the Nieuport 28's robust takeoff performance was equally stunning: "With the chocks pulled and the Gnôme winding up, it's like a Clydesdale or Percheron pulling for there is no doubt as to the old engine's raw horsepower – I know of no other aircraft except the Boeing F4BI (P-12) that has such complete and instant response. The tail is up in 15 feet of forward roll, and the rudder is needed to overcome torque, though the actual torque is nothing like the hair-raising fables of the World War I-type pulp magazines. The climb is spectacular, and the steep-climbing turn gives not the slightest evidence of payoff."[8]

Pilots used a variety of methods to check that the engine was oiling properly. Apart from the smell of castor oil that Frank Tallman found overwhelming, an obvious solution was to look down to the right at the oil pulsator and note oil pulsations (some pilots could also get a pretty accurate fix on the engine rpms by gauging the oil pulsations). One could also note the accumulation of oil on the windshield, or on the leading edges of the wing. Jim Appleby had several simpler methods to check oiling: "stick your arm out into the slipstream" or "blip the switch [the coupé button], then turn around and look for the trail of blue smoke after the blip switch is released."[9] Ingesting castor oil mist remained a problem, unless, as Frank Tallman suggested, one wore "a nice tight, pressure-type oxygen mask"; Tallman found the smell of castor oil "overwhelming."[10]

C. Cruise

The aircraft can be flown on two ignition settings for cruise. Setting of 3 gives 85–90 mph, and setting of 4 gives top speed [of] 120 mph. STRAIGHT AND LEVEL [S/L]: There is no elevator trim fitted and approximately 5 lbs. push is required for S/L on setting of 4. With application of power, there is a nose up tendency, this being more marked with an aft C of G. The aircraft is longitudinally stable with the elevators being effective throughout the speed range. Lateral stability is neutral and the ailerons become very heavy above 90 mph. Turns to the left are much faster than to the right due to the torque effect of the engine. Sideslip angles of up to 30 degrees were made to the left and right and were controllable though the rudder tended to trail with the airflow.[11]

Jim Appleby had flown the SPAD VII and XIII, and he appreciated the structural strength of the SPAD in relation to the more fragile Nieuport 28 (this, of course, did not pertain to the improved, and more structurally sound, Nieuport 28 reproduction that Appleby designed and built). The forward and side visibility in a SPAD XIII was better than that of the Nieuport 28; because of the stagger of the SPAD's wings, you could look down and see more of the terrain. The

Historic Aircraft Collection's Nieuport 28A reproduction, in flight at Old Warden Aerodrome in the early 1990s. Guy Black

Jim Appleby making a low pass near the photographer. This Nieuport 28 was later acquired by Jim Hall in 1968 at the Movieland of the Air Museum auction, under the auspices of Parke-Bernet Galleries Inc. Jim Appleby

Nieuport could accelerate faster in straight and level flight and also enter into a dive faster than the SPAD. But the SPAD could catch up in about 500 feet and speed past the Nieuport, for no contemporary fighter was faster than the SPAD XIII in a dive. Jim Appleby, however, characterized the flying qualities of the SPAD XIII in much the same way as the pilots who flew it during the First World War: "It flew like a brick ----house."[12]

D. Stalls and VNE

There is no stall-warning device fitted. Stalls were carried out at both ranges of C of G with no speed differences. The stall warning, in the form of airframe buffet, occurred at 50–55 mph, and the stall itself, [at] 38–42 mph, [with] power off. At the stall, nose drop occurred first, followed by left wing to an angle of 15 degrees. Height loss was estimated at 150 feet. No spins were carried out.

There is no official VNE [do not exceed speed] for the Nieuport 28, but the example was flown to 140 mph with no control problems. The engine RPM of 1450 was achieved. The control forces became very heavy above 100 mph.[13]

The Nieuport 28 had a well-deserved reputation for agility and handling. The airplane performed chandelles and loops beautifully, but with offset rudder at the top to counteract torque; the power of the 160 hp Gnôme thrust the airplane easily up and over the top of the loop. Stalls were straightforward unless full back elevator was applied. Snap rolls were OK to the left but not attempted to the right because of the torque. This maneuver should not be done with a rotary engine because it could break the crankshaft.

The rudder and elevator controls were well-balanced and very effective, but the aileron response, because of the wide gap between the wing and ailerons, was not. This adversely affected the roll rate of the airplane: "It was easy to get into an Immelmann, but lack of aileron efficiency made it difficult to get out."[14] Jim Appleby felt that an effective "gap seal," one that would not disturb air flow or restrict free movement of the aileron, would greatly enhance the roll-rate efficiency of the Nieuport 28. But for roll performance he preferred the Sopwith Pup, which had ailerons on both top and bottom wings and was over 350 pounds lighter than the Nieuport 28.

Frank Tallman complained about the excessive heat generated by the Gnôme rotary engine: "The big Gnôme gives off heat like a cast-iron stove in a New England store in winter. It's so d--- hot, you're sure the ship is afire."[15] Jim Appleby explained that Tallman's Nieuport 28, unlike the aircraft that Dick King flew, lacked a heat deflector on the back of the firewall, which directed the heat down and out of the rear of the cowl. Lanky pilots in 1918 had also complained about engine heat, but only if they stretched their boots forward too close to the firewall.

Tallman's clipped-wing Nieuport 28 was also missing the "infamous cut-out [selector] switch," (too complicated, according to Jim Appleby) but was equipped with an airspeed indicator, oil pressure gauge and altimeter.[16] Cole Palen's Nieuport 28, as flown by Dick King, was still equipped with the multiposition selector switch (the function of which will be described fully in Appendix C) in addition to the blip switch (coupé), which temporarily cut out the engine. Use of the blip and/or selector switch would sometimes alarm spectators on the ground: "None of these people had ever heard a rotary engine run

A shot of the modified instrument panel of the Movieland of the Air Museum's Nieuport 28.

before and [they] didn't realize that the cutting out of the engine was a normal occurrence and was the only way the pilot has of controlling the cruising and descending of the aeroplane."[17]

III. Return to Base

A. Approach, Landing, and Taxiing

A 'blipping' approach, using a setting of 4, was found to be more favourable because the engine tends to oil and flood with low ignition setting being used for more than 30 seconds. Speed on the approach used is 60–65 mph and control of speed [is] good up to the flare. Forward visibility at the flare is poor and little swing is noticed on the rollout. The aircraft has a strong weathercock tendency, and therefore, should always be landed into the wind. Landing roll is 100 yards on flat, short grass with no wind.

The aircraft can be taxied with no assistance in light winds by use of a blast of power over the rudder. The help of a wing tip runner is recommended in any wind over 5 knots. The aircraft has no nose-over tendency on short grass, however, it has a spreader bar between the wheels some 12" high, and so taxiing or landing in long grass should be avoided.[18]

Landing the Nieuport 28 was a breeze: "The Nieuport glides and flares on landing so smoothly … ."[19] Frank Tallman credited the Nieuport 28's rudder: "Thanks to the graceful and generous rudder, you don't have to make the rudder correction on landing that you do with both the SPAD and the Fokker D.VII."[20] Jim Appleby agreed: "The rudder is fully effective [until the aircraft slows] to a walk."[21]

The consensus among these latter-day pilots was that the Nieuport 28 was, with the exception of attention given to engine control, a delight to fly. Dick King, echoing the sentiments of wartime Air Service squadron commander Harold Hartney, may have summed it up best: "It is a beautiful aeroplane to fly because you fit into it like a glove and you become an extension of the machine."[22]

Appendix B
The Design Evolution of the Nieuport 28

Background

The wartime fortunes of the Société Anonyme des Établissements Nieuport may have peaked with the introduction of the Nieuport 17 in April 1916. This lightweight sesquiplane fighter, equipped with a single Vickers machine gun and powered by a 110 hp Le Rhône rotary engine, saw widespread service with France's Aviation Militaire (serving principally with Army cooperation units) and Allied air forces including those of Britain, Italy, Russia, and Romania. The Nieuport Company's market position would not be sustained, however, for future Allied requirements would increasingly be met by other, more innovative designs. Gustave Delage and the Nieuport Company struggled to prevent competitive designs (particularly the SPAD VII and XIII), from dominating the fighter market; for the time being, Delage responded by making incremental changes in his basic sesquiplane design and experimenting with new configurations of engine and airframe.

The Nieuport 27 was the culmination of Nieuport's long line of V-strut fighters; its maximum speed of 116 mph at sea level and ceiling of 18,200 feet made it only marginally better than the Nieuport 17, but inferior to the SPAD VII, now equipped with a high-compression 180 hp engine. The operational life of the Nieuport 11 to 27 series of sesquiplane fighters on the Western Front was approximately thirty months; but for the production problems encountered with the SPAD VII, the life of Nieuport's sesquiplane series would have been substantially diminished.

During much of 1917, the Nieuport Company experimented with different fighter designs, with Delage seeking the right combination of engine (principally Le Rhône or Clergêt rotaries), wing (mono-, bi-, and triplanes, with varying wing area), fuselage (standard frame, faired, or monocoque), tail assembly, and other structural details. While none of these experimental fighters reached production, some of their evolutionary design characteristics would take form in future Nieuport fighters, among them, the Nieuport 28.

Below: The Nieuport 27, the last in a long line of Nieuport sesquiplanes. The tail assembly and fuselage design of the Nieuport 27 is evident in the later design of the Nieuport 28.

Bottom: This unnumbered Nieuport fighter illustrates the transition to the broader chord, twin-spar lower wing of Nieuport's newer fighter designs. This experimental fighter was powered by a Le Rhône rotary engine. S.H.A.A. via William Nungesser

NIEUPORT 28 PROTOTYPES AND PRODUCTION MODELS EXTERIOR DISTINGUISHING FEATURES

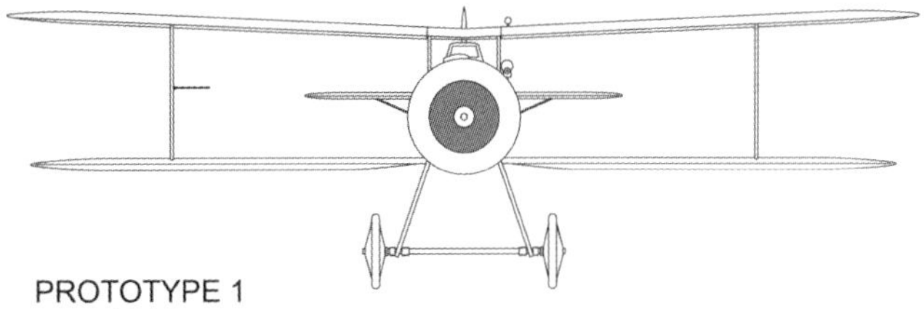

PROTOTYPE 1
June 1917
Total dihedral on upper wing only. Serial number 4434. Provision for one Vickers machine gun. Venturi mounted on top wing.

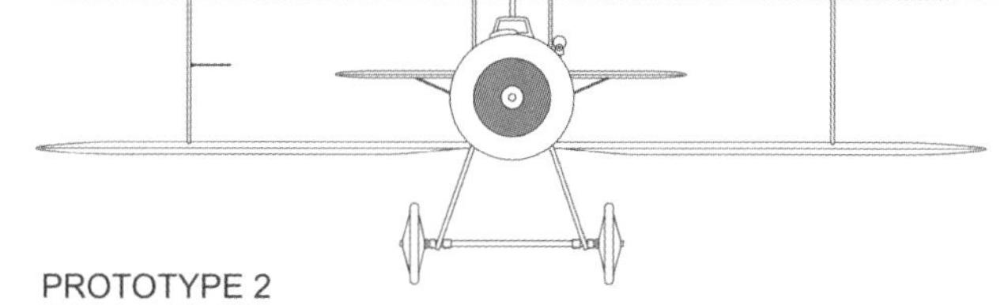

PROTOTYPE 2
October 1917
No dihedral. Serial number unknown. Provision for one Vickers machine gun. Venturi mounted on top wing.

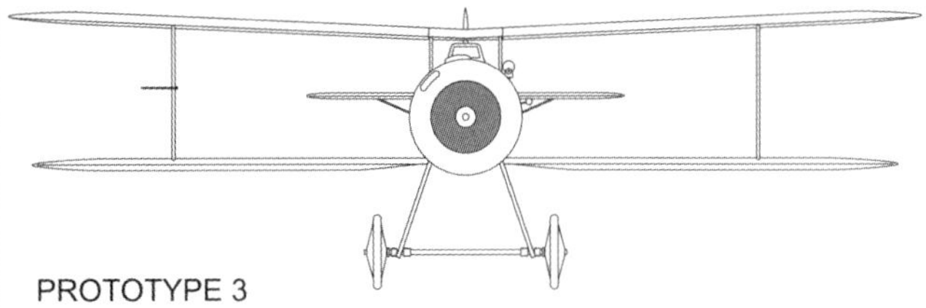

PROTOTYPE 3
November 1917
Total dihedral. Serial number 6125. Provision for one Vickers machine gun. Venturi mounted on port side of fuselage. Additional prototypes were built with total dihedral.

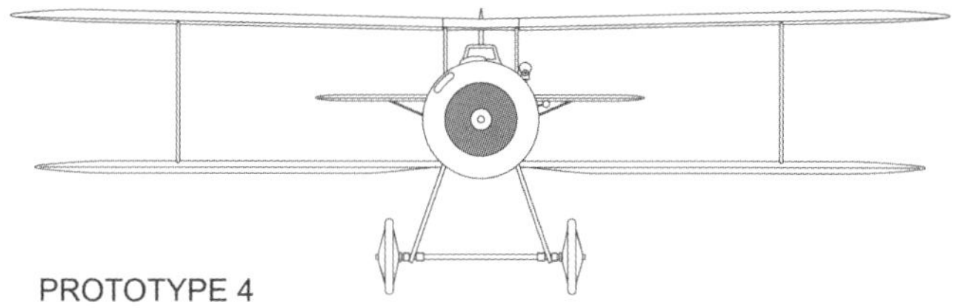

PROTOTYPE 4
November 1917
Half dihedral. Provision for one Vickers machine gun. Serial number unknown. Venturi mounted on port side of fuselage. Doubled lift wires introduced for added strength.

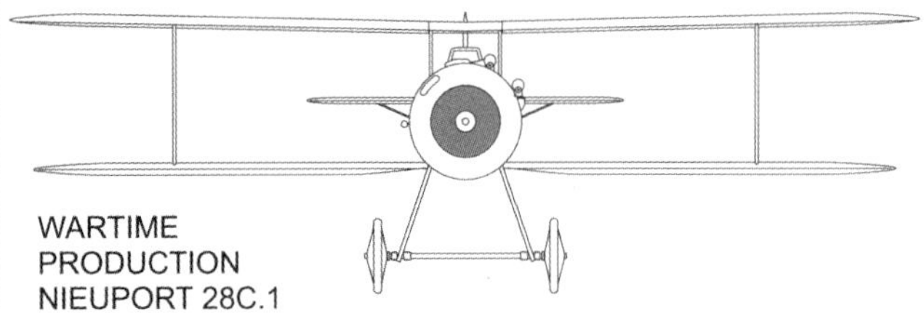

WARTIME PRODUCTION NIEUPORT 28C.1
From December 1917
Half dihedral. Provision for two Vickers machine gun. Venturi mounted on starboard side of fuselage.

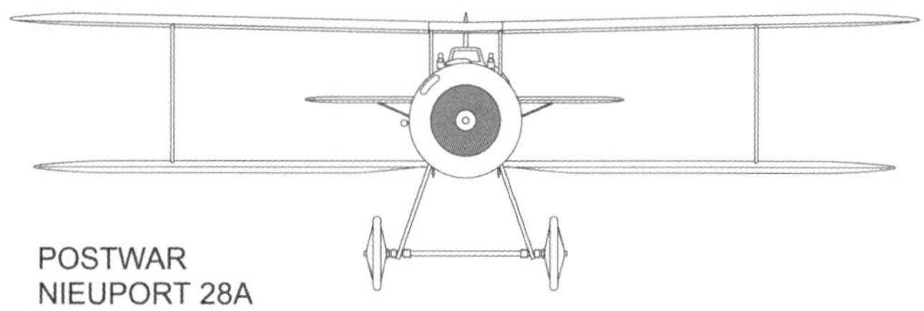

POSTWAR NIEUPORT 28A
From October 1918
Half dihedral. Modified version of wartime production Nieuport 28C.1. Provision for two Marlin machine guns. Venturi mounted on starboard side of fuselage.

Nieuport 28

It has frequently been observed that the Nieuport 28 represented a significant break with past design concepts. Equipped with the more powerful 160 hp Gnôme monosoupape 9N rotary engine, the aircraft had a fully faired fuselage with two-spar upper and lower wings of unequal chord, braced by parallel interplane struts. Other distinguishing features (to be explored fully in the following appendix) included ailerons on the lower wings, fully elliptical wing tips, and a tail unit that had its origins in the Nieuport 24, all of which contributed to what many consider an exceptionally elegant airplane.

The Nieuport 28 represented a break between Nieuport's sesquiplane fighters and the radically different and highly successful Nieuport 29 that followed it, in the process reclaiming the fighter market for Nieuport in the postwar era. In mid-1917, Delage and other aircraft designers and airmen were already paying close attention to the ongoing development of the 300 hp ungeared Hispano-Suiza, the engine that would ultimately power the Nieuport 29. In the meantime, testing of the first prototypes of the lightweight, single-bay Nieuport 28 fighter was under way.

Nie. 28C1 (Nieuport 28, Chasse [fighter], single place), serial number N.4434, was first tested by the Section Technique de l'Aéronautique (STAé), on 5-6 June 1917. With a change of its Levasseur propeller it was tested again, with similar results, one week later. With a load of 228 kilograms and powered by a Gnôme monosoupape 9N rotary engine, the aircraft established a maximum speed of 209 kph (1,450 rpm at 2,000 meters), reaching that altitude in 4.5 minutes. Maximum altitude achieved was 6,700 meters, with minimum horizontal speed near the ground of 106 kph at 750 rpm.[1]

Opposite
Top: N.4434, the first prototype of the Nieuport 28, first flew in June 1917. This aircraft, equipped with a single Vickers machine gun mounted on the upper longeron, featured an upper wing with total dihedral (dièdre total). S.H.A.A. via William Nungesser

Center: This photograph of N.4434 clearly shows the twin spars and ailerons on the lower wing, which were major departures from Nieuport's earlier sesquiplane designs. S.H.A.A. via William Nungesser

Bottom: This is the patent drawing for the Brevet d'Invention, No. 503,610, that the Nieuport Company applied for on 31 July 1917. The patent drawing illustrates a Nieuport 28 prototype that features total dihedral and a slight degree of sweepback of both upper and lower wings. This was one of a number of wing configurations that Gustave Delage was testing. S.H.A.A. via Bernard Klaeyle

N
4434

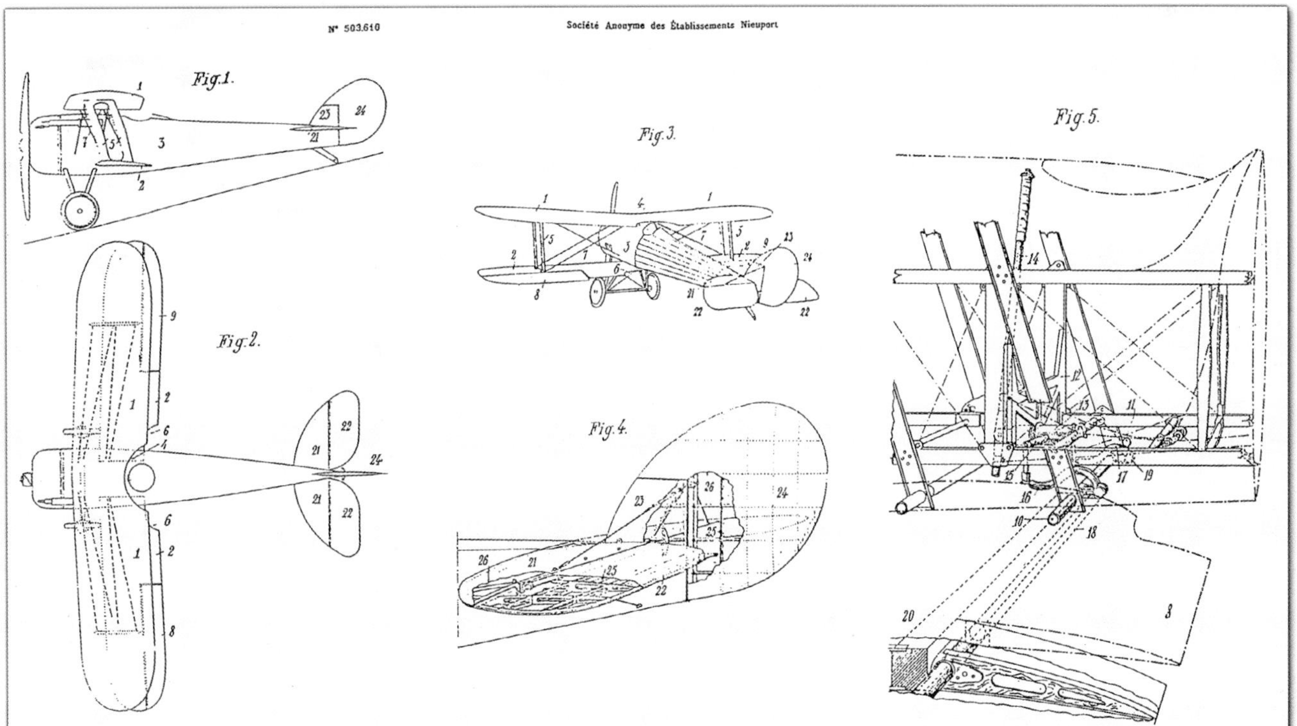
N° 503.610
Société Anonyme des Établissements Nieuport
Fig.1.
Fig.2.
Fig.3.
Fig.4.
Fig.5.

An unnumbered Nieuport 28 prototype with no dihedral, referred to in French as dièdre nul. S.H.A.A. via William Nungesser

On 31 July 1917, the Nieuport Company applied for a patent for the Nieuport 28. Brevet d'Invention No. 503,610 described the main features of the aircraft as having "ailerons on the lower wing, enhanced pilot's view from the low set upper wing with dihedral, flat profile in the central part of the upper wing, elliptical wing tips, [and] wooden tail surfaces." [2] The patent drawings portray an aircraft similar to the first prototype, N.4434, but with a slight sweepback on the upper and lower wings. This design feature, evident on a Clergêt 11E-engine-powered fighter (not a Nieuport 28) that appeared several months later, suggested that Delage was attempting to improve longitudinal (pitch) stability. However, this feature did not improve handling qualities, and it was subsequently abandoned.

Seeking to optimize the aircraft's lateral (roll) stability, Gustave Delage tested different wing configurations. Several aircraft (N.6125, N.6128, N.6132, and N.6133) in addition to N.4434, were built with dièdre total (full dihedral) while other known prototypes incorporated diédre nul (no dihedral) or ½ diédre (one-half or semi-dihedral).[3] Delage finally settled on ½ dihedral for the production version of the Nieuport 28.

In order to establish an optimal rate of climb, Delage tested several propellers, each with a different angle of pitch.

In an effort to improve roll-rate efficiency, Delage later experimented with ailerons on both top and bottom wings. Ailerons were of normal chord, but shorter span than those found on the standardized Nieuport 28, and the top aileron was activated by a connecting rod. While this configuration appeared on several Nieuport 28s (including the modified prototype N.6134 and two aircraft given to Argentina after the war), it was also found on precursors and prototypes of the Nieuport 29. This modification, however, was never standardized on production models of the Nieuport 28, 28A, or the Nieuport 29.

Early prototypes of the Nieuport 28 (N.6134 excluded) had an oil-tank capacity of 20 liters and a total fuel-tank capacity of 115 liters – a main fuel tank of 65 liters ahead of the pilot and 25-liter fuel tanks on either side of the pilot's seat. A Weyman exhauster fed fuel from

A side view of dièdre nul, with a single Vickers machine gun mounted on the upper left longeron. S.H.A.A. via William Nungesser

the reserve tanks to the main tank; the venturi actuating the Weyman mechanism was placed in several different positions before it was permanently ensconced on the starboard side of the fuselage just aft of the engine cowl. A single Vickers machine gun, fed by a cloth belt containing 500 rounds, was installed.

In August 1917, the United States contracted for 2,000 SPAD XIII fighters, equipped with 200 hp Hispano-Suiza engines, and 1,500 fighters of either the experimental SPAD XV monocoque or the Nieuport 28, both of the latter fighters powered with the Gnôme monosoupape rotary engine. (The August 1917 contract was later cancelled, due to nonperformance on both sides.) At the time the single-gunned prototype Nieuports were being tested, the two-gunned Morane-Saulnier A1, (later designated MoS 29) was also undergoing testing at Villacoublay. Initial results on the Gnôme-powered Morane monoplane fighter were promising.

The twin-gunned SPAD XIII had entered front-line service, but in small numbers, as its 200 hp Hispano-Suiza engine, while successful on the test bench, encountered almost insurmountable problems once it entered production. The more powerful engine required reduction gearing in order to tap the increased power from higher crankshaft speeds. The attempts to rectify cooling, lubrication, carburetor, and metal tempering (of the gears), problems associated with the geared engine, was a laborious engineering effort, and delayed widespread introduction of the new fighter. By the third quarter of 1917, the 200 hp Hispano-Suiza engine was already considered inadequate in combating high-flying German reconnaissance aircraft.

The introduction of a direct-drive, high-compression 180 hp Hispano-Suiza engine into the SPAD VII prolonged production of the SPAD VII for a considerable time; it also provided an interim solution to the dearth of SPAD XIIIs. Increased compression ultimately provided the solution to improving the performance of the 200 hp geared engine of the SPAD XIII. With redesigned and improved carburetion, valves, strengthened crankshaft, and lubrication, the high-compression, geared 220 hp Hispano-Suiza engine became the standard power plant for the SPAD XIII ... but the bugs were never completely ironed out during the course of its operational existence.

In the late fall of 1917, the engine debate (or crisis, as some called it) was still unresolved, and would remain so until well into the following year. There were problems with the Gnôme rotary, and very serious problems with the geared Hispano-Suiza engine: "it was

Another Nieuport 28 prototype featuring a total dihedral upper wing like N.4434. Distinctive camouflage appears on this prototype. The next three photographs are of the same aircraft taken at different angles. S.H.A.A. via William Nungesser

S.H.A.A. via William Nungesser

S.H.A.A. via William Nungesser

S.H.A.A. via William Nungesser

reported that two-thirds of all aircraft powered by the 200-hp Hispano-Suiza engine were grounded owing to engine defects."[4]

General Pétain had decreed on 17 October 1917 that Nieuport fighters powered by 120 hp engines were now inferior to German fighters, and would be replaced by the Nieuport 28, Morane-Saulnier 29, or SPAD XIII, depending on availability. At this juncture, American observers were betting on the Morane-Saulnier 29 to win best of class among the Gnôme rotary-engine fighters (the Gnôme-powered SPAD XV monocoque fighter had failed its tests by this time, and had been rejected), as reported by General Pershing in typical cablese to the United States: "Morane monoplane Gnome one fifty engine superior to all Greatest speed any single seater pursuit airplane Second in climb only to Martinside [sic – Pershing may have been referring to the Martinsyde Buzzard, then under development in the UK] experimental machine Other characteristics excellent stability perfect landing speed better than other Gnome engine scouts In future other Gnome airplanes may equal but do not think will excel Morane monoplane."[5]

These were the prevailing conditions in November 1917, when the STAè undertook comparative maneuverability testing of three Nieuport 28 prototypes, each having a different wing configuration. The ½ dihedral (½ dièdre) prototype emerged as the preferred configuration.

Second Lieutenant Bourgeois flew the ½ dihedral Nieuport 28 prototype at Villacoublay on 7 November 1917. The following day it was tested again, this time by Second Lieutenant Canivet.[6] Equipped with a 150 hp Gnôme (Type Omega 6) monosoupape engine with Chauvière Series 47652 propeller affixed, both pilots reported "good" action on the controls, "easy" reaction of the controls, and "good" stability in each axis of flight. Both pilots commented on the ease of operation on the ground and the rapidity with which the airplane took to the air. Landing was pronounced equally good as the aircraft flattened easily, rolled very little (the metal-shod skid was effective), and alighted slowly. Second Lieutenant Canivet reported that the visibility was "Good in the rear, fairly poor below, and mediocre above, as the top plane is fairly high above the pilot's head."[7]

On 13 November 1917, pilot Mallard tested the performance of the ½ dihedral Nieuport 28 prototype that pilots Bourgeois and Canivet had flown days earlier. With a useful load of 228 kilograms, Mallard reached a speed of 200 kph (at 1,410 rpms) at an altitude of 2,000 meters. Speed at 5,000 meters and 1,350 rpms was clocked at 185 kph. Rate of climb in minutes, in 1,000-meter increments, was 2:35 (to 1,000 meters), 5:30 (2,000 meters), 9:00 (3,000 meters), 14:00 (4,000 meters), and 21:15 to an altitude of 5,000 meters. The ceiling established was 6,750 meters.

It was reported on 18 December 1917 that "a prototype Nieuport 28 C1 Gn. [Gnôme] 9Nc [160 hp] is being tested with semi-dihedral [½ dihedral] waiting for an engine."[8] During the same month, another Nieuport fighter, quite similar in exterior appearance to the Nieuport 28, was also undergoing testing. This aircraft, mentioned earlier in this appendix, was powered by a 200 hp Clergêt rotary engine, and

Above: This Nieuport experimental fighter looked like a derivative of the Nieuport 28, but had several features – monocoque fuselage and tail surfaces – that were similar to the Nieuport 29. The wings on this single-gun fighter have no dihedral and the position of the single set of cabane struts restricted forward visibility, as well as providing less structural integrity. S.H.A.A. via William Nungesser

Below: Clearly derived from the Nieuport 28, this experimental fighter was armed with two Vickers machine guns and powered by a 200 hp Clergêt rotary engine. It did not enter production because its performance was only marginally better than that of the SPAD VII. S.H.A.A. via William Nungesser

incorporated twin Vickers machine guns, reputedly the first Nieuport fighter to carry two guns.[9] The performance of the Clergêt-powered fighter was no better than the SPAD VII, and consequently it never reached production. Other experiments with monoplane fighter prototypes equipped with the Gnôme monosoupape or 180 hp Le Rhône 9R rotary engine proved equally unsuccessful, however.[10]

The following events, presented in detail in Chapter 3, are worth reviewing, for the conjunction of these events determined that the Nieuport 28 would not suffer the same fate as Nieuport's other failed experimental fighters.

In late December 1917, a further refinement of the ½ dihedral Nieuport 28 finally produced a two-gunned fighter. This modification required removing the 25-liter reserve tank to the left of the pilot; the right reserve tank remained in place. The Nieuport Company tooled up in anticipation of production orders on the Nieuport 28.

As related in Chapter 3, French projections for aircraft at the front by April 1918 numbered 4,022, with bombers and fighters being given priority. By early 1918, some French escadrilles were being converted to the Morane monoplane fighter, and the SPAD XIII was beginning to be mass-produced by the Société Anonyme Pour L'Aviation et ses Dérivés (SPAD). The French government had contracted with eight other French manufacturers to manufacture the SPAD XIII, but there were production delays. As a result, French fighter projections for April 1918, set in the fall of 1917, would not be reached. However, French aviation requirements remained paramount.

Allied air services were gearing up to meet the threat of Germany's "Amerika Program" and the growing threat of massive German offensives expected for early spring 1918. The pressure was building on Brigadier General Benjamin Foulois, Chief of Air Service, AEF, to equip and field the nascent US Air Service.

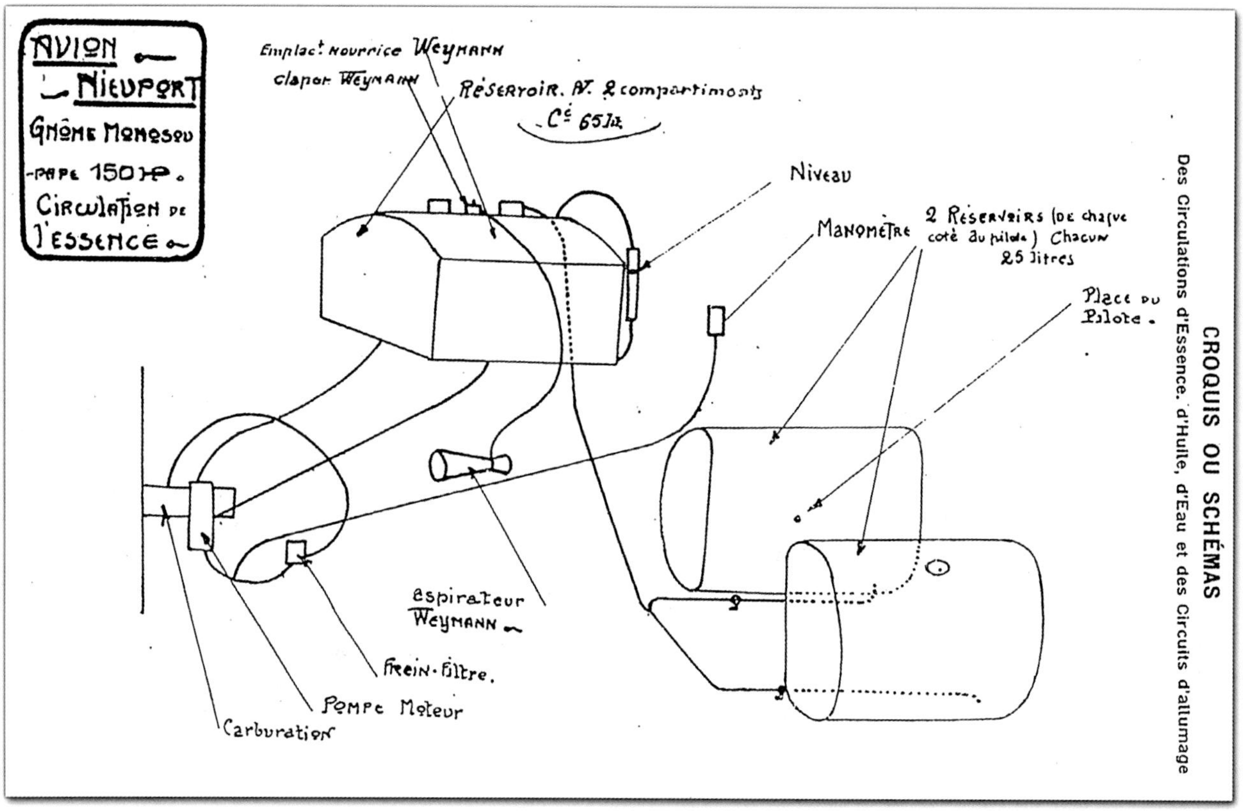
AVION — NIEUPORT
Gnôme Monosoupape 150 HP.
Circulation de l'essence
Emplact nourrice Weymann
clapet Weymann
Réservoir AV. 2 compartiments
Ce 65 lit.
Niveau
Manomètre
2 Réservoirs (de chaque coté du pilote) Chacun 25 litres
Place du Pilote
Espirateur Weymann
Frein-filtre.
Pompe Moteur
Carburation
CROQUIS OU SCHÉMAS
Des Circulations d'Essence, d'Huile, d'Eau et des Circuits d'allumage

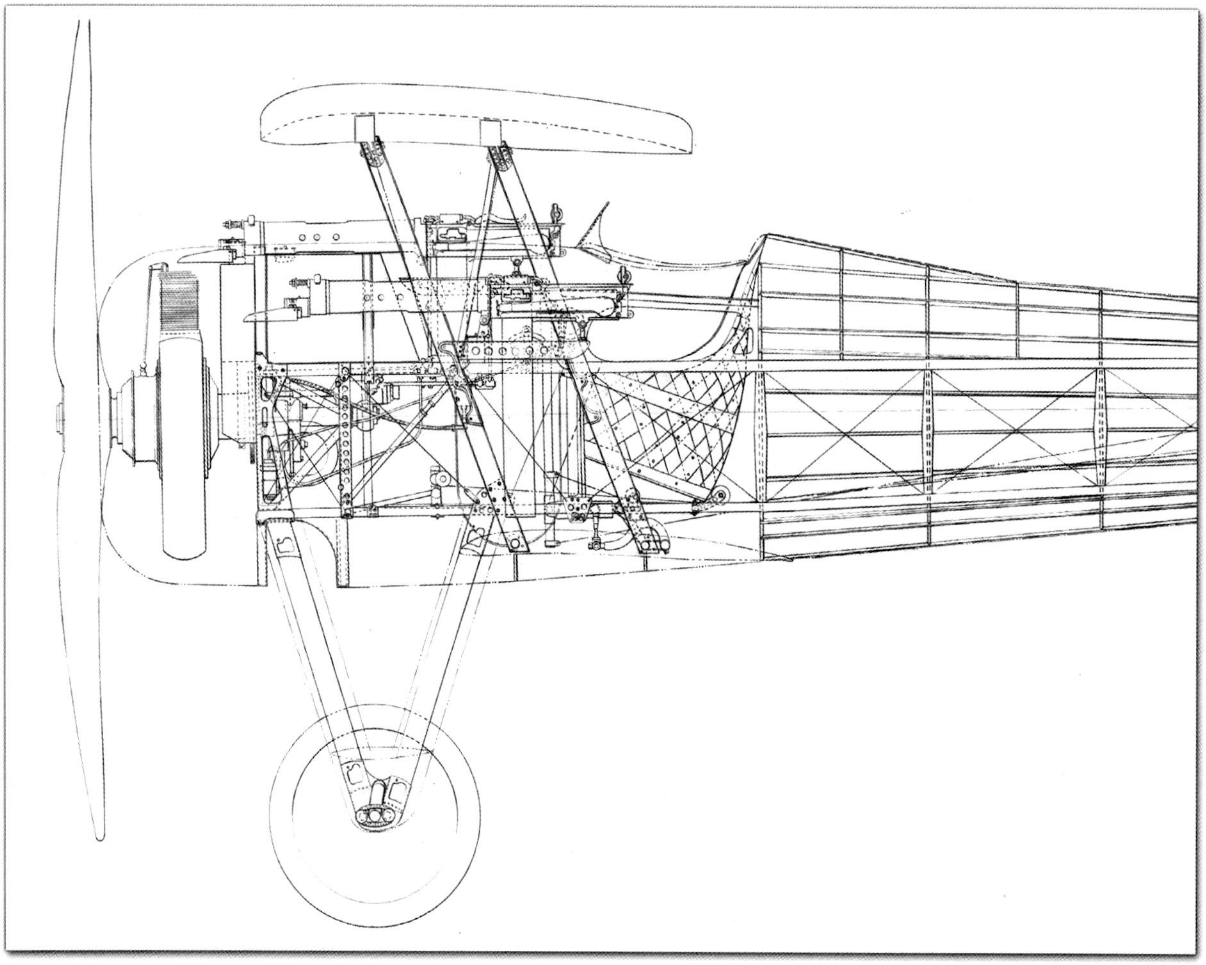

On 16 February 1918, Brigadier General Foulois made a formal request to the French government for front-line aircraft, specifying the latest types, including the SPAD XIII. Foulois was highly displeased with what was offered in response: Dorand A.R. 1s, Sopwith 1 ½ Strutters, and now-obsolete Nieuport 27 fighters. But he was prepared to take the lot, and a contract for delivery of thirty-six Nieuport 27s, including other aircraft, was formalized as Contract F-12 on 23 January 1918. Shortly thereafter, General Pershing abrogated the August 1917 aircraft contract with the French government, ostensibly for nonperformance on both sides.

On 21 February, M. Dumesnil, le Sous-Secrétaire d'État de l'Aéronautique Militaire et Maritime, informed Brigadier General Foulois that thirty-six Nieuport 28 fighters would be provided on Contract F-12, in place of the Nieuport 27s. This was a momentous decision for the US Air Service and the Nieuport Company, and perhaps a small victory for Brigadier General Foulois as well. In addition to the promise of – untested in combat – Nieuport 28s, the French government allocated 600 Morane-Saulnier 29 fighters to the Air Service, for delivery commencing midyear. On 7 March 1918 the US Air Service received the first eighteen of 208 wartime-production Nieuport 28s.

As a footnote to the delivery of the first Nieuport 28s, on 8 March, a Morane-Saulnier monoplane fighter, flown by an American Lafayette Flying Corps pilot, suffered wing failure and crashed, killing the pilot. This was not the first, nor the last, fatal result of wing failure (as this had occurred on 26 February and again on 11 May) suffered by this highly touted fighter. As a result, however, the type was withdrawn from front-line service.

As related in Chapter 4, wing failure, although never resulting in a fatality, was the primary reason for terminating the Nieuport 28's combat career. In spite of its brief period of combat, the Nieuport 28 had built up a strong constituency among pilots, principally those pilots

Opposite
Top: This is the fuel-system arrangement for the single-gunned Nieuport 28 prototypes. Note that reserve fuel tanks sit on either side of the pilot's seat. The tank to the left of the pilot was removed when the two-gunned version was developed. The other side-mounted tank was later removed to the belly position when the wartime production design was modified, and was designated the Nieuport 28A. Charles Woolley

Bottom: This drawing shows the twin Vickers gun arrangement of the wartime-production Nieuport 28 fighter. S.H.A.A. via William Nungesser

of the 147th and 27th Aero Squadrons. In view of the cancellation of the Morane contract and the continuing scarcity of SPAD XIII fighters, the Air Service was therefore receptive to suggestions for continuing production of the Nieuport 28 for use as advanced trainers. These aircraft, however, would incorporate modifications that resulted from experience gained during combat operations.

On 19 June, Brigadier General Foulois cabled Lieutenant Colonel Dunwoody, Assistant to the Chief of Air Service, AEF: "In view of present military emergencies and large [twenty-three] number of changes contemplated in Nieuport 28, recommend you do not cancel contract [A.S. 5365, dated 2 May 1918] for six hundred Nieuport [28s]. Insist, however, you institute most rigid system of inspection of all planes and engines at factories and before planes and engines leave Orly... ."[11]

A list of these modifications (see illustration identifying principal modifications in Appendix C) was discussed among representatives of the US Air Service, the French Air Service, the Gnôme Company,

Below: Without guns and still sporting French colors, this Nieuport 28 (believed to be N.6137) was the first of the type to be delivered to the U.S. Air Service for the 95th Aero Squadron in mid-March 1918. N.6137 was one of the Nieuport 28s lost in a hangar fire at Villeneuve-les-Vertus on 31 March. Don Brady

A Nieuport 28A trainer at Carlstrom Field after the war. Florida State Archives

and the Société Anonyme de Construction Aéronautique (S.A.C.A.) Company. (The Nieuport Company had licensed the Nieuport 28 in order to focus on development of the Nieuport 29.) Several of the modifications – replacing fuel lines, strengthening landing gear, and possibly strengthening the wings' leading edges as well – were already under way in the field. Now these modifications would be incorporated in the new design, to be known as the *Nieuport 28A*, so titled on a blueprint of the modified aircraft done by Lieutenant Henry Babcock, USAS, in October 1918.

In a memorandum to Brigadier General Foulois, dated 3 October 1918, Major John Satterfield, Air Service, AEF, stated: "We have in process of construction 600 Nieuport 28[s]. It is promised that 50 will be delivered by November 1st and one hundred per month thereafter. According to our usual experience, we do not anticipate that deliveries would begin quite as soon as promised."[12]

Satterfield's prediction was correct. For unexplained reasons, the order for 600 Nieuport 28A advanced trainers had been moved from S.A.C.A. to Établissements Lioré et Olivier (LeO). The first modified aircraft emerged from LeO's factory for testing at Orly Field on or about 18 October, but the contract was canceled less than one month later, with the signing of the Armistice. After contract-termination negotiations with the French government, the Air Service accepted, and shipped to the USA, eighty-eight Nieuport 28As.

Nieuport 29

In July 1918 Major General Mason M. Patrick, Chief of Air Service, AEF, reported: "Developments in design and performance of pursuit planes are so rapid that it is quite impossible to say definitely at the present time of just what type of machine the [seventeen squadrons

Below: An unsuccessful step along the way to the vaunted Nieuport 29, this experimental fighter was powered by a variant of the Lorraine-Dietrich V-8 engine with a four-blade propeller fitted. The forward visibility of this single-bay aircraft was severely restricted by the machine guns and radiator mounted in front of the cockpit. S.H.A.A. via William Nungesser

due to become operational during February–June 1919] will be made up; but from present indications, it seems possible that those at least which are constituted during the first quarter of 1919, will be either Sopwith-Dolphins, Martinsydes [Buzzard], or the new modified SPAD type."[13] During the same month, these fighters, each powered with the 8Fb, 300 hp Hispano-Suiza engine, entered a comparative test along with an unnamed Nieuport prototype that was also equipped with the 300 hp Hispano-Suiza engine. The Nieuport prototype bested its competitors, except for the Martinsyde Buzzard that climbed to 5,000 meters almost two minutes quicker.[14]

The Nieuport 29 prototype developed, but too slowly to enter combat before the war ended. Conditions in postwar France, like those in the United States, impeded sales of new military aircraft because the French government still held large stocks of war-surplus military aircraft. In 1921, the French government proposed a novel solution to this problem: induce "industry to purchase surplus stocks *en bloc,* sell them, and give the government a 60 percent share of the proceeds."[15] Among the fighters that Société Anonyme Nieuport-Astra (Nieuport had merged with the Astra firm in 1921) purchased were small stocks of Nieuport 28As; these surplus fighters (advertised with 180 hp Le Rhône rotary engines) were listed for sale in the company catalog alongside the most modern Nieuport designs as late as 1924.

The production version of the Nieuport 29, considered by many to be Gustave Delage's finest fighter design, was one of the most successful fighters throughout the 1920s. Itself a radical departure in airframe and engine from the fighter that immediately preceded it, the Nieuport 29 embraced the V-8 cylinder, liquid-cooled, in-line 300 hp engine, and featured a monocoque fuselage with integral fin, two-bay biplane structure with long-span ailerons on the lower wings, plus two independently synchronized Vickers machine guns. Pilot reports lauded the handling characteristics of the aircraft, much as they had done for its predecessor, the elegant Nieuport 28.

Deliveries of Nieuport 29s to French units began in February 1921. By 1925, they were serving in twenty-five (out of thirty) French escadrilles, and also in the air services of Italy, Belgium, Spain, Sweden, Japan, and Argentina.[16]

An early prototype of the Nieuport 29, N.12002 (shown here), differed in several ways from the production-version Nieuport 29, which was fitted with an enlarged rudder and narrow-chord, long-span ailerons on the bottom wings, in place of ailerons on top and bottom wings (note the faint outline of the Eiffel Tower in the background of this photo). The Nieuport 29, powered by the 300 hp Hispano-Suiza engine, equipped 25 French fighter squadrons by 1925; it also saw service with the air forces of a number of other countries. This aircraft is shown in a postwar Nieuport advertisement. L'Aéronautique Pendant la Guerre Mondiale (author's collection)

Appendix C
The Nieuport 28: General Characteristics and Specifications

The following description of the Nieuport 28's airframe and propulsion system is derived from contemporary US Air Service and Royal Air Force documents.[1] These documents were translated from the original French materials, and dimensions given are in metric. ***Note:*** *Information presented in italics highlights the differences between the wartime-production Nieuport 28 fighter and the postwar-production Nieuport 28A trainer.*

The Airframe

DESCRIPTION OF THE AIRPLANE – The N XXVIII airplane is a single-seater biplane with a tractor screw worked by a 160 hp motor [Gnôme monosoupape]. It is fitted with two Vickers machine guns firing through the propeller. *Two American-designed and -manufactured Marlin machine guns, positioned between the cabane struts, equipped the Nieuport 28A.*

FUSELAGE – The fuselage consists of a beam of rectangular section formed of 4 spruce and ash longerons in the front part [lower longerons] braced by wooden uprights and crosspieces, the whole crossbraced by means of piano wire. The beam ends at the back in a sole spruce upright, on which are fixed the hinged joint fittings of the rudder. The whole front part of the fuselage consists of the engine plate supports, the tanks, the controls, the seat of the wing struts, the machine guns with their accessories, the landing gear. The rear part has elastic empennages and tailskid.

The fuselage, from the rear to the back of the pilot, is covered with fabric stretched on rods maintained plumb with the bays by laminated fuselage ribs, so as to give to the fuselage a polygon section with small sides, approaching a circular form.

From the back of the pilot to the front it is fitted with cowls of molded and fabric-covered wood, which can be easily dismounted for taking out the tanks or any important repairs in this part. *Because of delamination problems encountered with the two-ply cowl panels, they were replaced with compressed-paper cowl panels on the Nieuport 28A.* Moreover, those cowls have inspection doors, which allow inspecting all the important parts.

This view, also of N.6212, shows the external machine-gun mount, pilot's seat, and flare-gun box to the left and rear of the pilot's seat. R.L. Cavanagh

This photograph clearly shows the wire-braced box-girder construction of the fuselage of the Nieuport 28. Formers and stringers gave the slim, conical fuselage an elegant appearance. R.L. Cavanagh

James Ashenden's N.6212 after repair by Swiss technicians and prior to being re-covered, offers an excellent view of the structure of the Nieuport 28. The reserve "saddle" tank is seen aft of the main fuel tank and to the right of the cockpit. The tank was moved to the belly position on the Nieuport 28A. R.L. Cavanagh

CHASSIS – The landing gear is formed of two V struts fixed to the fuselage and joined at their top by two tube crosspieces, having in the center the hinges of the mobile axles and at the ends rubber cord shock absorbers. The planes formed by the front branches of these V struts are crossbraced to ensure the undeformability of the system. Moreover, a cable running from the cross-knot of the crossbracing maintains the joints of the axles and prevents flexion of the crossed tubes.
The wheels are of standard type 650 x 80, with fabric-covered flange completing the landing gear, which is suitably streamlined by an aluminum fairing covering the struts and tube crosspieces.

TAILSKID – A tailskid, of the type known as elastic, is hinge-jointed on the lower crosspiece of the fuselage section. To the top of this tailskid, penetrating to the inside of the fuselage, are fastened the rubber shock absorbers, which are fastened at the other end onto the crosspiece of the preceding section.

CONTROLS – The aileron and elevator controls are made with a steel-tube vertical lever [control stick], which is jointed near the lower end into a fork, made one with it by means of a horizontal tube rudder-bar of the aileron levers.

The upper end has a pushrod contact and two levers for control of the machine gun. The upper end of the lever, which is grasped by the hand, is covered with a rubber sleeve. The elevator cables start directly from this lever.

The rudder cables start from a rudder-bar worked by the feet. This rudder-bar is formed of two half-cylinders of soldered sheet steel, and hinged in the center on a vertical shaft fitted to a cross-member which, by its shape when turned back, permits varying the distance between the seat and the foot-rest by 50 mm. The pilot's heels slide over two walnut foot-rests.

WING STRUTS – Two duralumin U struts of 56 x 20 x 20/10 with a vertical incline of 30 [degrees], suitably fixed to the fuselage and spacers, ensure the fastening of the upper and lower planes. The outer part of these struts is streamlined by an aluminum fairing.

PROPELLER – A propeller is directly fitted on the nose of the motor.

WINGS – The upper planes, with a chord of 1 m 300 [1.3 meters] of rectangular shape with an elliptical outside end, consist of two pine beams of trapezoidal section, onto which are fitted all the 1,300 mm ribs which form the outline of the wing, which end in front and at the rear on a border, which gives the wing its contour. [It should be noted again that this document was translated from French and dimensions given are metric. In some cases, the dimensions are absent or incomplete, and may be incorrect.]

The beams, separated by 340mm, bear the fastenings of the cables and the fixings of the wing struts; at these points the gap is obtained by steel tubes; along the length of the wing, one rib out of two forms a caisson to resist compression stress, and the whole is crossbraced by piano wires.

The leading edge of the front border to the front beam is covered with laminated [ply]wood, glued and nailed to the nose of the ribs and the complementary ribs [false noses]. *In order to strengthen the leading edge of the top wing of the Nieuport 28A, wooden battens, measuring 32.5 mm x 2 mm, were glued and nailed to the plywood sheathing into each standard and compression rib.*

The lower planes, with a chord of 1 m, have similar arrangements, but in addition receive the ailerons – movable surfaces consisting of a

This view of a Nieuport 28 based at McCook Field shows the mounts and ammunition boxes for both Vickers machineguns, tachometer (the only fixed instrument), and the smaller version of the windscreen. This may have been the only wartime-production Nieuport 28 to be shipped to the U.S. from France. R.L. Cavanagh

Internally mounted tailskid. R.L. Cavanagh

A closer view of the Nieuport 28's wing structure. R.L. Cavanagh

series of ribs fastened to a tube controlled from the inside of the fuselage and turning in the sorb-wood bearings fastened to the rear wing beam. The planes are covered with linen, doped, and varnished.

EMPENNAGE – The rear surfaces consist of a wooden frame covered with molded wood panels.

The frame consists of a principal beam, an edge fixing the outer limit, and a series of small ribs so assembled that they form a system of squares. The panels are made of two thicknesses of wood cut 8/10 mm thick, and of 50 mm-wide strips of tulipwood glued across the grain over a mold. These panels are nailed to the ribs of the frame and glued to the edge and the beam. The whole is varnished and fabric-covered.

The elevator has a duralumin tube half-sunk into the principal beam; this tube revolves in the turned bearings, fitted in the rear beam of the tailplane, but easily dismounted with keys. The fin is fixed on the fuselage by means of a tube sunk into the rear part, which, prolonged, penetrates into the end fittings of the fuselage. This tube has a part at its end which serves as a hinge-joint of the rudder, the lower-end fitting of the fuselage being made to receive the other hinged joint.

HEATING – A generator of the type controlled by a propeller is fitted on the right upper plane [the pylon for securing the generator on the right upper wing can often be observed in contemporary photographs, however, the generator itself was rarely, if ever, installed]. The energy which it supplies is transmitted by conductors ad hoc to a terminal fixed on the right upper longeron of the fuselage near the pilot. The wires which are connected to the heating equipment run from this terminal.

WIRELESS – The planes [wings], as well as the fuselage, are metal-plated so that wireless messages can be received.

The following drawings highlight the external features of the Nieuport 28 fighter and the modifications made to the Nieuport 28A trainer.

The Gnôme 9N rotary engine is mounted forward of the oil tank, firewall, and main fuel tank. The cap strips defining the wing ribs are visible on the underside of the wing. R.L. Cavanagh

The pylon atop the upper wing was used to secure a generator. Most pylons were removed from the aircraft, as generators were rarely, if ever, used on the Nieuport 28 during the war. R.L. Cavanagh

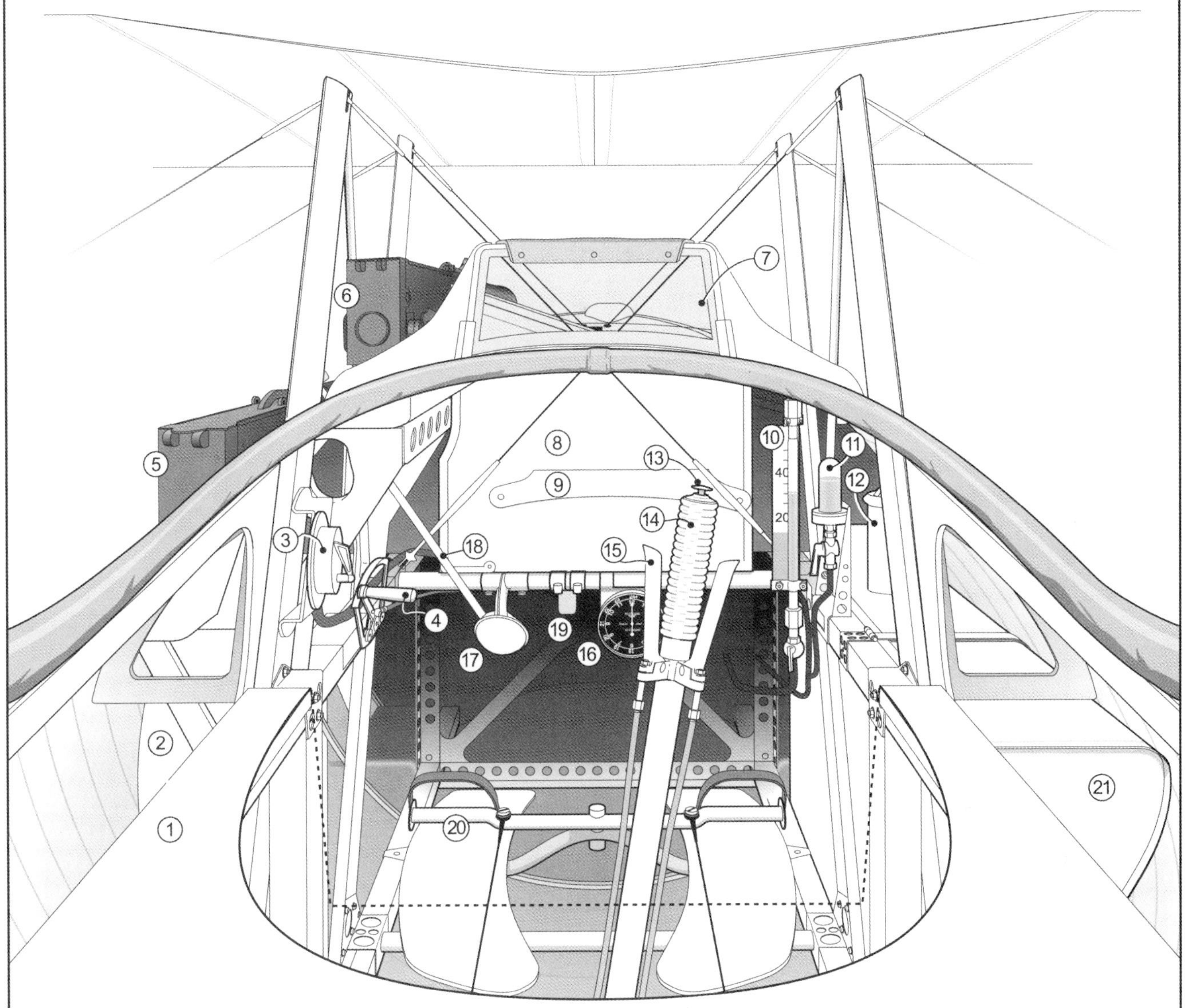

NIEUPORT 28 COCKPIT

KEY

1 Ply deck around seat. Seat outline indicated by broken line
2 Ammunition box for side mounted machine gun.
3 Ignition selector switch
4 Fuel adjustment quadrant
5 Side mounted Vickers machine gun
6 Top mounted Vickers machine gun
7 Windshield. Top edge fitted with leather padding
8 Ammunition box for top mounted machine gun
9 Rub plate on ammunition box
10 Fuel sight gauge
11 Oil pulsator
12 Filler for fuel reserve tank
13 Coupe button on control column
14 Control column hand grip
15 Machine gun triggers
16 Jaeger Tachometer
17 Leather padding protection on 90° joint (MG sychronization gear)
18 Oscillating rod (MG sychronization gear)
19 90° joint bracket (MG sychronization gear) for top mounted machine gun
20 Rudder bar
21 Reserve fuel tank

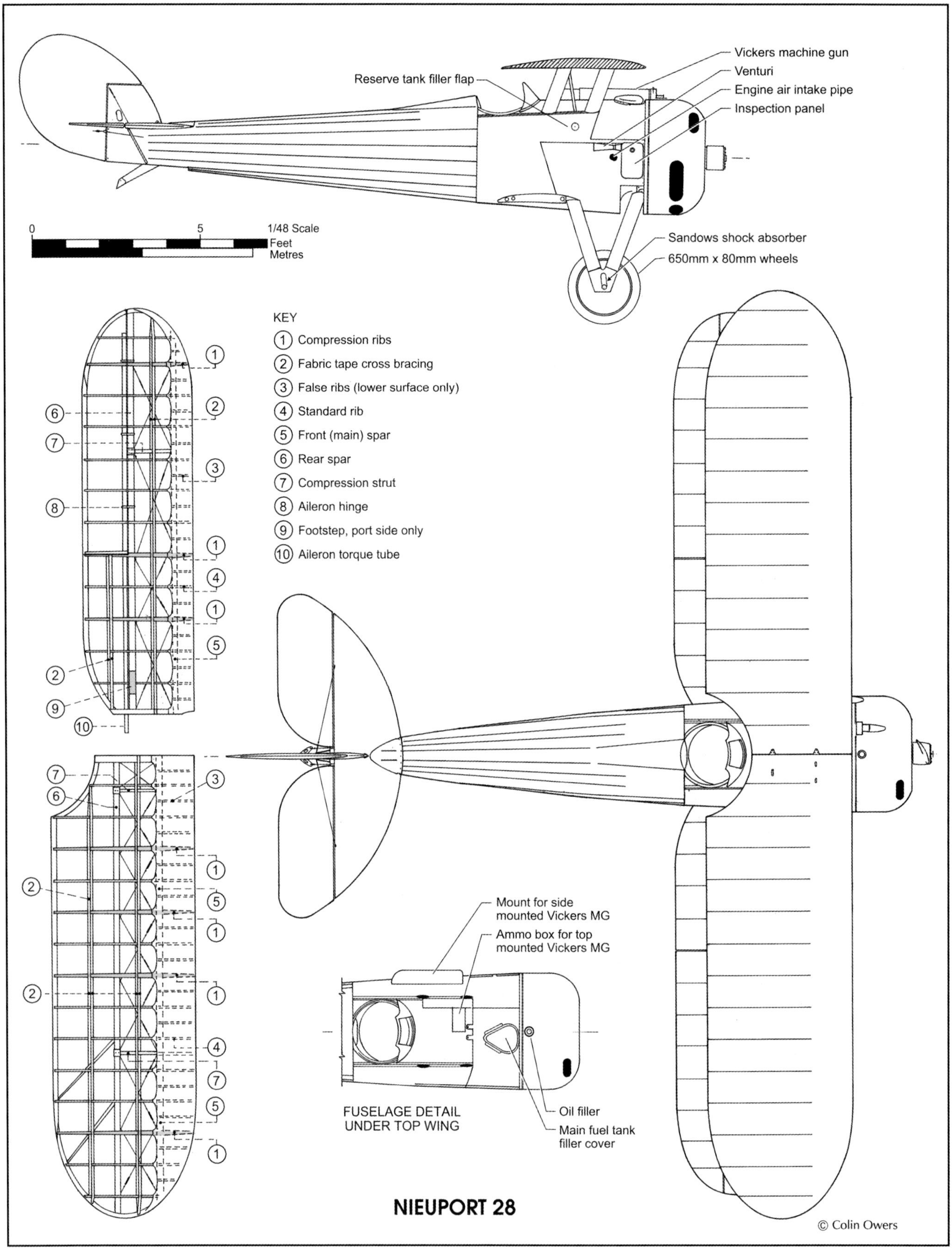
Reserve tank filler flap
Vickers machine gun
Venturi
Engine air intake pipe
Inspection panel
0
5
1/48 Scale
Feet
Metres
Sandows shock absorber
650mm x 80mm wheels
KEY
(1) Compression ribs
(2) Fabric tape cross bracing
(3) False ribs (lower surface only)
(4) Standard rib
(5) Front (main) spar
(6) Rear spar
(7) Compression strut
(8) Aileron hinge
(9) Footstep, port side only
(10) Aileron torque tube
Mount for side mounted Vickers MG
Ammo box for top mounted Vickers MG
FUSELAGE DETAIL UNDER TOP WING
Oil filler
Main fuel tank filler cover
NIEUPORT 28
© Colin Owers

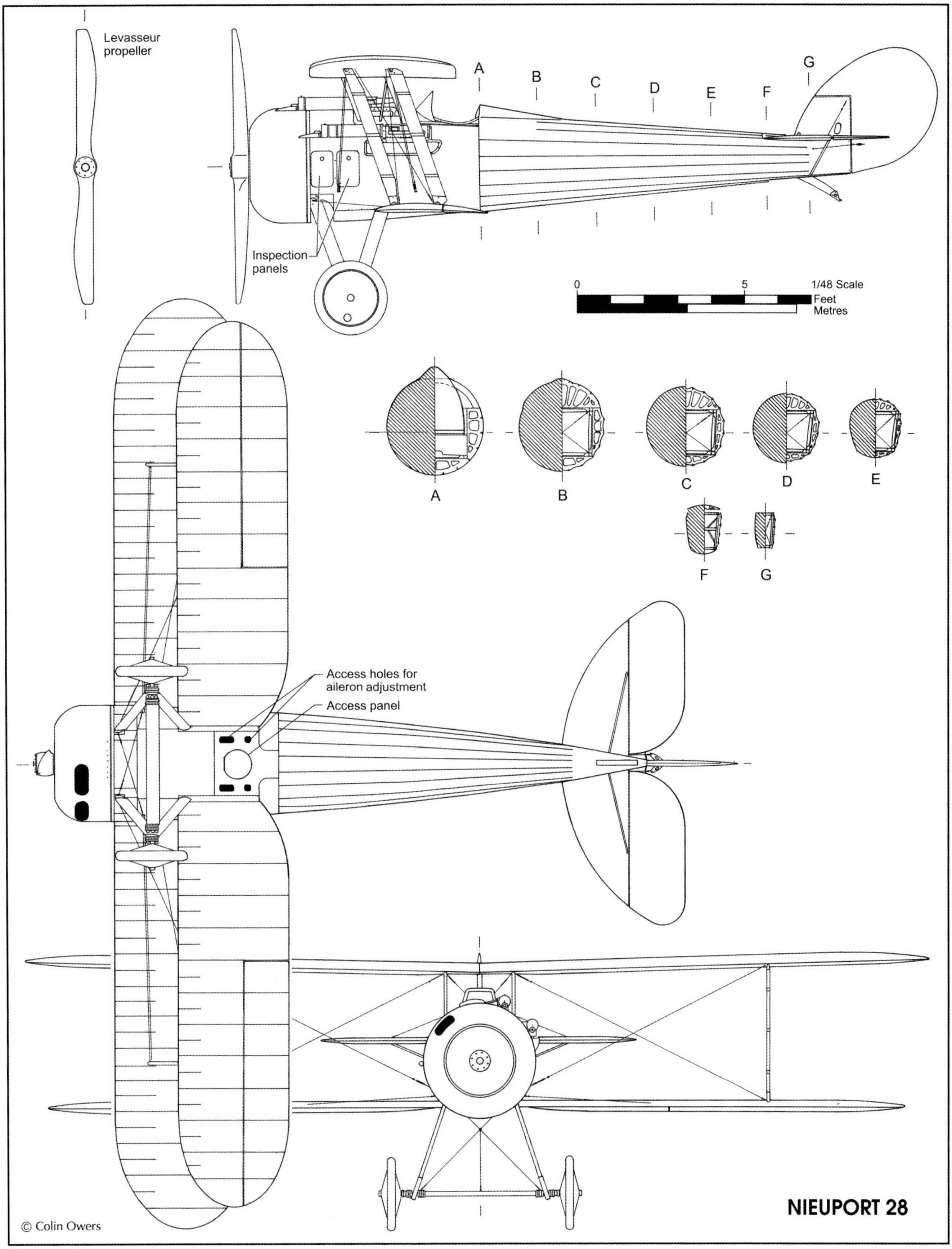
Levasseur propeller
A
B
C
D
E
F
G
Inspection panels
0
5
1/48 Scale
Feet
Metres
A
B
C
D
E
F
G
Access holes for aileron adjustment
Access panel
NIEUPORT 28
© Colin Owers

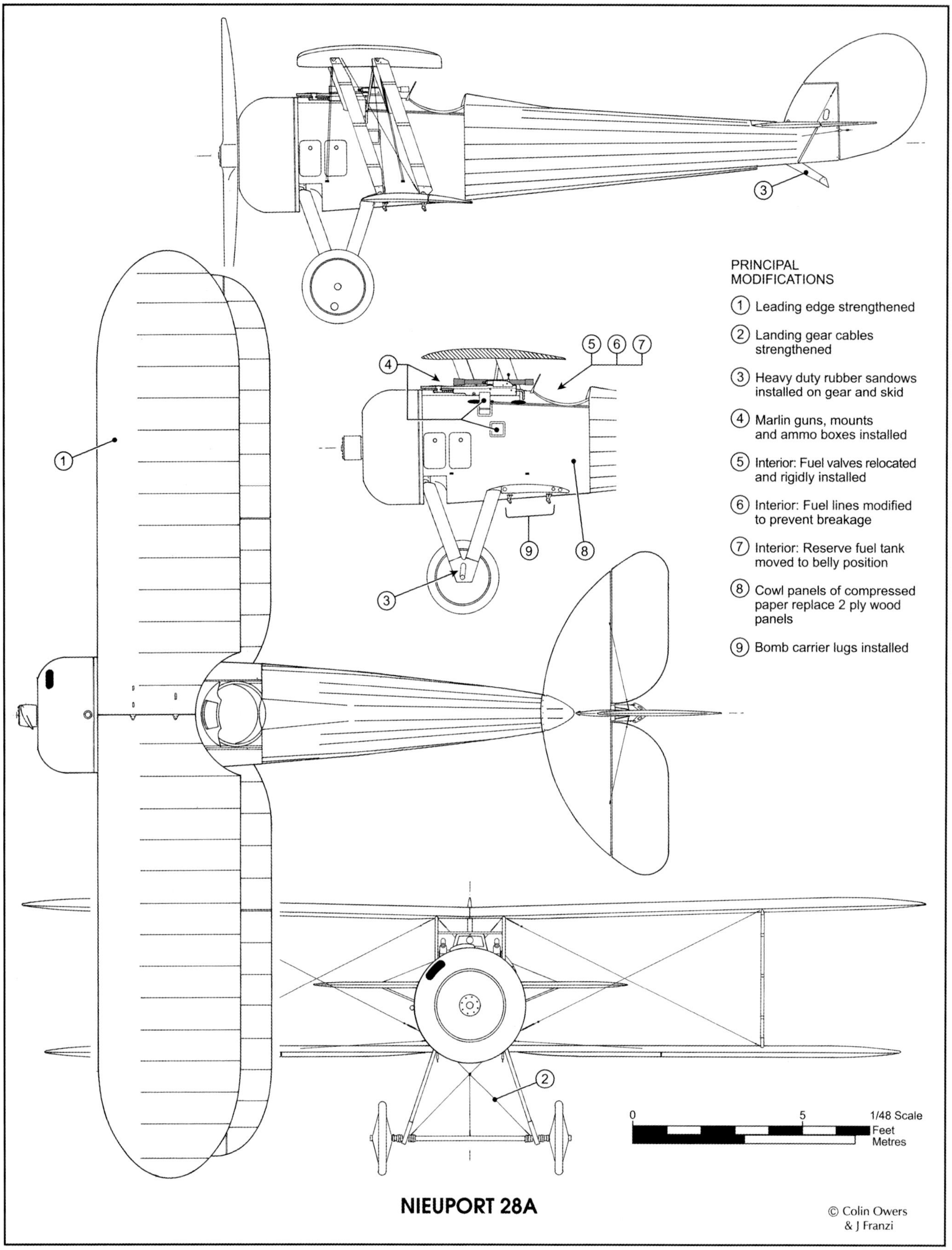
PRINCIPAL MODIFICATIONS
1 Leading edge strengthened
2 Landing gear cables strengthened
3 Heavy duty rubber sandows installed on gear and skid
4 Marlin guns, mounts and ammo boxes installed
5 Interior: Fuel valves relocated and rigidly installed
6 Interior: Fuel lines modified to prevent breakage
7 Interior: Reserve fuel tank moved to belly position
8 Cowl panels of compressed paper replace 2 ply wood panels
9 Bomb carrier lugs installed
0
5
1/48 Scale
Feet
Metres
NIEUPORT 28A
© Colin Owers & J Franzi

The Motor

MOTOR – 160 hp Gnôme monosoupape, 9 cylinders. The motor is mounted overhanging on a steel plate terminating the front fuselage, which holds the motor support flange. Another plate, placed at 280 mm from the former, holds the anchor plate as well as the bronze boxes for synchronization of the machine-gun firing.

The motor has as accessories: two magnetos, an oil pump, a gasoline pump, ignition selector switches coupled with a controller permitting the motor to run at slow speed by suppressing ignition in all or some of the cylinders, an oil dome [also known as an oil pulsator] fixed where the pilot can see it for lubrication control. *In the new motors, the usual brake filter is replaced by an adjustable spray nozzle called the rotary spray nozzle, which enables a portion of the piping to be suppressed.*

Partial cutaway of finely machined Gnôme 9N rotary engine. R.L. Cavanagh

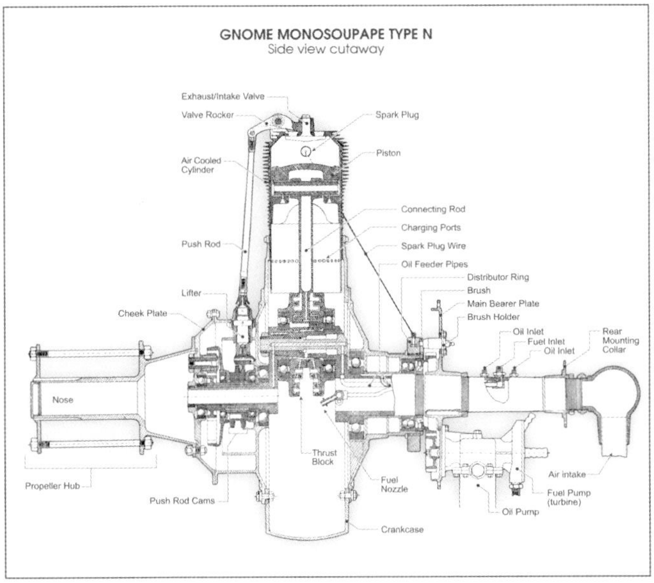

TANKS – Oil: Of leaded sheet-iron, with a capacity of 25 liters, ring shaped and fixed under the motor cowl so as to keep the oil fluid.

Gasoline: A service tank containing 85 liters under pressure from the motor is completed by an auxiliary ["saddle" tank, with a 40-liter capacity, located to the right of the pilot]. *The configuration in the Nieuport 28A is different; in this case the reserve tank, containing 37 liters, is fitted under the fuselage, the gasoline mounting from the lower tank to the upper one by a Weyman exhauster, and of an emergency hand pump (Guer et Mansuy system), in case the former stopped working.*

Top right: Note location of the reserve, or "saddle", tank as found on the wartime-production Nieuport 28.

Right: The reserve "belly" tank (seen between the foot rests) as found on the Nieuport 28A.

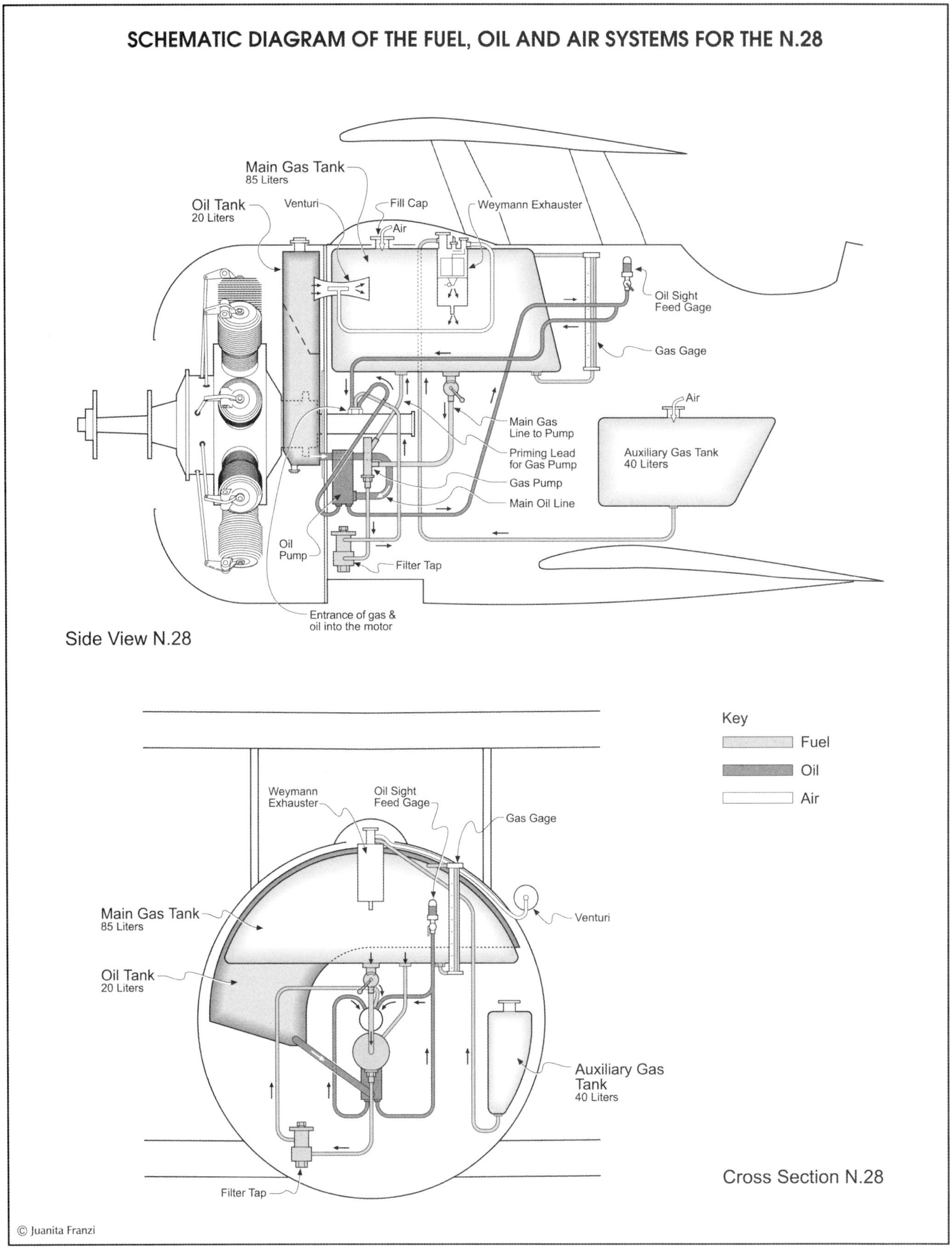
SCHEMATIC DIAGRAM OF THE FUEL, OIL AND AIR SYSTEMS FOR THE N.28
Main Gas Tank
85 Liters
Oil Tank
20 Liters
Venturi
Fill Cap
Air
Weymann Exhauster
Oil Sight
Feed Gage
Gas Gage
Air
Main Gas
Line to Pump
Priming Lead
for Gas Pump
Gas Pump
Main Oil Line
Auxiliary Gas Tank
40 Liters
Oil
Pump
Filter Tap
Entrance of gas &
oil into the motor
Side View N.28
Key
Fuel
Oil
Air
Weymann
Exhauster
Oil Sight
Feed Gage
Gas Gage
Main Gas Tank
85 Liters
Venturi
Oil Tank
20 Liters
Auxiliary Gas
Tank
40 Liters
Filter Tap
Cross Section N.28
© Juanita Franzi

OIL PIPING – One tube running from the tank to the oil pump; two tubes from the pump to the motor; on one of these pumps there is a branch running to the dome [oil pulsator].

GASOLINE PIPING [see drawing below]

A. Tube of 14 x 16 of the plug cock 13, fitted on the gravity tank with the gasoline pump.

B. Tube of [indecipherable] of the gasoline pump with the motor.

C. Tube of 4 x 6 of the pump with the tap fitted on the gravity tank (driving out of air bubbles).

D. Tube of [indecipherable] communication of the lower tank with the Weyman exhauster.

E. Tube of 4 x 6, communication of the exhauster with the venturi tube.

F. Tube of [indecipherable] running to the level.

G. Tube of 10 x 12 from the upper tank to the hand pump and the motor. [piping dimensions in report are unclear]

All the piping is made of annealed mild copper and answers exactly to the specifications required by the American Aviation Service in all that concerns its course inside the fuselage and its connections with the different parts. [The replacement of copper fuel lines had begun in the field before the Nieuport 28 was withdrawn from service. Seven copper fuel-line tubes, each with flexible connectors, comprised a shipset; these were being installed on each Nieuport 28 in service to eliminate the problem of fuel-line breakage due to engine vibration and improperly annealed copper fuel lines.]

This description of the Type N, 9 cylinder, 160 horsepower monosoupape Gnôme, commonly spoken of in English as the 150 horsepower, applies equally well to the Types NB and NC, "Type N" being the title by which this engine is generally known.

DESCRIPTION – The Gnôme monosoupape motor, Type N, is a rotary motor with 9 radial cylinders of 115 mm bore and 170 mm stroke. It is composed of a one-piece crankcase, into which are screwed the cylinders.

The Guer et Mansuy hand pump was accessible to the left rear of the pilot's seat. Also shown is the brace for the outside machine-gun mount and the ammunition box for the same gun.

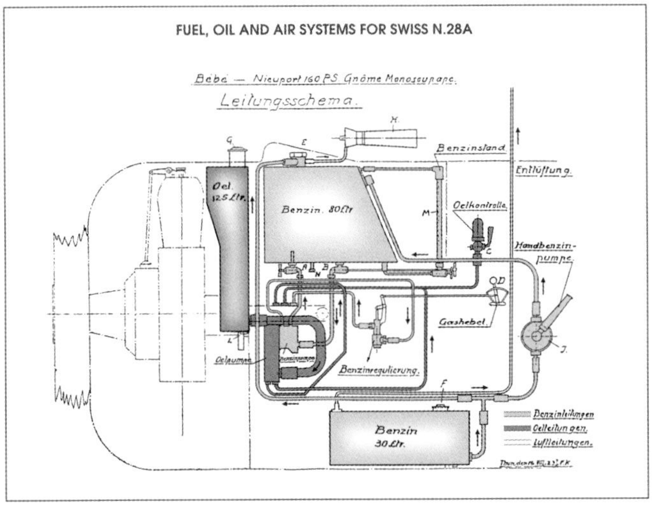

This Swiss drawing, c. 1923, of the fuel/oil system of the Nieuport 28A shows the reserve tank relocated to the belly position and the Guer et Mansuy hand pump used to transfer fuel from the belly tank to the main fuel tank. The legend at the bottom right of the drawing identifies the various (top to bottom, respectively) fuel, oil, and air lines. Also shown is the fuel quadrant and regulator governing the flow of fuel into the engine (see engine cutaway drawing). Note the main fuel shutoff valve, activated by the long rod with T-handle extending into the cockpit area. The shutoff valve at the base of the sight glass can be closed to prevent leakage from the sight glass.

The single-throw crankshaft is fixed and keyed in the main bearer plate, which serves as motor support. On this plate are mounted:

1. The magnetos [two].
2. The oil pump, carrying the gasoline pump.
3. The selector switch (to right magneto), with the tachometer drive.
4. The machine gun cam box, synchronizing system.

There are three valve cams on a single shaft, mounted on the crankshaft and driven at half-speed through satellite gears revolving with the motor. There is one pushrod for each cylinder, so that each cam controls three valves.

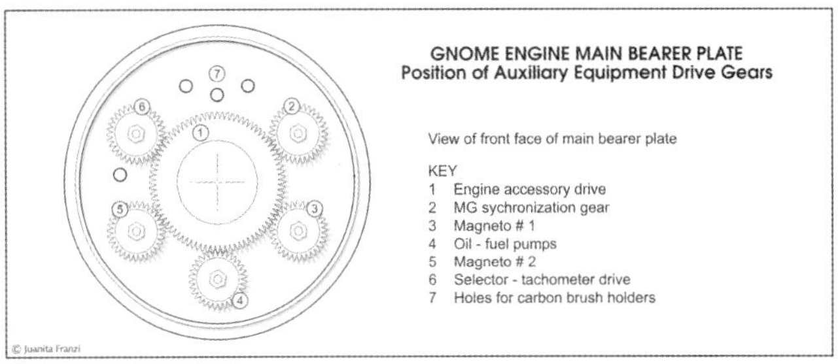

The motor has no intake valves, the supply of rich gas being automatically admitted by the pistons, near the bottom of the stroke. To get an idea of the working of this arrangement, a single cylinder may be considered, the crankcase being supposed, by way of illustration, to be fixed and the crankshaft as turning.

The cylinder is closed at the top by the exhaust valve, controlled by a cam, so shaped that the closing is delayed 145 degrees, allowing fresh air to enter through the valve after the exhaust stroke. The piston, continuing its stroke, uncovers the ports in the bottom part of the cylinder.

These ports form the communication between the cylinder and the inside of the crankcase. The gasoline and part of the necessary air for the mixture are taken into the crankcase through the hollow crankshaft. The principle of the motor is as follows: To draw in, by leaving the exhaust valve open beyond top dead center, the fresh air necessary to make a correct mixture with the very rich gas taken into the cylinder. To create the necessary partial vacuum to draw in the mixture, the exhaust valve closes a short time before the ports are uncovered.

Photograph of a Gnôme 9N cylinder. The top of the piston travels from a point just below the spark plugs down to a point just below the induction ports. One can clearly see the long stroke of this engine, giving it a torque rating of over 300 foot/pounds. The displacement of this engine is about 970 cubic inches, or about 15.8 liters. Also visible is the cast-iron liner pressed into the cylinder, slightly protruding from the bottom, as evidenced by a small chip broken from the liner. The cylinder is simply screwed into the crankcase, oriented in position by a circular key, and secured in place by the lock ring visible on this cylinder. Caption and photograph courtesy of Fred Murrin

CYCLE OF THE MOTOR – Let us consider a single cylinder, following it from the end of the compression stroke through the four cycles constituted by two complete revolutions:

1. Ignition, represented by point A. 20 degrees advanced*.
2. Power stroke, represented by arc B C.
3. Exhaust, represented by arc C DEF. The valve begins to open at C; thus the lead is 80 degrees.
4. Air intake, represented by arc F G H. Instead of closing after the top dead center as in ordinary motors, the valve remains open down to point H, during the descending stroke of the piston. This causes an intake of air into the cylinder, and the valve is completely closed only at point H, 35 degrees before the bottom dead center is reached.
5. During the descending stroke of the piston corresponding to arc H I, the valve being closed and the ports in the cylinder still covered by the piston, a partial vacuum is produced within the cylinder.
6. ADMISSION OF THE RICH MIXTURE. □ At point I [20° ahead of the lower dead center], the piston uncovers the ports in the cylinder during a time represented by arc I J. The rich mixture from the crankcase, drawn in by the partial vacuum of which we have just spoken, mixes within the cylinder with the air which has just been admitted, forming the explosive mixture.
7. COMPRESSION. – The ports again closing at J [in the diagram], the gas is compressed during the ascending stroke J K L of the piston, and is ignited at point L.

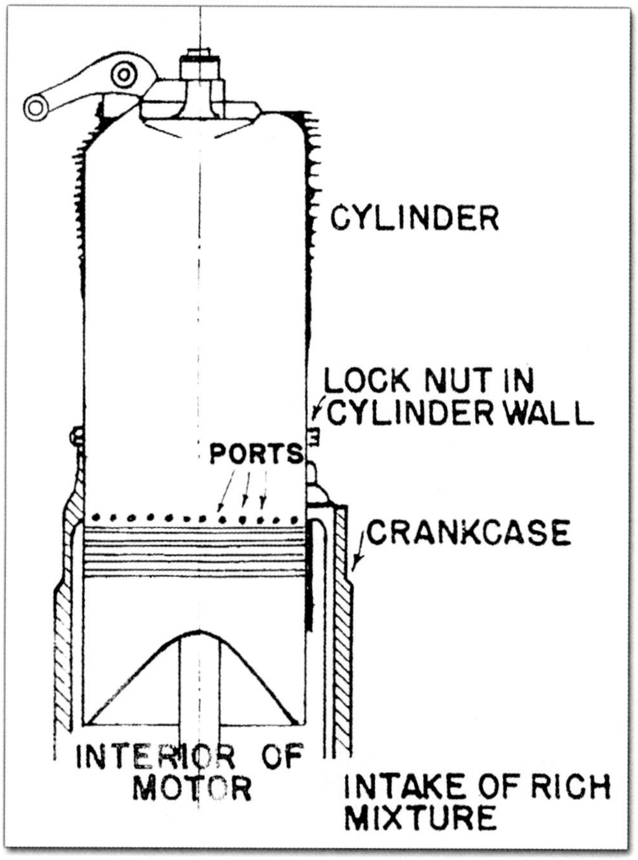

Drawing of a Gnôme 9N cylinder. Note position of piston allowing entry of fuel/oil mixture through the induction ports.

ADJUSTMENT
The angle between adjacent cylinders is 40°.

1. Ignition. – The ignition advance is 20°.

The motor being placed on its supports, a cylinder is brought around to the end of the compression stroke [valve closed], leaving it 20° ahead of dead center, a point which is reached when the bottom cylinder is vertical.
At this point, the contact breaker screws are adjusted so that the break is just beginning. This is done by unmeaning gears and re-meshing them in proper position with the motor drive wheel.

2. Timing the cam-gears. – The motor being mounted and keyed on the main bearer plate, the bolts fixing the cover on the cam case (cam box) are removed. A cylinder is brought into position for the exhaust opening (the lower cylinder vertical), and the cheek is turned to the left to bring the cam into contact with the pushrod of the cylinder chosen, and locked with two of the assembly bolts. It may occur here that the two holes are not exactly facing each other. The bolts may be placed by loosening slightly. The crankcase having 56 holes and the cheek 42, the error in regulating the cam cannot amount to more than 1°, more or less. Make sure of the adjustment by turning the motor over twice, and tighten the other bolts.

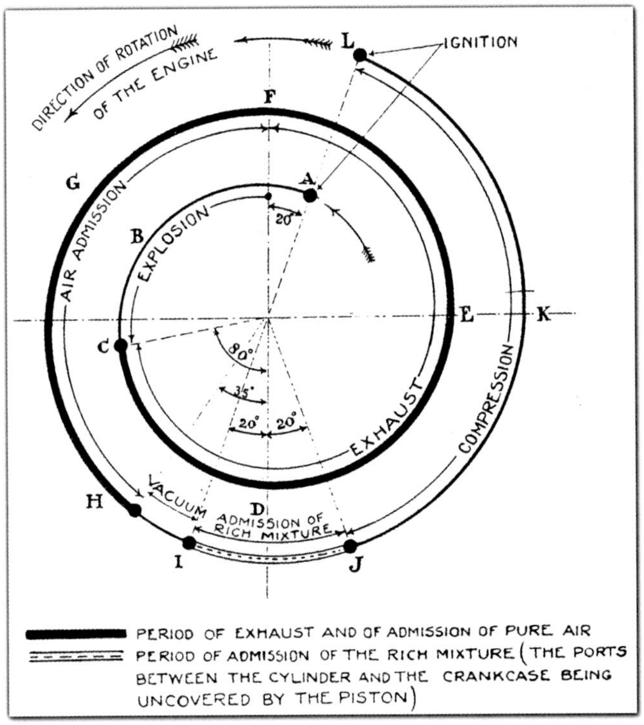

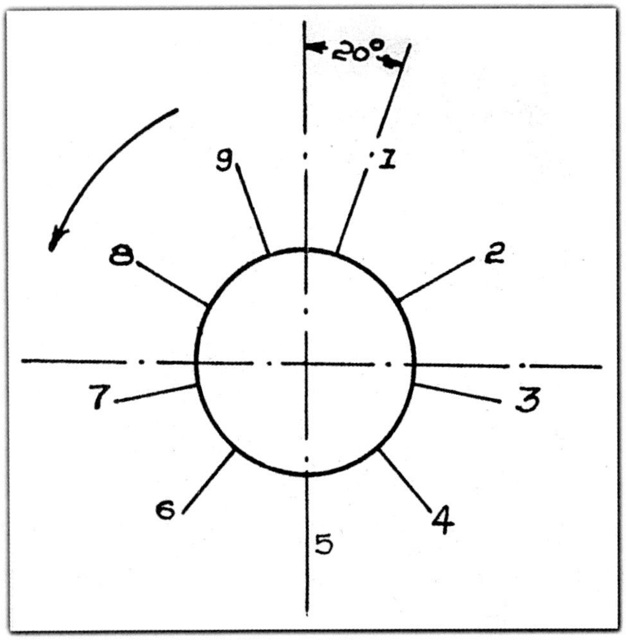

Above: Diagram illustrating four-cycle operation of Gnôme 9N rotary engine.

Top right: With the selector switch set at position 4, or full power, the firing order of the Gnôme 9N is: 1-3-5-7-9-2-4-6-8 and repeat.

The valve controls should have a play of 0.5 mm. To make sure of this, remove the upper yoke by taking out the pin. The valve being well-closed and the pushrod drawn back toward the camshaft, 0.5 mm of stagger should be observed between the respective holes in the yoke and rocker. To obtain exactly 0.5 mm of play, adjust the rod without play and then tighten down the knuckle tip by a half-turn.

MOUNTING

The N monosoupape motor is mounted overhanging, as shown in the illustration to the right.

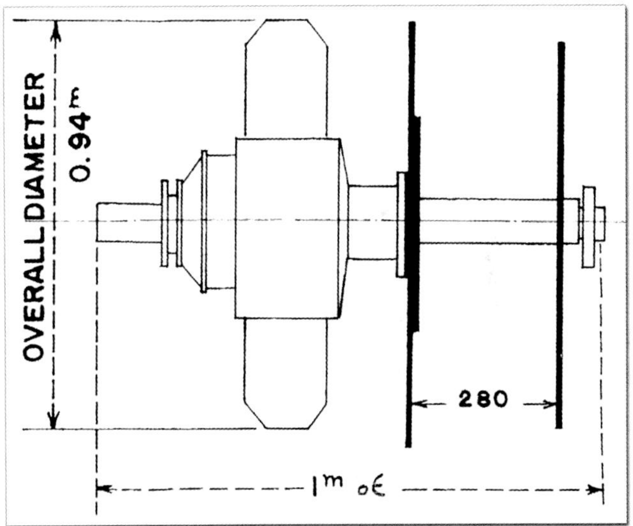

Gasoline Feed. – The gasoline is carried to the motor by the middle one of the three connections screwed to the upper part of the crankshaft. Feed is by a gasoline pump mounted on the shaft of the oil pump. Its output is regulated by a needle valve controlled by hand, by means of a lever sliding along a graduated sector.

The intake of gasoline to the pump from the gravity tank is by a direct pipe, without bends or elbows. To avoid a loss of priming in the pump, it has been supplied with an air vent which is always open. This constant overflow naturally carries away gasoline, and it is consequently necessary to join the air outlet to the gravity tank by a pipe.

Oil Feed. – The oil is carried to the motor through two connections on either side of the gasoline connection on the crankshaft. The oil pumps of the N motor being equal in flow, the oil pump connections may be mounted indifferently on either of the oil connections.

The oil tank should be in a position to feed the pump by gravity. It is thus necessary that in all attitudes the airplane may assume in normal flight, the form of the tank and the placing of the piping shall

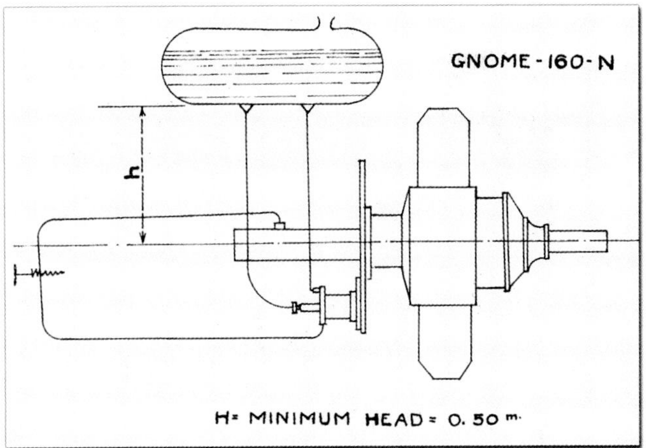

be such as to guarantee a continuous delivery of oil at the pump. An intermittent delivery of oil at the pump would have the serious consequences of unpriming the latter.

Priming the oil pump. – Make sure that the oil pump is primed before starting the motor:

(a) If the motor has just been mounted for the first time.
(b) If the gravity oil tank has been emptied.

In this case, open the oil cock of the tank and completely unscrew the plug in the upper part of the upper body of the pump. Wait until the oil flows from the opening thus made, unaccompanied by air bubbles. Then replace the plug.

Remarks – The quality of the castor oil used is very important for the proper working of the motor.

A special device for heating the oil can be mounted on the N motors as on ordinary motors, and prevents freezing up of the oil in the tank in cold weather or cold climates.

When the motor has just been mounted and before the two oil pipes are put into place, it is advisable to inject one or two syringes of oil into the shaft connections, to clear both these conduits within the motor of air. This will permit the flow of oil, unmixed with air, from the time the motor starts.

RUNNING

The correct propeller for a given machine is the one which, the motor giving full power and the machine in horizontal flight, revolves at 1,300 to 1,350 rpm.

A propeller test with the machine stationary can serve only to make sure of the regular running of the motor: a horizontal flight test is indispensable to find out the number of additional revolutions this propeller will give the motor over the figure shown by the stationary test. This test should be made not only for each series of machines, but for each individual airplane. This increase may vary, depending upon the airplane, from 50 to 250, or even 300 revolutions. What will determine the choice of a propeller will thus be, all other things being equal, the number of rpm of the motor upon which it is mounted. [It is] tested in horizontal flight in a straight line. This number of revolutions should never exceed 1,300 at 5,000 meters.

STARTING. – The injection of gasoline into the cylinders by way of the valves is unnecessary, the best method of starting being as follows: Turn the motor over by hand, so placing it that a cylinder with the valve open shall be vertical and on the bottom.

The ignition current being switched off, open up the gasoline sector until the gasoline begins to run out of the open valve. AT THIS MOMENT, CUT OFF THE GASOLINE INTAKE. With the current still cut off, turn the motor over twice by hand.

Switch on the ignition current and start, turning on the gasoline during the first explosions of the motor (if opened before, there is danger of flooding the motor with gasoline). Regulate the gasoline with the sector.

CAUTION. Never reduce the speed of the engine by throttling the gasoline supply. If you do, you will very likely "burn" the pistons. The Gnôme monosoupape engine is different from others in the respect that its throttle lever controls the quantity of gasoline only, and not the air. Partially closing the throttle, therefore, only WEAKENS THE MIXTURE and this, if carried too far, makes it burn too slowly. With a slow-burning mixture, the MAXIMUM temperature is lower than if the mixture is just right, but the AVERAGE temperature is higher; and to make a long story short, the chief cause of burned pistons and cylinders in the Gnôme is TOO WEAK MIXTURE. Always set the throttle lever for the best possible mixture; that is, the mixture which will give highest possible speed at the altitude and under the weather conditions in which you are flying. To reduce the speed, use the selector switch; and do not hesitate to run for long periods with the selector switch in operation and the engine missing regularly.

The selector switch positioned on the left rear cabane strut. ***What is not shown is the "master switch" that is referred to in technical literature, but is not found in known photographs of the cockpit of the Nieuport 28.***

DESCENTS. – Descents can be made:

With the switch – for instance, in case of a descent of very short duration, e.g., near the ground. In this case, it is preferable, without touching the gasoline-flow sector, to switch on the current for periods as short as desired, but at short intervals.
Using the selector – The motor is run at reduced speed by the use of the selector, of which a complete description is given further on in the special notice at the end of the pamphlet.

FITTING OF THE MOTOR ON THE AIRPLANE/STARTING OF THE MOTOR.

Make certain that the oil pump has begun to work; if not, unscrew the oil pump plug-screw, let out the air, and re-screw the plug when the oil begins to flow outside. Verify the fastenings of the magneto cables, the selector, and contact.

The starting of the monosoupape motor is very easy, and the motor should start immediately after the first turn. The movements to be carried out are the following:

1. The pilot opens the tank needle-valve cock, without forgetting the cock for driving out the air, the filter brake remaining closed.

2. The mechanic says "Gasoline without contact" and the pilot opens wide the filter brake and puts in the iron part of the contact; the mechanic turns the propeller round several times by hand until he sees the gasoline flow by the valves.

3. The mechanic says "Close gasoline contact." As soon as the gasoline flows, the pilot closes the filter brake and pushes in the bone part of the contact. The mechanic starts the motor, which begins to work with the gasoline remaining in the cylinders.

From the first explosion, the pilot gradually opens the filter brake until he has found the right adjustment point when the motor turns smoothly without chattering. If the motor does not start, renew the priming as at the beginning, and facilitate the arrival of the gasoline by a few movements of the hand pump.

In winter it is important that the motor should not be clogged with gasoline, as excess gasoline flows outside the cylinders and catches fire at the first explosion. Whenever this happens, all that is necessary is to tightly close the gasoline lever handle without cutting the contact; the little gasoline there is outside is consumed in a few revolutions and is put out at once without danger.

This cannot be done except on the ground after priming. In flight there cannot be an excess of gasoline, the flow of the gasoline pump being gradual, according to the number of revolutions of the motor, and even for pick-ups, after having cut off the engine, the air current is sufficient to drive the gasoline. The point of adjustment can vary slightly according to the temperature and the atmospheric pressure. Too much or too little gasoline produces chattering. The right carburetion once found, make the selector take No. 1 or 2 position, to permit removing the blocks and maneuvering the airplane. During the time No. 1 or 2 contact is in the selector, the gasoline lever handle must not be touched.

SELECTOR – The motor, having cylinders bored throughout, is at this moment under atmospheric pressure by means of the crankcase and of the inner air suction tube, the valve having remained open during nearly all the time of aspiration, the cylinder being under a pressure very near to the atmospheric pressure before the piston comes out of the orifice. Under these conditions, the cylinder capacity is always complete and has always need of a quantity of gasoline in proportion to the quantity of oxygen admitted, inversely proportional to the altitude. In other ways the quantity of gasoline is kept proportional to the number of revolutions by a gasoline impeller controlled by the motor itself.

A motor working in this way cannot have a slow speed. This disadvantage has to be counteracted by use of the selector. The selector consists of a lever handle put at the disposal of the pilot, which can be put in five different positions: 0, 1, 2, 3, 4. Into this selector the wire of the mass of the magneto passes, and the selector cuts off ignition from all the cylindrical parts, according to the following law.

A further word about the functions of the selector and master switches:[2]

The following paragraphs have been added to remove any confusion about the functions of the selector and master switch and the firing sequence of the cylinders.

The "master" switch, wired only to the left magneto, is an on-off switch for that magneto. When the master switch is turned on, the left magneto sends impulses to one set of spark plugs, of which each of the nine cylinders have two. The purpose of the master switch and left magneto, (which are independent of the selector switch, right magneto, and second set of spark plugs) is to simply provide a redundant magneto system.

The functions of the master switch and selector switch are apparent in the flight procedure for the Nieuport 28:

> Start with both magnetos 'on' (master switch on and selector switch at position 4). Once the engine comes to full power and fuel is adjusted to give proper mixture, turn master switch 'off' and turn selector switch to position 3, then 2, then 1. Taxi using positions 2 and 3 alternately to maintain slow taxi until turned into the wind.
>
> On take off, progress to position 4, pausing for about 1-2 seconds at each position. Once on position 4, the pilot reaches down and turns on the master switch to make the left magneto go into service. Now the engine is running at full song on both magnetos. Note that any time the pilot wishes to make use of the selector qualities, he must turn off the left magneto. He normally patrolled in this manner, running at full speed.
>
> So, consequently, when the pilot is on final approach to landing, he must turn off the master switch [which governs the left magneto] and use the selector switch to regulate his landing speed. The use of the blip [coupé] was discouraged and not often necessary to use with a Gnôme 9N, even during landing.[3]

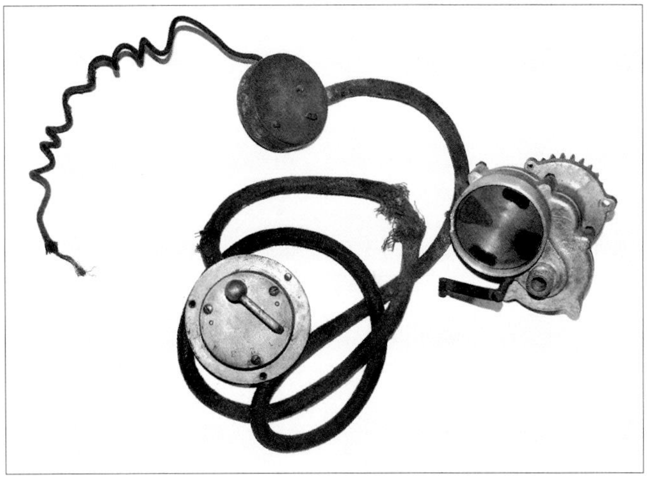

The selector switch on the left with five positions – 0 to 4 – marked on the face and electrical cord to selector switch drive unit on the right, which controls the rpm of the Gnôme 9N rotary engine. The rotating disc, with four nonconductive surfaces on which five small carbon brushes ride, acts as a spark "interrupter," grounding the leading magneto at selected intervals, depending on the selector switch setting. Also visible is the selector/tachometer drive gear (see drawing of the Gnôme engine main bearer plate). Caption and photograph courtesy of Fred Murrin

The cylinder firing order as determined by the selector switch settings is as follows:

Terminal 4: The right magneto sends impulses every four cycles: the engine is at full power.
[The following shows firing order in position 4, with * signifying a repeat.]

1-3-5-7-9-2-4-6-8*1-3-5-7-9-2-4-6-8*1-3-5-7-9-2-4-6-8*

Terminal 3: The right magneto sends impulses every eight cycles: the engine is at half power.

1----5----9----4----8----3----7----2----6----*1----5----9----4----8----3----7----2----6*

Terminal 2: The right magneto sends impulses every sixteen cycles: the engine is at one-quarter power.

1--------9--------8--------7--------6--------5--------4--------3--------2--------*

Terminal 1: The right magneto impulses every thirty-two cycles: the engine is at one-eighth power.

1---------------8---------------6---------------4---------------2---------------9---------------7---------------5---------------3---------------*

Terminal 0: The selector switch ignition is cut off.

During maneuver of the selector, the gasoline flow must be allowed to continue in all the cylinders, even in those which are not ignited, in consequence, the gasoline lever handle must not be touched, to make the speed slow with the selector.

This maneuver of the selector has the disadvantage of wasting a portion of the gasoline, but it has the advantage of being extremely convenient and no mistakes can be made while it is being used; the pick-ups of the motor are very sharp. Under these conditions the pilot is free from all trouble concerning the motor, and can fix his attention entirely on the flight or on the landing.

SPEEDS – The different speeds obtained by means of the selector of ignition are:

	a) On the Bench	B) In Flight
Terminal 1	460 Revs	500 Revs
Terminal 2	620 Revs	750 Revs
Terminal 3	900 Revs	1100 Revs
Terminal 4	1300 Revs	1400/1450 Revs

The propellers can make on the bench between 1,230 and 1,350 revolutions. Some lose in rearing, others gain. The climb should begin at about 1,300 revolutions. The speed of the airplane is, therefore, about 110 to 130 km per hour on its climbing flight. The motor loses about 110 revolutions between horizontal flight on the ground and horizontal flight at 5,000. For example, 1,470 revs on the ground and 1,360 at 5,000. The airplane loses from 20 to 25 km between the same heights.

REGIME OF THE SELECTOR

Position 4: Flight in full power (170 hp)
Position 3: Reduced speed, but maneuver still good (170 hp)
Position 2: Horizontal flight, but tangent (25 hp)
Position 1: Descent of airplane (10 hp)
Position 0: Cut off

PARTICULAR PRECAUTIONS TO BE TAKEN ************
Before each flight, make sure that:

1. The propeller is solidly fixed on its hub.
2. The cowl belt is well stretched.
3. The wheel caps are well pinned.
4. The wheels are well lubricated and turn freely.
5. The fastenings of the tailplane and the rudder are in place and carefully fixed.
6. The elevator and rudder cables are in good condition and well- stretched.
7. The hinged joints of all the controls are well greased and the working of them is smooth (aileron bearing, direction bearing, control stick, elevator bearing, etc.).
8. The gasoline and oil piping are in good condition, the durits not damaged, and the connections well tightened up.
9. The ignition cables are well-fastened to the magneto and the selector. The fitting of the propeller on the motor for machine-gun firing is correct.
10. When the motor is running, that the contact is perfect, the oil mounts in the dome, and lubrication is evenly made, judging from the escape of oil on the inside walls of the cowl.
11. That the cocks do not close of themselves owing to vibration.

After each flight:

Place the motor so that one valve is open below, to allow sending out the oil which is inside the motor.
Verify carefully the tension of the wire bracing cables.
Lubricate all the hinge-joints and all the bearings.
Clean the motor cowl.

Upkeep

The dismounting just indicated suffices for complete cleaning of the motor. This should be done after about 50 hours of flight. The proper regulation of gasoline in flight is, it may be remarked, the most important factor in keeping the motor in good condition.

The rest of the cleaning operation is very simple:

(A) Wash in gasoline all such pieces as the cam gearing, camshaft, roller, ball bearings, piston rings, etc. In the course of reassembling, these same pieces should be oiled with a brush (using castor oil), especially the parts inside the cam gearing: rollers, pins of rockers, etc.

(B) Make sure that none of the oil holes or channels are stopped.

(C) Clean the upper parts of the pistons by light scraping, and make sure that the bottom of these, inside, have no deposits of carbonized oil, a thing likely to occur from the use of castor oil of poor quality. Clean the oil holes of the pistons and the grooves for the rings.

(D) Clean the cylinder flanges (with fine emery paper), being sure that no traces of rust remain. Make sure frequently that the oil is getting to the pin of the valve lever properly, carefully cleaning the oil inlet which passes through this lever, and seeing to it that the holes of the socket pins are not stopped and that the oil passes freely through the pushrod.

The valves do not need to be ground. The head turns on its seat while the motor is running, and this rotation is in general sufficient to constantly assure its proper seating.

REMARKS: When a motor is to be transported by rail or road, or when it is to remain for a long time in the hangar or a storehouse, IT IS RECOMMENDED: that the pushrods be removed, so that all the valves being closed, no dust can get to the inside of the motor.

It is well after a flight to so place the motor that a cylinder with an open valve is vertical and in the bottom, so as to drain the oil out of the motor after stopping.

Putting kerosene in the cylinders is not indispensable; it should always be done when the motor is cold, and very slowly, so that the kerosene shall not get to the inside of the motor by way of the ports in the cylinders.

Stripping

STRIPPING OF THE PROPELLER – Remove the screws of the bolts of the propeller hub nose. Take out the reinforcing plate, remove the propeller, and place it as much as possible removed from the sun and moisture.

STRIPPING OF THE COWLING – Remove the assembling bolts of the fixing plate with the lug and safety bolts. Remove the plug of the oil tank. Turn the cowl to loosen the groove of the oil tank. Take it out by working gently, twisting alternately in one direction and then in the other.

Mechanics of the 147th Aero Squadron at work on Lieutenant Charles "Pip" Porter's N.6250, which was crashed by Lieutenant Thomas Abernethy. Engine overhauls and wing replacements on the Nieuport 28 were much simpler and far quicker than on the SPAD XIII. R.L. Cavanagh

STRIPPING OF THE MOTOR – Remove the connections of the piping going to the different parts fixed on the plate: oil pump, gasoline pump, the connections of the lighting wires with the magnetos and the selector.

Remove these different parts:

Dismount the tube bringing air to the motor.
Release the nuts of the rear flange.
Put a plug under the nose of the motor.
Remove the attachment bolts of the front motor support flange and the locknut of the rear flange.
Take out the motor, place it on its special support, and add to it all the accessories.

STRIPPING OF THE OIL TANK – The motor being taken out, the oil tank is removed by raising, in order to take it from the front bow of the cowl support.

UPPER TANK –

Remove the right machine gun.
Remove the collimator.
Remove the motor cowl.
Take out the dismountable holder by removing it from the grooves.
Take out the piping durits.
Unplug the belts and the fixing cable.
Take out the tank, first lifting it slightly to disengage the plugs, then laterally.

LOWER TANK –

Remove the lower cowl, taking out the screws that hold it.
Remove the pipe durits.
Unfasten the belts.

STRIPPING THE MACHINE GUNS – Remove the front and rear support shafts. Remove the machine guns.

STRIPPING THE WHEELS – Unscrew the axle plugs after having removed the pins, taking care not to strain if the threading shows a tendency to grip, for fear of twisting the hinged fork. Take out the wheels.

STRIPPING OF THE AXLES –

Remove the wheels.
Take off the axle-cover.
Take off the rubber cords.
Take off the hinge-jointed pin.
Take out the axle.

STRIPPING OF THE LANDING-GEAR FRAME –

1. When it is necessary to remove the struts:

Take out the plugs which fix them to the upper thimble.
Unscrew the plugs which hold the thimbles.
Remove the frame.

2. When it is not necessary to remove the struts:

Take out the plugs which lock them in the forks of the landing gear.
Remove the fixed shaft.

Assembly

ASSEMBLING OF THE MOTOR –

Strip the magnetos, oil pump, machine gun control.
Put the motor in place; hold it under the nose by a peg.
Fix the 18 spark plugs.

Lock the nuts of the anchor plate.
Wedge the magnetos, oil pump, machine-gun control.
Connect the gasoline and oil pipings.
Verify the priming of the oil pump with the small tap made for that purpose on the upper part.
Verify the electric circuit.

ASSEMBLING OF THE COWL – Place the cowl on the motor. Engage it in the bow by turning it until it strikes against it. Fit in the spring blade; stretch it. Screw up the oil tank plug.

ASSEMBLING OF THE PROPELLER – Place the propeller before the bolts of the hub nose. Enlarge the holes, if necessary. Place the reinforcement plate. Bolt.

ASSEMBLING OF THE OIL TANK – Done in the same way, but in the opposite order from that of stripping.

ASSEMBLING OF THE GASOLINE TANK – In the same way, but in the inverse order from that of stripping.

Mount the machine guns.

ASSEMBLING THE WINGS —

1. Preparation:
Adjust the cellule uprights in their housings and bore the fitting holes corresponding to those of the fittings; adjust the length of the tubes of the lower central plane, which in a new airplane are too long. If the fabric covering which is fitted is new, mark exactly the position of the lower assembling bolt holes in relation to those already bored in the centering tubes of the central lower plane.

2. Assembling:
Place the lower wings by fitting in the ferrules on the tubes of the lower central plane.

Rest the end of the wing on a trestle, so as to bring it about horizontal.

Place the upper wings by carefully fixing the fittings to the ends of the wing struts. If the hole is not bored in the fittings, bore it on the spot.

Fix in the assemblage bolts, not forgetting to pass through the crossbracing cables of the wing struts and the non-carrying cables.

Put in place the cellule uprights.

Bring all the cables without.

3. Adjustments:
The mean theoretical incidence is 1°, i.e., 1.7%. Therefore, set the duralumin wing struts so that this incidence exists at the wing sockets. It is sufficient to keep the wing chord at the different ribs parallel to the initial cord. Place the fuselage horizontal.

Adjust in the longitudinal direction by means of the goniometer placed on the upper fuselage longerons of the pilot's post, or better still, on a special scale adapted from end to end of the tailplane, the axis of which is found in the line of flight.

Adjust in the transversal direction by placing the goniometer on a ruler resting on the two upper longerons of the fuselage at the pilot's post. It is advisable to raise the machine in front with screw jackets and set it under the V of the chassis, so as to ensure its immobility. True up the lower planes by means of cables; with the goniometer, make sure that the incidence is the same everywhere, that the trailing edge is trued up well with the leading edge, and that all the lines are perfectly horizontal. Adjust the cabane by working on the middle crossbracings so that the duralumin struts are strictly parallel among themselves in a vertical plane. Above all, avoid a beginning of transversal bolting. Adjust the lifting cables by leaving the trestles under the lower planes so as to make all the box ribs of the upper edge touch closely.

Bore holes for the assemblage bolts in the ferrules of the upper plane beam. Pass the bolts through.

Evenly stretch all the cables, taking care not to change the position of the lower wing; the upper wing should by its construction be accurately trued in relation to its origin.

Bore the fixing hole of the lower wing and pass the bolts through.

If after trial the machine should have a tendency to nosedive, it can be corrected, preferably by increasing the incidence of the upper plane by acting on the rear cellule strut, which can be adjusted, as well as on the corresponding cable, without touching the lower plane. If, however, the incidence on the upper plane exceeds 140, it will be necessary to act in the inverse sense on the lower plane, so as to divide the correction.

ADJUSTMENT OF THE AILERONS – The hand control lever being in the vertical plane of the machine, the rear edge of the ailerons should be on the right and left in the prolongation of the rear edges of the planes. In this position, stop the aileron control lever by tightening the bolts and secure with a nut.

EMPENNAGE —

Put the tailplane in place by setting the rear hook in its housing by a front and back movement, making it rest on its brackets.

Temporarily fix the inspection door by setting in the two front pins and place it on the T fitting, and by blocking the rear butterfly nut.

Fix the safety fittings.

Assemble the elevator by setting the fine rods of the bearings in their housing and keying them up.

Make certain that the keys can be still further tightened up when the base of the bearings fits perfectly on the beam.

In this fitting, the ends of the elevator cables are in place when fixed on the control lever.

Assemble the fin by setting the rear tube in the bearings of the end fittings, and by fastening it onto the front fitting and onto the upper fitting of the tail.

Hook the cables of the tailplane wire-bracing system and adjust them for truing up this latter, so as to make it parallel to the front beam of the upper planes.

Hook the elevator cables by temporarily dismounting the inspection door and uniting the 2 turnbuckles by their boxes. Adjust the cables in such a way that the rudder makes an angle of 30° when climbing and 22° when descending.

Lock the turnbuckles and replace the inspection door as indicated.

Put the rudder in place by setting it from above to below in its bearings, and by fastening it by washers and pins to the lower bearing.

Fasten the rudder control cables, and adjust so that when the rudder-bar is perpendicular to the axis of the fuselage, the rudder is in the prolongation of the fuselage as is.

Armament

The Nieuport 28 Fighter

Introduced by Vickers Ltd. as the Model 1908 "Light Pattern" machine gun, the British War Department adopted the weapon in 1912 as the Gun, Machine, .303, Mark I. The water-cooled ground-gun version of the .303 Mark I equipped, in small numbers, the first contingents of the British Expeditionary Force in 1914; Vickers would be hard-pressed throughout the war to meet the burgeoning demand for this weapon.

By 1918, approximately one-third of all Vickers machine guns was being produced for Allied aerial combat.[4] Vickers aircraft machine guns differed from ground guns in several important ways: elimination of the water cooling system reduced weight by nine pounds, the jacket was louvered to allow free flow of air to cool the barrel, handgrips and ground sights were removed and a loading handle was installed to facilitate cocking, adoption of Prideaux disintegrating metal links dispensed with the troublesome fabric ammunition belt, and a trigger motor device was installed to allow the machine gun to integrate and function with a synchronizing system.

As the guns were in short supply, only one worn Vickers .303 machine gun could initially be supplied for each newly delivered Nieuport 28 fighter of the First Pursuit Group. American pilots were at a substantial disadvantage in combat while equipped with only one machine gun, and this situation was exacerbated by the frequency of gun stoppages – the biggest cause of mission aborts.

Some stoppages could be fixed in the air with immediate working of the loading handle, but other problems necessitated a prudent return to base. Poor calibration of the synchronizer, defective ammunition, excessive friction due to congealed oil or poor fit of parts, excessive weight of fusee spring, broken lock or firing pin, worn barrel, and poor loading of ammunition or misshapen links were some of the problems that pilots encountered in the heat of battle. However, care and maintenance of the machine-gun system improved markedly with time and experience, and with additional supplies of machine guns available, some pilots were loath to give up the Vickers for the American Marlin machine guns that equipped the SPAD XIII.

The cyclic rate of the Vickers .303 machine gun was 500 rounds per minute and accurate range was approximately 1,100 yards.

The following full-page drawings illustrate the Nieuport 28's synchronization gear and explain its function.

An 11mm Vickers machine gun was designed for use with incendiary and tracer ammunition for attacking observation balloons. The muzzle velocity was somewhat lower than that of the service ammunition, but it was sufficient to enable an attack at relatively long range. Pilots were advised to carry a special set of orders specifying that they were equipped with this gun armed with incendiary ammunition, while on a mission to attack observation balloons (and, presumably, not enemy aircraft).

The Nieuport 28A Trainer

The armament of the [Nieuport 28A trainer] airplane consists of two Marlin machine guns fitted between the two duralumin wing struts on a level with the upper cowling. They are fed by two ammunition cases, one of which is placed on the outside of the spare, and the other between the crossbracing of the front and rear bays. The ejection of the cartridge cases and links of the left machine-gun is made into a box which takes them outside through a duct of suitable section; the right machine-gun links are directly ejected outside, the cartridge-cases are

Close-up of Vickers machine-gun installation. The inboard gun has a muzzle shield to prevent cracking of the metal cowl due to hot muzzle blast. National Archives

Lieutenant Claudius A.M. Roberts, armaments officer of the 147th Aero Squadron, is seen adjusting a Vickers machine gun. Note venturi at the leading edge of the lower left wing. Charles Woolley

Contemporary photograph of the interior of a Nieuport 28 cockpit showing the control stick with triggers for the twin Vickers machine guns, Jaeger tachometer affixed to the horizontal bar, horizontal rub rail affixed to the ammunition box behind the control stick, and oscillating rod angling to the left outboard Vickers machine gun. The leather padding to protect the pilot's knee covers the 90° oscillating rod joint from the machine-gun synchronizing gear. National Air and Space Museum, Smithsonian Institution (SI 86-10427)

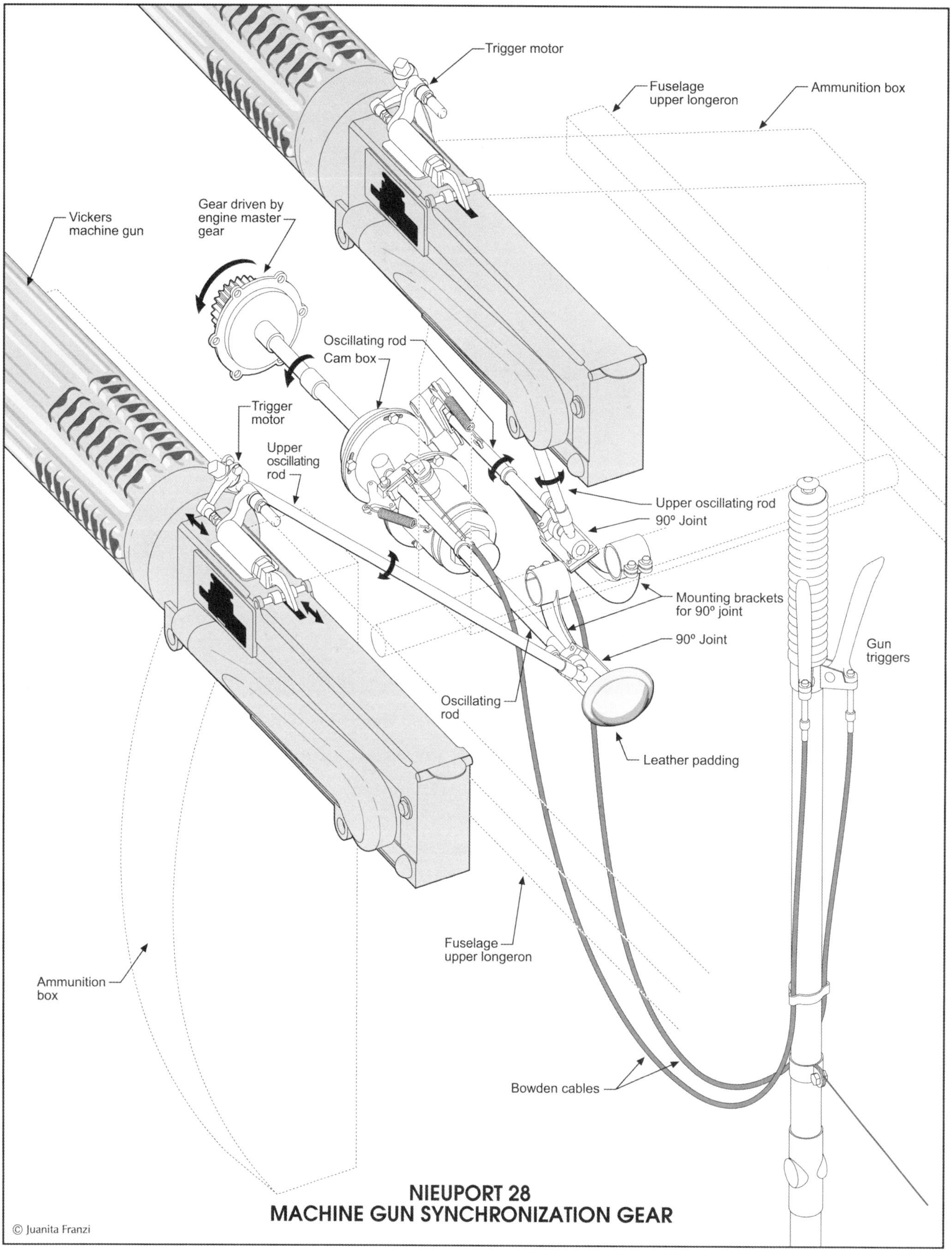
Trigger motor
Fuselage upper longeron
Ammunition box
Vickers machine gun
Gear driven by engine master gear
Oscillating rod
Cam box
Trigger motor
Upper oscillating rod
Upper oscillating rod
90° Joint
Mounting brackets for 90° joint
90° Joint
Gun triggers
Oscillating rod
Leather padding
Fuselage upper longeron
Ammunition box
Bowden cables
NIEUPORT 28
MACHINE GUN SYNCHRONIZATION GEAR
© Juanita Franzi

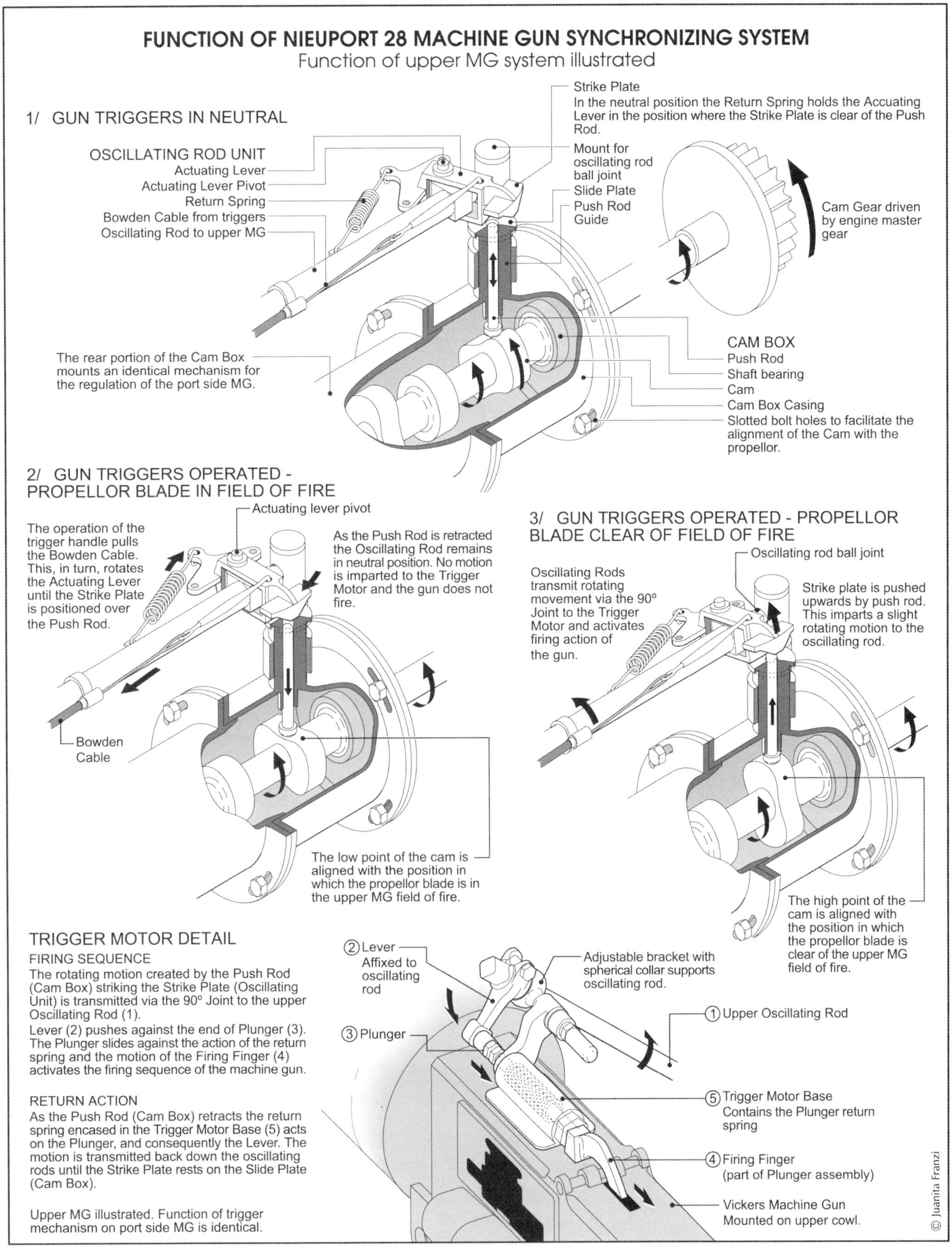
FUNCTION OF NIEUPORT 28 MACHINE GUN SYNCHRONIZING SYSTEM
Function of upper MG system illustrated
1/ GUN TRIGGERS IN NEUTRAL
Strike Plate
In the neutral position the Return Spring holds the Accuating Lever in the position where the Strike Plate is clear of the Push Rod.
OSCILLATING ROD UNIT
Actuating Lever
Actuating Lever Pivot
Return Spring
Bowden Cable from triggers
Oscillating Rod to upper MG
Mount for oscillating rod ball joint
Slide Plate
Push Rod Guide
Cam Gear driven by engine master gear
The rear portion of the Cam Box mounts an identical mechanism for the regulation of the port side MG.
CAM BOX
Push Rod
Shaft bearing
Cam
Cam Box Casing
Slotted bolt holes to facilitate the alignment of the Cam with the propellor.
2/ GUN TRIGGERS OPERATED - PROPELLOR BLADE IN FIELD OF FIRE
Actuating lever pivot
The operation of the trigger handle pulls the Bowden Cable. This, in turn, rotates the Actuating Lever until the Strike Plate is positioned over the Push Rod.
As the Push Rod is retracted the Oscillating Rod remains in neutral position. No motion is imparted to the Trigger Motor and the gun does not fire.
Bowden Cable
The low point of the cam is aligned with the position in which the propellor blade is in the upper MG field of fire.
3/ GUN TRIGGERS OPERATED - PROPELLOR BLADE CLEAR OF FIELD OF FIRE
Oscillating rod ball joint
Oscillating Rods transmit rotating movement via the 90° Joint to the Trigger Motor and activates firing action of the gun.
Strike plate is pushed upwards by push rod. This imparts a slight rotating motion to the oscillating rod.
The high point of the cam is aligned with the position in which the propellor blade is clear of the upper MG field of fire.
TRIGGER MOTOR DETAIL
FIRING SEQUENCE
The rotating motion created by the Push Rod (Cam Box) striking the Strike Plate (Oscillating Unit) is transmitted via the 90° Joint to the upper Oscillating Rod (1).
Lever (2) pushes against the end of Plunger (3). The Plunger slides against the action of the return spring and the motion of the Firing Finger (4) activates the firing sequence of the machine gun.
RETURN ACTION
As the Push Rod (Cam Box) retracts the return spring encased in the Trigger Motor Base (5) acts on the Plunger, and consequently the Lever. The motion is transmitted back down the oscillating rods until the Strike Plate rests on the Slide Plate (Cam Box).
Upper MG illustrated. Function of trigger mechanism on port side MG is identical.
(2) Lever Affixed to oscillating rod
(3) Plunger
Adjustable bracket with spherical collar supports oscillating rod.
(1) Upper Oscillating Rod
(5) Trigger Motor Base Contains the Plunger return spring
(4) Firing Finger (part of Plunger assembly)
Vickers Machine Gun Mounted on upper cowl.
© Juanita Franzi

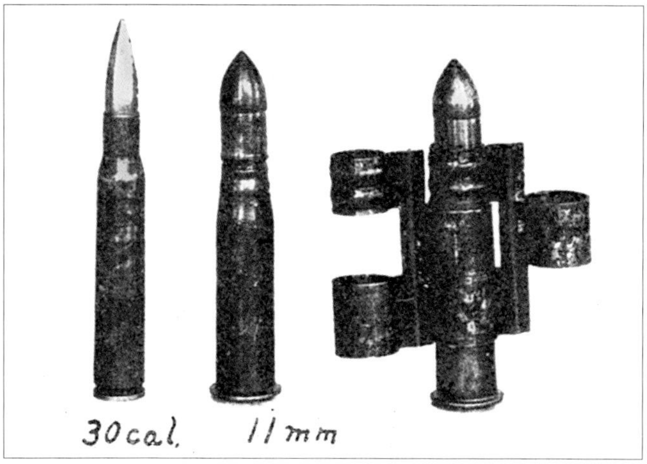

The Vickers machine gun was modified to fire 11 mm incendiary or tracer ammunition for use in attacking observation balloons. An 11 mm cartridge is compared here with a .30 caliber cartridge, and the 11 mm cartridge on the right is fixed in a metallic link, one element of a Prideaux disintegrating link belt. Handbook of Aircraft Armament 1918

This photograph of a Nieuport 28A undergoing modification for shipboard use at the Naval Aircraft Factory clearly shows the twin Marlin machine-gun installation, with unit sight positioned between the guns. Also visible are the .30 caliber ammunition boxes and a telegraph key, visible to the right of the tachometer. National Archives

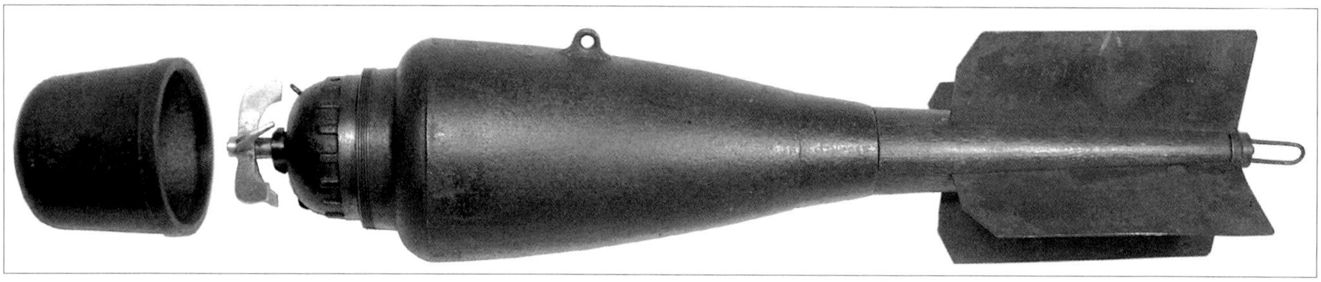

The bomb carrier (see following illustration) was used to carry four Cooper anti- personnel fragmentation bombs of the type shown above. Cooper bombs (the American copy was designated MARK II-B Fragmentation Bomb) each weighed nineteen pounds and were equipped with a fuse mechanism designed to explode on contact with the ground. Bomb fragments covered an area of forty yards or more. There is no evidence that bombs were dropped in combat by the Nieuport 28A, although similar carriers for Cooper bombs were installed and successfully used on some SPAD XIII fighters during the war. Bomb-carrier attachment lugs are still found on some surviving Nieuport 28As.

received in a box and then taken outside, so that they do not hit the pilot, no matter what the position of the airplane may be.

The Marlin machine gun weighed twenty-two pounds and had a rate of fire of 680 rounds per minute. The gun was lighter and had a faster cyclic rate than the Vickers. The Vickers' cyclic rate could be increased to 850 rounds per minute, however, with the addition of the Hyland muzzle booster.

First Pursuit Group pilots demonstrated the efficacy of ground attack during the Meuse-Argonne Offensive, where ground strafing and fragmentation bombs dropped from SPAD XIII fighters were used effectively on concentrations of German troops and supply columns. This was a mode of attack favored by the RAF and adopted by the American Air Service, but decried by the French: "The French Aviation has long since rejected the principle of the single-seater bombing plane, and has adopted, exclusively, multi-seaters, generally two-seaters. As a matter of fact, it is to be carried on at the same time as the handling of the machine and engine. The bombing should be carried out by an expert operator having the freedom of movement necessary for fixing the target, helping the pilot to fly exactly over the spot, working the fighting device, working the controls of the bomb-releaser, and if necessary, defending himself against the enemy."[5]

Major General Patrick rejected this notion, believing that there were occasions when small fragmentation bombs, dropped from fighters, could be used to good effect. In fact, tests were already under way to install and test a bomb carrier, capable of carrying four Cooper fragmentation bombs, on the Nieuport 28. Following a trial on 13 August 1918, the installation was approved and recommended as standard equipment for the Nieuport 28.

Although there is no evidence of the Nieuport 28 bomb-carrier installation being used in combat, evidence of the bomb-carrier attachment lugs is still found on the undersides of some surviving Nieuport 28As.

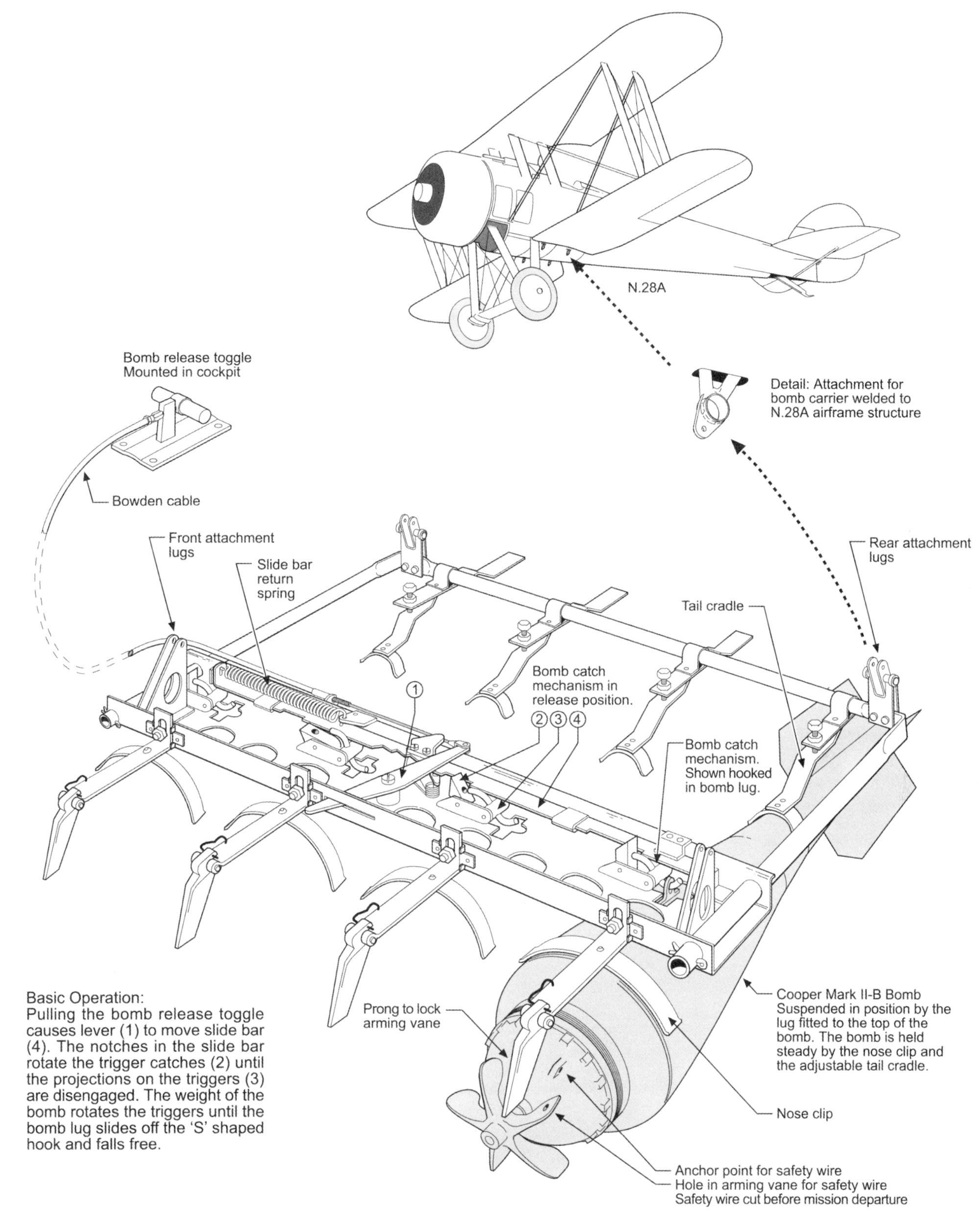

BOMB CARRIER INSTALLATION ON N.28A

Other Standard Equipment on the Nieuport 28 and Nieuport 28A

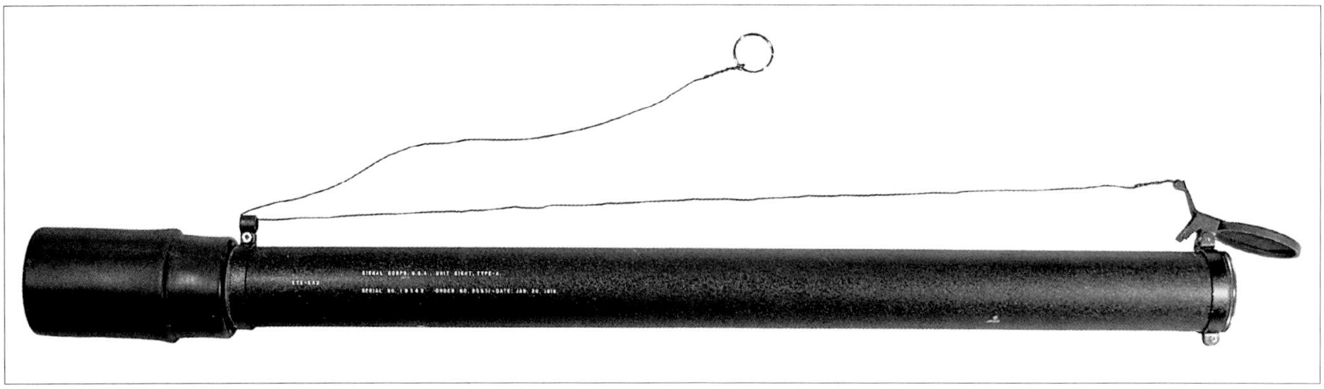

The unit sight, two inches in diameter and twenty-five inches in length, is an optical sight with no magnification. Within the sight is a sighting ring that allows quick sighting of the target, irrespective of where the pilot's eye is aligned against the sight. Graticulation within the lens allows the pilot to make an approximate calculation of the speed of the enemy airplane. Handbook of Aircraft Armament 1918

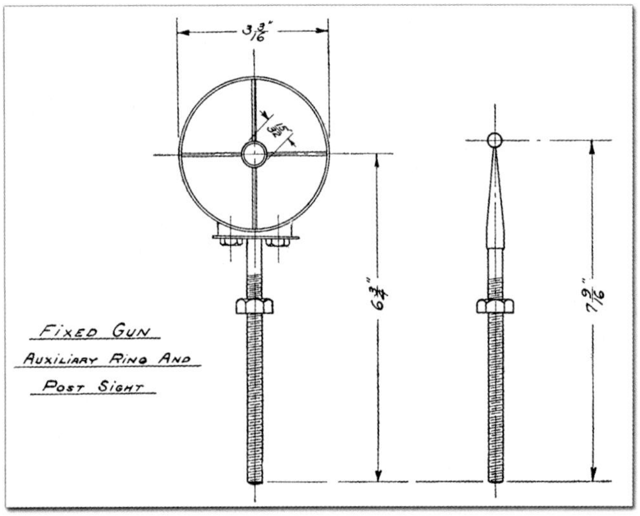

Auxiliary ring and post sights were used in conjunction with the unit sight. Handbook of Aircraft Armament 1918

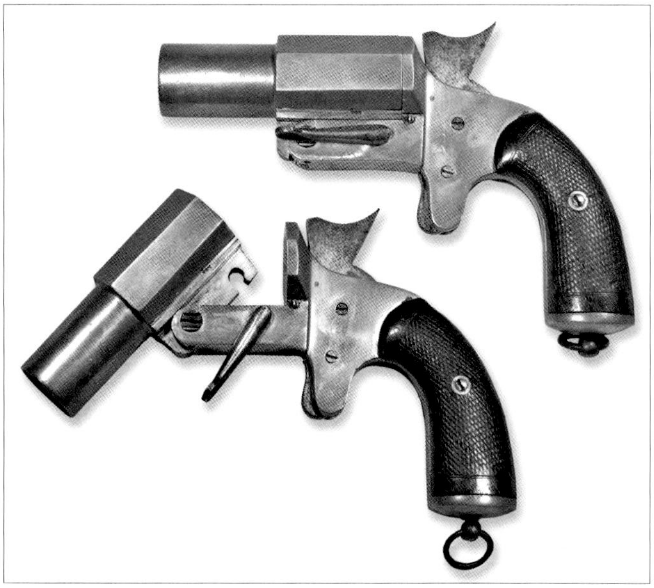

A French flare gun, of the type carried aboard the Nieuport 28 for signaling purposes.

Specifications and General Characteristics[6]

Type: Chasing biplane, single seater
Engine: 150 Gnôme, monovalve
Appendix D
Military Category

SUMMARY OF RESULTS

	Kg	Lbs
Weight when empty:	436.00	961
Load:	152.00	335
Combustible [fuel and oil]:	110.00	242
Total weight:	698.00	1538
Weight per square meter:	43.60	96
Weight per RF:	4.36	9.6
(160 hp at 1,300 revolutions)		

DIMENSIONS

Maximum span:	8.16 m	26 feet, 9 ¼ inches
Maximum length	6.40 m	21 feet
Total height:	2.50 m	8 feet, 1 ¾ inches

Height of axis of propeller above the ground:
(a) airplane at rest: 1.6 m
(b) airplane in line of flight: 5 m

CELLULE [WINGS]

Biplane type
Retreat [sweepback] angle: -0-
Dihedral angle of upper wing: upper wing 1° 30'
Dihedral angle of lower wing: -0-
Relative position of the planes: upper wing staggered 15°
Gap: 1.2 m
Upper plane [surface]: Span: 8.1 m; Depth: 1.3 m
Lower plane [surface]: Span: 7.8 m; Depth: 1 m
Total lifting surface [net]: 16 sq. m

AILERONS

Arrangement: 2 ailerons on the lower plane
Dimensions: Length: 2.14 m; Depth: .4 m
Distance from the center of the ailerons to the axis of the airplane: 2.7 m

HORIZONTAL EMPENNAGE

Fixed part: non-adjustable – Surface 1.08 sq. m
Movable part: 2 panels worked together: Surface 2.24 sq. m
Distance from the stabilizer joint to the entering [leading] edge of the wing: 4.5 m

VERTICAL EMPENNAGE

Drift in 2 parts, lower and upper, surface: lower and upper, Surface .14 sq. m
Vertical rudder: Surface: .76 sq. m
Distance from the joint of the rudder to the leading edge of the wing: 4.65 m

FUSELAGE: Section of main frame: Dimensions: D. 1 m; Surface: .78 m

LANDING CHASSIS

Number of wheels: 2; Gauge: 1.6 m; Shock absorber: Sandows
Brake device: None

VARIOUS: Fuselage, longerons, uprights, and cross pieces of spruce with piano wire stays.

MOTOR GROUP

Engine: Monovalve Gnôme
Type: 9 cylinders, rotary
Power: 160 hp at 1,200 revolutions
Magnetos: two
Starting device: starting with propeller

OIL TANKS

Number:	1
Weight of capacity of oil:	20 liters
Weight of empty tank:	Kind of metal: 5 kilos; Leaded sheet iron
Kind of oil:	Castor oil
Device for reheating oil:	Tank behind engine
Device for testing oiling:	Glass bell

GASOLINE TANKS

Number:	2
Weight or capacity of gasoline:	125 liters
Weight of tank, Metal used:	25 kilos; lead coated sheet iron
Level indicator:	Glass tube
System of feeding:	Weyman exhauster
Place of gasoline tanks:	1 in front of pilot; 1 at side of pilot

REVOLUTION COUNTER: Mark, number, place: Jaeger, 1, in front of pilot

ENGINE CONTROLS

Gasoline:	1 hand lever
Gas:	None
Air:	None
Altimeter corrector:	None

TYPES OF CONTROLS

Commander's post:	Principal: 1
Elevation:	Lever
Lateral control:	Lever
Steering:	Foot bar
Engine:	Contact on lever

ARMAMENT: 2 Vickers machine guns

LOAD

Pilot:	80 kg
Instrument:	7 kg
Total load:	152 kg

NIEUPORT 28

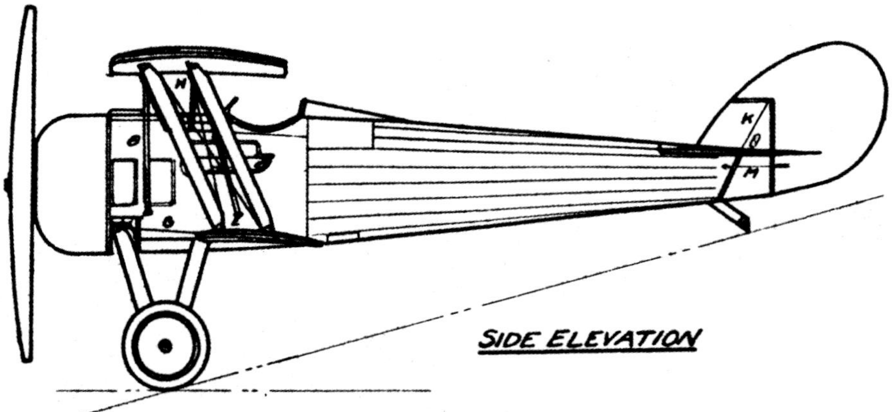

SIDE ELEVATION

INCIDENCE - INFERIOR

	Right Angle	Right Reading	Left Angle	Left Reading
At fuselage	2° to 2°-10'	35 to 38 m.m.	2° to 2°-10'	35 to 38 m.m.
At wing extremity	2° to 2°-10'	35 to 38 m.m.	2° to 2°-10'	35 to 38 m.m.

INCIDENCE - SUPERIOR

	Right Angle	Right Reading	Left Angle	Left Reading
At fuselage	1°-30' to 2°	34 to 45 m.m.	1°-30' to 2°	34 to 45 m.m.
At wing extremity	1°-30' to 2°	34 to 45 m.m.	1°-30' to 2°	34 to 45 m.m.

STAGGER At fuselage At wing strut

AILERON DROOP

FUSELAGE TOP LONGERONS ALIGNMENT

Level longitudinally and transversely at cockpit

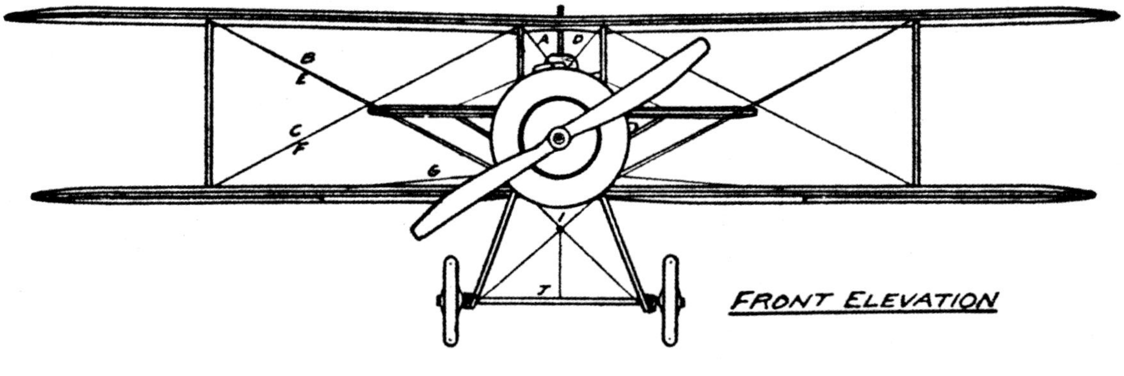

FRONT ELEVATION

DIHEDRAL inferior - 0 superior

WING BRACING

DESCRIPTION	FRONT TRUSS SUFFIX	FRONT TRUSS DIAM.	FRONT TRUSS SINGLE or DOUBLE	REAR TRUSS SUFFIX	REAR TRUSS DIAM.	REAR TRUSS SINGLE or DOUBLE
Center section cables	A	3 1/2 m.m.	Single	D	4 1/2 mm.	single
Flying cables	B	4 m.m.	Double	E	4 m.m.	Double
Ground cables	C	4 1/2 m.m.	Single	F	4 1/2 mm	Single
EXTERNAL DRIFT CABLES	G	3 1/2 m.m.	Single			
INCIDENCE CABLES - SUFFIX	H	DIAM.	Single			

UNDERCARRIAGE BRACING

DESCRIPTION	SUFFIX	DIAM.	SINGLE or DOUBLE
Cross bracing cables	I	4 1/2 m.m.	Single
Joining cables	J	3 1/2 m.m.	Single

TAIL BRACING - SUFFIX K GAGE Single

FUSELAGE WIRES

CONFIDENTIAL
OFFICIAL INFORMATION

INSPECTION DEPT. 8-30-18 N-60

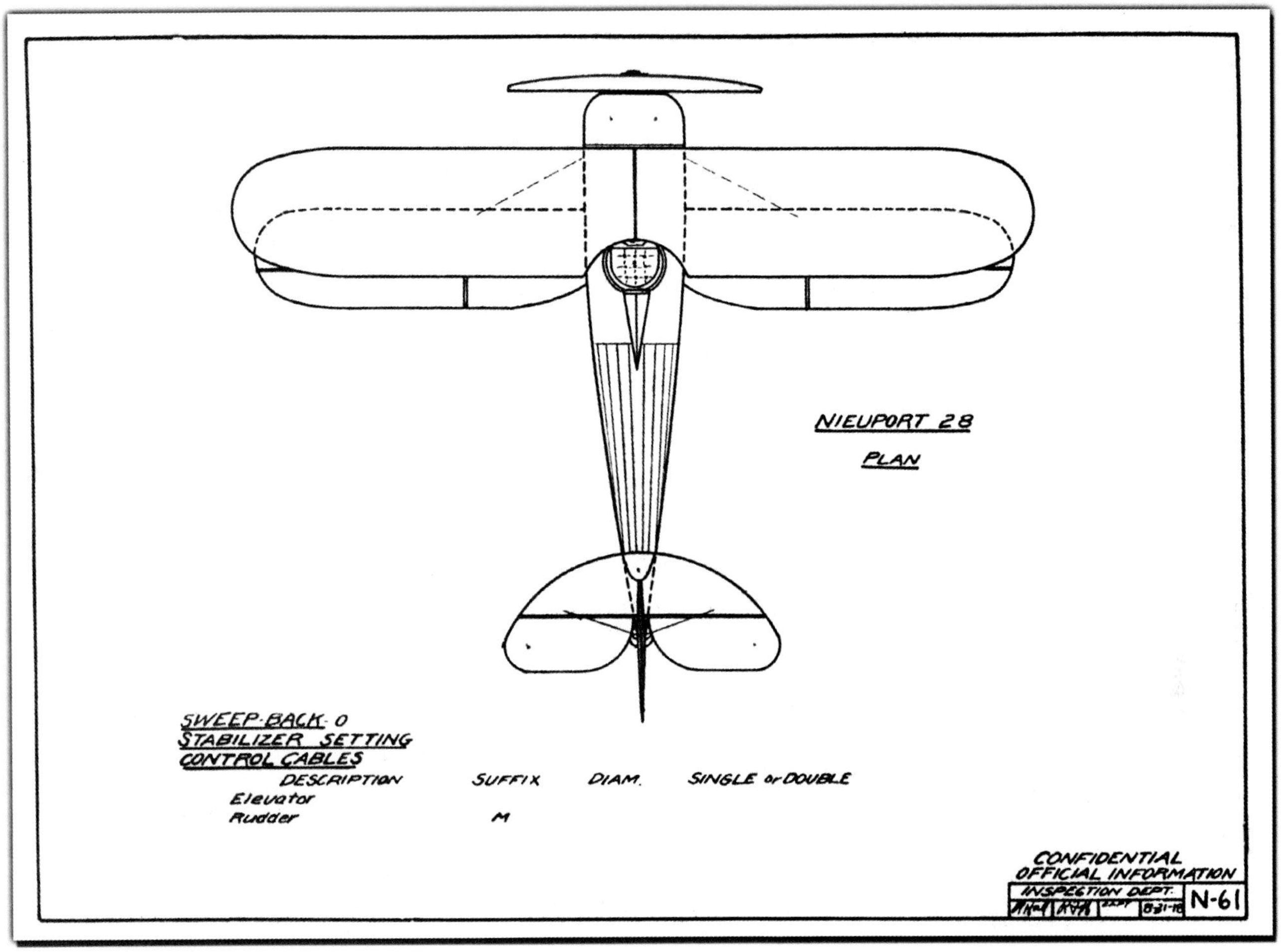

Weight of gasoline:	90 kg
Weight of oil:	20 kg
Total combustible:	110 kg

TOTAL MILITARY LOAD:
Load plus weight of combustible: 262 kg

TOTAL WEIGHT: 698 kg

PERFORMANCE[7]

Maximum speed: 122 mph at 6,560 feet
Climb rate: 5.5 minutes to reach 6,560 feet
Climb rate: 14 minutes to reach 14,000 feet
Ceiling: 19,000 feet
Endurance: 1 1/2 hours

Appendix D
Destined to Fail: The Nieuport 28 Wing

Several weeks after the glorious twin victories scored by Air Service pilots on Sunday, 14 April 1918, Colonel Billy Mitchell lauded the Nieuport 28 fighter and recommended "that its construction and that of the Gnome monosoupape [single valve] motor be continued with all speed for the use of the American Air Service in France."[1] The following month, however, brought a dramatic reversal of fortune for the Nieuport 28, as pilots of the 94th and the recently combat-activated 95th Aero Squadrons began to experience engine fires and catastrophic wing failures with the nimble, French-built fighter.

As related in an earlier chapter, Lieutenant Jimmy Meissner was the first Air Service pilot to encounter wing failure; this occurred on 2 May 1918, moments after Meissner's victim began a fatal spin to earth. Other pilots soon followed suit, with Captain Hall and Lieutenants Rickenbacker, Casgrain, Meissner (again), and Heinrichs all experiencing the same terrifying "crack" as the leading edge of the top wing of their Nieuports tore away, taking ribbons of fabric with it. None of these accidents was fatal, but the die was cast. On 12 June 1918, in a memorandum to the Chief of the American Air Service, Brigadier General Benjamin Foulois urgently recommended that "immediate steps be taken to replace all aeroplanes of this type [Nieuport 28], by one place SPADs, or an equally efficient and reliable British type."[2]

Unlike the SPAD XIII, which had an extraordinarily long gestation period, the Nieuport 28 fighter entered combat virtually untested. Some of the problems, such as the replacement of weak landing-gear wires, were quickly taken care of in the field; a more serious problem with engine fires was dealt with by proper training and onsite replacement of improperly annealed copper fuel lines. The frequency of wing failures in May and early June 1918 was an entirely different matter; the problem was hushed up while squadron officers debated the cause of an apparently defective wing and attempted to fix it. The problem, however, could not be remedied because the true cause of the wing failures was not understood at the time; understanding would come only after the war, when aerodynamicists were at last able to achieve and analyze accurate information about the characteristics of airflow and the resulting aerodynamic pressures on the wing at different attitudes and velocities.

What the Designers Knew – and When

The Nieuport Company had a tradition of building light, highly maneuverable fighter planes, and the Nieuport 28 was no exception. Earlier Nieuport designs, such as models 11, 17, and other variants, were supplied to many Allied air services, and were considered among the most outstanding fighters of the war. The Nieuport 28, designed in 1917, used a heavier and more powerful engine than its predecessor designs and required a larger wing area and a two-spar upper and lower wing to carry the added load. The Nieuport 28 continued to employ a thin wing design that was characteristic of the majority of World War I fighters, including the Sopwith Camel and the SPAD XIII, which replaced the Nieuport 28.

Allied airplane designers thought, *or rather intuited*, that a thin wing was a more efficient design (i.e., resulted in less drag, which would improve the lift/drag ratio), and experiments utilizing primitive wind tunnels seemed to corroborate their judgment. However, these early, low-velocity wind tunnels using small-scale airplane models could not realistically simulate the actual conditions of flight.

• • •

Allied observers were confounded when they encountered the Fokker Dr.1 and Fokker D.VII, both sporting thick wings, with the top wing of the D.VII being "extremely deep compared with any modern standard."[3] With uncharacteristic verboseness, the British editor of *Flight Magazine* stated: "A [thick wing] section like the Fokker is not generally credited with any very high efficiency, but the mere fact that it has been retained in a design, examples of which have been built not more than three months ago, would certainly appear to indicate that it has not been found in practice to be so inferior as to outweigh any other advantages that may attend its employment."[4]

Allied aerodynamicists learned only after the war of the work that was done during wartime in Germany by Dr. Hugo Junkers, to develop a wing thick enough to contain the bracing necessary to carry

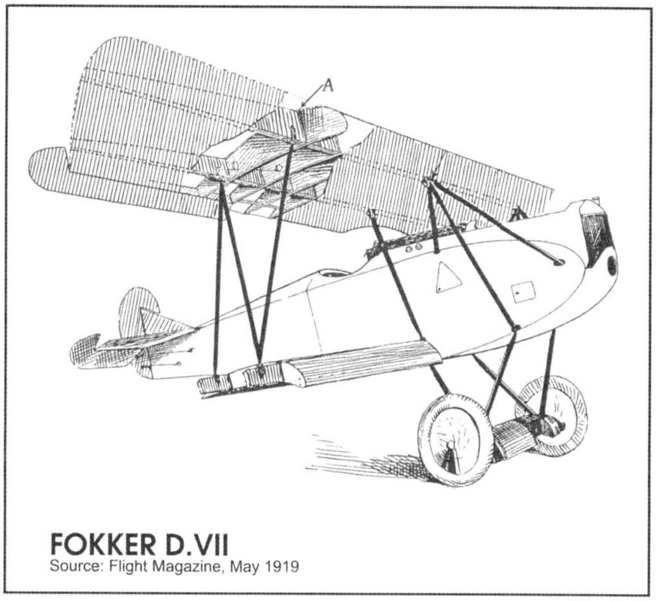

Fokker D.VII with cutaway wing. Flight Magazine, May 1919

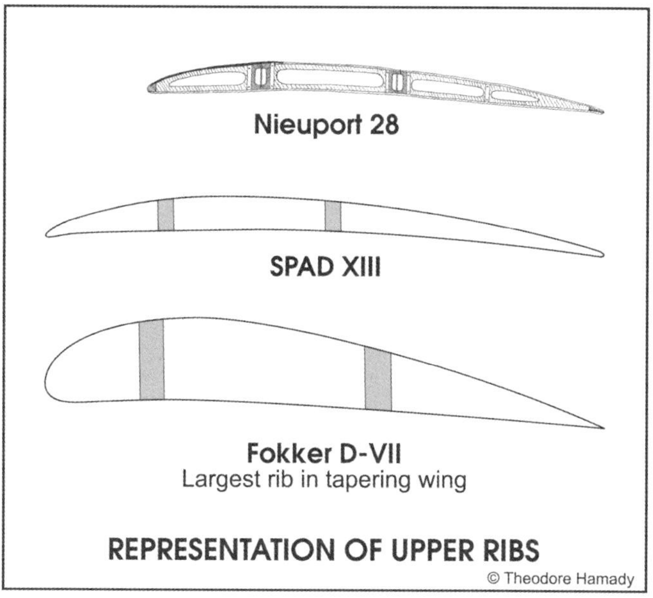

Comparative views in scale of top wing ribs of the Nieuport 28, SPAD XIII, and Fokker D.VII (inboard rib of tapered upper wing).

the load. Anthony Fokker, who had flown Junkers' first thick-wing aircraft, the J-1, adapted the thick wing for the Dr.1 and the D.VII, and after May 1918, Allied pilots became well-acquainted with the exceptional climb rate, maneuverability, and ease of control of the Fokker D.VII, but they had little understanding about how and why the thick wing contributed to improved performance and handling.

The contemporary illustration of a Fokker D.VII (above left) clearly shows the placement of a thick rib (A) on front and rear spars that tapered toward the wing tips. The drawings on the left (drawn roughly to scale) contrast the thin standard upper-wing ribs of the Nieuport 28 (top) and the SPAD XIII (middle), with the thick center section Fokker D.VII rib. Note the position of the front and rear spar on each rib.

The SPAD XIII, which replaced the Nieuport 28 in Air Service squadrons, had half again as many ribs across a wing span slightly longer than that of the Nieuport 28. This provided better load distribution, but at a price. The SPAD XIII was designed for strength and speed, but had flight characteristics "like a brick," according to the pilots who flew it. John D. Anderson Jr., in his book *A History of Aerodynamics*, states that the "SPAD had a relatively high speed at 134 mph because of its powerful engine that simply overcame the relatively poor aerodynamic features."[5]

• • •

The problem resulted from the inability of these early wind tunnels to produce a full-scale Reynolds number, thereby validating conditions of actual flight. In the 1880s, Osborne Reynolds (1842–1912) of the University of Manchester had derived a ratio, thereafter known as the Reynolds number, from experiments conducted with water flowing through pipes. Reynolds concluded from his experiments that a flow pattern (of water, in his experiments) over a scale model and over a full-size object of the same shape would be the same (hence, a full-scale Reynolds number) if a certain flow parameter (the ratio: pVd/, where p = density of the fluid, V = velocity of the fluid, and Φ = fluid viscosity) were the same for both. Reynolds numbers later became a critical factor (with the substitution of air for water in the formula) in the testing of aircraft models in wind tunnels.[6] But full-scale Reynolds numbers could only be achieved if the wind tunnel could produce the requisite velocity and density of the flow of air over the scale model being tested. Anything less, and the resulting low Reynolds number could lead airfoil designers in the wrong direction, as Professor John D. Anderson Jr. pointed out in his book, *A History of Aerodynamics*.[7] One such misdirection was the perpetuation of the thin airfoil. Anderson states that aerodynamicists traditionally intuited that thick airfoils would produce more drag than thin airfoils, and early wind-tunnel tests by the Wright brothers and others seemed to validate that notion. However, it is now known that the finding is valid only at low Reynolds numbers.

Given the designers' predilection and knowledge at the time, the Nieuport 28's thin wing was clearly designed for lightness, maneuverability, and speed at the expense of strength.

The left and right upper wings were joined at the aircraft's centerline. Fourteen ribs on each upper wing transferred the load from the fabric wing covering (not shown) to the two hollow box spars constructed of spruce. In addition to this load transfer function, the ribs gave the wing proper camber or aerodynamic shape. Four of the ribs were compression ribs and were of stronger construction, to oppose the pressure of the bracing wires angled between the main and rear spars. Metal-tube struts provided additional bracing between the spars and also attachment points for interplane struts between the upper and lower wings. Nose ribs, also called false ribs, were interspersed in front of the main spar between the standard and compression ribs, and helped retain the correct shape of the airfoil and also provided additional strength to the leading edge. A three-ply birch veneer was added to the top of the wing to strengthen the leading edge, or entering edge, as it was then called. Spruce leading and trailing edge strips and ash wing tips defined the graceful planform of the Nieuport 28 wing.

The drawing depicting a standard rib warrants careful scrutiny, for it suggests why the Nieuport 28 top wing was prone to failure.

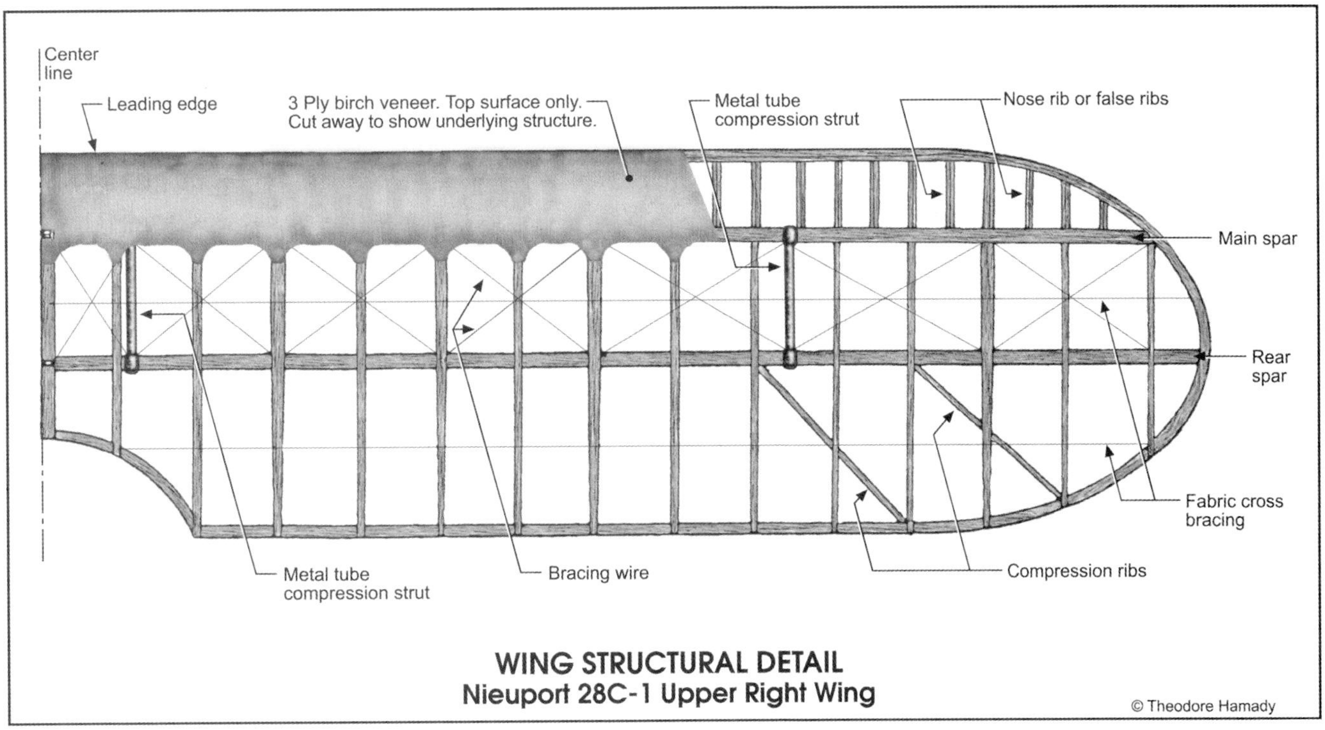

Structural detail of the Nieuport 28's upper right wing.

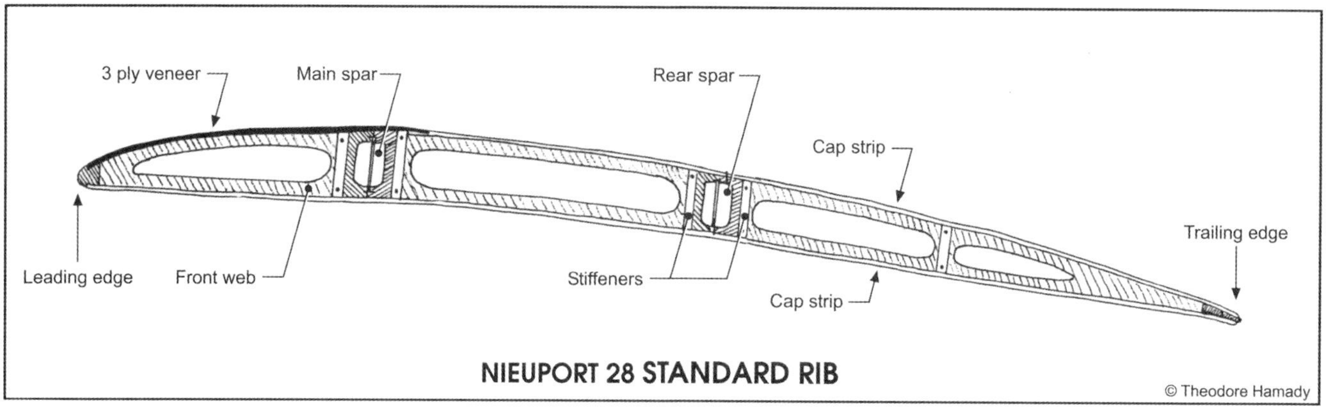

Side view of a Nieuport 28 upper wing standard rib.

The standard rib of the Nieuport 28's upper wing comprises cap strips made of 5/8" x 1/8" ash and encapsulated the 5/32" thick poplar webs with a thin veneer on the top front surface. The compression ribs had wider and thicker cap strips and were boxed in the center section for added strength.

The inside of the thin, narrow cap strips was grooved to hold the webs and nailed in place. The bottom cap strip extended from the trailing edge to the leading edge, but the top cap strip extended only to the rear of the main spar, where it was slightly cut down to accept the rear portion of the three-ply veneer protecting the leading edge.

The poplar webs were contained between the upper and lower cap strips, poplar being a suitable wood to withstand compression stress. The webs were cut out for lightness and had vertical stiffeners glued and nailed to them at various points along the rib to prevent the webs from bending and splitting.

The veneer was nailed and glued to the leading edge and nailed into the top of the front web and top of the main spar. Note that the front web was not attached directly to the main spar, although some original ribs did reveal that two small nails were driven at a 45° angle through the stiffener and web into the front spar, though this was hardly an adequate means of attachment.

After the wing components were assembled, the wing was covered with fine linen fabric that was double-stitched and seamed at the leading edge, and then doped. To maintain the proper airfoil profile, the fabric, tautened by the application of dope, was stitched between the bottom and top cap strips, and then painted.

Now consider what happened to James Meissner, Eddie Rickenbacker, and others in May and early June 1918. When Meissner returned on 2 May to his aerodrome at Gengoult after landing safely at another Allied aerodrome, he reported that he had had a collision with his adversary that caused the leading edge of the wing to tear away.[8] Meissner's report was questioned by Captain Du Doré, a member of the Aeronautic Section of the French army and a liaison officer at Gengoult Aerodrome. Du Doré believed that the "wing [leading edge is] too weak; it gives way, the ribs between the [leading] edge and the central longeron [main spar] breaks the cloth, [which] tears off, and the wing loses the covering completely."[9] Du Doré urgently recommended that the leading edge of the upper wing be reinforced.

American Air Service officers weighed in with their analyses of the problem with the upper wings of the Nieuport 28. In a communication dated early June 1918 to the Chief of the Air Service, First Army, First Pursuit Group Commander Major B. M. Atkinson expressed his opinion that the "weak construction in [the] upper wing [was] due to both spars being too close to the middle," and further noted that "upon redressing from a steep dive, the leading edge [would collapse], carrying away the fabric of the upper surface of the wing."[10] Major John Huffer, commander of the 94th Aero Squadron, attributed the problem to the veneer on the leading edge of the wing. Huffer believed that exposure to the sun would warp the veneer and loosen it from the spar underneath, which would cause it to break away under the strain of recovery from a high-speed dive.[11] A fix of the upper wing, which was perhaps suggested by Major Huffer, was later undertaken. The fix involved gluing and nailing a thirteen-inch-long contoured wood strip, or batten, as some called it, through the leading-edge veneer and into the main spar and web of each standard and compression rib. This was done, presumably, to hold the veneer more securely in place.

Gluing and nailing these battens (wooden strips perpendicular to the leading edge), through the plywood veneer and into the web of the wing rib beneath, was thought at the time to be an appropriate solution to the problem of wing failure. This fix helped to secure the top veneer, but the real problem was later found to be elsewhere.

Fabric Stripping

Clearly, these officers did not believe that the Nieuport 28's wing failures originated with a fabric break. This notion – so closely associated with the Nieuport 28 – that the wing fabric stripped away during an abrupt recovery from a high speed dive, is correct, insofar as it occurred only *after the wing's leading edge failed first,* and flew off in a slipstream, pulling streamers of fabric with it.

The notion of "fabric stripping" may have originated with a postwar article by James Norman Hall, who had experienced wing failure while flying with the 94th Aero Squadron. Hall described his experience as follows: "While diving vertically upon the enemy near-

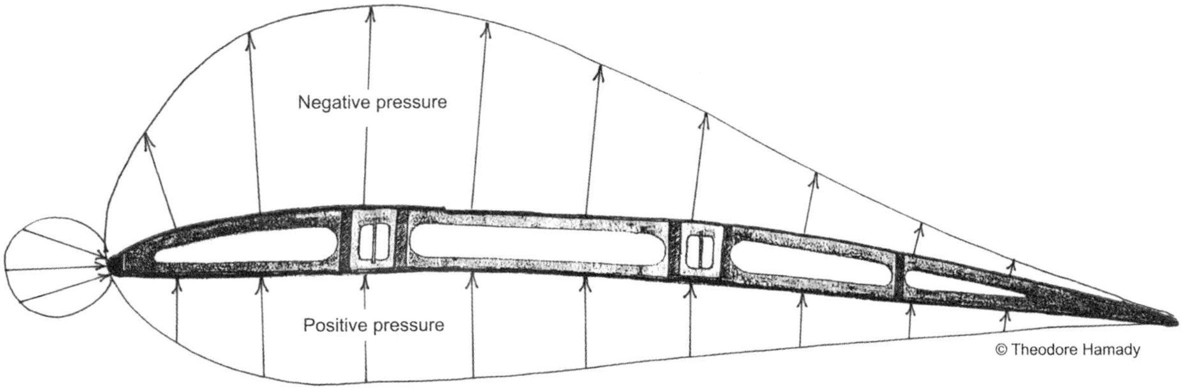

Pressure vectors on a standard rib with the airplane cruising at the same angle of attack. Pressures are negative above the wing and negative below, relative to the ambient pressure.

est me, the fabric covering the upper surface of my upper right plane [wing] burst along the leading edge, throwing the plane completely out of balance."[12] It is unknown why Hall described the incident in this manner, because he was later shown a photograph of his crashed airplane (see this photograph in Chapter 4) that clearly showed the upper right wing's leading edge had collapsed, and part of the remaining structure was hanging down within the fabric, which was still partially intact.

Captain Eddie Rickenbacker contributed to the inaccuracy of the record. In his postwar memoir, written with the help of a ghostwriter, Rickenbacker recounted James Meissner's experience on 2 May 1918. "So furious had been his downward plunge that the force of the wind's pressure had torn away the fragile covering of both his upper wings."[13] Rickenbacker knew better, but perhaps failed to convey an accurate account to his ghostwriter.

During congressional hearings held in 1919, Meissner and Rickenbacker were both questioned about the problems with the Nieuport 28 wing by Congressman James Frear. Meissner stated that the problem was due to "a weakness at the entering [leading] edge," and Rickenbacker confirmed Meissner's statement, testifying that the problem was "due to the defective construction [of the leading edge] where it was attached to the upper spar."[14] It is interesting to note that Congressman Frear seemed predisposed to understand the problem of the Nieuport 28 wing as "a parting of the cloth from the wings,"[15] clearly, an understandable observation from someone with little understanding of airplane structures and aerodynamic forces.

With the benefit of aeronautical knowledge acquired in the postwar years, the factors that caused the upper wing of the Nieuport 28 to fail can now be examined. The drawing provided gives a representation of the lift or pressure forces on a Nieuport 28 upper wing standard rib when the airplane is cruising at a small angle of attack. The length of the lines, called vectors, represent the magnitude of those pressures relative to the ambient pressure. The vector arrows pointing away from the wing surface illustrate pressures less than ambient (these pressures were then called suction, or more commonly, negative pressure), and vector arrows pointing to the wing surface illustrate pressures greater than ambient pressure (commonly called positive pressure). Wartime airplane designers were aware that the centers of these pressures would move forward along the chordline (a line drawn from the leading edge to the trailing edge of the wing) at a high angle of attack (climb) and shift to the rear when the angle of attack decreased.[16] The designers believed that the length of this travel took place from the midpoint along the chordline forward to about one-third the distance from the wing's leading edge. This was the area where the greatest pressures were thought to occur, and it corresponded to where the main and rear spars were placed to encompass the area of these higher pressures along the chordline under varying airspeeds and angles of attack. Only after the war would these pressure distributions be measured, and found to be more intense and closer to the leading edge than had previously been thought.

All of the pilots who encountered wing failure were diving at high speed moments before the failure of the upper wing occurred. An accurate representation of the pressures on the upper wing rib during recovery from a steep dive would show pressures of far greater magnitude, far forward along the chordline, and with negative pressures both above and below the wing's leading edge. Now, follow Lieutenant Eddie Rickenbacker in his high-speed dive, encountering the "crack of doom" as his upper wing collapsed and the sudden violent vrille, or spin, that followed:

> I believe I should have followed my first target all the way to the ground regardless of the consequences, so desperately had I determined to get him. So I, perhaps, prolonged my terrific speed a trifle too long. As the enemy plane fell off and began to flutter, I pulled my stick back close into my seat and began a sharp climb. The notorious weakness of the Nieuport quickly announced itself. A ripping crash that sounded like the crack of doom to my ears told me that the sudden strain had collapsed my right wing. The entire spread of canvas over the top wing was torn off by the wind and disappeared behind me. Deprived of any supporting surface on this side, the Nieuport turned over on her right side. The tail was forced up despite all my efforts with the joystick and rudder ... I was caught in a vrille [spin]... .[17]

In every recorded instance of failure of the Nieuport 28's upper wing, the entire leading edge broke clearly forward of the main spar. Several

Opposite: Lieutenant Eddie Rickenbacker attempts to recover, after the leading edge of his upper right wing has failed. Michael O'Neal Above: This drawing illustrates Eddie Rickenbacker's maneuver that resulted in wing failure. Considerable stress was imposed on the upper wing as a result of Rickenbacker's dive recovery – with the magnitude of the upward G force being a function of the abruptness of his transition from a high-speed dive to a climbing turn. Greater stress was imposed on the climbing wing – in this case, the upper right wing – which failed. Michael O'Neal

obvious questions occur at this point: why did one upper wing fail and not both, as in James Meissner's case on 2 May 1918; and why did most right upper wings fail instead of the left wings, as in Waldo Heinrichs' case on 1 June? One answer is that one of the upper wings may have already been damaged and an abrupt maneuver would break the wing's leading edge completely. A more likely answer is that it was prudent for fighter pilots to roll out of a dive to the left or the right (most always to the left in a Nieuport 28 because of the torque of the rotary engine), thereby presenting a potential attacker with a more difficult deflection shot. The high wing in an aileron roll would incur a higher load and break, especially during an abrupt pullout, leaving the other upper wing intact. It appears that Eddie Rickenbacker rolled up sharply to the left out of his steep dive, breaking the leading edge of the upper right wing in the process, and then fell sharply to the right in a violent spin, as lift was lost on the right wing.[18]

James Meissner's experience on 2 May 1918 was slightly different from Rickenbacker's or the other pilots'. Meissner entered a precipitous dive straight ahead at high speed to avoid colliding with his adversary, a risk common to inexperienced pilots who became fixated on their target. He then pulled back sharply – too sharply – on the stick in a straight up recovery, and in an instant, the leading edge along the entire span of the upper wing failed with a loud crack and broke away. The damage to both upper wings was relatively symmetrical, and Meissner managed to control his airplane without falling off into a spin. Ironically, another design feature of the Nieuport 28 (that the ailerons were placed on the lower wings) enabled Meissner and others who encountered failure of the upper wings to manage at least a survivable, controlled crash once the failure had occurred. Had the ailerons been placed on the upper wings, the loss of the leading edge and resultant torn fabric would have altered the airflow over the damaged wing, rendering the ailerons less effective and making the airplane difficult to control.

The upper wing of the Nieuport 28 failed because the wing rib failed in its function of transferring the heavy loads encountered at the leading edge of the wing to the main spar. The portion of the rib forward of the main spar was poorly designed, and so structurally weak as to concentrate the shear and bending moment force on the veneer above the wing and the very thin cap strip below. These structures were inadequate to the task. The fix, which involving nailing and gluing a wood strip or batten atop the veneer adopted after the spate of accidents, added nominal strength to the top of the leading edge of the upper wing. But it did not address what was principally lacking in the rib construction. A shear tie is required to securely tie the web to the spar and to add the necessary rigidity forward of the main spar to manage the heavy shear and bending forces.[19] Extending the top cap strip forward to the leading edge would have added strength to the entering edge with a minimal weight penalty.

Some officers believed that the wing's leading edge stuck out too far forward of the main spar. (James Meissner said this during his appearance before the congressional committee referred to earlier.)

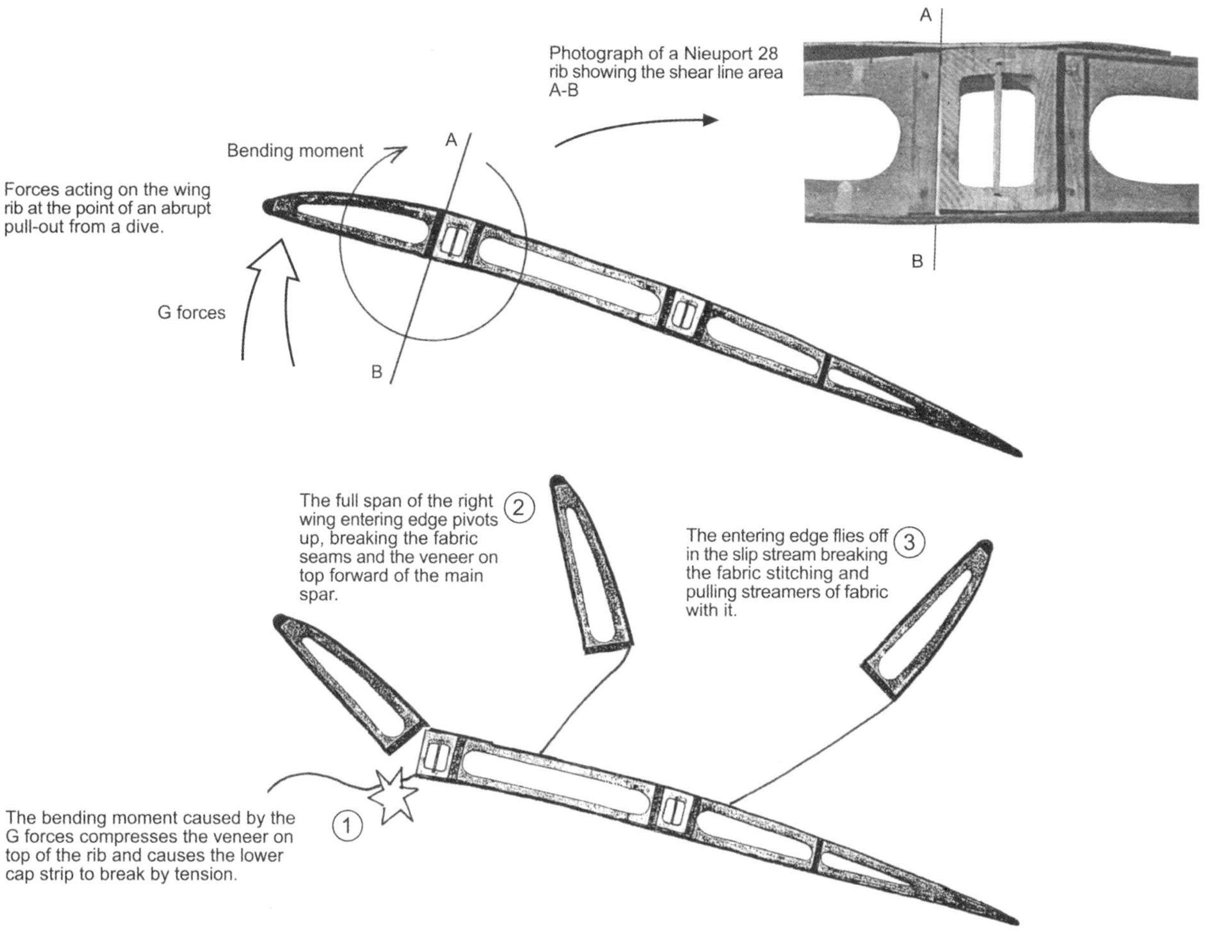

WING FAILURE SEQUENCE
The failure sequence of Eddie Rickenbacker's upper right wing at the moment of his abrupt pull-out of a steep dive.

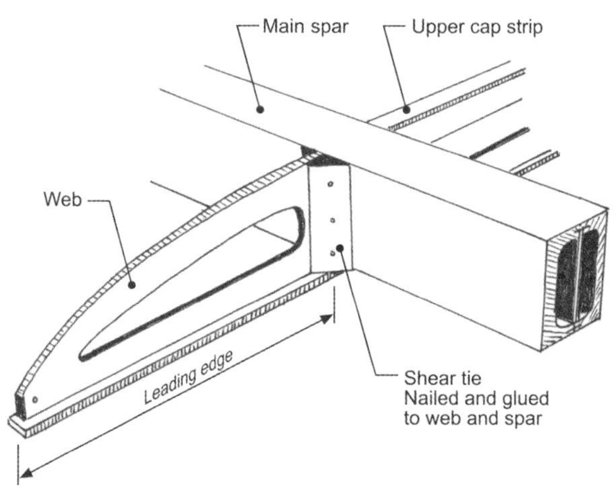

BLOCK SHEAR TIE
Example of a triangular block shear tie that would help transfer the shear force from the web to the spar

Opposite
Top: This drawing illustrates the failure sequence of Rickenbacker's upper right wing at the moment of his abrupt pullout from a steep dive. The upper illustration shows the shear line A-B and the bending moment caused by G forces encountered during the pullout: the veneer forward of the main spar is compressed and the rib's lower cap strip breaks by tension (1). The leading edge then pivots up, breaking the fabric seam (2) and the veneer forward of the main spar, which flies off in the slipstream, breaking the fabric stitching (3), and pulling streamers of fabric with it. This action occurred at the same instant across the entire span of the upper right wing.

Bottom left: Eddie Rickenbacker looks stricken, after his near disaster with wing failure. R.L. Cavanagh

Bottom right: Example of a triangular block shear tie, nailed and glued to the web and spar, that would help transfer the shear force from the fragile web to the spar.

A postwar caution to airfoil designers held that the leading edge should be as short and rigid as possible. There is some evidence that a secure attachment of the leading edge to the main spar was a more important consideration than the length of the leading edge itself.[20] However, there is no evidence that the Air Service considered these modifications at the time that the problems with the Nieuport 28's upper wings occurred.

Other factors contributed to the failure of the Nieuport 28's upper wing. These factors included a strict adherence by the airplane designers to the thin wing philosophy, and the resultant sacrifice of strength to achieve lightness and thinness. The designers were also hampered by a lack of knowledge of pressure distributions or loads along the chord and span of the wing under varying conditions of flight. As standard test procedure, the Section Technique de l'Aéronautique performed static testing (using sand bags layered on until the wings failed) of the Nieuport 28's wings under positive and negative loads, and the test results were reported to the Nieuport Company.[21] However, there is no evidence that the critical leading edge of the wing was tested under load. If the French authorities knew of the problem, they apparently did not inform the American Air Service or caution American pilots.

Poor wartime workmanship and materials were also contributing factors. During the restoration of a Nieuport 28 at the National Air and Space Museum's Paul Garber Facility (1995–2000), the restoration team found evidence of carelessly driven nails in examples of original wing ribs that weakened the rib and also minimal use of casein glue (a derivative of milk curd), which is not waterproof.[22]

Ultimately, the inexperienced pilots of the 94th and 95th Aero Squadrons were responsible for destroying the fragile upper wings of the Nieuport 28 by overstressing them in the heat of combat. The wing of any aircraft will fail if it exceeds its design limitations. Major Harold Hartney, commanding officer of the 27th Aero Squadron, was well-aware of this when he directed his pilots to avoid the abrupt maneuvers that brought about the collapse of the fragile wing: "Early in my flying career I had observed that it [the wing] was the weakest point in all these early airplanes, and I warned the boys about it. In fact, on one annoying occasion, I had to send to the rear a pilot who refused to believe that I knew what I was talking about in this manner and crudely pulled back his stick at the end of a dive."[23]

With the possible exception of Lieutenant William Plyler of the 27th Aero Squadron, all of the pilots of the 27th and 147th Aero Squadrons were spared the frightening experience of wing failure, due to the firm orders and proper instructions dispensed by their commanding officers, Majors Harold Hartney and Geoffrey Bonnell.

The Problem Persists – But Is Finally Resolved

The Nieuport 28 was not the only Air Service fighter to encounter upper-wing failure while undergoing high-stress flight maneuvers. On 19 July 1921, Lieutenant Clark was killed when his Curtiss-built Orenco D-1 crashed at Ellington Field, Texas. The cause of the accident was attributed "to the failure of the upper right wing leading edge, causing the wing to fall back and up, thereby creating excessive drag and loss of control."[24] Clark's fatal accident and discoveries of faulty workmanship in his aircraft induced other pilots to refuse to fly the Orenco D-1 any longer. The type was subsequently removed from service.

Lieutenant J. A. Macready's report of an accident at McCook Field on 30 March 1921 while flying a Boeing-built MB-3 sounds ominously familiar:

The top view of an upper right wing of a Curtiss-built Orenco D-1 after a nonfatal crash. R.L. Cavanagh

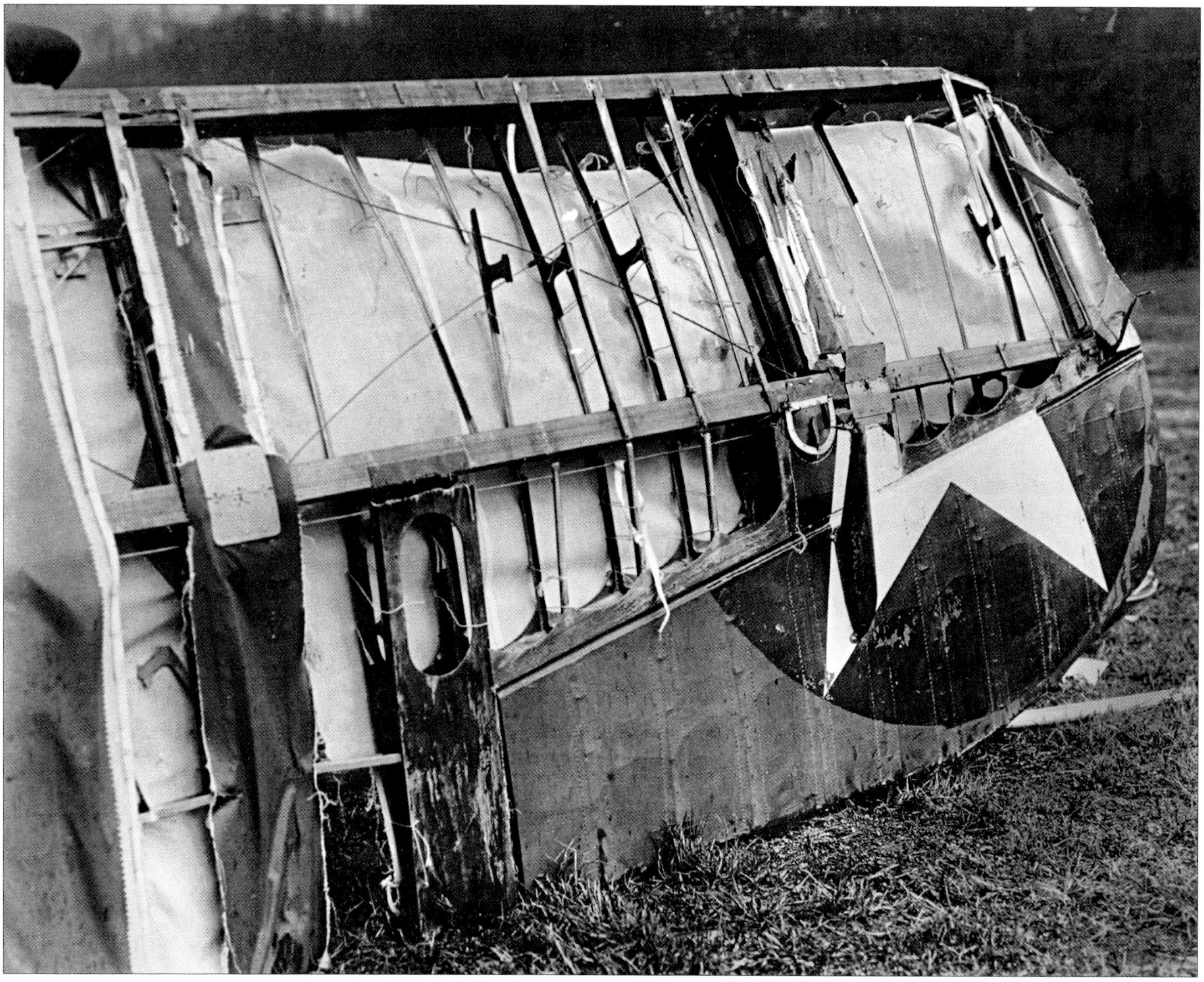

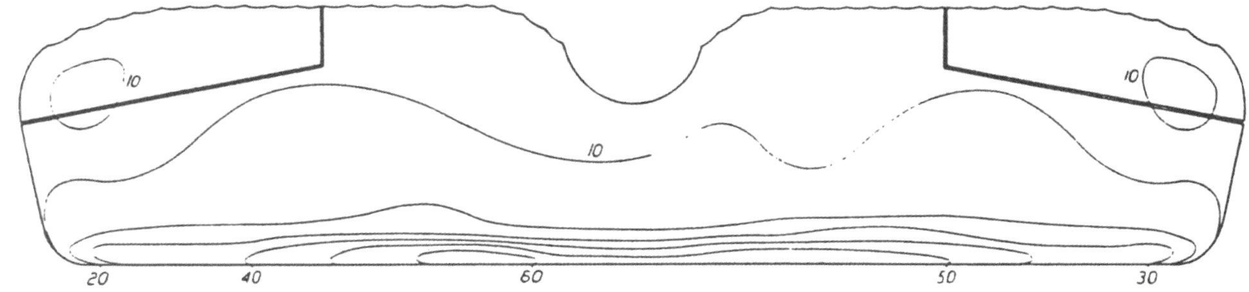

Steady flight at 70mph and 1,000 RPM

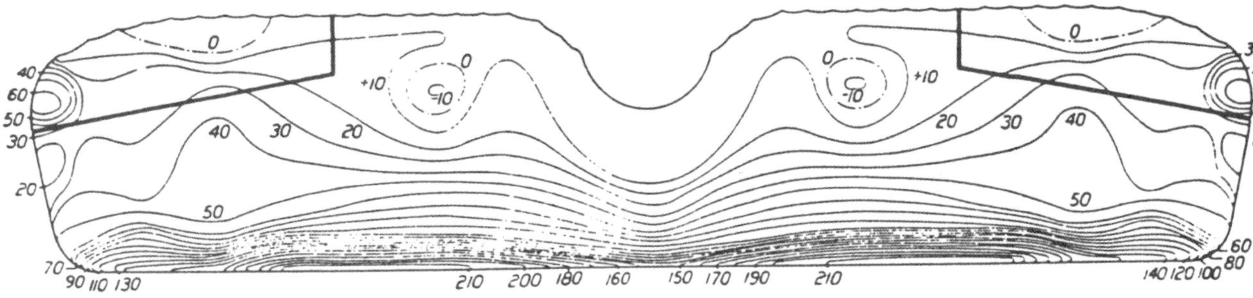

Vertical bank at 150mph and 1,900 RPM

AIR PRESSURE LIFT CONTOURS

Air pressure or lift contours plotted on a top plan view of the wing of a specially modified Boeing MB-3. The top plan view shows the moderate pressures encountered in steady flight. The lower plan view shows the distribution of potentially destructive pressures encountered in a vertical bank.

Source: NACA Report #193, Pressure Distribution Over the Wing of an MB-3 Airplane in Flight

> [T]he MB-3 is a fast pursuit airplane. One of my duties was to test the maneuverability as a fighting airplane. The dive on the enemy is one of the primary functions of combat. With this in mind, and also to note the effectiveness of the closed shutters, I dove the plane at a very steep angle with the power off. I was carefully studying the airplane as it dove, intending to keep a margin of safety and refraining from any quick movements of the controls that would cause undue strains or stresses.
>
> Suddenly I heard a terrific report or crashing sound and felt the plane heavily jarred. I thought that the propeller had broken and crashed into a wing. The pilot can see the top of the top wing from his seat. Looking up, I observed that practically the entire top of the wing was gone, and that webs and woodwork was bare with the fabric stripped from them. The entire leading edge of the wing had collapsed and stripped the top fabric from the wing, leaving it with almost no lift or sustaining power.[25]

Opposite
Top: A Boeing MB-3 (serial number N63341), after a test flight by Lieutenant J.A. Macready at McCook Field on 30 March 1921. Macready dove with power off at a steep angle, and avoided any abrupt control movement; however, the heavy download encountered in the dive was sufficient to shear off the upper wing's entire leading edge forward of the main spar. R.L. Cavanagh

Bottom: A view of the top of the upper right wing of Macready's MB-3, showing the leading edge gone forward of the main spar, broken ribs in the center section, and much of the fabric missing from the top of the wing. Note that the fabric remains on the bottom of the wing. R.L. Cavanagh

Above: Air pressure or lift contours plotted on plan views of the top of the upper wing of the specially modified Boeing MB-3. The upper illustration shows the moderate pressures that the MB-3 encountered while the aircraft was in steady flight at 70 mph and 1,000 rpm. The bottom illustration shows the distribution of potentially destructive pressures encountered when the aircraft was in a vertical bank at 150 mph and 1,900 rpm. NACA Report #193, Pressure Distribution over the Wings of an MB-3 Airplane in Flight

The Curtiss Orenco D-1 and the Boeing MB-3, like the Nieuport 28, incorporated a thin wing design. These postwar accidents and memories of the wartime travails of the Nieuport 28 induced the Air Service to fund an investigation, to determine the distribution of load over the wings of a high-speed airplane under all conditions of flight. That research was conducted at Langley Field, Virginia, under the auspices of the National Advisory Committee for Aeronautics (NACA). It was the first time that pressures were measured across the entire span and chord of the wing. Using a specially modified MB-3, which included the addition of beefed-up rib structures, recording manometers placed in the fuselage took measurements from holes cut in the wing surface at air speeds of 70, 115, and 145 miles per hour at closed, medium, and full throttle, under conditions of steady flight. These tests were undertaken during three maneuvers: a roll, a flattening out of a dive, and a vertical bank at 150 mph.

NACA Executive Committee Chairman Joseph S. Ames made a preliminary report on the findings of the NACA pressure-distribution tests when he delivered the annual Wilbur Wright Lecture to the aeronautical community in 1923.[26] Ames illustrated the results of the tests with contour charts that showed a significant pressure increase and shift forward toward the wing's leading edge as the MB-3 maneuvered sharply at higher speeds. Ames commented that the results of the pressure-distribution tests would be of great use to the airplane designer.[27] Professor Ames also mentioned the inauguration of the Variable Density Wind Tunnel (VDT) at Langley Field, an event that had a significant impact on the progress of airplane design. The air density within this innovative wind tunnel could be compressed up to 20 atmospheres (roughly 300 psi), and the resultant airflow could at last produce realistic test measurements indicating true aerodynamic flight. Ames concluded his remarks by stating that "if the use of these scale effect methods justifies our present hopes, we shall be able in a comparatively short time to place at the disposal of the aircraft designer a wealth of information which should increase markedly the accuracy of his work."[28]

John D. Anderson Jr. would later note the real impact of the VDT: "When it became operational in 1922, [the VDT] was the first wind tunnel capable of testing airfoils, wings, and complete airplane configurations under the conditions of full-scale Reynolds numbers. With that facility, the NACA leapfrogged over all other existing wind tunnels, and the experimental data obtained with the VDT made the United States the undisputed leader in applied aerodynamics for the next 15 years. The product of the VDT and the results of the NACA pressure distribution tests would have far-reaching effects on wing testing and design."[29]

John D. Anderson Jr. also noted that with the undertaking of extensive testing of airfoils at the VDT, "by 1925, the advantage of relatively thick airfoils over the very thin shapes characteristic of most World War One airplanes was widely recognized."[30]

By the mid-1920s, the US Air Service began to routinely test the leading edges of wings and fixed control surfaces on all military airplanes, and especially on highly maneuverable fighters. This was done to test the reactions of those surfaces "to shear and bending during maneuvers such as a roll when high local stresses are imposed on the section forward of the main spar."[31] One can speculate that had the same tests been performed on the wings of the Nieuport 28 in 1917, the elegant and beloved (by many) Nieuport 28 fighter might have remained in combat far longer than its short-lived wartime use of four months.

Appendix E
Production Orders, Deliveries, and Known Serial Numbers

Production Orders[1]

Order#	Order Date	Number Ordered	Received	Purpose
F-12	1/23/18	36	36	Pursuit work (1)
A.S. 5061	2/6/18	36	36	Pursuit work
A.S. 5244	4/6/18	12	12	Replacement aircraft
A.S. 5244	"	2	2	Training
A.S. 5244	"	1	1	Sample shipped to USA (2)
A.S. 5222	3/23/18	216	110	Replacement aircraft (3)
A.S. 5365	5/2/18	600	(4)	Advanced training aircraft
A.S. 5759	7/10/18			Unassembled wing parts; Shipped to Washington (5)

(1) This order originally called for 36 Nieuport 27 fighters, later replaced with Nieuport 28s. See Chapter 3 for more details.

(2) This late-production Nieuport 28, believed to be serial number N.6298, may have been the only wartime-production aircraft to reach the USA. It is likely the aircraft that was redesignated as P-38 after being received for testing at McCook Field in Ohio.

(3) Although no record of cancellation was found, Brigadier General Foulois' 12 June directive to "replace all aeroplanes of this type" (see Chapter 4 for details) resulted in only partial delivery of this final order for wartime-production Nieuport 28s.

(4) After initial discussions with S.A.C.A., this order for Nieuport 28A advanced trainers was ultimately awarded, in October 1918, to Lioré et Olivier (see Chapter 6 and Appendix B for details). Eighty-nine Nieuport 28As were accepted, and eighty-eight of those were ultimately shipped to the USA.

(5) This may have been a replacement cellule set – or a modified cellule set that was sent to the USA for evaluation and testing.

Deliveries of Wartime-Production Nieuport 28 Fighters to the Air Service, AEF[2]

March 1918	37
April 1918	18
May 1918	103
June 1918	18
July 1918	19
August 1918	13
Total	**208***

*This total may not reflect the single Nieuport 28 shipped to the USA.

As noted in Chapter 6, the AEF accepted eighty-nine new Nieuport 28A trainers at Romorantin as part of the final Liquidation Settlement; eighty-eight of these aircraft were crated and shipped to the USA in August 1919.

Nieuport 28 and Nieuport 28A List of Known Serial Numbers

Disposition and other codes provided under the "Remarks" column are defined as follows:

B = Burned
C = Condemned
L = Lost over lines or due to enemy action
R = Returned to depot (First Air Depot, Orly, or any other)
S = Salvaged at First Air Depot
T = Transferred to another unit
W = Wrecked or destroyed in accident

Axxx = French commercial registrations
CGTx = Compagnie Génerale Transaérienne (French commercial registrations)
FAA = Fuerza Aérea Argentina
ICGT = French commercial registration for N.6134
KIA = Killed in action
KIC = Killed in crash
Lant Flt = Atlantic Fleet, US Navy
NASSD = Naval Air Station San Diego
POW = Prisoner of war
w/e = Week ending
WIA = Wounded in action

1 AD = First Air Depot
1 Exp Field = First Experimental Field
1 PG − First Pursuit Group
2 AIC = Second Air Instruction Center
3 AIC = Third Air Instruction Center
94th, 95th, 147th, and 27th Aero Squadrons constitute the First Pursuit Group

Other airplanes listed have French military or civilian registrations.

A single italicized date indicates the presence of the airplane on that date only; a pair of italicized dates indicates that the airplane was present at that location between those two dates.

Serial No.	Unit No.	Side	Pilot(s)	Earliest Date	Latest	Remarks Date
4434						first prototype
5325	Orly					aluminum
6125						prototype; dièdre total (short cabane struts)
6128	AEFB				1/23/23	destroyed 1/23/23; dièdre total
6132						prototype
6133	ADEZ					
6134						
6134	ICGT					French markings; five-color camouflage
6137	95 AS		Sewell	*3/12/18*	*3/12/18*	T
6137	94 AS				3/31/18	B-hangar fire at Villeneuve-les-Vertus
6138	95 AS		Buckley	*3/12/18*	*3/12/18*	T
6138	94 AS	0	Peterson; Chapman	*4/15/18*	5/3/18	L-Chapman KIA in flames
6140	95 AS		McLanahan	*3/12/18*	*3/12/18*	T
6140	94 AS	9	Chapman		4/20/18	R
6141	95 AS		Blodgett	*3/12/18*	5/17/18	L-damaged in hangar fire 3/31/1918
6142	95 AS	13	Taylor	*3/12/18*	*3/12/18*	T
6142	94 AS	23	Hill	4/21/18	5/27/18	W-crashed behind lines near Rambucourt
6143					3/?/18	W-smashed by hangar collapse due to snow at Villacoublay
6144	95 AS	14	Casgrain	*3/12/18*	*3/12/18*	T
6144	94 AS	8	Meissner; Cates	4/21/18		wing failure – twice
6145	147 AS	10	O'Neill	6/2/18	8/13/18	R
6145	3 AIC	1391		8/16/18	*9/23/18*	
6146						test machine; no cowling
6147					w/e 8/21	R-returned from front
6147	3 AIC	1402		8/18/18	*9/30/18*	
6148	95 AS		Richards	*3/12/18*	*3/12/18*	T
6148	94 AS	13	Taylor	*4/15/18*	6/7/18	C
6148	147 AS			8/10/18	8/13/18	R
6149	95 AS	2	Woolley	*3/12/18*	*3/12/18*	T
6149	94 AS	21	Chapman; Campbell	4/21/18	5/19/18	W-Eastman wrecked at Ménil-la-Tour 5/19/18
6150	95 AS		Curtis	*3/12/18*	*3/12/18*	T
6150	94 AS				3/31/18	C-damaged in hangar fire; to Romorantin
6151	95 AS		Quick	*3/12/18*	*3/12/18*	T
6151	94 AS	14	Cunningham; Eastman	*4/15/18*	*6/25/18*	W-Cunningham rolled over; Chalmers broke landing gear at Dogneville
6152	95 AS			*5/5/18*		to Romorantin
6153	95 AS		Buford	*3/12/18*	*3/12/18*	T
6153	94 AS	17	Hall	*4/15/18*	5/7/18	L-Hall POW
6154	95 AS		Fisher	*3/12/18*	*3/12/18*	T
6154	94 AS	7	Gude; Sherry	*4/15/18*		
6155	95 AS	6	McLanahan	*5/5/18*	*5/11/18*	
6156	95 AS			*5/7/18*		
6157	27 AS	8	Hoover		7/28/18	S-"Becky" from 1st Mobile Park to Saint-Cyr
6158	95 AS	10	Heinrichs	*3/12/18*	*3/12/18*	T
6158	94 AS	0	Campbell	4/21/18	5/7/18	

6159	94 AS	12	Peterson; Rickenbacher; Zacharias		*4/15/18*	to Saint-Cyr 7/13/1918
6159	3 AIC	1362		8/5/18		
6160	95 AS	8	Heinrichs	5/15/18		C-upper wing failure, no injuries; to Romorantin
6162	95 AS			5/15/18		T-to 27 AS
6162	27 AS				8/3/18	T-to 147 AS
6162	147 AS			8/3/18	8/14/18	R-to Orly
6162	3 AIC	1407			*9/28/18*	
6163	95 AS		Jones	*3/12/18*	*3/12/18*	T-to 94 AS
6163	94 AS	9	Cunningham	4/21/18		
6163	3 AIC	1446		8/21/18	*10/17/18*	
6164	94 AS	10	Campbell	*4/14/18*	5/5/18	R
6164	3 AIC	1633		11/ /18	*12/12/18*	
6165	95 AS		Rhodes	*3/12/18*	*3/12/18*	T-to 94 AS
6165	94 AS		Eastman	4/12/18	4/12/18	W-wrecked on landing at Gengoult
6166	94 AS				3/31/18	B-hangar fire at Villeneuve-les-Vertus
6168	94 AS	5	Wentworth	*4/15/18*		R-to 1 AD
6168	1 AD	5	Morlan			to Saint-Cyr
6169	95 AS		H. R. Hall	*3/12/18*	*3/12/18*	T
6169	94 AS	1	Huffer; Rickenbacker	*4/15/18*	6/25/18	C-wing failure, 5/17/18
6171	95 AS			*5/6/18*	7/17/18	T-to 147 AS
6171	147 AS		Raible	7/17/18	7/25/18	W-wrecked by Raible
6172	94 AS	6	Marr	*4/15/18*	5/10/18	W-cartwheeled on field by Marr; to Romorantin
6174	95 AS			*5/5/18*		
6174	3 AIC	1625		*11/ /18*		
6175	95 AS		Thompson		7/5/18	L-Thompson KIA
6176	95 AS			*5/5/18*		
6177	95 AS	14	Roosevelt		7/14/18	L-Roosevelt KIA by Uffz. Gräper
6178	94 AS	16	Davis; Lufbery	*4/15/18*	5/19/18	L-Lufbery KIA
6179	94 AS	11	Chambers	*4/15/18*	7/1/18	L-Tittman severely wounded; down in Allied lines
6180	94 AS	18	Green; Sherry; Prinz	*4/15/18*	6/9/18	C
6181	94 AS	15	Loomis; Jeffers	*4/15/18*		
6182	95 AS			*5/5/18*		R-returned from front w/e 8/21/18
6182	3 AIC	1409		8/20/18	*9/24/18*	
6183	3 AIC	1567		10/14/18	*11/2/18*	
6184	94 AS	3	Winslow	*4/14/18*	5/21/18	C
6185	95 AS	15	McKeown	*3/12/18*	*3/12/18*	T-to 94 AS
6185	94 AS	10	Kurtz	4/21/18	5/22/18	L-Kurtz KIC; burned near field
6187	95 AS			5/15/18		T-in French markings
6187	27 AS				8/2/18	T
6187	147 AS		Bronson	8/2/18		R
6187	3 AIC	1429		8/25/18		
6188						B-French markings
6189	94 AS	6	Marr; Winslow	5/10/18	6/24/18	W-wrecked by Cates; shipped to Saint-Cyr 8/17/18
6190	95 AS			5/5/18		
6191	95 AS			6/16/18		
6193	94 AS	2	Lufbery; Davis	*4/15/18*	6/2/18	L-Davis KIA in flames
6194	95 AS			5/5/18		R-to Romorantin
6195	94 AS	8	Meissner	*4/15/18*	4/20/18	R-to 1 AD
6196	95 AS			5/6/18		R-to Romorantin
6197	27 AS					R-to Romorantin
6198	95 AS					to Romorantin
6199	95 AS				7/17/18	T-to 147 AS
6199	147 AS	3	Abernethy	7/17/18	7/30/18	W-Abernethy rolled over; to Saint-Cyr
6201	94 AS	20		6/30/18	7/14/18	T
6201	27 AS	3	Norton; Martin	7/14/18		W-normal-spaced cocardes
6203	147 AS		Robertson	6/15/18	6/28/18	W-wrecked by Robertson west of Cheoric
6204	27 AS				8/2/18	T-to 147 AS
6204	147 AS		Ennis	8/2/18	8/14/18	R-to Saints w/e 7/17/18; to Orly
6206	147 AS	3	Abernethy	7/3/18	7/15/18	L-dn. by v.Bülow J.36 NW of Combois; to Saint-Cyr 8/17/18

6207	147 AS	19	Robertson; Porter	6/10/18	6/25/18	W-wrecked by Porter at LaChapelle; to Romorantin
6208	95 AS	11	Buford?	*5/10/18*	*5/10/18*	to Romorantin
6209	147 AS		Raible	6/15/18	6/24/18	W-wrecked by Raible at Cerossmace; to Romorantin
6210	147 AS		Cassard	6/2/18	7/16/18	L-Cassard KIA at Dormans; rudder and insignia tacked to tree
6211	147 AS	16	Brotherton	6/2/18	6/25/18	W-crashed by Brotherton at Manspach; to Romorantin
6212	147 AS		Ashenden	6/10/18	6/25/18	L-down at Derendingen, Switzerland; interned
6214	27 AS	5				
6215	3 AIC			10/14/18		normal-spaced cocardes; subject of official photos
6217	3 AIC	1610			*11/ /18*	
6218	27 AS		Plyler		6/13/18	L-brought down near Lorry, S of Goin, by Flg. Bunning of Kest 3; Plyler POW
6219	95 AS	7			7/17/18	T-to 147 AS
6219	147 AS		Herron	7/17/18	8/13/18	W-Lt. Milham, ferry pilot, KIC at Saints
6220	3 AIC	1632		11/ /18		
6222	95 AS	14	Taylor	*5/11/18*	*5/11/18*	
6225	3 AIC			4/18/18	4/18/18	W-forced landing at Vierzon; wings, landing gear demolished
6227	94 AS			7/3/18	7/9/18	W-*"Lt. Prinz crashed at French Park"?*
6229	3 AIC	900		*4/16/18*	*10/31/18*	photographed with René Fonck
6230	95 AS				5/9/18	T
6230	94 AS	4	Smyth	5/9/18	7/13/18	R-normal-spaced cocardes; to Saint-Cyr 8/6/18
6232	94 AS		Robertson	7/6/18	7/14/18	T-to 147 AS
6232	147 AS	5		7/14/18	8/14/18	R-to Orly
6232	3 AIC	1392		8/16/18	*9/23/18*	
6233	147 AS	18	Harmon	6/2/18	6/4/18	W-Harmon wrecked near Toul
6234	27 AS	9	Elliott		7/2/18	L-dn. near Etrépilly-Verdilly by Jasta 10; Elliott KIA, buried at Chacrise, Aisne
6235	147 AS	14	Stevens	6/2/18	8/9/18	W-normal-spaced cocardes; wrecked by Simon
6236	95 AS	6				
6236	94 AS	17	Marr; Wentworth	5/9/18	7/9/18	W-Wentworth wrecked in landing
6238	95 AS					T-from 95 AS
6238	27 AS				8/3/18	T-to 147 AS
6238	147 AS	19	Brew	8/3/18	8/15/18	W-wrecked by Brew at Saints; to Saint-Cyr
6239	3 AIC	1626		11/ /18		close-spaced cocardes
6240	147 AS		Robertson	6/2/18	6/2/18	W-crashed by Robertson at Épinal; to Romorantin
6241	1 PG					27 AS?
6243	94 AS					
6244	95 AS			5/7/18	7/17/18	T-to 147 AS
6244	147 AS	16	McDermott	7/17/18	8/12/18	W-crashed at May-en-Multien/Hammonville; to Saint-Cyr
6245	95 AS			5/7/18		
6245	3 AIC	1390		8/15/18	*10/8/18*	W-wrecked west of Vierzon
6246	94 AS			6/30/18	7/6/18	W
6247	1 PG					27 AS?
6247	3 AIC	1440		8/27/18	*10/9/18*	
6248	27 AS				5/21/18	R-to 1 AD for repair
6250	147 AS	2	C. P. Porter	6/2/18	6/8/18	W-normal-spaced cocardes; to Romorantin
6252	3 AIC	1830		11/27/18	*12/3/18*	at Orly 6/19/18
6253	94 AS			6/30/18	7/14/18	T
6253	147 AS	20	Wells	7/14/18	7/16/18	W-wrecked by Wells at Basseville; to Saint-Cyr
6254	1 Exp Fld			w/e 7/17		cocardes under upper wings!
6254	94 AS	5	Meissner	6/14/18	*6/24/18*	to Saints w/e 7/17/18
6254	147 AS		Willard	7/17/18	8/14/18	R
6254	3 AIC	1393		8/16/18	*10/22/18*	
6255	27 AS			w/e 7/17	8/2/18	T-to 147 AS

6255	147 AS		Simon	8/2/18	8/14/18	R
6255	3 AIC	1400		8/16/18	*9/15/18*	
6256	147 AS	15	K. L. Porter	6/2/18	8/13/18	R
6256	3 AIC	1415		8/20/18	*9/23/18*	
6257	147 AS		Simonds	6/10/18	8/14/18	R
6257	3 AIC	1475		9/4/18		
6258	27 AS		Schmitt		5/30/18	B-burned in hangar fire at Epiez
6259	27 AS		Hunt		8/1/18	L-dn. Brameille; Udet of Jasta 4; Hunt KIA, buried near Chateau de Vizley
6260	94 AS	20	Cunningham; Eastman	6/1/18	6/28/18	W-wrecked by Eastman on flight to Touquin
6262	147 AS	4	Shawhan	6/2/18	6/13/18	W-wrecked by Shawhan at Fide Burley; to Romorantin
6263	3 AIC	1598		10/23/18	*10/30/18*	
6264	147 AS	12	Parry	6/2/18	7/8/18	L-Parry KIA; vicinity of Fismes
6265						French markings; at La Cheppe
6266	147 AS		Healy	6/2/18	6/2/18	W-wrecked by Healy at Epiez
6267	27 AS?			7/20/18		probably 27 AS
6269	147 AS	2	Ennis	6/2/18	7/18/18	S-engine seized while landing at Saints; to Saint-Cyr 8/6/18
6270	27 AS			7/17/18	7/17/18	T-to 147 AS
6270	147 AS		Raible	7/17/18	7/30/18	W-crashed on takeoff from Saints; to Saint-Cyr
6271	94 AS	7	Tittman	6/14/18	6/24/18	C-forced landing at Vesoul; to Romorantin
6271	3 AIC	1629		11/ /18		
6272	94 AS				7/21/18	T-to 147 AS
6272	147 AS			7/21/18	7/21/18	S-salvaged on receipt from 94 AS
6273	3 AIC	1474		9/4/18	*10/3/18*	
6274						to Romorantin
6275	94 AS	2	Loomis	6/1/18	7/14/18	T-to 27 AS
6275	27 AS	17	Sands	7/14/18	8/1/18	L-between Arcy and Bruys or over Cuiry-Housse; Jessen, Jasta 4; Sands KIA in flames by Ltn.derR. Emil Rolff, Jasta 6
6276	27 AS	2				from First Air Depot to Saint-Cyr 8/17/1918
6277	147 AS	11	Lawrence	6/2/18	6/4/18	W-crashed by Lawrence in vicinity of Neufchâteau
6279	147 AS	4	McDermott	6/2/18	6/20/18	W-crashed by McDermott in vicinity of Gondreville
6280	147 AS	3	Abernethy	6/2/18	6/25/18	W-crashed by Abernethy at Toul
6281	147 AS	8	Jones	6/2/18	8/14/18	R
6281	3 AIC	1416		8/21/18		
6282						
6283	94 AS	16	Rickenbacker	5/28/18		
6285	27 AS	10	Harkins	7/26/18	8/5/18	W-shipped from 1st Mobile Park to Saint-Cyr 8/9/18
6287	147 AS	17	Bronson	8/2/18	7/27/18	W-crashed by Simon at Créteil; to Saint-Cyr 7/30/18
6288						French markings; to Orly 8/31/18
6289	147 AS	13	White	6/2/18	7/5/18	W-crashed by Brew at Rebais
6290						from 1st Mobile Park to Saint-Cyr 8/17/18
6292	95 AS				7/18/18	T
6292	147 AS		Muther	7/18/18	7/25/18	W-crashed by Muther at Saints; to Saint-Cyr 7/30/18
6293	27 AS		McArthur		7/20/18	L-brought down at Fismes or Oulchy; McArthur KIA, buried at Origny-en-Thiérache
6294	147 AS	13	White	7/5/18	8/15/18	R-close-spaced cocardes
6294	3 AIC	1443		8/28/18	*10/31/18*	
6295	27 AS?			w/e 7/17		to Saints w/e 7/17/18
6296	27 AS		Norton	w/e 7/17	7/20/18	L-Norton WIA; d. 7/23
6297	94 AS	3	Green	6/1/18	7/14/18	T-to 147 AS
6297	147 AS	12	Muther	7/14/18	8/13/18	R
6297	3 AIC	1567		10/14/18	*10/30/18*	
6298	McCook F	P-38				tested at McCook Field; close-spaced cocardes

6299	95 AS				7/18/18	T-to 147 AS
6299	147 AS		Love	7/18/18	8/13/18	R
6299	3 AIC	1401		8/16/18		
6300	147 AS		Stevens	7/20/18	7/31/18	L-Stevens KIA, vicinity of Fere-en-Tarédenois
6301	95 AS	16				to 27 AS
6301	27 AS	16			ca. 7/20/18	from 95 AS; tricolor stripes
6302	27 AS	*5?*	Gunn		7/16/18	L-vicinity of Dormans - Condé-en-Brie; Uffz. Schneck of Jasta 9; Gunn KIA
6303	27 AS?					R-returned from front w/e 8/21/18
6303	3 AIC	1410		8/20/18	*11/1/18*	
6304						from 1st Mobile Park to Saint-Cyr 8/17/18
6305	147 AS		McDermott	6/29/18	7/16/18	W-crashed by Brew at Francheville; to Saint-Cyr 8/6/18
6306						to 1 AD 6/22/18
6307	147 AS	2	Raible	6/29/18	7/16/18	W-crashed by Raible at Saints; to Saint-Cyr 9/17/18
6308	147 AS		Healy	6/29/18	7/5/18	W-crashed by Healy at Merville
6309	3 AIC	1472		*10/3/18*	*10/3/18*	
6310	3 AIC	1856		12/8/18		
6311						to 1 AD 6/22/18
6312	147 AS	6	C. P. Porter	7/1/18	8/13/18	R
6312	3 AIC	1394		8/16/18		
6313	1 AD			6/23/18	7/18/18	R-damaged at 1 AD; return to Orly
6314	147 AS		Simon	7/1/18	7/6/18	W-crashed by Simon at Touquin
6315	3 AIC	1473		9/4/18	*10/30/18*	
6316	27 AS	20	Miller	*7/20/18*	8/3/18	T-"TERTIOUS"; to 147 AS
6316	147 AS	3	Abernethy	8/3/18	8/14/18	R
6316	3 AIC	1444		8/28/18	*10/2/18*	
6317	3 AIC	1436		8/27/18	*10/12/18*	
6318	27 AS?			7/17/18		R-from 1st Mobile Park to Saint-Cyr 8/6/18
6319	147 AS	3	Abernethy	8/8/18	8/14/18	R
6319	3 AIC	1445		8/28/18	*10/15/18*	
6320	3 AIC	1857		12/8/18	2/17/19	S-at Orly 7/15/18
6321	3 AIC	1439		8/27/18	*10/17/18*	
6322	3 AIC	1483		9/9/18	*10/2/18*	
6323	3 AIC	1441		8/27/18	*10/10/18*	
6324	3 AIC	1437		8/27/18	*10/22/18*	
6325					7/17/18	W-forced landing at Marles, motor failure; damaged
6327	3 AIC	1438		8/27/18	*10/8/18*	
6328	3 AIC	1442		8/28/18	*10/11/18*	photographed at 2 AIC
6329	3 AIC	1461		9/2/18	*10/9/18*	
6330	3 AIC	1448		8/30/18		
6333	147 AS		Harmon	7/20/18	8/9/18	W-wrecked by Harmon at Saints; to Saint-Cyr 9/17/18
6334	147 AS	16	Brotherton	7/11/18	8/14/18	R-snake motif on white cowl
6334	3 AIC	1395		8/16/18	*9/24/18*	
6335	27 AS			7/17/18	8/2/18	T-to 147 AS
6335	147 AS		Raible	8/2/18	8/14/18	R
6335	3 AIC	1397		8/16/18		
6336	3 AIC	1432		8/26/18	*9/20/18*	
6337	3 AIC			8/30/18		brought in from Field Services
6338	FAA		Ten. B. Matienzo	*5/28/19*	5/28/19	L-trans-Andes attempt; wrecked elev. 4,450 m.; Matienzo perished
6339	FAA			*5/28/19*	*5/28/19*	to Argentina; grounded in 1926; used for official performance tests; Report No. 24
6341	27 AS			7/17/18	8/2/18	T-to 147 AS
6341	147 AS		K. L. Porter	8/2/18	8/14/18	R
6341	3 AIC	1396		8/16/18	*10/15/18*	
6342	3 AIC	1431		8/26/18	*10/8/18*	
6346	27 AS					to Romorantin
6347	27 AS	3	Wanamaker		7/2/18	L-brought down at Bois St. Germaine

						by Udet of Jasta 4; Wanamaker POW
6349	94 AS	13	Taylor	6/1/18	7/14/18	T-to 147 AS
6349	147 AS		Harmon	7/14/18	7/20/18	W-wrecked by Harmon at Saints; to Saint-Cyr 8/6/18
6350	27 AS					to Romorantin
6351	94 AS		Eastman	*7/2/18*	7/2/18	W-Eastman crashed new plane at La Ferté-Gaucher
6352						constructed by Nieuport
6353	3 AIC	1694		*11/ /18*	*12/3/18*	
6355						from 1st Mobile Park to Saint-Cyr 7/19/18
6356	1 PG			6/13/18		close-spaced cocardes; constructed by Nieuport; **last N.28 to USAS/AEF**
6364	Lant Flt			1/20/20	6/20/20	W-became A-5797; USS Pennsylvania, Hampton Roads; **first US Nieuport 28A**
6366						five-color camouflage; new rudder format
6367						Bob Rust parts in USA
6373	McCook F.					camouflaged
6378	NASSD			4/28/20	1/18/21	C-became A-5805; sold to E. S. Daugherty, Long Beach, CA, 8/8/2
6426	NASSD			4/28/20	1/18/21	C-became A-5801; USS Texas; sold to E. H. Rogers 8/8/21
6432				10/ /18		lower-right wing; 10-18
6433	Carlstrom		Chris Ford; Lt. Grey	ca. 4/20	ca. 7/21	W-khaki paint; Indian head in diamond; repainted and wrecked, Carlstrom Field
6434						W-khaki paint; crashed on nose; new rudder format
6437	NASSD			4/28/20	1/18/21	C-became A-5804; sold to E. H. Rogers 8/8/21
6440	Carlstrom					modified 213 AS insignia
6442	Lant Flt			1/2/20	2/28/21	C-became A-5796; USS Oklahoma; USS Nevada
6456	NASSD			4/28/20	8/2/22	became A-5803; USS Mississippi; for sale 5/6/22 - $200
6458	NASSD			2/9/20	8/2/22	became A-5800; USS New Mexico; for sale 5/6/22 - $200
6461	Lant Flt		Pride	12/29/19	3/17/20	W-became A-5794; USS Arizona; wrecked Santa Cruz del Sur, Cuba
6462	NASSD			2/9/20	8/2/22	C-became A-5802; USS Idaho; condemned 5/6/22
6465				11/ /18		lower-left wing; 11-18
6472	Lant Flt			1/2/20	2/28/21	C-became A-5795; USS Oklahoma
6477	Lant Flt			1/2/20	4/1/20	L-became A-5798; USS Pennsylvania; USS Nevada; lost at sea
6488	Lant Flt			1/2/20	1/28/20	W-became A-5799; USS Nevada
6493						Bob Rust parts in USA
6497						fuselage
6507						striped fuselage; modified 213 AS insignia
6514	AEDV					per Bernard Klaeyle
	CGTA					
6522	CGTI					Compagnie Générale Transaérienne
6526	CGTY					Compagnie Générale Transaérienne
6531						US Army Museum
6536	CGTO					Compagnie Générale Transaérienne
6548	ADCO		Fronval			
6566	AEDX					
6569	AEEC					American 80 hp
6579	AEET					
6606						one of 14 Swiss N.28As
7046						

The following airplanes were salvaged by the US Army, AEF, and sold to Emile Hervet, Société Générale, at Romorantin on 29 August 1919: serial numbers 7047, 7048, 7049, 7050, 7075, 7076, 7077, 7078, 7079, 7080, 7081, 7082, 7084.

7092	AGDN?		Nieuport 28A; surveyed at McCook Field 14 January 1924
7093	AGDN?		
7099	AGAJ		
7103		2/?/19	upper-left wing; stamped 2-19
7108	AGAI		
7110	AGDO		
7111	AGAK		
7226		2/?/19	upper-right wing, stamped 2-19
7633			R. Rust, wing manuf. 4/19

This list, compiled by Alan D. Toelle and kindly shared with the author, is a work in progress.

Appendix F
Colors and Markings

To prevent dangerous confusion with enemy markings and to conform to general plan of our Allies, recommend marking of [American] aeroplane wings as follows: Red circle with diameter equal to chord, inner blue circle diameter two thirds of chord, center white circle diameter one third of chord. Rudder markings vertical red white and blue stripes starting at rudder post. – Brigadier General W. L. Kenly[1]

During the War

The familiar white star in a blue circle would not be seen on American aircraft flying over the Western Front during World War I: Brigadier General Benjamin Foulois explained why, "On the Western Front particularly, any airplane which is not marked plainly with a circle, is regarded as hostile and fired on, and it is believed that the marking recommended in the United States [the white star in a blue circle] is dangerous and should not be used."[2] Under the circumstances, the US Air Service, AEF, was induced to adopt a cocarde, or roundel, with red-blue-white concentric circles as its new national insignia. With the exception of the revised US national insignia and the later-reversed rudder stripes to red, white and blue, American military aircraft largely conformed to the colors of the Aviation Militaire, for the French government supplied almost three-quarters of the fighters, bombers, and observation planes used by the Air Service on the Western Front during the war.[3]

French aircraft of 1916 had been finished in aluminum powder mixed with yellow pigment, giving rise to the term "The Yellow Period," or were clear-doped with metal panels and cowls left untreated.[4] Later aircraft, such as the Nieuport 17, were finished in aluminum (pigmented) dope, known as d'enduit métallisé, with the cowlings left in natural metal. This appears to be the finish of the first Nieuport 28 prototype, N.4434, as pictured in the profile section.

The next color scheme, adopted in October 1917, was the five-color camouflage pattern; this utilized colored aluminum dope that had been developed and patented by Société Nauton Frères et de Marsac.[5] Combat aircraft (as opposed to training planes that did not require camouflage) were given first and second coats of plain dope, and after each coat had thoroughly dried (and been rubbed with ground glass to ensure a good surface for the first application of colored dope), the first coat of colored dope was applied in the approved camouflage pattern. After drying, the surface was rubbed again, before application of a second coat of colored dope. No further rubbing was necessary before applying the fifth and final, finishing coat of plain dope. It is interesting to note that after fourteen days, the weight of the dried dope was approximately 100 grams per square meter – after three months, the weight dropped to 80 grams per square meter.[6]

Early-production Nieuport 28 fighters, delivered to the Air Service in March and April 1918, came in the factory-applied, standard five-color, French cellulose-acetate dope camouflage pattern. Metal surfaces were painted with Ripolin, believed to be an oil-base paint.[7] Initially, cocardes of equal diameter were painted on both sides of the upper wing; this was a throwback to the Nieuport sequiplane design, where the bottom, narrow-chord wing could not display a cocarde large enough to be readily seen. A cocarde of smaller diameter was painted on the bottom of the lower wings. Black letter and number decals, designating the aircraft type (28) and serial number, were affixed on the cabane struts (type 28 only), underside of the wing tips, elevators, and at the rear of each side of the fuselage. "LEVER ICI" (LIFT HERE) decals were placed on both sides toward the rear of the fuselage. Serial data and aircraft specifications were painted on the rudder, along with the Nieuport logo (see the profile section later in this appendix). The Nieuport logo and weight specifications were found only on the port-side rudder.

The 147th Aero Squadron insignia pictured here was removed by the pilot, Lieutenant Thomas J. Abernethy, from Nieuport 28, N.6199 (#3), after he crashed on 30 July 1918. On the left is a swatch of brown overpaint, which follows the outline of the original camouflage. Factory-applied dark green paint is visible at the upper right. "Mickey" has two yellow overseas stripes on one leg and four dead rats at his feet. The outer two rats have Maltese crosses in yellow; the middle two rats were added after the insignia was removed, and signify later victories. Underlying visible blue paint reveals that this aircraft formerly belonged to the 95th Aero Squadron. (Thanks to Alan Toelle for providing this information.) Author's collection

Upon arrival of new Nieuport 28 fighters at the squadron, French cocardes and rudder stripes were quickly painted over in American colors, with various shades of blue being used. Initially, the rudder stripes were repainted white-blue-red, with serial numbers sometimes reapplied to the white panel, but this was later changed to red-white-blue, with blue at the trailing edge.

After receiving their new fighters, pilots enthusiastically began to add squadron insignia. According to an official *Air Service Bulletin* dated 6 May 1918, this addition required that the squadron first have been "officially accredited with three enemy planes brought down in aerial combat, or immediately upon receiving citation in orders from higher authority for distinguished service".[8] In addition, the Chief of Air Service directed that "all airplanes in a squadron shall be numbered serially from 1 up to 19 [the range of numbers increased later when the number of fighters per squadron was increased from eighteen to twenty-four], these numbers to be painted in black paint and large enough to be distinguished from a distance. They shall be painted on both sides of the fuselage near the stabilizer, on the underside of the right lower wing, and on the right top side of the upper wing."[9] Flight commanders' and deputy flight commanders' aircraft were to be identified with streamers attached to the lower wing tips and/or the rudder, and squadron commanders' aircraft would be identified with "two bands of red, white, and blue stripes running diagonally from the rear of the cockpit to the rear of the fuselage at the foot of the rudder post."[10] Additional markings included distinctive squadron markings on top and bottom wings.

Pilots added personal touches, painting unique and colorful cowl designs (or adopting standard cowl designs for each flight) and different colors on the wheel covers, and also affixing Liberty Bond posters and painting names of sweethearts or fraternities, Masonic symbols, mottoes, etc. (see the profile section). These latter markings, however, were to be confined to a space not more than six by six inches square and not aft of the cockpit.[11] Lieutenant Douglas Campbell's N.6164 is illustrated in the profile section as it appeared on Sunday, 14 April 1918, still in French colors, but with the beginning of a distinctive cowl design and the "Hat in the Ring" squadron insignia proudly painted on.

Beginning with serial number N.6201, Nieuport 28 fighters were delivered from the Nieuport factory to the squadrons in American colors, and with the cocarde eliminated from the underside of the top wing. Illustrations in the profile section show the basic pattern of finishes and markings as delivered during this period, with upper surfaces finished in chestnut brown, light and dark green, beige and black, and "ecru" or light yellow on the bottom surfaces. This pattern would remain virtually unchanged until the cocardes and the black footprint on the top right wing were moved inboard, only to revert to the former position later in the production run. When Nieuport 28 fighters were transferred from one squadron to another, the old squadron insignia and numbers were painted over, but this usually left some evidence of the aircraft's former self. Second Lieutenant Abernethy's 147th Aero Squadron insignia, "Who Said Rats!" cut from his crashed airplane and pictured on the first page of this appendix, shows the blue color of the 95th Aero Squadron's oval peeking through in spots.

Wartime deliveries of Nieuport 28 fighters to the US Air Service began with serial number N.6125 and ended in August 1918, with what is believed to have been N.6356.

Postwar Colors

Postwar deliveries of Nieuport 28As to the Air Service from Lioré et Olivier (serial numbers range from approximately N.6364 to approximately N.6566) displayed several minor variations from the wartime color scheme – these included cocardes with a darker blue color, black footprint on top right wing reverted to its former position, and a different style of legend on the tail. The Nieuport logo was also gone.

On 4 October 1918 the Air Service "standardized the use of cellulose acetate dope on all combat and training aircraft" with "a protective covering on all doped fabric [to be] either pigmented oil varnish or a pigmented dope"[12] Similar to the British PC 10 specification, the mixture of yellow ochre and lamp black resulted in a dark brown color then referred to as olive brown wing enamel. Weight was a consideration, for according to the new specification, four coats of dope were not to exceed two and seven-tenths ounces per square yard of surface.[13]

Lioré et Olivier delivered some Nieuport 28As to the Air Service, AEF, in five-color camouflage, before changing over to the new color specifications – hence some of the aircraft delivered to the United States in 1919 appear in each scheme. The Nieuport 28As still sported the wartime cocarde (see profile section), as deliveries from Lioré et Olivier had ceased before the War Department ordered a reversion to the "star-in-circle" design in May 1919.[14] Some contemporary photographs show that the Air Service retained the cocarde while the Nieuport 28A was in brief service as an advanced trainer.

When twelve Nieuport 28As were received at the Naval Aircraft Factory from the Air Service in December 1919, some of the aircraft were in wartime camouflage and others in olive brown. After extensive modifications were made to the aircraft to prepare them for shipboard duty, they were painted overall in Aluminum Enamel, a pigmented spar varnish. This change was made "because the reflective value [of the aluminum finish] maintained the fabric at a considerably lower temperature which lengthened the life of the fabric."[15] Following the lead of the Air Service, the navy directed that all naval aircraft revert to the use of the star-in-circle national insignia and blue-white-red rudder stripes on the rudder, with red at the trailing edge (as illustrated in the profile section).

Nieuport 28 Prototype

Prototype Number 1 N.4434
Villacoublay, France, June 1917

The first prototype Nieuport 28 featured total dihedral on the upper wing and was equipped with only one Vickers machine gun mounted on the portside upper longeron. Finished in aluminum dope, or d' enduit metallise, cocardes of equal diameter to those on top were painted on the underside of the upper wing tips; this practice was discarded later in the production run. Note the louvers behind the cowl and the venturi atop the upper wing.

A standardized production model of the Nieuport 28 C.1 emerged six months later, with provision for two Vickers machine guns and painted in five-color camouflage.

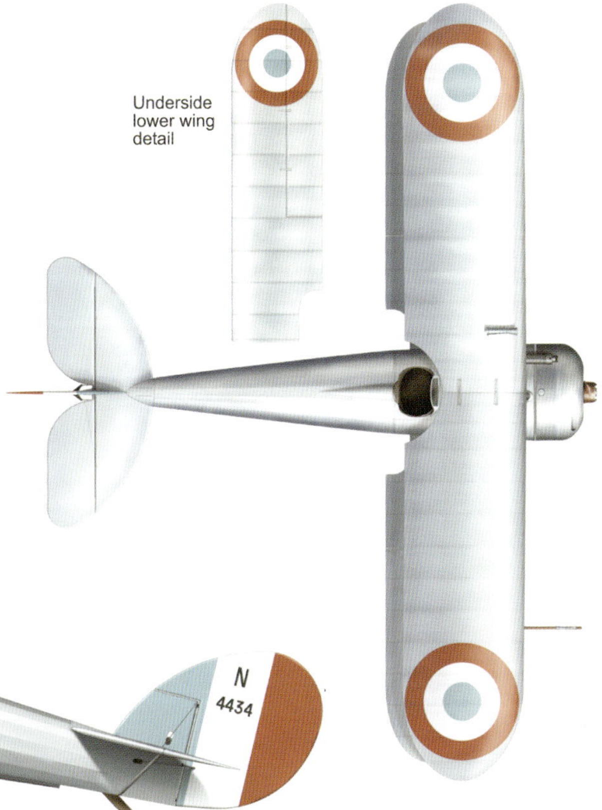

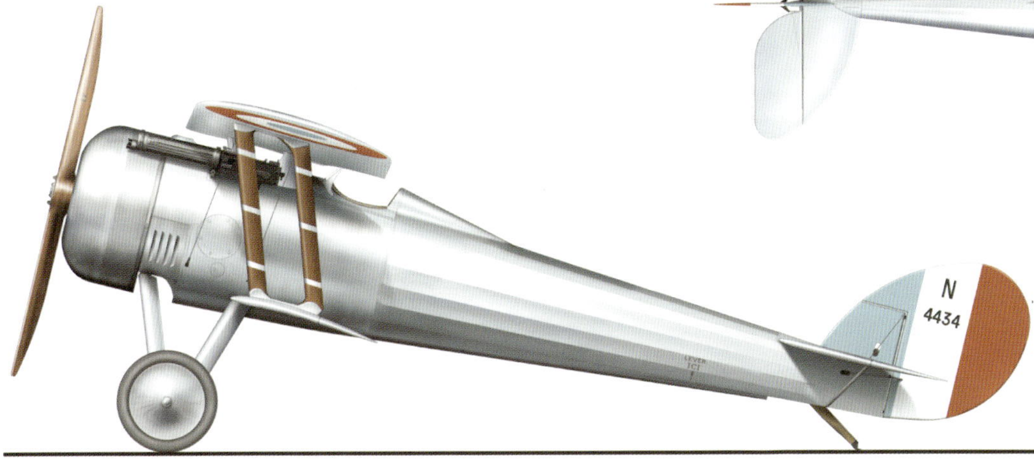

Artwork © Juanita Franzi

94th Aero Squadron

Nieuport 28 N.6164 Lieutenant Douglas Campbell
Gengoult Aerodrome, Toul, France, 16 April 1918

Lieutenant Campbell's N.6164 as it appeared to the press several days after Campbell's and Winslow's dramatic twin victories on Sunday, April 14, 1918. N.6144 is still in French colors but has the 94th Aero Squadron's "Hat in the Ring" insignia displayed and the beginnings of Campbell's distinctive "orange peel" design on the cowl. Dark green paint on the fuselage covers repairs done to this aircraft after the hangar fire at Villeneuve on 31 March. The familiar photograph of Campbell's and Winslow's Nieuport 28s was published in news media throughout the United States weeks after they achieved the first victories for the 94th Aero Squadron.

Lieutenant Campbell's squadron number 10 and the black peels on the cowl were added later to N.6164 and this is how the aircraft has been most often portrayed.

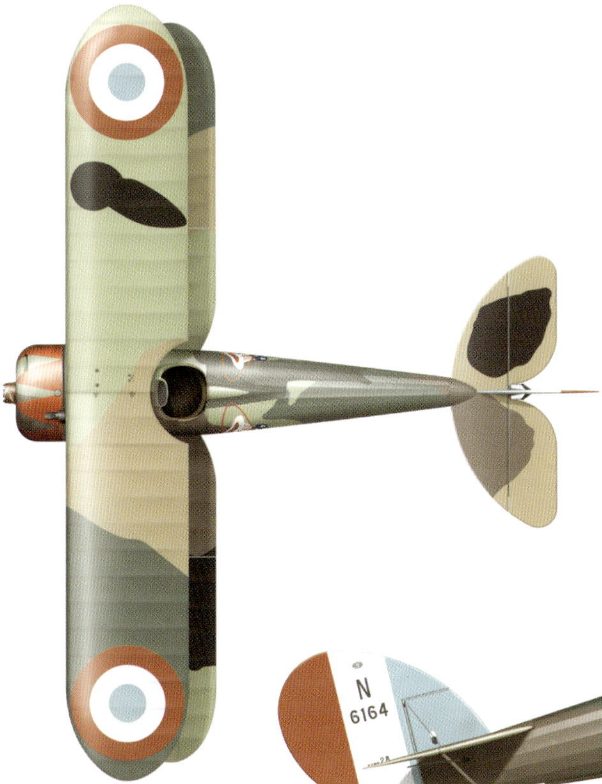

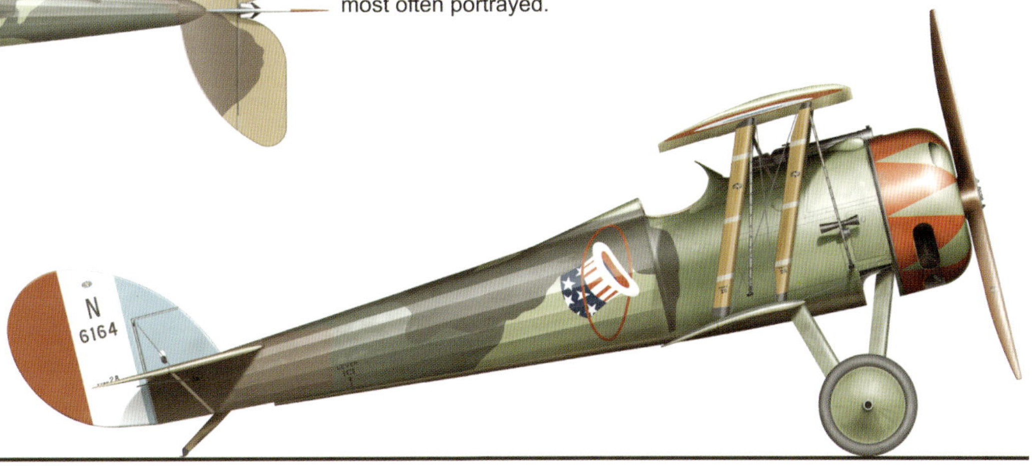

Nieuport 28 and 28A Colors and Markings

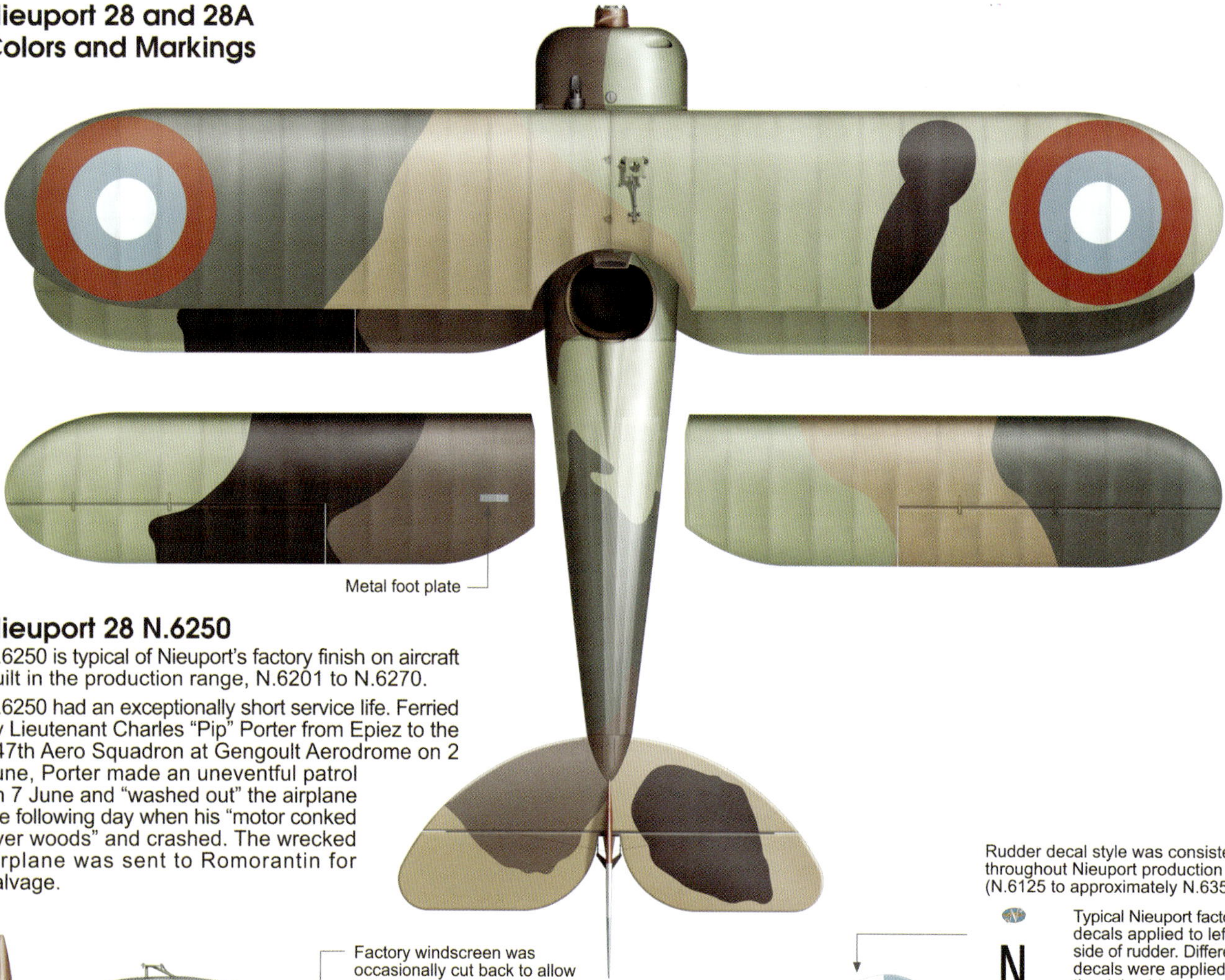

Nieuport 28 N.6250

N.6250 is typical of Nieuport's factory finish on aircraft built in the production range, N.6201 to N.6270.

N.6250 had an exceptionally short service life. Ferried by Lieutenant Charles "Pip" Porter from Epiez to the 147th Aero Squadron at Gengoult Aerodrome on 2 June, Porter made an uneventful patrol on 7 June and "washed out" the airplane the following day when his "motor conked over woods" and crashed. The wrecked airplane was sent to Romorantin for salvage.

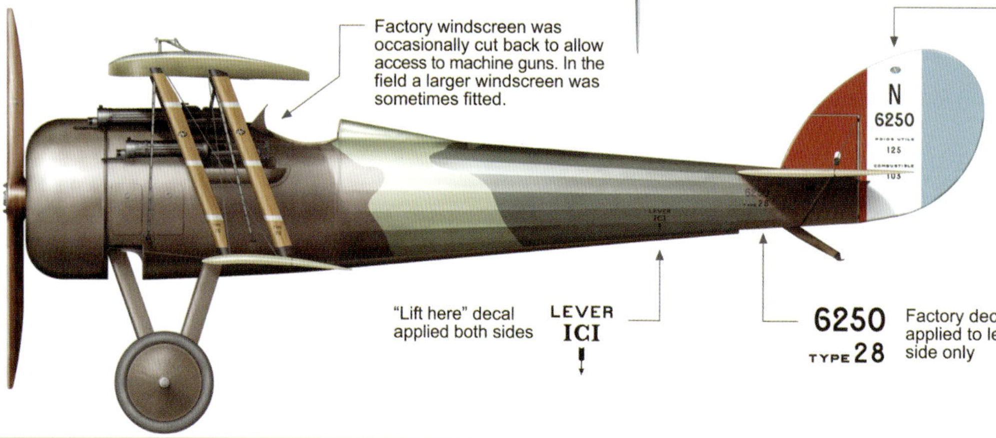

Profile artwork © Juanita Franzi

COLOR TABLE

Color references are provided as a guide. Original paint contained aluminum powder and cannot be accurately replicated using printed color charts. Research and color matching by Alan Toelle.

Paint Type	Swatch	French Color		Methuen	Munsell	CMYK			
Acellos Dope		Vert Fonce	Dark Green	30/4F3/5	10Y/3.5/1.5	18c	7m	36y	59k
		Vert Clair	Light Green	30/4D/E4/5	10Y/4.5/2.5	8c	4m	35y	37k
		Marron	Chestnut Brown	7E/F4	7.5YR/4.1/1.4	9c	19m	25y	58k
		Beige	Beige	5D6	1Y/5.3/4.2	0c	20m	55y	40k
		Ecru	Light Yellow	5D4	2.5Y/6.0/4.0	0c	0m	37y	38k
National Markings		Rouge	Insignia Red	9C8	7.5R/4.5/9.0	0c	70m	66y	35k
		Bleu	Insignia Blue	24D/E3	10BG/6.0/3.0	33c	4m	8y	20k
Ripolin Enamel		Vert Clair	Light Green	30D7		16c	0m	42y	36k
		Marron	Chestnut Brown	7F5		6c	32m	29y	70k

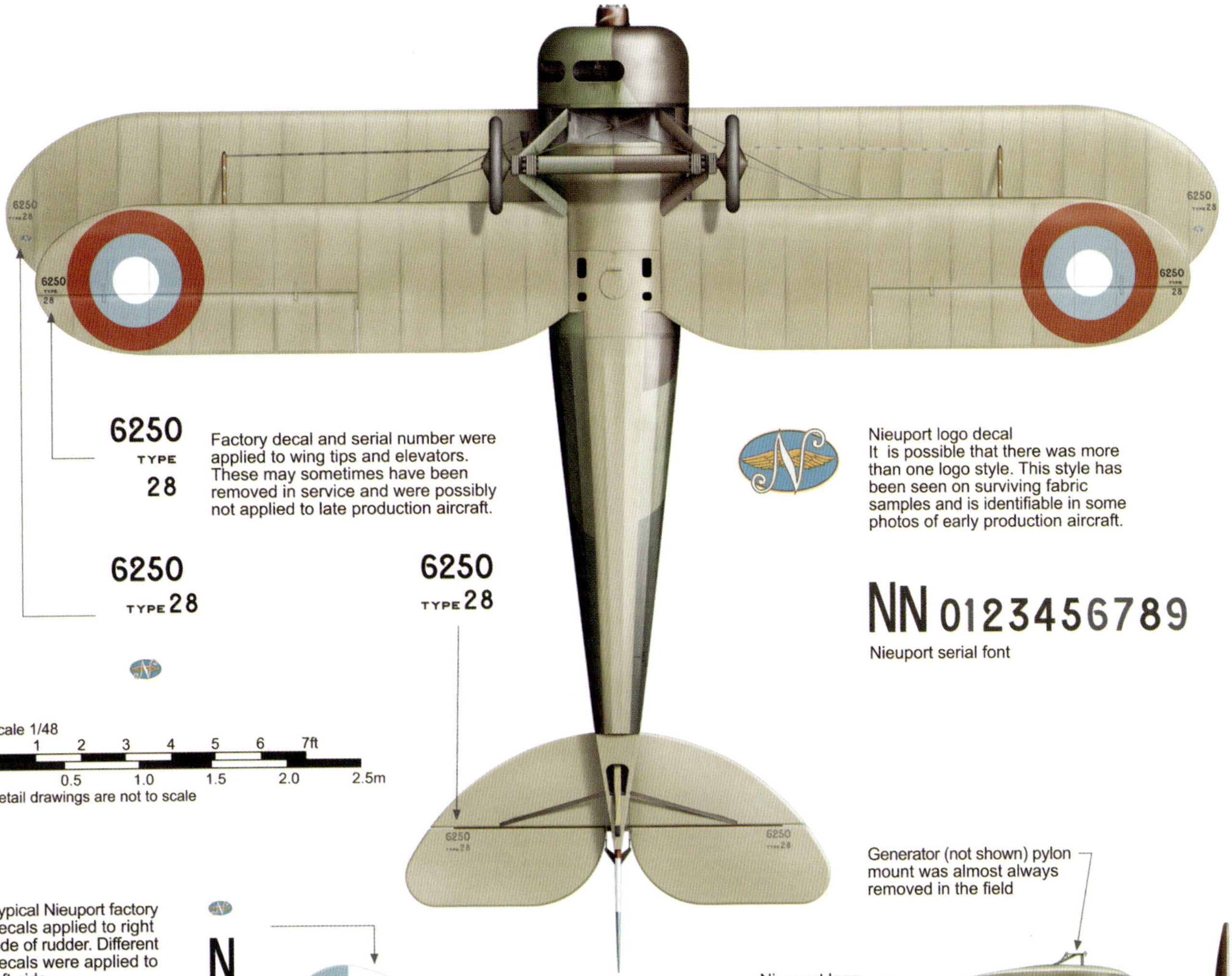

6250
TYPE
28

Factory decal and serial number were applied to wing tips and elevators. These may sometimes have been removed in service and were possibly not applied to late production aircraft.

6250
TYPE 28

6250
TYPE 28

Nieuport logo decal
It is possible that there was more than one logo style. This style has been seen on surviving fabric samples and is identifiable in some photos of early production aircraft.

NN 0123456789
Nieuport serial font

Scale 1/48
0 1 2 3 4 5 6 7ft
0 0.5 1.0 1.5 2.0 2.5m
Detail drawings are not to scale

Generator (not shown) pylon mount was almost always removed in the field

Typical Nieuport factory decals applied to right side of rudder. Different decals were applied to left side.

Company logo was not always applied

N
6250

TYPE 28

Nieuport logo

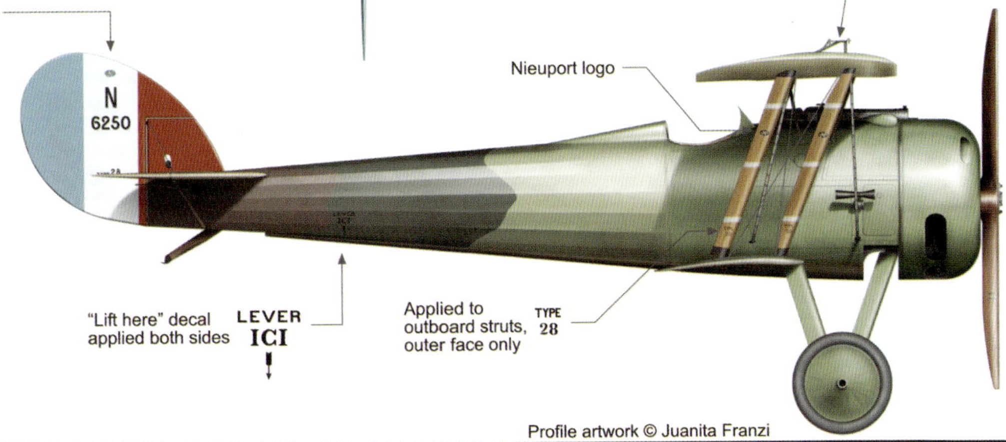

"Lift here" decal applied both sides

LEVER
ICI

Applied to outboard struts, outer face only

TYPE
28

Profile artwork © Juanita Franzi

Lioré et Olivier Rudder Decals

Lioré et Olivier applied the same decals to both sides of rudder.
Two variations have been identified

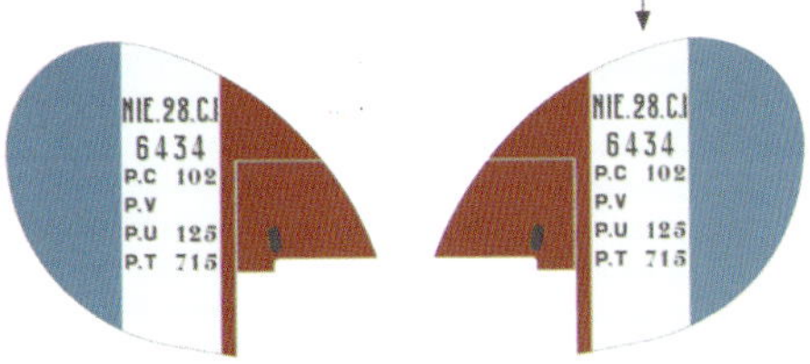

	Alternative style
NIE.28.C.I	NIE 28 CI
6434	6366
P.C 102	PC 102
P.V	PV
P.U 125	PU 125
P.T 715	PT 715
Additional examples 01234	Additional examples 6789

Detail artwork © Alan Toelle

Levasseur logo
Applied to front face of both blades

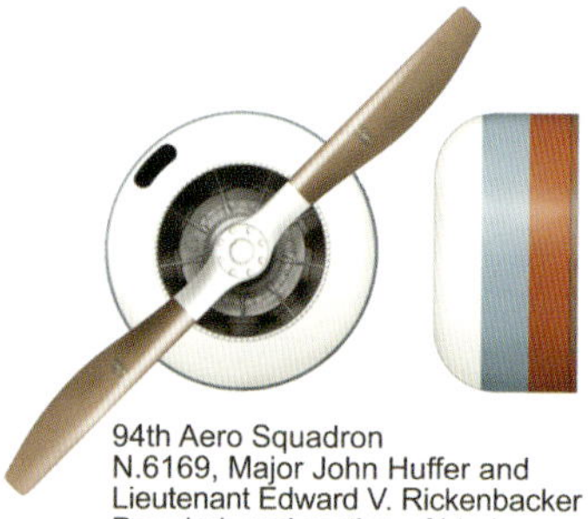

94th Aero Squadron
N.6169, Major John Huffer and Lieutenant Edward V. Rickenbacker
Prop hub and portion of blades painted white

Examples of Squadron Cowl Markings

1/48 scale

The 94th and 95th Aero Squadron Flights were referred to by number codes while the 27th and 147th Squadrons used letter codes, "A," "B," and "C," following British practice

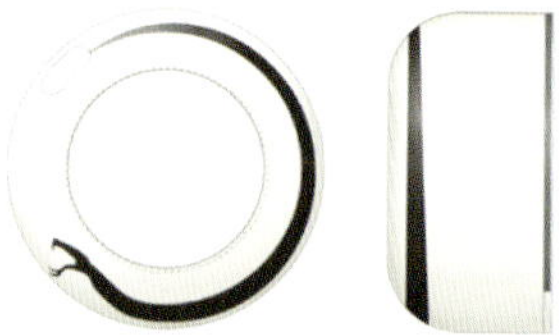

147th Aero Squadron
"B" Flight
Second Lieutenant William E. Brotherton

94th Aero Squadron
N.6164, Lieutenant Douglas Campbell
Completed cowl design

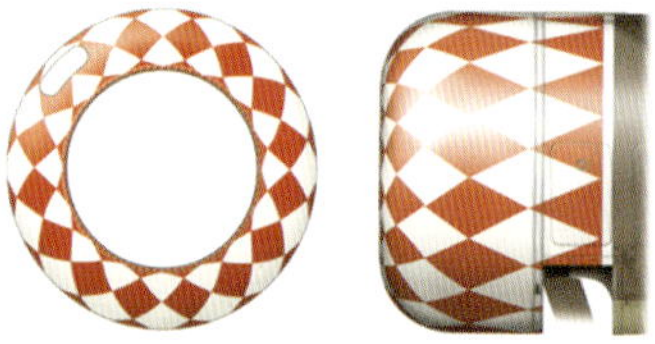

95th Aero Squadron
1st Flight

95th Aero Squadron
2nd Flight

95th Aero Squadron
3rd Flight

Profile and cowl artwork © Juanita Franzi

Variations in Factory Application of Camouflage and National Markings

Detail artwork © Alan Toelle

Details not to scale

N.6125 to N.6200
Constructed by Nieuport
Cocardes and rudder in French colors
Cocardes above and below the upper wing

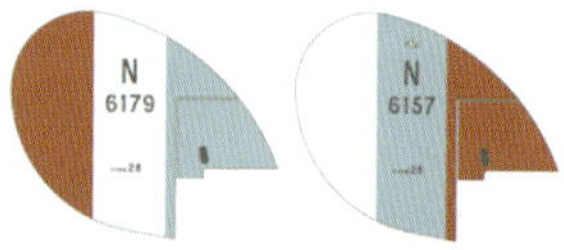

Typical rudder · Rare example

Wing underside

In the field, cocardes and rudder were generally soon overpainted in American colors
Shade of blue varied

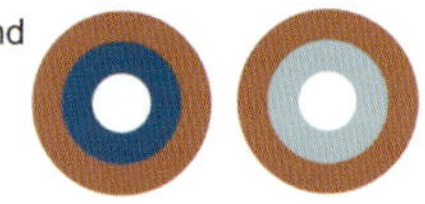

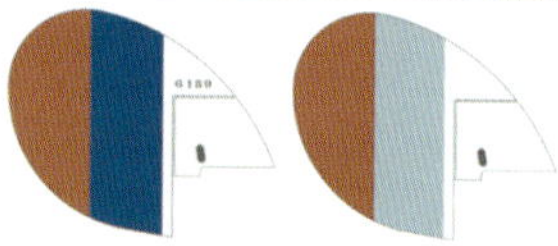

N.6201 to approximately N.6270
Constructed by Nieuport
Cocardes and rudder in American colors
Cocardes no longer applied to the upperwing underside

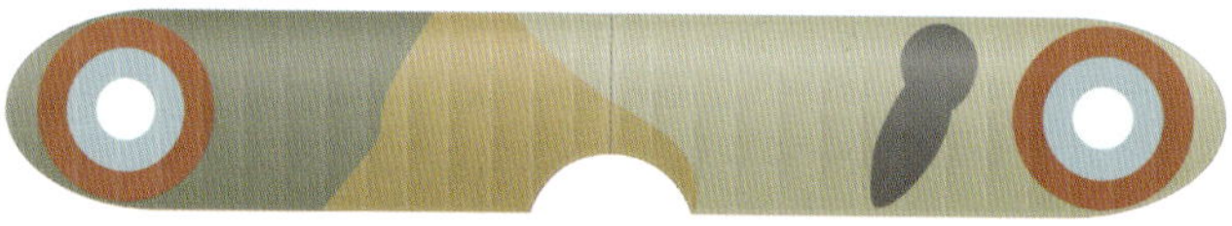

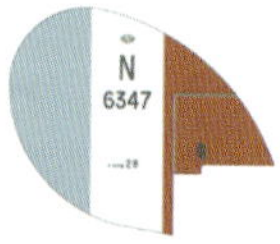

American rudder colors applicable to Nieuport constructed aircraft from N.6201 to approximately N.6356

N.6271 to approximately N.6356
Constructed by Nieuport
Cocardes and rudder in American colors
Camouflage "footprint" and cockade moved inboard

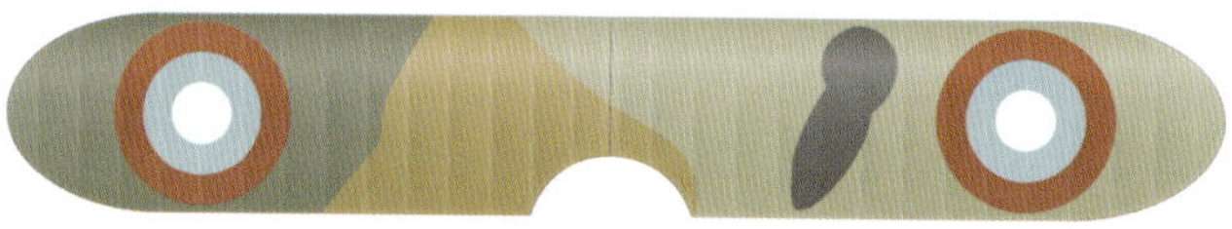

Approximately N.6364 to approximately N.6566
Constructed by Lioré et Olivier
Cocardes and rudder in American colors
Left wing camouflage moved inboard
Cocarde in the inboard position

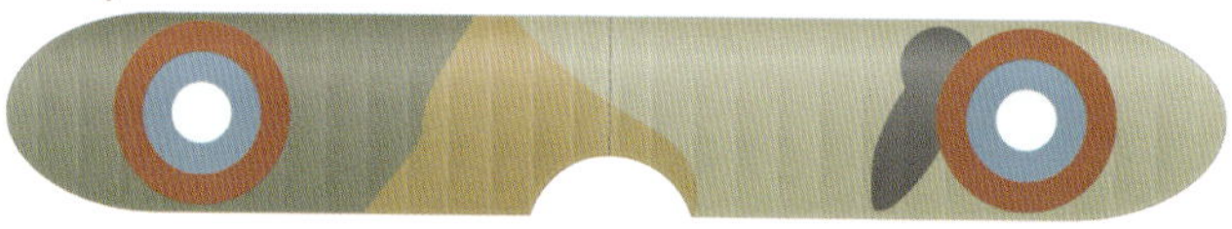

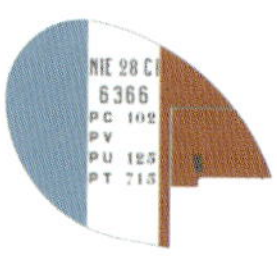

95th Aero Squadron

Nieuport 28 N.6160 Lieutenant Waldo Heinrichs
Gengoult Aerodrome, Toul, France, April 1918

Featuring scarlet and gold spirals on the cowl identifying the 2nd Flight of the 95th Aero Squadron, Lieutenant Heinrichs was piloting this Nieuport 28, squadron number 8, when he experienced wing failure of the upper left wing on 2 June 1918. Lieutenant Heinrichs survived this event but was later downed and taken prisoner in September.

Note Heinrich's personal marking of his initial in a square just aft of the headrest on the fuselage. French cocardes have been overpainted with the new US Air Service colors and French rudder stripes have been repainted (from the rudder post): white, blue, red. The serial number is clearly marked on the rudder.

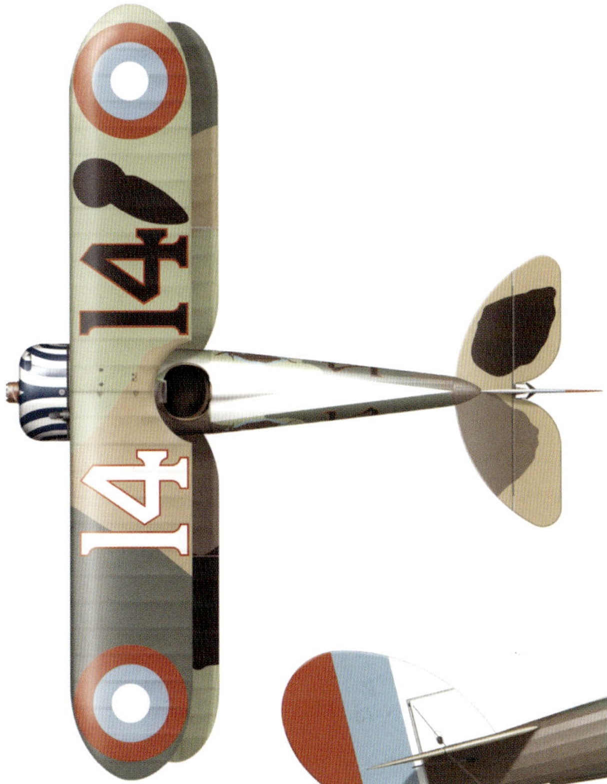

95th Aero Squadron

Nieuport 28 N.6177 Lieutenant Quentin T. Roosevelt
Saints Aerodrome, Chateau-Thierry Sector, France, July 1918

Dark blue and white concentric circles on the cowl identify Lieutenant Roosevelt's Nieuport 28 as belonging to 3rd Flight with "Jake," the squadron mascot, portrayed as the squadron's kicking mule insignia. Cocardes are painted under the upper wings and the squadron number, 14, is painted on both sides of the fuselage and twice on the top wing. The white numerals were added after the squadron moved to the Chateau-Thierry sector in late June. The white turtledeck may suggest flight leader markings but that is uncertain.

Lieutenant Quentin Roosevelt scored his first and only victory in this aircraft on 10 July 1918; he was killed in action four days later.

27th Aero Squadron

Nieuport 28 N.6302 Lieutenant Clifford A. McElvain
Saints Aerodrome, Chateau-Thierry Sector, France, July 1918

Lieutenant McElvain's Nieuport 28 bears the squadron number 5 and a Masonic emblem under the lower Vickers machine gun mount. The 27th Aero Squadron, unlike the 95th and 147th Aero Squadrons, did not identify their Nieuports by flight assignment by painting the cowls a distinctive color or design. However, checkerboard markings on the wings identify the 27th Aero Squadron.

Lieutenant Malcolm R. Gunn was KIA on 16 July while flying N.6302. Lieutenant McElvain, a member of "A" Flight of the 27th, was downed and taken prisoner on 1 August ("The Black Day of the 27th") while flying another Nieuport 28 fighter.

Artwork © Juanita Franzi

27th Aero Squadron

Nieuport 28 N.6157 Lieutenant William J. Hoover
Saints Aerodrome, Chateau-Thierry Sector, France, July 1918

"Becky," Hoover's N.6157, squadron number 8, featured an imposing "Screaming Eagle" of the 27th Aero Squadron, an insignia inspired by the Anheuser-Busch logo. The squadron's checkerboard marking appears on the wing. The upper wing has been replaced as evidenced by the close-spaced cocardes.

Note that the rudder stripes on this early production Nieuport 28 have been painted in an unusual, red-blue-white, or reverse scheme. It also appears that the port and starboard fuselage numbers were slightly offset, possibly as a result of over painting earlier markings.

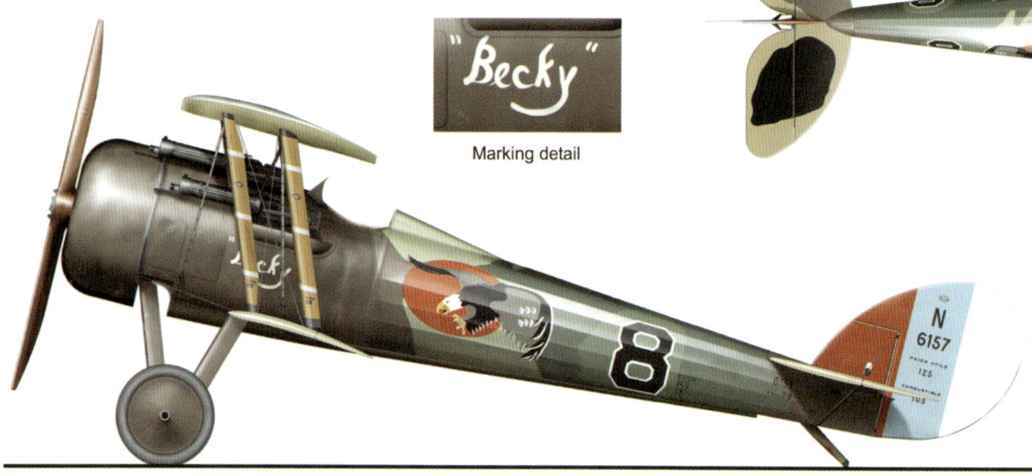

Marking detail

147th Aero Squadron

Nieuport 28 N.6256 Second Lieutenant Kenneth L. Porter
Saints Aerodrome, Chateau-Thierry Sector, France, July 1918

Ken Porter spent many combat hours piloting N.6256, squadron number 15, from early June until shortly before it was returned to Orly on 13 August 1918. The blue cowl signifies that Porter was a member of "C" Flight of the 147th Aero Squadron, red and white being the colors of "A" Flight and "B" Flight respectively.

Of special interest is the hinged compartment that was fitted behind the cockpit, a feature that appears in several examples in this serial number range.

The Cairn Terrier, "Mickey" insignia, painted on 147th Aero Squadron aircraft varied in size and were sometimes personalized with the addition of service stripes, dead rats signifying victory credits, or medals awarded to the pilot.

Artwork © Juanita Franzi

147th Aero Squadron

Nieuport 28 N.6334 Second Lieutenant William E. Brotherton
Saints Aerodrome, Chateau-Thierry Sector, France, July 1918

A black snake coils around the white cowl ("B" Flight) of Second Lieutenant Brotherton's Nieuport 28. Brotherton flew N.6334, squadron number 16, from 11 July until it was returned to Orly on 14 August. William "Bedroll" Brotherton was KIA on 10 October 1918 while flying a SPAD XIII.

Air Service Pilots School

Nieuport 28A Serial number 6440
Carlstrom Field, Arcadia, Florida, 1920

Carlstrom Field in Florida and March Field in California were the principal pilot training fields in 1920. This training aircraft is painted with olive brown pigmented cellulose acetate dope in accordance with Spec. 24. 100-G, dated 4 October 1918. The cocarde, adopted on 11 January 1918, is retained, although the reversion to the star-in-circle insignia had been made official in May 1919. The rudder stripes, however, have reverted to their earlier positioning of blue, white, with red at the tail of the rudder. Reminiscent of the deactivated 213th Aero Squadron, the insignia is noteworthy because Major Christopher Ford, Officer in Charge of Flying and Training at Carlstrom, had been a member of the 213th in August and September 1918.

Note that the fabric wheel covers, inspection panels and landing gear strut fairings have been removed and the rudder and vertical stabilizer ribs, lacking veneer covering, are clearly defined under the fabric. The propeller appears to be a British Lang Propeller Company copy of the usual Levasseur propeller. The Lang copy had fabric-covered tips.

Ship-plane Unit, Atlantic Fleet, USS Arizona

Nieuport 28A Serial number N.6461, BuNo 5794
Lieutenant (junior grade) Alfred "Mel" Pride
On maneuvers off the coast of Cuba, March 1920

Painted overall in aluminum enamel, except for the cowl which is left unpainted, this aircraft was equipped with a fabric covered wooden hydrovane and rubberized fabric air bags to be deployed in the event of ditching. The generator atop the upper wing powered the wireless radio and the unit gun sight is retained although the twin Marlin machine guns have been removed. The "circle in a star within a circle" national insignia (the reversion to the prewar insignia was made official by the Navy on 19 August 1919) is painted on the left upper wing although prevailing regulations called for the insignia to be painted at both wing tips.

This aircraft was surveyed after being ditched on 17 March 1920.

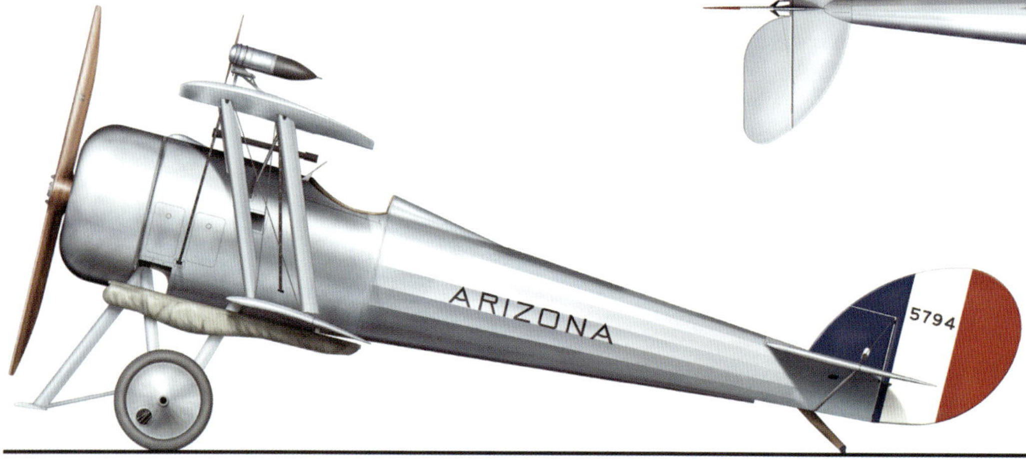

Fliegertruppe

Nieuport 28A Bébé Swiss No. 688
Thun, Switzerland, 1924

Fliegertruppe repaired and tested Lieutenant James Ashenden's crashed Nieuport 28 and were sufficiently impressed with its performance to buy fourteen Nieuport 28A trainers from Nieuport Astra in 1923-24. Number 688 is one of a series numbered 685-698, and is painted in the Swiss colors of the day. Note the venturi atop the upper left wing and the simple, rounded windscreen.

Lieutenant Ashenden's Nieuport 28 (N.6212, renumbered 607) also saw brief service (1923-1925) as a trainer. Number 688 is now on permanent display at the Verkehrshaus der Schweiz in Lucerne, Switzerland.

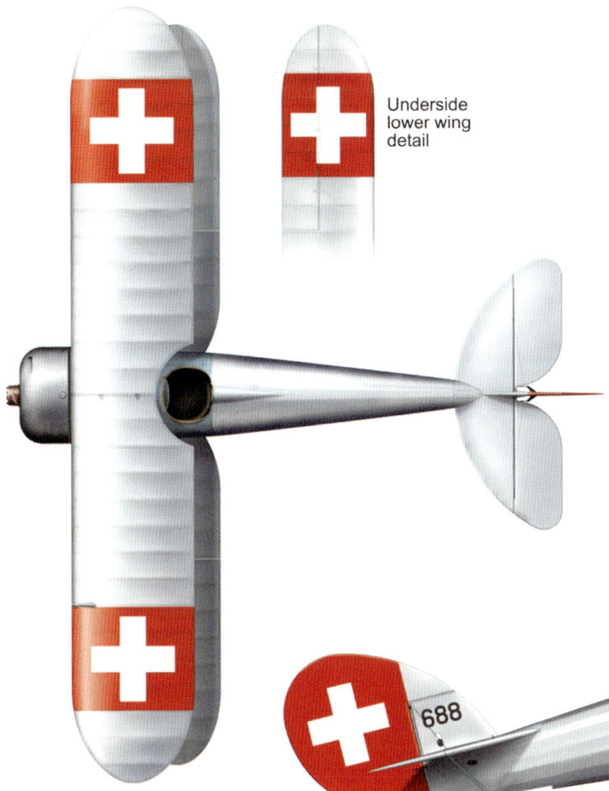

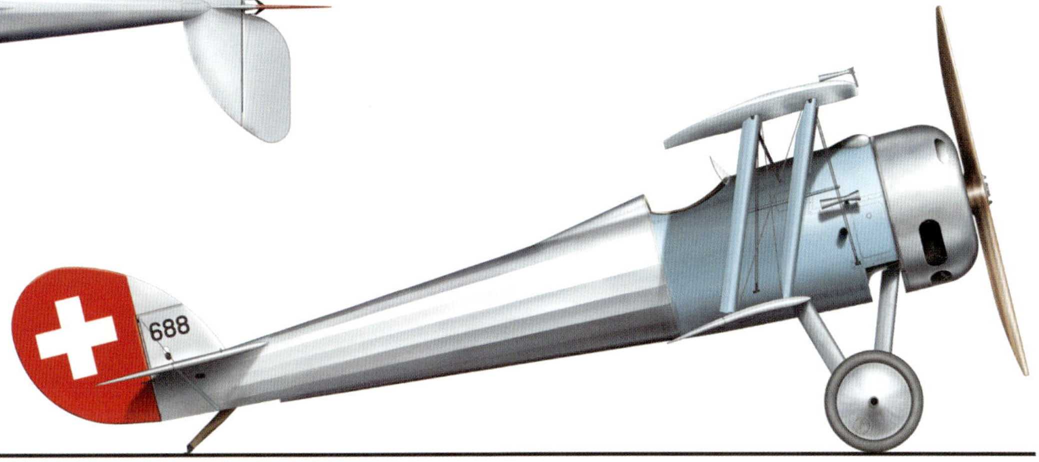

Artwork © Juanita Franzi

Fuerza Aérea Argentina

Nieuport 28 N.6338 Teniente Benjamin Matienzo
Escuela Militar de Aviación, El Palomar, Argentina,
circa March 1919

Both of the late production Nieuport 28s (N.6338 and N.6339) supplied to the Fuerza Aérea Argentina, retained standard wartime camouflage but were equipped with non standard, short span ailerons on top and bottom wings. Pushrods, connected to the lower ailerons, activated the upper set of ailerons. This configuration, intended to improve roll moment, was tested but never adopted as standard by Nieuport.

Contemporary photographs show that Argentine colors were painted on wings and tail, but the sun emblem is absent. Some reports suggest that this aircraft was painted red and given the number 1 prior to Teniente Matienzo's tragic attempt to cross the Andes in May 1919.

Lieutenant James A. Meissner's
Nieuport 28 N.6144
94th Aero Squadron, 15 May 1918

Jimmy Meissner's N.6144

Lieutenant James Armand Meissner's Nieuport 28 is illustrated in the profile section as it appeared on 15 May 1918, the day Meissner received the Croix de Guerre for his first victory, scored two weeks earlier. What follows is a brief history of Jimmy Meissner's association with N.6144.[16]

On 12 March 1918, Lieutenant Wilfred Casgrain was assigned to fly Nieuport 28, serial number N.6144, as a member of the third flight of the 95th Aero Squadron. However, 6144 was retained by the 95th for only a short time before the squadron was ordered to Cazeaux to take gunnery training. The airplane sat idle at Epiez until it, and other Nieuports 28s of the 95th, were retrieved by the 94th Aero Squadron.

Lieutenant Jimmy Meissner took possession of N.6144 on 21 April, noting in his diary, "mine is 6144, good bus." Jimmy flew several alert missions with no results between 21 April and 2 May, and accompanied Lieutenant Alan Winslow on a "fun flight," where he did barrel rolls over the aerodrome, causing those on the ground to think that he had gotten a Boche.

Jimmy made some modifications to his Nieuport 28, including installation of a larger windshield and replacing the landing-gear wires with thicker gauge wires. Meissner's mechanics added the "Hat in the Ring" insignia (note that the ring is a golden yellow, rather than the more familiar red – this was revealed by spectrographic analysis by NASM technicians), a dark color number 14, and a distinctive silver and red zigzag pattern on the cowl, and finally affixed a half-sheet, Third Liberty Bond Drive poster to the top of the lower right wing.

Jimmy Meissner's 6144 experienced wing failure (described fully in Chapter 4) for the first time on 2 May 1918, but the aircraft was quickly repaired, as he noted in his diary entry for 6 May: "my plane fixed up again, new wings & motor overhauled. Tested it out & lined up gun." Meissner flew an alert mission the next day but nosed over upon landing, and 6144 was again out of commission. With a new set of wings, propeller, and rudder repair, 6144 also received a new squadron number, changed from the dark #14 to a white #8. The cowl also was repainted in a slightly modified zigzag pattern, as depicted in the profile section.

Meissner and 6144 were relatively idle the following week, with several uneventful alerts and limited flying because of bad weather. On 12 May, he noted in his diary that he had "roamed thru the woods with Thorne Taylor in [the] after[noon], looking at birds' nests and flowers."

A few days later, 15 May was a busy day for the 94th and a red-letter day for David Peterson, who bagged two enemy planes during an hourlong patrol. Ken Marr had a successful encounter with a "biplace" and Reed Chambers downed a balloon, but neither he nor Marr received confirmation for their claims. Jimmy Meissner and Thorne Taylor attacked three Albatros fighters and a "biplace," but broke off quickly to return to Gengoult Aerodrome after Meissner's machine gun jammed.

After an eventful morning, General Gerard, Commander of the Eighth French Army, and other dignitaries arrived at the aerodrome in the afternoon to present the Croix de Guerre to David Peterson, Eddie Rickenbacker, and Jimmy Meissner. After the award ceremony, Meissner, in the company of Billy Mitchell, David Peterson, Raoul Lufbery, and Rickenbacker, flew a twenty-minute exhibition flight over the aerodrome.

The following day, Meissner and 6144 chased a drifting balloon but couldn't catch it; he then attacked a tethered observation balloon, causing the observer to jump, but he failed to destroy the balloon.

The next ten days were quiet, with few alerts flown and another departure from combat when Meissner's single machine gun jammed.

Jimmy Meissner wrote the following caption on the back of this photograph, dated 19 June 1918: "Mechanics and self by faithful #8 [N.6144]. In the graveyard now after 60 hours flying, many combats and 3 Boche, broken by a new pilot." The Glasebrook Foundation

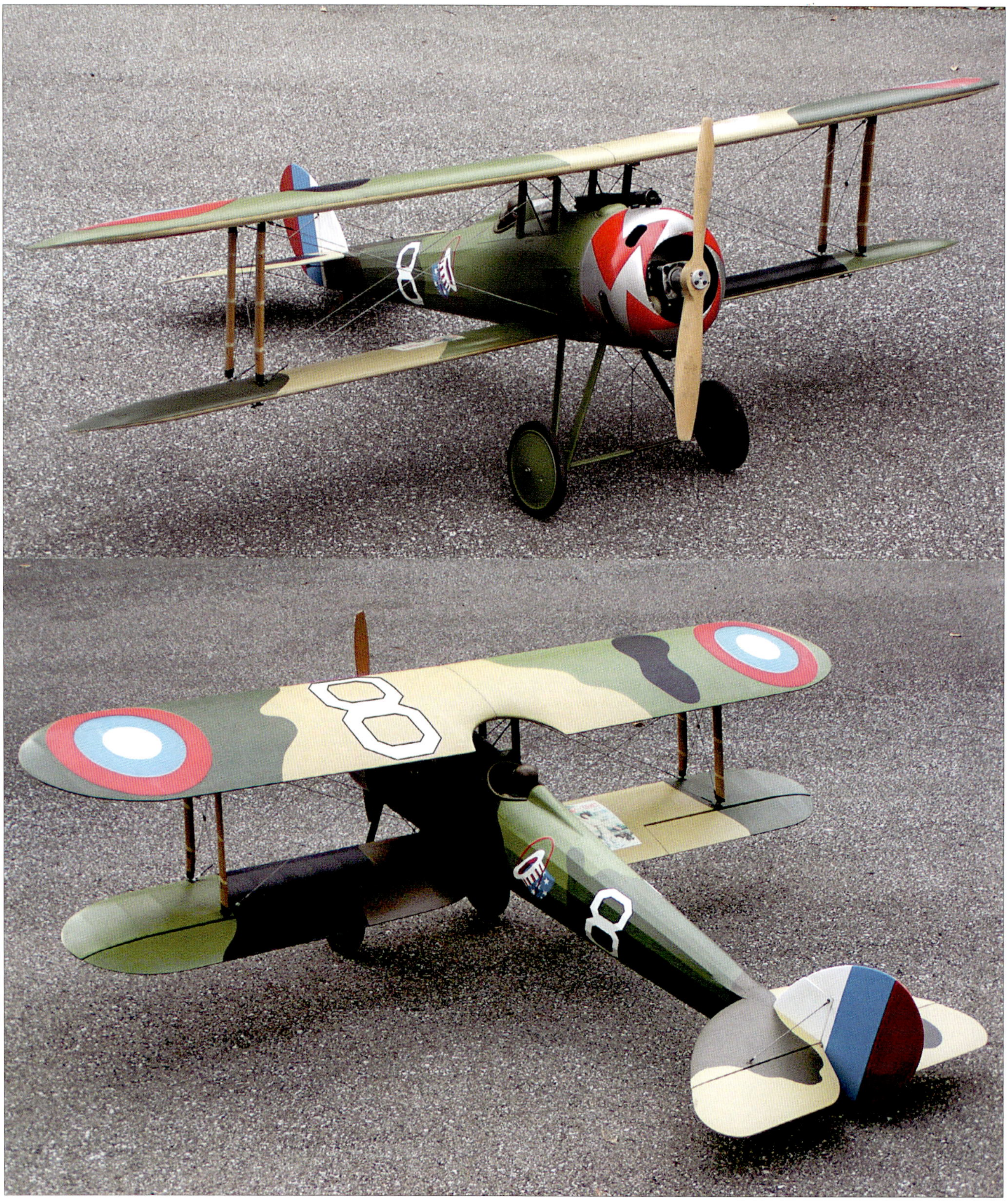

James Suchy built this exquisite Nieuport 28 radio-controlled model and painted it in Jimmy Meissner's colors. Constructed from a BALSA USA kit, this 1:4 scale model features an eighty-inch wingspan, length of sixty-one inches, and weight of twelve to fourteen pounds. James Suchy

During this brief, quiet interlude for Meissner, Douglas Campbell scored his third and fourth victories, and shared his fifth with Eddie Rickenbacker. However, the squadron lost Raoul Lufbery and Paul Kurtz.

Jimmy Meissner and 6144 scored again on 30 May, but experienced wing failure a second time during this combat. The airplane was quickly repaired. Jimmy recorded: "Bus O.K. by eve".

A second machine gun was finally installed on 6144 on 7 June. The following day, Meissner had an unsuccessful encounter with a Hannover that was flown by a "very Clever pilot" who "got away cold." Bad weather the next few days gave the pilots of the 94th "rest for our tired nerves."

On 13 June, Meissner and 6144 flew their last combat together: "Taylor, Winslow, and I went out on voluntary patrol at 7:15. Archies showed us a Hannover biplace S.W. of St. Mihiel at 8. Chased it to Thiaucourt firing frequently, there at 8:15, it started to maneuver & we got it. 3 of us together, in flames, upside down! Saw it crash. Confirmed."

Jimmy Meissner's association with 6144 ended the next day. "Turned old No. 6144 [over] to Cates [new man] & took new bus 6254 for self." By all accounts, his association with 6144 had been successful for both pilot and airplane. Jimmy Meissner had been credited with 2.33 enemy aircraft while flying 6144 and 6144 had suffered – and survived – major damage on three separate occasions.

James Armand Meissner was soon promoted to captain, and transferred from the 94th Aero Squadron to become the new commanding officer of the 147th Aero Squadron. Ironically, for the squadron that had clung most devotedly to its Nieuport 28 fighters, Meissner's first task as CO was to wean the 147th's pilots away from their beloved Nieuport 28s and teach them how to effectively employ the SPAD XIII in battle. It was an uphill fight.

Modeling the Nieuport 28

Highly popular with modelers and model collectors, Nieuport 28 model kits and ready-built static models are available in a variety of media, including balsa, plastic, mahogany, and diecast, and in a variety of scales, from the awesome 1:4 scale Proctor radio-controlled (RC) kit, with eighty-inch wingspan (and weight of 16.5 pounds), to the diminutive 1:64 Model Power diecast plane. Available Nieuport 28 kits, including those kits that are no longer in production, can readily be found on the Internet.

WW1 AERO, The Journal of the Early Aeroplane (World War I Aeroplanes Inc., Poughkeepsie, NY) and *Windsock International*, a bimonthly publication of Albatros Productions Ltd. (Berkhamsted, Hertfordshire, UK), offer a wealth of information and tips to modelers of World War I aircraft. Modelers can also utilize the excellent Aerodrome Web site (http://www.theaerodrome.com/) to gather and exchange information.

NOTES

Chapter 1

1. Theodore Hamady, "The First Victory," *Air Force*, April 1988, 68-73. Quoting Alan Winslow letter dated 17 April 1918 to his parents, from the Donald Winslow Family Collection.

2. James A. Meissner, "Diary," entry dated 14 April 1918, Lafayette Foundation Collection, Denver, CO.

3. Hamady, "The First Victory," 69.

4. Jack R. Eder, ed., *Let's Go Where the Action Is: The Wartime Experiences of Douglas Campbell* (Knightstown, IN: JaaRE Publishing, 1984), 55-59.

5. Douglas Campbell of Cos Cob, Connecticut, in an interview with the author in May 1981.

6. Eder, *Let's Go Where the Action Is*, 55-59.

7. Hamady, "The First Victory," 71.

8. "Summary of Air Information: Air Intelligence Bulletin," (GHQAEF [General Headquarters, American Expeditionary Force], Second Section, General Staff, Serial No. 2., 19 April 1918), 27.

9. Hamady, "The First Victory," 71.

10. Colonel Corbiere, Commander of the Troops of the Place de Toul, letter, to Major Huffer, commanding the American Squadron 94, 14 April 1918. *History of the First Pursuit Group, 1917-1936* (Selfridge Field, Mt. Clemens, MI: First Pursuit Group, 1938), 47.

11. Colonel William Mitchell, Chief of Air Service, 1st Army Corps, letter, to Commanding Officer, 94th Aero (Pursuit) Squadron, 3 May 1918. Copy in author's collection.

12. Brigadier General William Mitchell, *Memoirs of World War I* (New York: Random House, 1960), 191.

13. Colonel William Mitchell, telegram, to Brigadier General Benjamin Foulois, Air Service, AEF, Paris, file 1559, Record Group 120, National Archives at College Park, MD.

Chapter 2

1. C. G. Grey, ed., *Aeroplane*, August 1914

2. John H. Morrow Jr., *The Great War in the Air* (Washington, DC: Smithsonian Institution Press, 1993), 252.

3. Ibid., 33.

4. Robert Wohl, *A Passion for Wings: Aviation and the Western Imagination, 1908-1918* (New Haven, CT: Yale University Press, 1994), 205.

5. Morrow, *Great War in the Air*, 15.

6. Ibid., 15.

7. R. Ernest Dupuy and Trevor N. Dupuy, *The Encyclopedia of Military History: From 3500 B.C. to the Present* (New York: Harper & Row, 1986), 917.

8. Morrow, *Great War in the Air*, 196.

9. Jon E. Lewis, ed., *The Mammoth Book of Eyewitness World War I* (New York: Carroll & Graf Publishers, 2003), 159.

10. Charles Christienne and Pierre Lissarragu, *A History of French Military Aviation* (Washington, DC: Smithsonian Institution Press, 1986), 96.

11. Léonard Rosenthal and others, *Nieuport: 1909-1950* (Clichy, France: Docavia/Editions Lariviere, ca 1997), 12.

12. John A. Chionchio, "Defeat by Design," *Air Enthusiast*, January-April 1989, 67-74.

13. Christienne and Lissarrague, *History of French Military Aviation*, 98.

14. Morrow, *Great War in the Air*, 152.

15. General Ernst von Hoeppner, *Germany's War in the Air* (Nashville, TN: Battery Press, 1994), 88.

16. Albert Deullin, French Ace, quotation furnished to author by Bernard Klaeyle and translated by O. Abi Mershed.

17. Hershel Smith, *A History of Aircraft Piston Engines* (Manhattan, KS: Sunflower University Press, 1994), 67.

18. Le General Commandant en Chef [Pétain] to le Sous-Secrétaire d'État de l'Aéronautique Militaire, Paris, 22 October 1917. Document from S.H.A.A. (Service Historique de l'Armée de l'Air) archives, sent to author by Bernard Klaeyle and translated by O. Abi Mershed.

19. Eric Lawson and Jane Lawson, *The First Air Campaign: August 1914 - November 1918* (Conshohocken, PA: Combined Books, 1996), 221.

Chapter 3

1. House Select Committee on Expenditures in the War Department, *Hearings Before Subcommittee No. 1 (Aviation)*, 66th Cong., 1st sess., 1919, serial 2, part 6, 387.

2. Frederick B. Rentschler, *An Account of Pratt & Whitney Aircraft Company, 1925-1950* (privately printed, 1950), 6. Author's collection.

3. I. B. Holley Jr., *Ideas and Weapons* (New Haven, CT: Yale University Press, 1953), 126.

4. Frederick Palmer, *Newton D. Baker: America at War*, vol. 1 (New York: Dodd, Mead & Company, 1931), 282.

5. Michael D. Doubler, *Closing with the Enemy: How GIs Fought the War in Europe, 1944-1945* (Lawrence, KS: University Press of Kansas, 1994), 8.

6. *Hearings Before Subcommittee No. 1*, serial 2, part 31, ix.

7. Ibid., viii.

8. "Leading Newspapers Ask for $1,000,000,000 for Huge Air Fleet of 100,000 Aeroplanes," *Aerial Age Weekly*, 18 June 1917, 449.

9. Palmer, *Newton D. Baker*, 293.

10. Major Joseph Tulasne, "America's Part in the Allies' Mastery of the Air," *National Geographic* 33, no. 1 (January 1918): 5.

11. General Ernst von Hoeppner, *Germany's War in the Air* (Nashville, TN: Battery Press, 1994), 132.

12. Report of Aeronautical Commission, Major R. C. Bolling to Chief Signal Officer of the Army, Washington, DC, 15 August 1917, vol. 24, p. 11 (National Archives Publication MM 990, roll 32), US Air Service Records, Record Group 120, National Archives at College Park, MD.

13. *Hearings Before Subcommittee No. 1*, serial 2, part 31, xlii.

14. Report of Aeronautical Commission, vol. 24, p. 4.

15. Memorandum from Captain Herbert Hughes, Engineering Intelligence Division, to Chief Signal Officer, Washington, DC, 24 August 1917, file 452.1, "Subject: Airplane Performance, French," US Air Service Records, RG 120, National Archives at College Park, MD.

16. Le General Commandant en Chef [Pétain] to le Sous-Secrétaire d'État de l'Aéronautique Militaire, Paris, 22 October 1917. Document from S.H.A.A. (Service Historique de l'Armée de l'Air) archives, sent to author by Bernard Klaeyle and translated by O. Abi Mershed.

17. Holley, *Ideas and Weapons*, 122.

18. Ibid.

19. *Hearings Before Subcommittee No. 1*, lxii.

20. Ibid., lx.

21. Ibid., xlix.

22. General Pétain to le Sous-Secrétaire d'État de l'Aéronautique Militaire, 22 October 1917.

23. Brigadier General B. D. Foulois, "Office Memorandum Regarding Organizational Changes," 12 December 1917, B. D. Foulois Papers, personal correspondence, Box 5, Manuscripts Division, Library of Congress.

24. Colonel R. C. Bolling to Captain J. A. Drexel, London, England, 29 December 1917, file 452.1, Programs, US Air Service Records, RG 120, National Archives at College Park, MD.

25. Brigadier General B. D. Foulois to Dr. Charles D. Walcott, 20 April 1918, Foulois Papers, Manuscripts Division, Library of Congress.

26. General Hageneau to Chief of Air Service [Foulois], American Expeditionary Force, 30 November 1917, file 452.1, US Air Service Records, RG 120, National Archives at College Park, MD.

27. General Pétain to le Sous-Secrétaire d'État de l'Aéronautique Militaire, 22 October 1917.

28. *Hearings Before Subcommittee No. 1*, lxiv.

29. Colonel R. C. Bolling to Brigadier General B. D. Foulois, 11 January 1918, Foulois Papers, Manuscripts Division, Library of Congress.

30. Brigadier General B. D. Foulois to M. le Sous-Secrétaire d'État de l'Aéronautique Militaire et Maritime, Paris, 23 January 1918, file 452.1, US Air Service Records, RG 120, National Archives at College Park, MD.

31. Chief of Air Service [Foulois], AEF, to Chief of Supply Department [Dunwoody], Air Service, 19 January 1918, file 452.1, US Air Service Records, RG 120, National Archives at College Park, MD.

32. Brigadier General B. D. Foulois, Chief of Air Service, AEF, to General Pershing, Commander in Chief, AEF, 14 February 1918, file 452.1, US Air Service Records, RG 120, National Archives at College Park, MD.

33. Le Sous-Secrétaire d'État de l'Aéronautique Militaire et Maritime to Brigadier General B. D. Foulois, 21 February 1918, file 452.1, US Air Service Records, RG 120, National Archives at College Park, MD.

34. Colonel R. C. Bolling to Brigadier General B. D. Foulois, 22 January 1918, Foulois Papers, Manuscripts Division, Library of Congress.

35. Charles Woolley, *First to the Front: The Aerial Adventures of 1st Lt. Waldo Heinrichs and the 95th Aero Squadron, 1917-1918* (Atglen, PA: Schiffer Publishing, 1999), 67.

36. Major General Mason M. Patrick, Chief of Air Service, AEF, *United States Army in the World War, 1917-1919: Reports of Commander-in-Chief, AEF, Staff Sections and Services* (Washington, DC: Historical Division, Department of the Army, US Government Printing Office, 1948), 290.

Chapter 4

1. "A General History of the 27th Aero Squadron," p. 33 (National Archives Publication MM 990, roll 16), US Air Service Records, Record Group 120, National Archives at College Park, MD.

2. Harold Buckley, *Squadron 95* (Paris: Obelisk Press, 1933), 30.

3. Ibid., 31.

4. A. J. Lynch, "Interview with Captain Douglas Campbell, 94th Aero Squadron, USAS," *Cross & Cockade Journal* 6, no. 1 (Spring 1965): 41.

5. "History of 95th Aero Squadron" (unpublished book), Lafayette Foundation Collection, Denver, CO, p. 5.

6. Lieutenant James A. Meissner, "Combined Diaries" (unpublished), entry dated 1 March 1918, Lafayette Foundation Collection, Denver, CO.

7. Charles Woolley, *First to the Front: The Aerial Adventures of 1st Lt. Waldo Heinrichs and the 95th Aero Squadron, 1917-1918* (Atglen, PA: Schiffer Publishing, 1999), 72.

8. Lieutenant Joseph Raible, "Combined Diaries" (unpublished), entry dated 16 May 1918, Lafayette Foundation Collection, Denver, CO.

9. Woolley, *First to the Front*, 72.

10. Buckley, *Squadron 95*, 34.

11. Meissner, "Combined Diaries," entry dated 5 April 1918.

12. Jack R. Eder, ed., *Let's Go Where the Action Is: The Wartime Experiences of Douglas Campbell* (Knightstown, IN: JaaRE Publishing, 1984), 48.

13. Lynch, "Interview with Captain Douglas Campbell," 36.

14. Buckley, *Squadron 95*, 77-78.

15. Royal Frey, "94th Aero Squadron" (unpublished history), Lafayette Foundation Collection, Denver, CO, p. 6.

16. Meissner, "Combined Diaries," entry dated 11 April 1918.

17. Ibid., entries dated 12-13 April 1918.

18. Ibid., entry dated 14 April 1918.

19. Kenneth Lee Porter and Colonel C. R. Glasebrook, "Combat Flight Commander" (unpublished history of the 147th Aero Squadron, USAS), Lafayette Foundation Collection, Denver, CO, p. 14.

20. Woolley, *First to the Front*, 92.

21. Kermit Roosevelt, ed., *Quentin Roosevelt: A Sketch with Letters* (New York: Charles Scribner's Sons, 1921), 159.

22. Captain Hamilton Coolidge, *Letters of an American Airman: Being the War Record of Capt. Hamilton Coolidge, 1917-1918* (Boston: privately printed, 1919), 152.

23. Lynch, "Interview with Captain Douglas Campbell," 39.

24. Frey, "94th Aero Squadron," 14.

25. Norman L. R. Franks, *Aircraft Versus Aircraft* (London: Grub Street, 1998), 52.

26. Norman L. R. Franks, Frank W. Bailey and Russell Guest, *Above the Lines: A Complete Record of the Fighter Aces of the German Air Service, Naval Air Service and Flanders Marine Corps, 1914-1918* (London: Grub Street, 1993), 51.

27. Buckley, *Squadron 95*, 56.

28. Lynch, "Interview with Captain Douglas Campbell," 35.

29. Colonel William Mitchell, telegram, to Brigadier General Benjamin Foulois, Chief of Air Service, AEF, Paris, file 1559, RG 120, National Archives at College Park, MD.

30. James A. Meissner, "Some New Experiences" (unpublished account of incident that occurred on 2 May 1918), Lafayette Foundation Collection, Denver, CO.

31. Meissner, "Combined Diaries," entry dated 2 May 1918.

32. Buckley, *Squadron 95*, 71.

33. House Select Committee on Expenditures in the War Department, *Hearings Before Subcommittee No. 1*, 66th Cong., 1st sess., 1919, vol. 3, 3804.

34. Theodore M. Hamady, "Destined to Fail: The Nieuport 28 Wing," *Air Power History* 46, no. 4 (Winter 1999): 12.

35. Information regarding William H. Plyler's combat on 13 June 1918 was kindly provided to the author on 26 August 2004, by Plyler's son, William, who lives in Kershaw, South Carolina.

36. Lynch, "Interview with Captain Douglas Campbell," 39.

37. *Hearings Before Subcommittee No. 1*, 3779.

38. Frey, "94th Aero Squadron," 22-25.

39. Frey's interview of two villagers from the village of Maron is found in his unpublished history, "94th Aero Squadron", p. 25-26; Lieutenant Eddie Rickenbacker's testimony about Lufbery's injuries is found in *Hearings Before Subcommittee No. 1*, p. 3803.

40. Royal D. Frey, "A.E.F. Combat Airfields and Monuments in France, WW I," *AAHS Journal* 17, no. 3 (Fall 1972): 196.

41. Lieutenant Colonel Harold Hartney, *Up and At 'Em* (Harrisburg, PA: Stackpole Sons, 1940), 144.

42. Meissner, "Combined Diaries," entry dated 3 June 1918.

43. Brigadier General Benjamin Foulois, Chief of Air Service, First Army, AEF, to Major General Mason Patrick, Chief of Air Service, AEF, 12 June 1918, file 336, RG 120, National Archives at College Park, MD.

44. Colonel William Mitchell, telegram, to Brigadier General Benjamin Foulois, Chief of Air Service, AEF, Paris, file 336, RG 120, National Archives at College Park, MD. At the time of receipt of Mitchell's telegram (dated 1 May 1918), Foulois had not, as yet, been relieved by Major General Mason Patrick as Chief of Air Service, AEF.

45. Roosevelt, *Quentin Roosevelt*, 164.

46. Hartney, *Up and At 'Em*, 144-145.

47. Ibid., 145.

48. J. M. Bruce, *Morane-Saulnier Type A1*, Windsock Mini Datafile 5 (Berkhamsted, UK: Albatros Productions, 1996), 3-4.

49. Lieutenant Colonel Halsey Dunwoody, Assistant to Chief of Air Service, AEF, telegram, to Brigadier General Benjamin Foulois, (no date, but about 17 June 1918), file 336, RG 120, National Archives at College Park, MD.

50. Brigadier General Benjamin Foulois, Chief of Air Service, First Army, telegram, to Lieutenant Colonel Halsey Dunwoody, 19 June 1918, file 336, RG 120, US Air Service Records, National Archives at College Park, MD.

51. Michael Howard, *The First World War* (New York: Oxford University Press, 2002), 121.

52. Ben Levandowski, "Jasta 26 During 'Operation Michael'," *Cross & Cockade Journal* 16, no. 4 (Winter 1975): 360.

53. Hartney, *Up and At 'Em*, 167.

54. Lieutenant Edward V. Rickenbacker, "Diary" (unpublished), entry dated 16 June 1918, Lafayette Foundation Collection, Denver, CO.

55. *General History of the 27th*, 33.

56. Victory credits and losses (KIA, WIA, and POW) are derived, respectively, from *USAF Historical Study No. 133, U.S. Air Service Victory Credits: World War I* (Maxwell Air Force Base, AL: Historical Research Division, Aerospace Studies Institute, Air University, 1969); and James J. Sloan Jr., *Wings of Honor: American Airmen in World War I* (Atglen, PA: Schiffer Publishing, 1994), 129-135.

57. Buckley, *Squadron 95*, 57.

58. "American Pursuit Aviation at Chateau-Thierry," chap. 2, p. 6 (National Archives Publication MM 990, roll 16), US Air Service Records, RG 120, National Archives at College Park, MD.

59. "History of the First Pursuit Group, 1917-1936" (unpublished), Lafayette Foundation Collection, Denver, CO, p. 77.

60. Hartney, *Up and At 'Em*, 167.

61. Frey, "94th Aero Squadron," 42, 43.

62. Hartney, *Up and At 'Em*, 171.

63. Ibid., 176.

64. Rickenbacker, "Diary," entry dated 4 July 1918.

65. Roosevelt, *Quentin Roosevelt*, 164.

66. Rickenbacker, "Diary," entry dated 9 July 1918.

67. Hartney, *Up and At 'Em*, 195.

68. James Parks, "History of the 147th Aero Squadron" (unpublished).

69. "Summary of Air Information: Air Intelligence Bulletin," (GHQAEF [General Headquarters, American Expeditionary Force], Second Section, General Staff, Serial No. 2., 19 April 1918), 121.

70. Hartney, *Up and At 'Em*, 180.

71. Buckley, *Squadron 95*, 81.

72. "American Pursuit Aviation," chap. 2, 10.

73. Ibid., 10.

74. 147th Pursuit Squadron, USAS, "Combat Operations Report: June 18, 1918 to November 23, 1918" (unpublished), copy in author's collection. Combat report of 15 July 1918, by Lieutenant George A. S. Robertson.

75. Ibid., combat report of 15 July 1918 by Lieutenant Thomas J. Abernethy.

76. Porter and Glasebrook, "Combat Flight Commander," 22.

77. Lieutenant William Brotherton, "Combined Diaries" (unpublished), entry dated 24 July 1918, Lafayette Foundation Collection, Denver, CO.

78. Hartney, *Up and At 'Em*, 190.

79. *General History of the 27th*, 150.

80. Alan Toelle, "An Analysis of the 27th Aero Squadron's Combat Operations on 1 August 1918" (unpublished), copy provided to author by Toelle, 1-5.

81. Ibid., 5.

82. "General History of the 27th," 264.

83. Ibid., 266.

84. Dave McElvain, "Clifford McElvain and the Black Day," copy provided to author by Alan Toelle.

85. *Tennessee, the Volunteer State* (S. J. Clark Publishing, 1923), 824.

86. McElvain, "Clifford McElvain and the Black Day."

87. Ibid.

88. Alfred Fleisher, "McElvain/Fleisher WW I Dogfight," copy provided to author by David A. McElvain.

89. Hartney, *Up and At 'Em*, 198.

90. R. Ernest Dupuy and Trevor N. Dupuy, *The Encyclopedia of Military History: From 3500 B.C. to the Present* (New York: Harper & Row, 1986), 982.

91. Meissner, "Combined Diaries," entry dated 3 August 1918.

92. 147th Pursuit Squadron, USAS, "Combat Operations Report: June 18, 1918 to November 23, 1918," entry for 17 August 1918.

93. "History of the First Pursuit Group," 96.

94. *USAF Historical Research Study No. 133, U.S. Air Service Victory Credits: World War I*, 68-80, and Sloan, Wings of Honor, 129-135.

95. Major General Mason M. Patrick, Chief of Air Service, AEF, *United States Army in the World War, 1917-1919: Reports of Commander-in-Chief, AEF, Staff Sections and Services* (Washington, DC: Historical Division, Department of the Army, US Government Printing Office, 1948), 230.

96. Maurer Maurer, ed., *The U.S. Air Service in World War I*, vol. 2 (Maxwell Air Force Base, AL: Simpson Historical Research Center, 1978), 242.

97. Ibid., 249.

Chapter 5

1. House Select Committee on Expenditures in the War Department, *Hearings Before Subcommittee No. 1 (Aviation)*, 66th Cong., 1st sess., 1919, vol. 3, serial 2, 3842.

2. Joseph Houston Eastman, "Diary of Joseph Houston Eastman," entry dated 12 June 1918, Joseph Houston Eastman Collection, Hoover Institution Archives, Stanford, CA.

3. Kenneth Lee Porter and Colonel C. R. Glasebrook, "Combat Flight Commander" (unpublished history of the 147th Aero Squadron, USAS), Lafayette Foundation Collection, Denver, CO, p. 23.

4. Maurer Maurer, ed., *The U.S. Air Service in World War I*, vol. 1 (Maxwell Air Force Base, AL: Simpson Historical Research Center, 1978), 40.

5. George R. Evans, "World War I Aircraft Performance Chart," *Cross & Cockade Journal* 11, no. 4 (Winter 1970): 370-371.

6. Ibid., 370.

7. Lieutenant Colonel Harold E. Hartney, *Up and At 'Em* (Harrisburg, PA: Stackpole Sons, 1940), 145-146.

8. Jack McCracken, "The Best World War I Fighter," *Over the Front* 14, no. 1 (Spring 1999): 50-59.

9. Kofl. 7 (Seventh German Army, Air Brigade), "Flugzeug aus dem Tatigeitsbericht des Kofl. 7 (Gegend Soissons)," dated 8 August 1918. Document kindly provided to the author by Peter M. Grosz and translated by Michael Neufeld at the National Air and Space Museum, Washington, DC.

10. Ibid.

11. McCracken, "The Best World War I Fighter," 58.

12. Ernst Udet's comments about the BMW motor type IIIa were published in *Motor* magazine in May/June 1919 (and translated by Alex Imrie). Greg VanWyngarden kindly provided an abstract of Udet's article to the author. The abstract also contained information on the rate of climb of Udet's own Fokker D.VIIF. His figures, which were not incorporated in the chapter, reveal a lower rate of climb (of approximately 20 percent), compared to factory figures. It appears that Evans and McCracken both used factory figures in making their calculations.

13. Captain Frank Burton, "Final Report Airplane Division," AEF, US Air Service, Technical Section, file 1998, Record Group 120, National Archives at College Park, MD.

14. John H. Morrow Jr., *German Air Power in World War I* (Lincoln, NE: University of Nebraska Press, 1982), 113.

15. Maurer, *U.S. Air Service in World War I*, vol. 1, 311.

16. "Pursuit Units," *Air Service Bulletin*, vol. 6, no. 287, 2 November 1918.

17. "A General History of the 27th Aero Squadron," p. 29 (National Archives Publication MM 990, roll 16), US Air Service Records, RG 120, National Archives at College Park, MD.

18. Ibid., 2.

19. Maurer, U.S. *Air Service in World War I*, vol. 1, 284.

20. H. Hugh Wynne, "Recollections of France: James Knowles, 95th Aero Squadron," *Cross & Cockade Journal* 10, no. 4 (Winter 1969): 356.

21. Maurer, *U.S. Air Service in World War I*, vol. 1, 288.

22. Richard Wenzl, Leutnant der Reserve, Jasta 6, *Richthofen-Flieger* (Karlsruhe, Germany: Badische Zeitung, c. 1930), 47. Translation by Peter Kilduff.

23. Maurer Maurer, ed., *The U.S. Air Service in World War I*, vol. 4 (Maxwell Air Force Base, AL: Simpson Historical Research Center, 1979), 84.

24. Maurer, *U.S. Air Service in World War I*, vol. 1, 322.

25. Captain Hamilton Coolidge, *Letters of an American Airman: Being the War Record of Capt. Hamilton Coolidge, 1917-1918* (Boston: privately printed, 1919), 219-220.

26. *Hearings Before Subcommittee No. 1*, serial 2, 3806.

27. General Ernst von Hoeppner, *Germany's War in the Air* (Nashville, TN: Battery Press, 1994), 156.

28. Maurer, *U.S. Air Service in World War I*, vol. 1, 311.

29. Hershel Smith, *A History of Aircraft Piston Engines* (Manhattan, KS: Sunflower University Press, 1994), 68.

30. Maurer, *U.S. Air Service in World War I*, vol. 1, 311.

31. Memorandum by Captain David McK. Peterson, "Instructions to Pilots,"1 November 1918, file 657, RG 120, National Archives at College Park, MD.

32. Eastman, "Diary of Joseph Houston Eastman," entry dated 24 July 1918.

33. Ibid., entry dated 29 June 1918.

34. Alan Toelle, untitled study comparing readiness and sortie efficiency of Nieuport 28 and SPAD XIII (unpublished). Copy of study given to author by Alan Toelle in 2001.

35. Ibid., 21.

36. Peterson, "Instructions to Pilots," 2.

37. Memorandum from Chief of Air Service to Assistant Chief of Air Service, Zone of Advance, Colombey-les-Belles, Subject: "Replacement of Airplanes," 15 October 1918, file 452.1, RG 120, National Archives at College Park, MD.

38. Memorandum from Major A. D. Butterfield to Chief, Technical Section, Subject: "Nieuport 28 Airplanes," 11 October 1918, file 452.1, RG 120, National Archives at College Park, MD.

39. Douglas Waller, *A Question of Loyalty* (New York: Harper Collins, 2004), 120.

40. Bert Frandsen, *Hat in the Ring* (Washington, DC: Smithsonian Books, 2003), 268.

41. Hartney, *Up and At 'Em*, 111-112.

42. Kofl. 7, "Flugzeug aus dem Tatigeitsbericht des Kofl. 7 (Gegend Soissons)."

43. Maurer, *U.S. Air Service in World War I*, vol. 4, 59. It should be noted that while the First Pursuit Group was operating the Nieuport 28 fighter, other American fighter squadrons were either serving under French command (the 103rd Aero Squadron was equipped with SPAD

XIIIs and still had some SPAD VIIs in service), or with the RAF. The American 17th and 148th Aero Squadrons, equipped with Sopwith Camels, remained with the British until the waning days of the war. The 22nd and 28th Aero Squadrons initially served with the RAF, but returned in time to participate in the St. Mihiel Offensive. At that time, they were re-equipped with SPAD XIIIs. The 139th Aero Squadron, equipped with SPAD XIIIs, became operational at Toul just prior to Château-Thierry; it remained at Toul, however, during July and August, and became the nucleus for the Second Pursuit Group.

44. Lieutenant Albert L. Deullin, "Pursuit Work in a Single Seater" in "Bulletin of the Information Section, Air Service, AEF," vol. 6, no. 255 (8 August 1918): 11.

45. Hartney, *Up and At 'Em*, 206.

46. Maurer, *U.S Air Service in World War I*, vol. 1, 335.

47. *Hearings Before Subcommittee No. 1*, serial 2, 3788-3789.

48. Phillip Roosevelt to Mrs. Relyea, personal correspondence, 11 October 1918. Letter kindly provided to author by Mrs. Eleanor Ford.

Chapter 6

1. Supplement to Report of Office of the Chief of Air Service, District of Paris, "Liquidation and Retrenchment," 21 January 1919, vol. 26, National Archives Publication MM 990, roll 32, US Air Service Records, Record Group 120, National Archives at College Park, MD.

2. Colonel Henry C. Whitehead, Air Service, Chief of Staff, telegram, to Major General Mason M. Patrick, Chief of Air Service, 12 November 1918, file 400.14, RG 120, National Archives at College Park, MD.

3. Memorandum from Lieutenant Colonel A. D. Butterfield, Chief of Material Division, to Colonel Aubrey Lippincott, Exhibit "E ... concerning sales of salvaged airplanes made in the AEF," 29 August 1919, file 1235, RG 120, National Archives at College Park, MD.

4. Memorandum from Major H. S. Bacon, Air Service, to Colonel Halsey E. Dunwoody, Subject: "Recommendation of Air Service Board, for Settlement of Contracts with the French Government for Miscellaneous Air Service Material on Order and Undelivered on November 11, 1918," 27 June 1919, file 1261, RG 120, National Archives at College Park, MD.

5. Memorandum from Major A. D. Butterfield, Air Service, Chief of Technical Section, to General Mason M. Patrick, Chief of Air Service, Subject: "Final Reports of Investigations of the Production in French Factories of Airplanes, Engines and Spares," 31 December 1918, p. 11, file 1998, RG 120, National Archives at College Park, MD.

6. Ibid.

7. "Nieuport 28 C.1," information sheet. Provided to author by Jim Appleby in November 1998.

8. Butterfield to Patrick, p. 11.

9. Memorandum from Lieutenant Colonel A. D. Butterfield, Chief of Technical Section, to Colonel Halsey Dunwoody, Subject: "Number of Airplanes to Be Received on Liquidation Settlement," 27 May 1919, file 1261, RG 120, National Archives at College Park, MD.

10. Memorandum from Second Lieutenant L. W. Moore, Office of Air Service Representative, AEF, Paris, to Lieutenant Colonel A. D. Butterfield, "... status of airplanes accepted by the US Air Service on the Liquidation Settlement," 22 August 1919, file 1261, RG 120, National Archives at College Park, MD.

11. "Air Service Airplane and Engine Distribution Reports," 19 June 1920. Data compiled from records at the National Archives by Lieutenant Colonel Kimbrough S. Brown and sent to the author via Robert L. Cavanagh on 5 August 1995.

12. "Activities of the Pilot School, Carlstrom Field, Arcadia, FL," *Air Service Newsletter* 20, p. 7. Copy provided to author by Robert L. Cavanagh.

13. "Sale of United States Army Surplus Aeronautical Equipment," c. 1920, Material Disposal and Salvage Division, Air Service, War Department, Room 1616, Munitions Building, Washington, DC. Copy provided to author by Bob Repich.

14. Secretary of the Navy Josephus Daniels, *Annual Report of the Secretary of the Navy: 1920* (Washington, DC: Government Printing Office, 1920), 44.

15. "Pilot School at Carlstrom Field, Arcadia, Florida, Busily Engaged in Instructional Work," *Air Service Newsletter* 19, p. 4. Copy provided to author by Robert L. Cavanagh.

16. Carlton D. Palmer to Fred D. Dickey Jr., letter, 22 December 1963. Copy provided by Mr. Dickey to author.

17. Director of the Air Service to Commanding Officer, Aviation General Supply Depot, Middletown PA, "Airplane and Engine Transfer Order," file 452.1, RG 18, National Archives at College Park, MD.

18. *Specifications for Nieuport 28* (Philadelphia: Naval Aircraft Factory, 14 April 1920). Copy provided to author by Hal Andrews.

19. Memorandum to Chief of Naval Operations, "Fleet Airplanes - Loading of," 16 December 1919, file Z-Z-11, RG 72, National Archives at Washington, DC.

20. Paul Stillwell, *Battleship Arizona, an Illustrated History* (Annapolis, MD: US Naval Institute, 1991), 52.

21. A. M. Pride to Fred Dickey Jr., letter, 21 January 1964. Copy provided by Mr. Dickey to author.

22. Ibid.

23. Ibid.

24. A. M. Pride to Fred Dickey Jr., letter, 6 February 1964. Copy provided by Mr. Dickey to author.

25. Daniels, *Annual Report*, 44.

26. Captain Rosario Rausa, USNR, "Pride of the Navy," *Journal of the National Museum of Naval Aviation Foundation* (Fall 1987): 9.

27. 147th Pursuit Squadron, USAS, "Combat Operations Report: June 18, 1918 to November 23, 1918" (unpublished), entry for 25 June 1918; and (unpublished) "History Of Nieuport 28 C-1, Serial Number 6212," the latter document courtesy of the Glasebrook Foundation, Arlington, VA.

28. "Fliegerlandung," Armeestab, Nachrichtensektion, An Generalstabchef, 28 Juni 1918, E27/13570Bd8, Schweiz Bundes-archiv, Bern, Switzerland. Translated by Daniel Richardson.

29. "History of Nieuport 28 C-1, Serial Number 6212."

30. 147th Pursuit Squadron, USAS, "Combat Operations Report," entry for 25 June 1918.

31. "Begleitheft für Flugzeuge, Flugzeug Nieuport Bébé, Nr. 607," Fliegermuseum Archiv, Dübendorf, Switzerland.

32. As late as 1924, Nieuport Astra was offering Nieuport 28 trainers in their catalog. Gregory Alegi explained that "Pierre-Etienne Flandin (1889-1958), the Undersecretary for Aeronautics and Air Transport from January 1920 to February 1921, devised a solution [to the glut of stocks of wartime aircraft] by persuading the industry to purchase surplus stocks *en bloc*, sell them and give the government a 60 percent share of the proceeds." Fliegertruppe benefited from this policy by acquiring fourteen Nieuport 28 trainers – seven at 15,000 Swiss francs each, and the balance at 10,000 Swiss francs each one year later. Information sources: Gregory Alegi, *Nieuport 29* (Berkhamsted, UK: Albatros Productions, 2003), Windsock Datafile

97, 3; and "Zuwachs Inventar (Jagdflugzeuge Nieuport Bébé)," via Fliegermuseum Archiv, Dübendorf, Switzerland.

33. Max Siegrist, *85 Jahre Berufsschule Amt und Limmattal Dietikon* (Dietikon, Markus Hummel & Co., 1985), 56-57, via Vehrkehrshaus der Schweiz, Lucerne, Switzerland. Translated by Daniel Richardson.

34. Marcelo Miranda, "The History of the Argentine Air Force," *AAHS Journal* 6, no. 1 (Spring 1961): 24-26.

35. Commodoro Ricardo Luis Quellet, ed., *Historia de la Fuerza Aérea Argentina*, TOMO 1 (Buenos Aires: Estudios Históricos, 1997), 25-27. Translated by Daniel Richardson.

36. Ibid., 293.

37. Ibid., 292-293.

38. Ibid., 293.

39. Ibid., 293.

40. Ibid., 305.

Chapter 7

1. Copies of US Navy "Aircraft Record" cards relating to operation and disposal of Nieuport 28 type aircraft were obtained from original records held at the archives of the United States Marine Corps Air/Ground Museum at Quantico, Virginia.

2. D. D. Hadfield, *Los Angeles Aeronautics: 1920-1929* (Inglewood, CA: Northrop University Press, 1973), 80.

3. Ibid., 45.

4. Eddie Martin (as told to Judy Liebeck and edited by Don and Vi Smith), *Just Call Me "Eddie": My Life as a Pioneer Pilot in Orange County California* (Irvine, CA: Print Network Publisher, 1998), 47. This privately printed book is a wonderful source of reminiscences about early aviation activities and pilots in the Southern California area.

5. Ibid., 47.

6. Ibid., 47-48.

7. Ibid., 49-50.

8. F. G. Schafer, "Hanging 'Round the Hangars," *Western Flying* 4, no. 4 (October 1927): 56.

9. Earle Ovington to Curtis Freshel, letter, 14 January 1924. Copy on Gallery of History, Autograph & Manuscript Dealer Web site, 6 May 2005, http://galleryofhistory.com/html/galleryhome.asp.

10. Contract between First National Properties Inc. and Garland Lincoln, date referenced as 10 March 1930. Provided to author by University of Southern California, Warner Brothers Archives, School of Cinema-Television.

11. Ibid.

12. Peter C. Rollins and John E. O'Connor, eds., *Hollywood's World War I Motion Picture Images*, "The Dawn Patrol and the World War I Air Combat Film Genre: An Exploration of American Values", by Dominick A. Pisano (Bowling Green, OH: Bowling Green State University Popular Press, 1997), 63.

13. "NASM/Historical A/C Listing, Aircraft Registration 2539," prepared by Dan Hagedorn, NASM archivist and historian, 22 February 1983. Copy given to author.

14. U.S. Department of Transportation, FAA Aircraft Registration Records, Aircraft Registration: N4728V, initially registered as R10415, Federal Aviation Administration, Aircraft Registration Branch (AVN-450), Oklahoma City, OK.

15. FAA Aircraft Registration Records, Aircraft Registration: 75W, Ivan R. Olsen Bill of Sale, 5 February 1930. Copy given to author by Daniel P. Hagedorn, NASM archivist and historian.

16. Ibid.

17. Jess Laughlin, "Dope on the Lincoln Stunt Plane," *Popular Aviation*, June 1937, 21-22.

18. Ibid., 22.

19. Rob Krehbiel of Hutchinson, Kansas, Letter to the Editor, *Air & Space* magazine, 10 November 1995. Copy provided to author.

20. H. Hugh Wynne, *Motion Picture Stunt Pilots and Hollywood's Classic Aviation Movies* (Missoula, MT: Pictorial Histories Publishing, 1987), 142-143.

21. Jim Greenwood and Maxine Greenwood, *Stunt Flying in the Movies* (Blue Ridge Summit, PA: Tab Books, 1982), 69.

22. James H. Farmer, *Celluloid Wings: The Impact of Movies on Aviation* (Blue Ridge Summit, PA: Tab Books, 1984), 320.

23. A mystery remains regarding the exact origin of the fourth Nieuport 28, which clearly stands out in the 1938 *The Dawn Patrol* lineup. Hugh Wynne noted that the contract Garland Lincoln had for *Hell in the Heavens* (described on page 142 of his book, *Motion Picture Stunt Pilots and Hollywood's Classic Aviation Movies*) called for a fourth Nieuport, but photo evidence of this aircraft is lacking. In addition, only three Nieuport 28s are lined up during the later filming of *Men with Wings* – two I-strut and one N-strut Nieuport 28s that Lincoln had possessed in prior films. Dan Hagedorn, NASM archivist and historian, noted that Nieuport 28, #2539, had been sold by Garland Lincoln on 2 October 1937 to Ed Erickson of Mines Field in Inglewood, California, who then sold the aircraft to Paul Mantz's United Air Services Ltd. (no date is given for this transaction), before it went to Paramount Pictures shortly before filming for *Men with Wings* began. It is reported that Lincoln's former Nieuport 28s required considerable rebuilding before they could be used as static displays for *Men with Wings*. Paul Mantz is seen photographed in a Nieuport 28 with the number "4" painted on its fuselage, and this was the only Nieuport 28 reported to have flown in the film. Don Dwiggins, author of *Hollywood Pilot: The Biography of Paul Mantz* (Garden City, NY: Doubleday, 1967), wrote that "in other parts of the country, he [Mantz] located a French Nieuport with a rotary engine ... and several other vintage planes for Wellman's epic" (Dwiggins, 59). In any case, Dwiggins also notes (on page 183) that Mantz's collection of antique aircraft, stored at his ranch in 1944, included: "four Nieuports, three DeHavillands, two SPADS, and one each, Eberhardt pursuit, Orenco, Thomas Morse Scout, 1910 Curtiss pusher, Fokker D. VII, Moth, Jenny, and a Martin Special."

24. Rollins and O'Connor, *Hollywood's World War I Motion Picture Images*, 75.

25. Farmer, *Celluloid Wings*, 125.

26. Ibid., 126.

27. Ibid., 290-339.

Chapter 8

1. Peter L. Jakab and Theodore M. Hamady, "The History of the NASM Nieuport 28," *WW I AERO* 174 (November 2001): 26.

2. Ibid., 29.

3. Donald Brady of Hayward, California, letter to author, 6 July 2005.

4. Ibid.

5. Ibid.

6. Robert Mikesh, *Restoring Museum Aircraft* (Shrewsbury, England: Airlife Publishing, 1997), 11.

7. Paul Mantz wrote to Cole Palen shortly after Palen purchased the Nieuport 28 from him. Responding to Palen's request for more information in order to establish proper title prior to registering the airplane, Mantz told him that the aircraft was one of four that he had purchased from Paramount Pictures in 1941. The letter is found in U.S. Department of Transportation, FAA Aircraft Registration Records, Aircraft Registration: N4123A, Federal Aviation Administration, Aircraft Registration Branch (AVN-450), Oklahoma City, OK.

8. Ibid.

9. Ray Folsom of Paso Robles, California, telephone interview by author, 5 July 2005.

10. "NASM/Historical A/C Listing, Nieuport 28, Aircraft Registration No. 2539," 22 February 1983. Copy given to author by NASM archivist and historian Daniel P. Hagedorn.

11. Christie's Auction Catalog: *The Contents of WINGS AND WHEELS MUSEUM, Orlando, Florida, Sunday 6 December 1981*, 88. Copy given to author by Jim Appleby.

12. Jim Appleby, telephone interview by author, 13 October 2005.

13. Colonel G. B. Jarrett, USAR (retired), "The First Museum," *AAHS Journal* 19, no. 2 (Summer 1974): 115.

14. Zona Appleby of Yucca Valley, California, e-mail message to author, 17 October 2005. Jim and Zona Appleby kindly provided much of the background information about the origin of Nieuport 28 restorations and reproductions found in the USA.

15. Andrew King, telephone interview by author, 1 December 2005.

Appendix A

1. Frank Tallman, *Flying the Old Planes* (Garden City, NY: Doubleday, 1973), 56.

2. Jim Appleby of Yucca Valley, California, interview by the author, 14 November 1998.

3. Members of the Historic Aircraft Collection (UK), "NIEUPORT BSKS - N.28C" (no date or pagination). Copy provided to author by the US Army Aviation Museum, Fort Rucker, Alabama. The aircraft, formerly BSKS, is now exhibited in this museum. (BSKS refers to the UK registration for this Nieuport.)

4. Dick King, in a draft of his recollections of flying old planes including the Nieuport 28, at Old Rhinebeck Aerodrome in Old Rhinebeck, New York. A copy of this work is in the Nieuport 28 curatorial file, Aeronautics Department, National Air and Space Museum, Smithsonian Institution, Washington, DC. Richard King, with Stephan Wilkinson, later published his recollections in *The Skies over Rhinebeck: A Pilot's Story* (Red Hook, NY: Jostens, 1997).

5. "NIEUPORT BSKS - N.28C."

6. Appleby, interview.

7. "NIEUPORT BSKS - N.28C."

8. Tallman, *Flying the Old Planes*, 59.

9. Appleby, interview.

10. Tallman, *Flying the Old Planes*, 60.

11. "NIEUPORT BSKS - N.28C."

12. Appleby, interview.

13. "NIEUPORT BSKS - N.28C."

14. Appleby, interview.

15. Tallman, *Flying the Old Planes*, 59.

16. Ibid.

17. King, draft recollections.

18. "NIEUPORT BSKS - N.28C."

19. King, draft recollections.

20. Tallman, *Flying the Old Planes*, 61.

21. Appleby, interview.

22. King, draft recollections.

Appendix B

1. Section Technique de l'Aéronautique, Rapport No. 12, "Annexe No. 1, Essais Effectués avec l'Avion Spécimen Nie. 28 C1 (Diédre total). No. 4434," June 1917. US Air Service Records, entry 312.1, Record Group 120, National Archives at College Park, MD.

2. Bernard Klaeyle, "Nieuport Nie 28 C1, Chronology of the Development of the Nieuport 28 Fighter" (unpublished). A copy of this log and a copy of the patent (No. 503,610) for the first prototype Nieuport 28 were kindly provided by Mr. Klaeyle to the author.

3. Ibid.

4. J. M. Bruce, *SPAD 13.C1*, Windsock Datafile 32 (Berkhamsted, UK: Albatros Productions, 1992), 3-4.

5. General John J. Pershing, Commander in Chief, AEF, to GHQ, Washington, DC, cable, 5 October 1917, "Engines," US Air Service Records, entry 639, RG 120, National Archives at College Park, MD.

6. Section Technique de l'Aéronautique, Rapport No. 12, "L'Examen et les Essais de l'Avion Nieuport – diédre," 6.

7. Ibid.

8. Klaeyle, "Chronology," 6.

9. J. M. Bruce, *Nieuport Aircraft of World War One* (London: Arms and Armour Press, 1988), 50.

10. Ibid., 51.

11. Chief of Air Service, AEF (Foulois), to Chief, Supply Department, Air Service (Dunwoody), cable, 19 June 1918, "Replacements," US Air Service Records, entry 400.6, RG 120, National Archives at College Park, MD.

12. Memorandum from Major John Satterfield, Supply Department, Air Service, AEF, to (Brigadier) General Foulois, 3 October 1918, US Air Service Records, entry 223.3, RG 120, National Archives at College Park, MD.

13. Memorandum from Major General Mason Patrick, Chief of Air Service, AEF, (having replaced Brigadier General Foulois), to Chief of Staff, GHQ, AEF, 12 July 1918, "Provisions for Adequate Pursuit Aviation," US Air Service Records, entry 412.1, RG 120, National Archives at College Park, MD.

14. Ibid.

15. Gregory Alegi, *Nieuport 29+*, Windsock Datafile 97 (Berkhamsted, UK: Albatros Productions, 2003), 1.

16. Ibid., 3.

Appendix C

1. Information on the structure and engine of the Nieuport 28 is compiled from two documents: "Airplane N XXVIII," Translation No. F. 2493, entry D52.1/29, Record Group 120, National Archives at College Park, MD, and "Gnome Monosoupape ENGINE, Type N, 9 Cylinder, 160 HP," *Air Service Bulletin*, Information Section, Air Service, American Expeditionary Force, vol. 4, no. 155 (23 November 1918), author's collection. Information on ordnance is found in *Handbook of Aircraft Armament* (Washington, DC: Bureau of Aircraft Production, Air Service, US Army, Government Printing Office, 1918), 35-65.

2. I am indebted to Fred Murrin, who provided me with an excellent description of the function of the Nieuport 28's selector and master switches (via letter dated 23 February 2006).

3. Ibid.

4. Dolf L. Goldsmith, *The Grand Old Lady of No Man's Land: The Vickers Machine Gun* (Cobourg, Ontario, Canada: Collector Grade Publications, 1994), 113.

5. Memorandum from Under-Secretary of State for Military and Naval Aviation, to Major General Mason Patrick, Chief of Air Service, AEF, 6 August 1918, US Air Service Records, entry 384.3, RG 120, National Archives at College Park, MD.

6. "Airplane N XXVIII."

7. Nieuport 28 performance figures are derived from George R. Evans' article, "World War I Aircraft Performance Chart," *Cross & Cockade Journal* 11, no. 4 (Winter 1970): 370-371.

Appendix D

1. Colonel William Mitchell to Brigadier General Benjamin Foulois, Chief of Air Service, First Army, AEF, telegram, file 1559, Record Group 120, National Archives at College Park, MD.

2. Memorandum from Brigadier General Benjamin Foulois, Chief of Air Service, First Army, AEF, to Chief of Air Service, AEF, 12 June 1918, file 336, RG 120, National Archives at College Park, MD.

3. Editor, "Fokker Biplane of Recent Type," *Flight Magazine*, 25 July 1918, 839.

4. John D. Anderson Jr., *A History of Aerodynamics and Its Impact on Flying Machines* (New York: Cambridge University Press, 1997), 308.

5. Anderson, *History of Aerodynamics*.

6. James R. Hansen, *Engineer in Charge: A History of the Langley Aeronautical Laboratory, 1917-1958* (Washington, DC: National Aeronautics and Space Administration, 1987), 69-72.

7. Anderson, *History of Aerodynamics*, 262.

8. The testimonies of James A. Meissner and Edward V. Rickenbacker are found in the report of the House Select Committee on Expenditures in the War Department, *Hearings Before Subcommittee No. 1 (Aviation)*, 66th Cong., 2nd sess., 1920, vol. 3, pp. 3778-3780, 3804.

9. Memorandum from Captain Du Doré, Aeronautic Section of the French Mission, French Army, to Chief of Air Service, AEF, 8 June 1918, file 1559, RG 120, National Archives at College Park, MD.

10. Memorandum from Major B. M. Atkinson, Commander, First Pursuit Group, Air Service, AEF, to Chief of Air Service, First Army, AEF, 9 June 1918, file 1559, RG 120, National Archives at College Park, MD.

11. Memorandum from Major John W. F. M. Huffer, Air Service, to Chief of Air Service, AEF, 10 June 1918, "Report of Nieuport '28' Planes," file 1559, RG 120, National Archives at College Park, MD.

12. James Norman Hall, "The Splintered Wing, A Chapter from the Journal of a Prisoner of War," *Air Service Journal* (April 1919): 11-15.

13. Captain Eddie V. Rickenbacker, *Fighting the Flying Circus* (New York City: Frederick A. Stokes, 1919), 77.

14. *Hearings Before Subcommittee No. 1*, 3779.

15. Ibid.

16. A. J. Pippard and Captain J. Lawrence Pritchard Sutton, *Aeroplane Structures* (London: Longmans, Green & Company, 1919). This is an excellent early book on the aerodynamics of flight, and is the source of much of the data on aerodynamics contained in the text of this appendix. The authors had extensive experience in the UK during the war, supervising experimental aircraft designs from the standpoint of structural strength.

17. Rickenbacker, *Fighting the Flying Circus*, 49.

18. During a telephone conversation with the author on 21 April 1999, Jim Appleby (former chief pilot for Tallmantz Aviation) said that the elevator on the Nieuport 28 is very responsive, enabling the airplane to quickly transition to a dive or climb. Appleby also noted the Nieuport 28's ability to quickly accelerate in a dive. Both flight characteristics could be detrimental to the fragile Nieuport 28 wing, especially when heavy-handed pilots flew the plane. Appleby has many flying hours in both original and replica Nieuport 28s.

19. Pippard and Pritchard Sutton, *Aeroplane Structures*, 200.

20. During an interview by the author with Jim Appleby on 5 November 1999, at his home in Yucca Valley, California, Appleby discussed several modifications he made to the upper wings of two Nieuport 28 replicas that he had built. Using plans accurate to the original aircraft, Appleby installed shear ties on each wing rib and employed stronger cap strips, with the upper cap strip brought all the way forward to the leading edge. Appleby used Ceconite rather than aircraft linen, and stitched the Ceconite securely to the rib structure from leading to trailing edge. The wing profile and structure of an original aircraft was preserved and no extra ribs were used ... and these modifications were made with only a minor weight penalty. Jim Appleby has extensively-test flown both of these replica Nieuport 28s; one of these aircraft was clocked (by a T-6 chase plane) at speeds close to 200 mph in a steep dive. Both of Appleby's replica Nieuport 28s are in private hands, and have accumulated hundreds of hours without incident.

21. Rapports: "Sur les Essais Statiques de l'Avion Nieuport 28," 23 August 1917, and "Nieuport C.1 Lorraine Dietrich 275H," 3 July 1918, Aéronautique Militaire, Section Technique, file D52.1/10, Archives, National Air and Space Museum, Washington, DC.

22. The author, a research volunteer at the National Air and Space Museum (NASM), was the project researcher during the five-year restoration of NASM's Nieuport 28. During this period, the author examined original wing components of this aircraft and other original examples in the United States. The author's observations regarding the poor wartime workmanship are based on personal inspection of these components and consultation with Nieuport 28 experts Jim Appleby and Robert Rust Sr., as well as with members of NASM's restoration staff. An expanded version of the author's findings regarding the Nieuport 28's problems with wing failure was originally published as "Destined to Fail: The Nieuport 28 Wing," in *Air Power History* 46, no. 4 (Winter 1999): 4-19.

23. Lieutenant Colonel Harold E. Hartney, *Up and At 'Em* (Harrisburg, PA: Stackpole Sons, 1940), 145.

24. The information on the Curtiss-built Orenco D-1 and Lieutenant Macready's report on the Boeing MB-3 is found in McCook Field's Orenco and MB-3 Project Books, now held by the National Museum of the US Air Force, Research Division.

25. Ibid.

26. Joseph S. Ames, "Relation Between Aeronautical Research and Aircraft Design," Wilbur Wright Lecture, *Journal of the Royal Aeronautical Society* (31 May 1923): 381-404. The NACA report that Ames refers to was published in 1925 as NACA Report #193, *Pressure Distribution over the Wing of an MB-3 Airplane in Flight*.

27. One of the contour charts published in NACA Report #193 graphically illustrates the higher pressures or lift in the upper or high wing in an aileron roll (NACA Report #193, 198). This fact was referred to earlier in this Appendix as a possible explanation for why only the upper right, or left, wing's leading edge failed, depending on whether the pilot rolled out of his dive to the left or the right. The report also noted the presence of negative pressure or "suction" (which was a surprise to many) on the undersurfaces of the wings of high-speed aircraft, and advised that the undersurfaces at the entering and trailing edges be stiffened.

28. Ames, "Relation Between Aeronautical Research and Aircraft Design," 404.

29. Anderson, *History of Aerodynamics*, 310.

30. Ibid.

31. Alfred S. Niles, *Airplane Design* (Dayton, Ohio: Engineering Division, US Army Air Service, 1926), 471-472.

Appendix E

1. Air Service, AEF, Supply Section, Airplane-Motor Division, "Status of European Plane and Motor Order," report dated 3 August 1918, file 452.1-13A, Record Group 18, National Archives at College Park, MD.

2. "Airplanes Received by U.S. Air Service from all Sources, Exhibit A-1," RG 120, National Archives at College Park, MD.

Appendix F

1. Brigadier General W. L. Kenly, Chief of Air Service, AEF, to Adjutant General, AEF, cable, "Cablegram to Washington," 17 September 1917, file 452.1, Record Group 120, National Archives at College Park, MD.

2. Brigadier General B. D. Foulois, Chief of Air Service [AEF], to Commander in Chief, AEF, "Markings of United States Airplanes," file 452.1, RG 120, National Archives at College Park, MD.

3. This section draws extensively from the major work entitled "'Project Butterfly,' The Standard French Camouflage System of 1918," published in *Cross & Cockade Journal* in three parts: Part 1 – vol. 9, no. 1 (Spring 1968): 1-21; Part 2 – vol. 13, no. 2 (Summer 1972): 150-183; and Part 3 – vol. 13, no. 4 (Winter 1972): 325-356. The authors of this superb work were: J. L. Elman, H. D. Hastings, Bergen Hardesty, and Alan D. Toelle; additional important information on colors and markings of Nieuport 28 fighters was found in "94th Aero Squadron 'Hats in the Ring'," *Over the Front* 6, no. 1 (Summer 1991): 154-182. The authors of this work were: Jon Guttman, Alan D. Toelle, Howard Fisher, and Greg VanWyngarden.

4. J. M. Bruce, *Nieuport Fighters*, Windsock Datafile Special (Berkhamsted, UK: Albatros Productions, 1993), 45.

5. Ibid., pp. 42, 45.

6. Alan D. Toelle, "Fabric Specifications," report, 19 July 1998, Curators File (Nieuport 28), National Air and Space Museum, Washington, DC.

7. Ibid.

8. Robert D. Archer, *The Official Monogram US Army Air Service & Air Corps Aircraft Color Guide, Volume 1, 1908-1941* (Sturbridge, MA: Monogram Aviation Publications, 1995), 168.

9. Ibid., 168.

10. Ibid.

11. Ibid.

12. Ibid., 32.

13. Ibid.

14. Ibid., 126.

15. Major John M. Elliott, USMC (retired), *The Official Monogram US Navy & Marine Corps Aircraft Color Guide, Volume 1, 1911-1939* (Boylston, MA: Monogram Aviation Publications, 1987), 20-74.

16. The brief history of Jimmy Meissner's association with Nieuport 28, N.6144, is excerpted from an article by Theodore Hamady and Michael O'Neal, "National Air & Space Museum Nieuport!" *Windsock International* 17, no. 3 (May/June 2001): 32-36. The quotations in the article are from James Armand Meissner's World War I diary, now in the collection of the Lafayette Foundation, Denver, CO.

BIBLIOGRAPHY

Periodicals:

Cross & Cockade Journal, vols. 1-25, the Society of World War I Aero Historians.

Over the Front, vols. 1-20, the League of World War I Aviation Historians.

W W I AERO: The Journal of the Early Aeroplane, World War I Aeroplanes, Inc.

Air Power History, the Air Force Historical Foundation.

Reports:

Gorrell, Edgar S., colonel, et al. "A History of the U.S. Army Air Service, 1917-1923." Record Group 120, AEF, National Archives at College Park, MD.

"Summary of Air Information and Summary of Air Intelligence," March to November 1918. Second Section, General Staff, General Headquarters, American Expeditionary Force.

US Congress. House Select Committee on Expenditures in the War Department. *Hearings Before Subcommittee No. 1 (Aviation)*, 66th Congress, 1st sess., 1919; 2nd sess., 1920.

Books and Booklets:

Alegi, Gregory. *Nieuport 29*, Datafile 97, Windsock Datafiles. Berkhamsted, Hertfordshire, UK: Albatros Productions, 2003.

American Battle Monuments Commission. *American Armies and Battlefields in Europe*. Washington, DC: US Government Printing Office, 1938.

Anderson, John D., Jr. *A History of Aerodynamics and Its Impact on Flying Machines*. New York: Cambridge University Press, 1997.

Blodgett, Mabel Fuller. *Life and Letters of Richard Ashley Blodgett, First Lieutenant, United States Air Service*. Boston: privately printed, 1919.

Bruce, J. M. *Morane-Saulnier Type A1*, Mini Datafile 5, Windsock Datafiles. Berkhamsted, Hertfordshire, UK: Albatros Productions, 1996.

Bruce, J. M. *SPAD 13.C1*, Datafile 32, Windsock Datafiles. Berkhamsted, Hertfordshire, UK: Albatros Productions, 1992.

Buckley, Harold. *Squadron 95*. Paris: Obelisk Press, 1933.

Christienne, Charles, and Pierre Lissarrague. *A History of French Military Aviation*. Washington, DC: Smithsonian Institution Press, 1986.

Coffman, Edward M. *The War to End all Wars: The American Military Experience in World War I*. Lexington, KY: University Press of Kentucky, 1998.

Coolidge, Hamilton, captain. *Letters of an American Airman: Being the War Record of Capt. Hamilton Coolidge, 1917-1918*. Boston: privately printed, 1919.

De Brunoff, Maurice, ed. *L'Aéronautique Pendant la Guerre Mondiale*. Paris: M. de Brunoff, 1919.

Dupuy, R. Ernest, and Trevor N. Dupuy. *The Encyclopedia of Military History: From 3500 B.C. to the Present*. New York: Harper & Row, 1986.

Dwiggins, Don. *Hollywood Pilot: The Biography of Paul Mantz*. Garden City, NY: Doubleday & Co., 1967.

Eder, Jack R., ed. *Let's Go Where the Action Is! The Wartime Experiences of Douglas Campbell*. Knightstown, IN: JaaRE Publishing, 1984.

Esposito, Vincent J. *West Point Atlas of American Wars: 1900-1918*. New York: Henry Holt & Co., 1997.

Farmer, James H. *Celluloid Wings: The Impact of Movies on Aviation*. Blue Ridge Summit, PA: Tab Books, 1984.

Farwell, Byron. *Over There: The United States in the Great War, 1917-1918*. New York: W. W. Norton & Co., 1999.

Frandsen, Bert. *Hat in the Ring: The Birth of American Air Power in the Great War*. Washington, DC: Smithsonian Books, 2003.

Franks, Norman. *Dog Fight: Aerial Tactics of the Aces of World War I*. London: Greenhill Books, 2003.

Franks, Norman L. R., and Frank W. Bailey. *Over the Front: A Complete Record of the Fighter Aces and Units of the United States and French Air Services, 1914-1918*. London: Grub Street, 1992.

Franks, Norman, Frank Bailey, and Rick Duiven. *The Jasta Pilots: Detailed Listings and Histories, August 1916 - November 1918*. London: Grub Street, 1996.

Franks, Norman, Frank Bailey, and Rick Duiven. *The Jasta War Chronology: A Complete Listing of Claims and Losses, August 1916 - November 1918*. London: Grub Street, 1998.

Franks, Norman L. R., Frank W. Bailey, and Russell Guest. *Above the Lines: A Complete Record of the Fighter Aces of the German Air Service, Naval Air Service and Flanders Marine Corps, 1914-1918*. London: Grub Street, 1993.

Goldsmith, Dolf L. *The Grand Old Lady of No Man's Land: The Vickers Machine Gun*. Cobourg, Ontario, Canada: Collector Grade Publications, 1994.

Gorrell, Edgar S., colonel. *The Measure of America's World War Aeronautical Effort*. Burlington, VT: Norwich University, 1940.

Greenwood, Jim, and Maxine Greenwood. *Stunt Flying in the Movies*. Blue Ridge Summit, PA: Tab Books, 1982.

Grosz, P. M. *Pfalz D.IIIA*, Datafile 21, Windsock Datafiles. Berkhamsted, Hertfordshire, UK: Albatros Productions, 1995.

Grosz, P. M. *Rumpler C.1*, Datafile 79, Windsock Datafiles. Berkhamsted, Hertfordshire, UK: Albatros Productions, 2000.

Guttman, Jon. *Nieuport 28*, Datafile 36, Windsock Datafiles. Berkhamsted, Hertfordshire, UK: Albatros Productions, 1992.

Hadfield, D. D. *Los Angeles Aeronautics: 1920-1929*. Inglewood, CA: Northrop University Press, 1973.

Hartney, Harold E., lieutenant colonel. *Up and At 'Em*. Harrisburg, PA: Stackpole Sons, 1940.

Historical Division, Department of the Army. *United States Army in the World War: Reports of Commander-In-Chief, A.E.F., Staff Sections and Services*. Washington, DC: US Government Printing Office, 1948.

Historical Research Division, Air University. *USAF Historical Study No. 133: U.S. Air Service Victory Credits: World War I*. Maxwell AFB, AL: Aerospace Studies Institute, 1969.

Holley, I. B., Jr. *Ideas and Weapons: Exploitation of the Aerial Weapon by the United States During World War I: A Study in the Relationship of Technological Advance, Military Doctrine, and the Development of Weapons*. New Haven, CT: Yale University Press, 1953.

Kennett, Lee. *The First Air War, 1914-1918*. New York: Free Press, 1991.

Lawson, Eric, and Jane Lawson. *The First Air Campaign: August 1914-November 1918*. Conshohocken, PA: Combined Books, 1996.

Martin, Eddie. *Just Call Me "Eddie": My Life as a Pioneer Pilot in Orange County, California*. Irvine, CA: Print Network Publisher, 1998.

Massager, Louis, ed. *Livre d'Or de la Société Française Hispano-Suiza*. N.p.: Drager Frères, 1924.

Maurer, Maurer, ed. *The U.S. Air Service in World War I*. 4 vols. Maxwell AFB, AL: Albert F. Simpson Historical Research Center, 1978-1979.

Mikesh, Robert. *Restoring Museum Aircraft*. Shrewsbury, England: Airlife Publishing, 1997.

Mitchell, William, brigadier general. *Memoirs of World War I*. New York: Random House, 1956.

Morrow, John H., Jr. *German Air Power in World War I*. Lincoln, NE: University of Nebraska Press, 1982.

Morrow, John H., Jr. *The Great War in the Air: Military Aviation from 1900 to 1921*. Washington, DC: Smithsonian Institution Press, 1993.

Morse, William. *Rotary Engines of World War One*. Olney, Buckinghamshire, UK:

Nelson & Saunders Publishers, 1987.

Munson, Kenneth. *Aircraft of World War I*. London: Ian Allen, 1967.

Neumann, Georg Paul, major. *The German Air Force in the Great War*. London: Hodder and Stoughton, 1920.

Niles, Alfred S. *Airplane Design*. Dayton, OH: Engineering Division, US Army Air Service, 1926.

Palmer, Frederick. *Newton D. Baker: America at War*. 2 vols. New York: Dodd, Mead & Co., 1931.

Patrick, Mason M., major general. *The United States in the Air*. Garden City, NY: Doubleday & Co., 1928.

Pearson, Henry Greenleaf. *A Businessman in Uniform: Raynal Cawthorne Bolling*. New York: Duffield & Co., 1923.

Pippard, A. J., and Captain J. Lawrence Pritchard Sutton. *Aeroplane Structures*. London: Longmans, Green & Co., 1919.

Pommier, Gérard, and Bertrand Pommier. *Nieuport, 1875-1911: A Biography of Edouard Nieuport*. (Atglen, PA: Schiffer Publishing, 2002.

Quellet, Ricardo Luis, commodoro, ed. *Historia de la Fuerza Aérea Argentina*. 2 vols. Buenos Aires: Estudios Históricos, 1997.

Rickenbacker, Eddie V., captain. *Fighting the Flying Circus*. Garden City, NY: Doubleday & Co., 1965.

Rollins, Peter C., and John E. O'Connor, eds. *Hollywood's World War I Motion Picture Images*. Bowling Green, OH: Bowling Green State University Popular Press, 1997.

Roosevelt, Kermit, ed. *Quentin Roosevelt: A Sketch with Letters*. New York: Charles Scribner's Sons, 1921.

Rosenthal, Léonard, et al. *Nieuport: 1909-1950*. Clichy, France: Docavia/Editions Lariviere, 1997.

Sanger, Ray. *Nieuport Aircraft of World War One*. Ramsbury, Marlborough, Wiltshire, UK: Crowood Press, 2002.

Sloan, James J., Jr. *Wings of Honor: American Airmen in World War I*. Atglen, PA: Schiffer Publishing, 1994.

Smith, Hershel. *A History of Aircraft Piston Engines*. Manhattan, KS: Sunflower University Press, 1994.

Smith, Vi. *From Jennies to Jets: The Aviation History of Orange County*. Fullerton, CA: Sultana Press, 1974.

Stillwell, Paul. *Battleship Arizona, an Illustrated History*. Annapolis, MD: US Naval Institute, 1991.

Tallman, Frank. *Flying the Old Planes*. Garden City, NY: Doubleday & Co., 1973.

Thayer, Lucien H., lieutenant. *America's First Eagles: The Official History of the U.S. Air Service, A.E.F. (1917-1918)*. San Jose, CA: R. James Bender Publishing and Champlin Fighter Museum Press, 1983.

US War Department. *Battle Participation of Organizations of the American Expeditionary Force in France, Belgium, and Italy, 1917-1918*. Washington, DC: US Government Printing Office, 1920.

VanWyngarden, Greg. *Jagdgeschwader Nr II: Geschwader 'Berthold'*. Wellingborough, Northants, UK: Osprey Publishing, 2005.

VanWyngarden, Greg. *'Richthofen's Circus': Jagdgeschwader Nr 1*. Wellingborough, Northants, UK: Osprey Publishing, 2004.

von Hoeppner, Ernst, general. *Germany's War in the Air: The Development and Operations of German Military Aviation in the World War*. Nashville, TN: Battery Press, 1994.

Wohl, Robert. *A Passion for Wings: Aviation and the Western Imagination, 1908-1918*.

New Haven, CT: Yale University Press, 1994.

Woolley, Charles, with Bill Crawford. *Echoes of Eagles: A Son's Search for His Father and the Legacy of America's First Fighter Pilots*. New York: Dutton Group, 2003.

Woolley, Charles. *First to the Front: The Aerial Adventures of 1st Lt. Waldo Heinrichs and the 95th Aero Squadron, 1917-1918*. Atglen, PA: Schiffer Publishing, 1999.

Woolley, Charles. *The Hat in the Ring Gang: The Combat History of the 94th Aero Squadron in World War I*. Atglen, PA: Schiffer Publishing, 2001.

Wynne, H. Hugh. *Motion Picture Stunt Pilots and Hollywood's Classic Aviation Movies*. Missoula, MT: Pictorial Histories Publishing Co., 1987.

INDEX

Abernethy, Thomas J., 85, 125, 219, 249, 250
Ackermann, Robert, 126, 181
Albaugh, (American) Sergeant, 74
Almonacid, Vicente Almondos, 134
Ames, Joseph, 239, 240
Anderson, Jr., John D., 231, 240
Anthony, John R., 35
Appleby, James, 172, 176, 177, 184, 188, 189, 190, 191, 192
Appleby, Zona, 184
Arango, Javier, 184
Ashenden, James F., 125, 126, 130, 181, 204, 259,
Atkinson, Bert M., 50, 51, 67, 79, 87, 96, 108, 110, 232
Avery, Walter L., 86, 87, 104

Babcock, Henry, 202
Baker, Hobart "Hobey", 51
Baker, Newton Diehl, 38, 39
Ball, Albert, 33
Barés, Joseph, 26
Batt, Howard, 150
Baxter, Warner (actor), 146, 149
Beachey, Lincoln, 140
Beauchamp, Oliver T., 89, 90, 95
Béchéreau, Louis, 34
Bellamy, Ralph (actor), 150
Bertrandais, Victor, 83
Birkigt, Marc, 34, 35, 106
Bishop, William, Avery "Billy", 32, 33
Black, Guy, 175, 188
Blankenship, R. T., 123
Blériot, Louis, 21
Boelcke, Oswald, 27, 33
Bolle, Karl, 79
Bolling, Raynal C., 41, 42, 43, 45, 46, 47
Bonnell, Geoffrey H., 71, 72, 79, 86, 87, 108, 109
Bourgeois, (French) pilot, 198
Boswell, Perry, 176
Brady, Don, 167, 172
Bréguet, Louis, 25
Brotherton, William E., 87, 88, 125, 254, 257
Brown, Kimbrough, 168, 172
Buckler, Julius, 93
Buckley, Harold R., 50, 53, 61, 67, 75, 82
Buford, Jr., Edward "Ned", 56, 58
Burton, Frank, 102
Butterfield, A. D., 108

Cagney, James (actor), 155
Campbell, Courtney, 29
Campbell, Douglas P., 5, 11, 12, 13, 14, 15, 17, 18, 19, 20, 49, 50, 53, 54, 56, 58, 61, 62, 64, 68, 75, 103, 158, 170, 186, 250, 251, 254, 263
Campbell, Louise (actor), 150
Candelaria, Luis, 131
Canivet, (French) pilot, 198
Casgrain, Wilfrid V., 65, 66, 230, 261
Cassard, Daniel W., 83, 85, 87
Cates, Jr., Robert Z., 263
Chambers, Reed M., 10, 11, 56, 261
Champlin, Douglas, 177
Chaplin, Charlie (actor), 135
Chaplin, Sydney, 135
Chevalier, Godfrey de C., 120, 123, 124
Clapp, Kenneth, S., 89
Clark, Virginius, 48
Clark, (American) pilot, 237
Coffin, Howard, 38, 39
Coody, R. F., 177,
Cook, H. Weir, 56
Coolidge, Hamilton, "Ham", 58, 77, 105, 106
Corbiere, (French) Colonel, 19
Correa, Esteban, 182
Creeth, Bert, 135
Cunningham, Alfred L., 108
Daniels, Josephus, 117, 124
Daugherty, Earl S., 135, 136, 137
Davis, E. C., 137
Davis, Philip W., 62, 63, 64, 68, 70
Dawson, Leo H., 89
Delage, Gustave, 23, 25, 29, 32, 37, 42, 193, 194, 196, 203
de la Meurthe, Henri Deutsch, 23, 25
DeMille, Cecil B. (movie director), 137, 140
de Nieport (name later changed to Nieuport), Edouard, 21, 22, 23
de Rose, Charles, 29, 30, 32
d' Esperey, Franchet, 30
Devine, Andy, (actor), 150
Dix, Richard (actor), 144
Dollfuss, (Swiss) Doctor, 128
Donaldson, Donald W., 89, 91
Doolittle, Jimmy, 146
Doree, (American) Colonel, 85
Doubler, Michael, 38
Doyle, Ed, 184
DuDoré, (French) Captain, 67, 232
Dumesnil, (French) Under-Secretary, 47, 48, 201
Dunwoody, Halsey, 72, 112, 201

Earhart, Amelia, 135, 136
Eastman, Joseph K., 99, 106, 107
Eckhout, (American) navy pilot, 124
Elliot, Edward B., 78
Erickson, Ed, 174
Evans, George, 100
Evans, Madge (actor), 140

Farrell, Charles (actor), 140
Fechet, James, 139
Fehr, Anthony, 116
Fleisher, Alfred, 91, 92, 93, 95
Flynn, Errol (actor), 153, 154
Foch, Ferdinand, 81, 82

Fokker, Anthony, 27, 231
Folsom, Ray, 174, 179
Ford, Christopher, 258
Foulois, Benjamin D., 38, 39, 45, 47, 49, 70, 72, 99, 108, 199, 201, 202, 230, 241, 249
Frandsen, Bert, 108
Frear, James, 99, 233
Freeman, Ray, 137, 177
Frey, Arno, 146
Frey, Royal, 69
Friedrichs, (German) pilot, 78
Frommhertz, Hermann, 79
Frye, Jack, 137

Gamy, (French) artist, 21
Garros, Roland, 21, 22, 26, 27
Gerard, (French) General, 9, 261
Goebel, Art, 137
Gorrell, Edgar S., 43, 44, 45, 46
Goering, Hermann Wilhelm, 75, 77
Grant, Alfred A., 89
Gräper, Carl Emil, 83
Green, M. Edwin, 56
Grey, (American) pilot, 116
Grey, C.G., 21
Griffith, Andy (actor), 184
Gude, Oliver Jay, 56, 68, 69
Gunn, Malcolm B., 256
Guynemer, Georges, 29, 30, 32

Hageneau, (French) General, 45, 46, 47
Hale, Alan (actor), 155
Hall, G. H., 123
Hall, James Norman, 15, 54, 56, 60, 65, 103, 230, 232, 233
Hall, James, E., 172, 190
Hambleton, John A., 87
Hardendorf, (American) navy pilot, 123
Hardesty, Bergen, 167, 180
Hartney, Harold E., 70, 71, 78, 79, 80, 82, 94, 95, 96, 97, 100, 104, 108, 109, 110, 192, 237
Haviland, Willis B., 109, 124
Hawker, Lanoe, 33
Hawks, Howard, 140
Heinrichs, Waldo, 52, 65, 66, 230, 235, 255
Holley, I.B., 44
Hoover, William J., 80, 256
Hudson, Donald, 78, 89, 90
Huffer, John W. F. M., 18, 50, 51, 56, 67, 232, 254
Hughes, Herbert, 42, 43
Hughes, Howard, 139, 140, 143
Hunt, George, 95, 174, 179
Hunt, Jason L., 89

Immelmann, Max, 27

Jakab, Peter L., 159
Jarrett, George Burling, 167, 177, 179
Jones, Arthur H., 52
Junkers, Hugo, 230

Kenly, W. L., 249
Kensinger, Ned, 177
Kilduff, Peter, 5
Kindley, Field E., 99
King, Andrew, 184, 185, 186
King, Bill, 185
King, Dick, 185, 188, 189, 191, 192
Kinner, W. B., 137
Kirby, Maxwell, 106
Krebiel, Rob, 146
Kreutzer, Joseph, 140
Kurtz, Paul B., 263

Lauman, Arthur,78
Le Blanc, A., 23
Letzkus, E. A., 120
Lincoln, Garland, 139, 140 141, 142, 143, 144, 146, 147, 148, 149, 150, 151, 153, 154, 156, 158, 169, 172, 174, 176
Lincoln, Pauline, 143
Lindbergh, Charles A., 139
Loerzer, Bruno, 75
Loomis, William F., 56
Löwenhardt, Erich, 78
Lucher, (French) Minister, 45
Ludendorff, Erich, 78, 81, 95
Lufbery, Gervais Raoul, 15, 50, 51, 53, 54, 56, 68, 69, 70, 261, 263
Luke, Jr., Frank, 85, 89

MacMurray, Fred (actor), 150
Macready, J. A., 237, 239
Mallard, (French) pilot, 198
Mantz, Albert Paul, 146, 150, 151, 153, 155, 156, 167, 169, 170, 172, 174, 175, 188
Marr, Kenneth, 56, 62, 261
Martin, Richard, 89, 90, 95
Martin, Eddie, 135, 137, 138, 139
Matienzo, Benjamin, 131, 133, 134, 182, 259
Matthews, Helen, 125
Maxwell, Reginald, 79
McClure, Harry, 176
McCracken, Jack, 100, 101, 102
McElvain, Clifford A., 89, 91, 92, 93, 95, 256
McDonnell, Edward O., 118
Meier, Ernst, 128
Meissner, James Armand "Jimmy", 54, 55, 56, 62, 63, 64, 65, 66, 70, 74, 87, 95, 110, 158, 159, 160, 230, 232, 233, 235, 260, 261, 262
Menckhoff, Carl, 86, 87
Military and naval pilots who flew the Nieuport 28, 242-247
Milland, Ray (actor), 150
Miller, James E., 50, 52
Miler, Walter P., 89
Miller, Zenos R., 67, 95
Mitchell, William P. "Billy," 19, 20, 61, 62, 70, 97, 104, 108, 230, 261
Moné, Brent, 176

Moné, Kip, 176
Montenegro, Conchita (actor), 146
Moore, Tim, 175
Morgan, Dennis (actor), 155
Morrow, John, 102
Moseley, C. C., 138
Murphy, (American) navy pilot, 123

Navarre, Jean, 29, 30
Nevius, Ruliff V., 89
Nieuport, Charles, 21, 22, 23, 25
Niven, David (actor), 153, 154
Norton, Fred W., 78
Nungesser, Charles, 29, 30, 32, 169

O'Brien, Pat (actor), 150
Olsen, Ivan R. "Ole", 143
O'Neill, Ralph A., 86
Osborne, Jim, 184
Overton, Dolph, 175, 188
Ovington, Earle, 135, 137, 138, 139

Palen, James H. "Cole", 5, 157, 169, 170, 186, 189, 191
Parodi, Antonio, 131, 133
Parry, Maxwell O., 83, 84
Parsons, Edwin C. "Ted," 149, 177
Patrick, Mason Mathews, 49, 62, 70, 99, 108, 113, 135, 202, 224
Pawkett, Clarence "Jim", 184, 185
Pershing, John Joseph, 46, 47, 96, 108, 198, 201
Pétain, Henri, 46, 198
Peterson, David McKelvey, 10, 48, 75, 158, 261
Petty, Jim, 177
Plyler, William H., 67, 109, 237
Polk, Lawrence, N., 89
Porter, Charles "Pip," 125, 219, 252
Porter, Kenneth L., 86, 87, 99, 100, 125, 257
Preuss, Werner, 78
Pride, Alfred Melville "Mel", 119, 120, 122, 123, 124, 258
Prince, Norman, 32
Prinz, LeRoy J., 53

Quinney, Art, 180

Rabe, Hanns-Gerd, 5
Rankin, Charles, 82, 83, 106
Rathbone, Basil (actor), 153
Reber, Samuel, 38
Rentschler, Frederick, 38
Reynolds, Osborne, 231
Rhodes, Carlyle, 79
Ribot, (French Premier), 39
Rickenbacker, Edward V. "Eddie", 10, 11, 48, 53, 56, 58, 60, 62, 65, 66, 67, 68, 69, 74, 75, 80, 87, 103, 106, 109, 110, 158, 183, 230, 232, 233, 235, 236, 237, 254, 261, 263
Roberts, Claudius A., 221

Roberts, Ivan A., 89
Robertson, George A. S., 84, 85, 125, 183
Robertson, Jim, 183
Rogers, Emery H., 135, 137, 138, 143, 174
Rolff, Emil, 88, 89, 90
Roosevelt, Philip, 51
Roosevelt, Quentin, 80, 83, 84, 255
Roosevelt, Theodore, 83
Rust, Jr., Robert, 181
Rust, Sr., Robert, 177, 181
Ryder, Frank, 183

Sands, Charles B., 89, 95
Satterfield, John, 202
Saunders, John Monk, 139, 154
Schmitt, Ralph, 87
Schuler, Robert, 184
Schuster, Gunther, 92, 93
Sewall, Sumner P., 52
Sherry, Alden B., 77, 106
Simon, Heinrich, 15, 18
Simon, Jr., Louis C. "Red", 79
Smythe, Walter W., 56
Sorensen, Neal, 174
Squier, George, 39, 40, 41
Strähle, Paul, 5, 35
Suchy, James, 262
Swanson, Carl, 183
Sykes, James J., 89

Tallman, III, Frank, 155, 156, 167, 172, 174, 175, 176, 177, 179, 181, 185, 188, 189, 191, 192
Tate, Mike, 175
Tatje, (German) pilot, 125
Taylor, Thorne C., 261, 263
Taylor, William H. "Bill", 53
Thompson, Sidney P., 79
Tittman, Jr., Harold H., 78
Toelle, Alan, 107
Trenchard, Hugh, 80
Tulasne, Joseph, 40

Udet, Ernst, 77, 78, 91, 102
Unger, Ed, 135

Vasconcells, Jerry C., 89, 91
Vedrine, Jules, 23
Vickers, Johnny, 142, 143, 172
von Bülow-Bothkamp, Harry, 85
von Falkenhayn, Erich, 29
von Hindenburg, Paul, 34
von Hoeppner, Ernst, 34, 41, 106
von Hutier, Oscar, 72
von Kluck, Alexander, 25
von Richthofen, Manfred, 33, 34, 75

Wanamaker, Walter B., 78, 79
Walcott, Charles, 45
Walters, Paul, 54
Webster, Jim, 137
Weeks, Kermit, 174
Wehner, Joseph H., 89
Wellman, William A., 150
Wells, Howard, 180
Wentworth, Chuck, 184
Wentworth, John, 54, 56
Wenzl, Richard, 89, 104
Weyman, Charles, 22, 23
White, Jr., Wilbert W., 79, 87
Whiton, Arthur L., 89, 95
Whyte, Howard, 184, 185
Wilson, Thomas Woodrow, 38
Winslow, Alan F., 10, 11, 12, 13, 14, 15, 16, 17, 18, 19, 54, 56, 69, 88, 89, 103, 158, 251, 261, 263
Wold, Ernest G., 89, 91, 92
Wolfer, Jacob, 120, 122, 123
Womack, Press, 184, 185
Wooldridge, Harry, 183
Wooten, James, C. "Jimmy", 89, 91, 92
Wootton, Frank, 14
Wroniecki, Antoni, 16, 17, 18

York, Joe, 137

Zanni, Pedro, 131, 133